Orange Line 4 Grundkurs

für Klasse 8

Das Lehrbuch versteht sich als Gesamtangebot. Welche Texte und Aufgaben verpflichtend sind, wird durch die schulinternen Curricula festgelegt.

1. Auflage 978-3-12-548174-9 (fester Einband)
1. Auflage 978-3-12-548374-3 (flexibler Einband)

| 1 | 9 | 8 | 7 | 6 | 5 | | 26 | 25 | 24 | 23 | 22 |
| 1 | 9 | 8 | 7 | 6 | 5 | | 28 | 27 | 26 | 25 | 24 |

Alle Drucke dieser Auflage sind unverändert und können im Unterricht nebeneinander verwendet werden. Die letzte Zahl bezeichnet das Jahr des Druckes.

Herausgeber: Dr. Frank Haß, Kirchberg
Autorinnen und Autoren: Chris Caridia, London sowie
Jo Cummins, London; Wolfgang Hamm, Marktredwitz; **Dr. Andrea Jessen, Tamm;** Leonie Pohl, Gütersloh; Nadine Uesbeck, Dortmund; Anna Zagermann, Hattingen; Konstanze Zander, Großenehrich
Beratung: Brunhilde Biek, Leonberg; Karin Braun, Dortmund; Wilma Brings, Bedburg; Amanda Chisnell, Lollar; Sara Conway, Stuttgart; Ulf Degen, Braunschweig; Tanja Frank, Ulm; Sandra Haberland, Recklinghausen; Wolfgang Hamm, Marktredwitz; Ulrike Heringhaus, Altheim; Michael Herrmann, Ludwigsfelde; Christa Kathmann-Fuhrmann, Bonn; Dr. Margitta Kuty, Greifswald-Eldna; Grit Machut, Berlin; Michael Meisenzahl, Karlstadt; Beatrix Pierce, Eppingen; Annegret Preker-Franke, Bielefeld; Dr. Hubert Schwandt, Parchen; Christian Straukamp, Nordhorn; Ines van Hove, Oldenburg; Dieter Vilimek, Helmstadt-Bargen

Redaktion: Beate Jäger; Dr. Susanne Dyka, Nürnberg; Birgit Piefke-Wagner, Korntal-Münchingen
Herstellung: Ulrike Wursthorn

Umschlaggestaltung und Gestaltungskonzept: know idea, Freiburg; Koma Amok, Stuttgart
Umschlagfoto: Getty Images (The Image Bank), München; Getty Images (Photographer's Choice), München
Illustrationen: Marek Blaha, Offenbach; Kirill Chudinskiy, Köln sowie
Friederike Ablang, Berlin; Iris Blanck, Hamburg; Martina Burghardt-Vollhardt, Kamenz; Udo Clormann, Wiesbaden; Christian Dekelver, Weinstadt; Thorsten Droessler, Leipzig; Andreas Florian, Lübeck; Anke Fröhlich, Leipzig; Carolin Görtler, Immenstadt im Allgäu; Josef Hammen, Trierweiler; Christian Hansen, Berlin; Rob Harvey, Cirencester, GB; Carmen Hochmann, Bielefeld; Martin Hoffmann, Stuttgart; Yvonne Hoppe-Engbring, Steinfurt; Steffen Jähde, Sundhagen; Klett Archiv, Stuttgart; Hendrik Kranenberg, Drolshagen; Jeongsook Lee, Köln; Katja Leuschner, Halle; Helga Merkle, Albershausen; Lutz-Erich Müller, Leipzig; Axel Nicolai, Brauweiler; David Norman, Meerbusch; Liliane Oser, Hamburg; Sven Palmowski, Barcelona, Spain; Katja Rau, Fellbach; Anja Rieger, Berlin; Annika Sauerborn, Mainz; Sandra Schmidt, Berlin; Carolin Ina Schröter, Berlin; Friederike Schumann, Berlin; Birgit Tanck, Hamburg; Inge Voets, Berlin; Sylvia Wolf, Wiesbaden; Katrin Wolff, Wiesbaden; Steffen Wolff, Brohl-Lützing; Dorothee Wolters, Köln

Satz: Satzkiste GmbH, Stuttgart
Reproduktion: Schwabenrepro GmbH, Stuttgart
Druck: Firmengruppe APPL, aprinta druck, Wemding

Printed in Germany
ISBN 978-3-12-548174-9 (fester Einband)
ISBN 978-3-12-548374-3 (flexibler Einband)

Orange Line 4

Grundkurs

Herausgeber: Dr. Frank Haß

Ernst Klett Verlag
Stuttgart • Leipzig

Inhalt

L = Listening   S = Speaking   R = Reading   W = Writing   V = Viewing   I = Intercultural

Kompetenzen / Themen / Ich kann …	Fertigkeiten	Seite

L = Listening   S = Speaking   R = Reading   W = Writing   V = Viewing   I = Intercultural

Kompetenzen / Themen / Ich kann …	Fertigkeiten	Seite

So lernst du mit Orange Line

Hier zeige ich dir, wie du dich in deinem Buch gut zurechtfindest. Das Buch hat fünf Units (Kapitel). Jede Unit ist gleich aufgebaut.

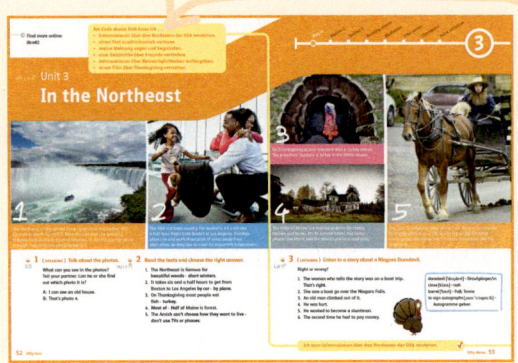

Way in

Hier steigst du in das neue Thema ein. Dazu gibt es auch einen kurzen Film.

Im gelben Kasten siehst du, was du in der *Unit* lernst.

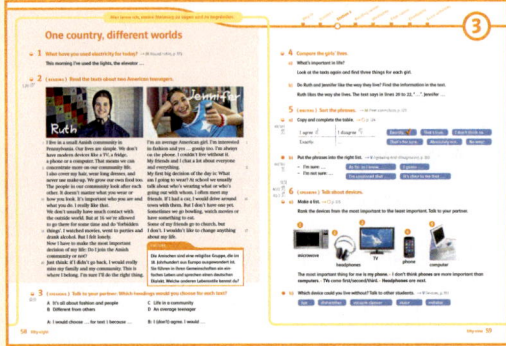

Stations

In jeder *Unit* gibt es zwei *Stations*, in denen du viele neue Dinge lernst. Diese Symbole zeigen dir, wie schwer die Übung ist und ob es im Anhang eine leichtere Variante gibt:

→ p. 137,

In der *Your turn*-Aufgabe kannst du zeigen, dass du alles verstanden hast, und deine eigenen Ideen einbringen.

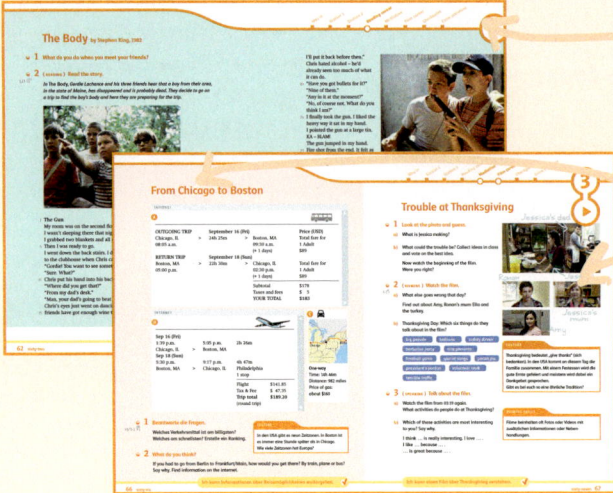

Reading corner

In der *Reading corner* gibt es verschiedene Geschichten und Sachtexte.

Mediation/Film corner

Auf der linken Seite geht es darum, englische Informationen auf Deutsch weiterzugeben oder umgekehrt.

In der *Film corner* geht es um einen englischen Film.

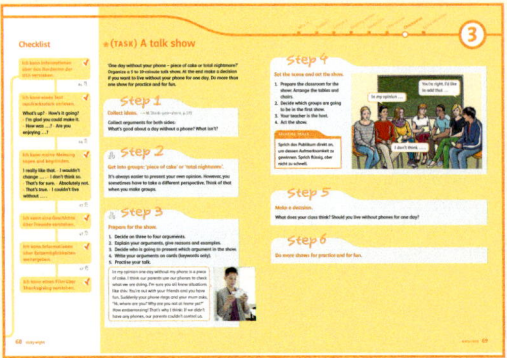

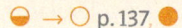

Checkpoint

Auf dieser Seite kannst du überprüfen, ob du in der *Unit* alles verstanden hast. In der *Checklist* sind alle Lernziele noch einmal aufgelistet.

Die Abschluss-Aufgabe (*task*) sollt ihr zu zweit oder in der Gruppe lösen.

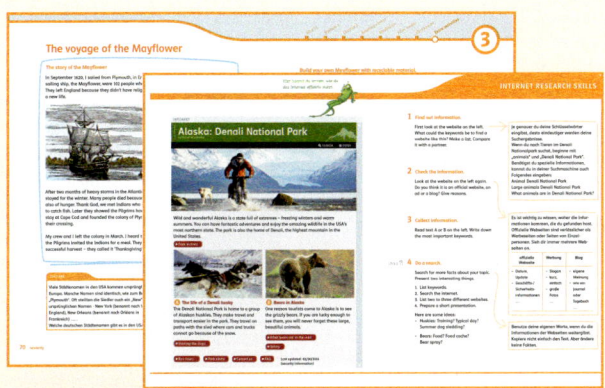

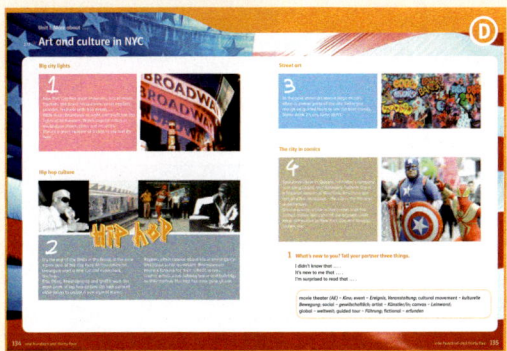

Extra activities

Hier findest du zwei Seiten mit besonderen Aktivitäten, z. B. einem Spiel.

Skills

Auf einige *Units* folgt eine Doppelseite, auf der du eine bestimmte Fertigkeit (*skill*) besonders trainieren kannst, also z. B. das Lesen, Schreiben, Sprechen oder Wörterbucharbeit.

More about

Hier findest du interessante weiterführende Informationen zur Region der Unit.

Im Anschluss an die fünf *Units* gibt es noch weitere nützliche Seiten:

Extra: Hier erwarten dich weitere Lesetexte und vieles mehr.

Grammar: Hier findest du alle Regeln und Erklärungen zur Grammatik sowie weitere Übungen.

Methods: Manche Übungen könnt ihr auf eine bestimmte Art und Weise bearbeiten.
Das erkennt ihr an diesem Symbol: → M
Wie es genau funktioniert, kannst du hier nachlesen.

Vocabulary: Im *Vocabulary* findest du alle neuen Wörter in der Reihenfolge, in der sie in der *Unit* auftauchen, und die wichtigsten Arbeitsanweisungen.
Im *Dictionary* sind die Wörter noch einmal alphabetisch aufgelistet: zuerst Englisch–Deutsch und dann Deutsch–Englisch.

Am Schluss des Buches findest du noch
- Sätze, die du im Unterricht sagen kannst, z. B. bei der Gruppenarbeit
- eine Liste mit den unregelmäßigen Verben.

Symbol	Erklärung
○ ◑ ●	leicht/mittel/schwer (Niveaudifferenzierung)
✳	individualisierende Aufgabe (natürliche Differenzierung)
→ ○ p. 131	Verweis auf leichtere Parallelübung auf der *Diff corner*-Seite
↻ OR ↺	Aufgabe zur Auswahl (Wahldifferenzierung)
⚷	Entwicklung von Schlüsselkompetenzen
P	Hier entsteht ein Produkt für das Portfolio.
4/1 ↗	Verweis auf eine Übung im *Workbook*
→ G6, p. 163	Verweis auf den Grammatikanhang (*Grammar*)
→ M	Verweis auf die Methodenseite (*Methods*)
→ V	Verweis zum Wortfeld im Vokabular (*Vocabulary*)
👥	Partnerarbeit
👥👥	Gruppenarbeit
🎧	Verweis auf die Lehrer-CD (Audio)
🎬	Verweis auf die Lehrer-DVD (Film)
⊕ Find more online:	Code auf www.klett.de eingeben und Zusatzinformationen erhalten

Zoom in – The USA

Every year in fall the New England states shine in bright colors.

1

Denali (Mt. McKinley) is the highest mountain in Alaska and North America (6,190 m).

4

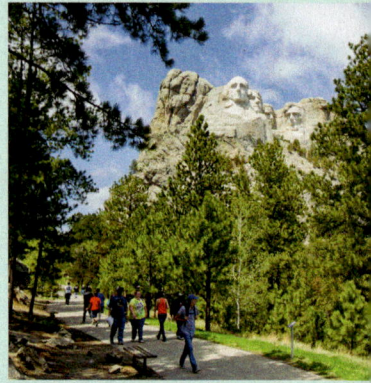

flag

rose

bald eagle

Name:	United States of America	Capital:	Washington D.C.
Population:	≈ 321,400,000 (July 2015)	States:	50
Area (total):	≈ 9,800,000 km²	Time zones:	9
	(≈ 3,600,000 sq.mi.)	Major rivers:	Mississippi, Missouri, Colorado
	(3rd largest country in the world)	Mountains:	Rocky Mountains,
Currency:	US dollar		Appalachian Mountains

The Midwest is a huge open area with lots of corn and soybean fields.

2

Hawaii is a surfer's paradise with perfect waves and white and black beaches.

3

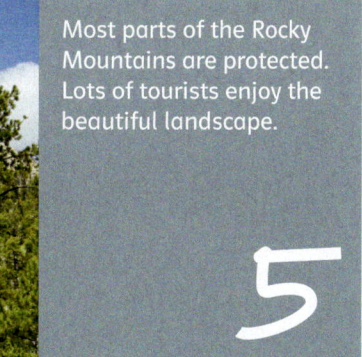

Most parts of the Rocky Mountains are protected. Lots of tourists enjoy the beautiful landscape.

5

In some parts of the American South there are swamps where alligators live.

6

☞☞ **1 Look at the photos and read the texts.**

What parts of the USA would you like to visit? Say why.

☞☞ **2 Look at the map at the back of the book. Find the answers.**

1. Name the countries that are north and south of the USA.
2. Name the oceans that are east and west of the USA.
3. Name the sea that's south of the states of Louisiana, Mississippi and Alabama.
4. Name the state that's in the Pacific Ocean, southwest of California.
5. Name the state that's to the northwest of Canada.
6. Find out the distances from north to south and east to west.

3 Look at the photos and choose one of the places.

Find out more about it on the internet. Present some interesting facts to the class.

1. Indiana: Indy 500
2. Kentucky: Fort Knox
3. Pennsylvania: Declaration of Independence
4. Washington: Space Needle, Seattle

3

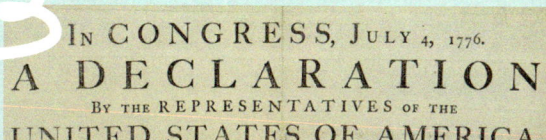

6

9

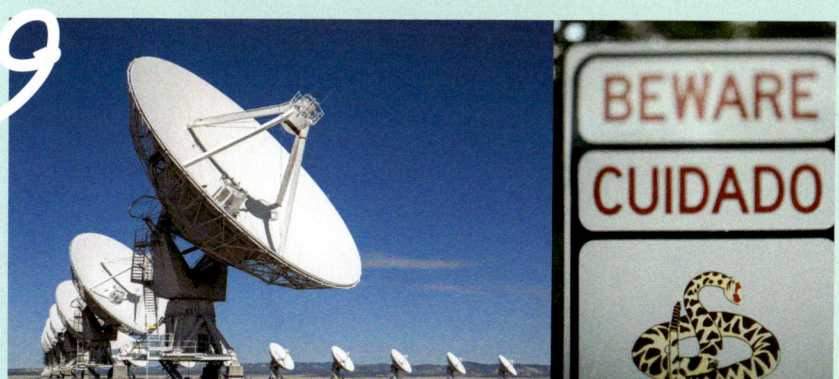

5. North Dakota: Sitting Bull
6. Alabama: US Space &
   Rocket Center, Huntsville
7. Colorado: Mesa Verde
8. Nevada: Las Vegas
9. New Mexico: Very Large
   Array

⊕ Find more online:
i8ce82

1 👆 1,1 ☞

Unit 1

Gateway NYC

1

New York City (NYC) is the biggest city in the United States. Over eight and a half million people live in its five boroughs: The Bronx, Brooklyn, Queens, Manhattan and Staten Island.

2

One World Trade Center is the tallest building on the New York City skyline and in the USA. It replaced the old World Trade Center after the attacks on September 11, 2001.

● 1 Look at the photos.

a) What do you know about New York City? The photos can help you.

b) Read the texts. Then match them with these phrases.

> sports in the USA

> a special tall building

> American culture

> the biggest city in the USA

> a symbol of hope

2/1–2 🗐

● 2 Check the sentences.

a) Right or wrong?

1. There are eight boroughs in New York City.
2. One World Trade Center is the tallest building in the USA.
3. People in New York don't like baseball very much.
4. Hip hop and street art started in New York.
5. The Statue of Liberty was made in the USA.

b) Correct the wrong sentences.

Baseball is one of the most popular sports in the USA, and New Yorkers love it.

New York is an important center for American culture. Music, theater, dance and art are all popular. Hip hop and street art started in New York.

The Statue of Liberty was a present from France to celebrate 100 years of American independence. For immigrants it became a symbol of hope.

3 (LISTENING) **Listen to a guided tour of One World Trade Center.**

1,2

Choose the right answer.

1. How many people died on September 11, 2001?
   almost 3,000 • almost 1,000
2. How many people saw the events on TV?
   over two million • over two billion
3. How long does it take to travel to the top?
   six minutes • 60 seconds
4. What do visitors watch in the elevators?
   a movie about the past of NYC • a movie about the past of the USA
5. Where does the electricity for the lights in the tower come from?
   the elevators • the wind

> billion ['bɪlɪən] – Milliarde
> event [ɪ'vent] – Ereignis
> elevator ['elɪveɪtə] – Aufzug; Lift
> top [tɒp] – Spitze
> light [laɪt] – Licht

Ich kann Informationen über New York verstehen. ✔

A taxi ride in NYC

1 (READING) **Read the text.**

1,3
3/1

1 **David Singh:** A traffic jam! It's always bad on the Brooklyn Bridge during rush hour. And last Monday they started roadwork here too. Did you know that it gets very
5 cold here in the winters? Two years ago we had so much snow. I didn't get into the city some days. I live in Queens, but I work in downtown Manhattan.
You can get a very good look at the New
10 York skyline from here. I never get tired of it – let me tell you about the sights.
That's One World Trade Center. Those skyscrapers over there are on Wall Street, the financial center of the world. Can you
15 see the Empire State Building? In the 1930s it was the tallest building in the world. The view of Manhattan from the top is really fantastic.
How long are you here for anyway? If you
20 only have one day in NYC, I say: buy a sandwich and a coffee and go for a walk in Central Park. There are lakes, playgrounds, a zoo and lots more.

Then take the subway at 86th Street and Lexington Avenue to Grand Central Station. 25
Around the corner you can get the best hot dogs in New York. In the afternoon you should go shopping and finish the day with a Broadway show.
The lights are green at last. Let's go. 30

2 **Collect the information.** → M Think-pair-share, p. 173

1. What's David's job?
2. Make a list of the places and buildings from the text.
3. Find the places or buildings on the map at the front of your book.

CULTURE

Man kann sich in Manhattan nicht verlaufen, wenn man auf die Straßennamen achtet. Avenues verlaufen von Nord nach Süd; Streets von Ost nach West.
Woher haben Straßen bei euch ihre Namen?

David Singh

3 Right or wrong? Find it in the text. → M Peer correction, p. 171

1. The traffic is bad during rush hour.
   That's **right.** *(lines 1–2) "It's always bad on the Brooklyn Bridge during rush hour."*
2. David lives in downtown Manhattan.
3. In the 1920s the Empire State Building was the tallest building in the world.
4. There's a zoo in Central Park.
5. You can get the best hot dogs around the corner of Grand Central Station.

4 Find the words.

a) **Choose the right word.** → ○ p. 114

| subway | avenue | skyline | playground | rush hour |

1. street • road • ——
2. taxi • bus • ——
3. park • lake • ——
4. traffic jam • roadwork • ——
5. skyscraper • tower • ——

b) **Match the words with the definitions.** → V City words, p. 179

| sidewalk | suburbs | construction site | parking lot |

1. you can leave your car there
2. where people can walk safely
3. a place where they are building something
4. people live here, away from the city center

5 (SPEAKING) Act as a guide.

3/2-3a) a) **Present what is on the map.** → ○ p. 114

Over there you can see ...

Don't miss ...   You must visit ...

Around the corner you can see ...

Look, there's ...

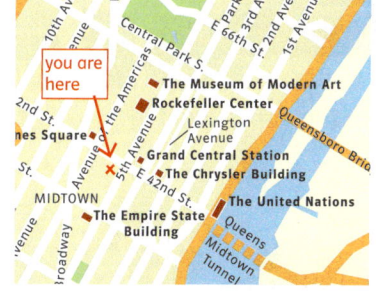

3/3b) b) **Show a visitor three places in your town. Bring a map or photos.** → V City guide, p. 183

In the distance you can see ...   Have a good look at ...   Right ahead are ...

CULTURE

Ein paar Wörter unterscheiden sich im britischen und amerikanischen Englisch. Schreibweise und Aussprache sind manchmal auch anders. Viele Sprecher mischen britisches und amerikanisches Englisch.	British	American
	town centre	downtown
	lift	elevator
	holidays	vacation

Language → G1, p. 158

Last Monday they started roadwork here.
Two years ago we had so much snow.
Did you know that?
I didn't get into the city.

Welche Zeitform ist das? Wie bildest du sie?
Welche Signalwörter kennst du für diese
Zeitform?

6 Complete the sentences. → M Bus stop, p. 168

4/4

1. The Statue of Liberty was a present from France in the 19th century. (be)
2. The Brooklyn Bridge —— on May 24, 1883. (open)
3. Grand Central Station —— its new name 'Grand Central Terminal' in 1913. (get)
4. In the 1980s Central Park —— a very safe place. (not be)
5. It —— eight years to build One World Trade Center, from 2004 to 2012. (take)
6. Two years ago schools in New York City —— because of heavy snow. (not open)

I was in NYC.
I wasn't in LA.
Were you there?

7 (WRITING) Tell the taxi driver's story.

a) Make sentences. Use the simple past. → ○ p. 114

4/5a)

Last winter …

Then …

1. be at the airport • get in
2. be cold • heavy snow
3. be in a traffic jam • talk to

When …

When …

4. arrive at the hotel • forget her saxophone
5. run to the hotel • look for her
6. give the saxophone back • be happy

1. Last winter I was at the airport. A woman …

b) Write an ending for the story. Here's one idea:

4/5b)

invite • concert • brilliant • great evening

8 (SPEAKING) **What did they do at One World Trade Center yesterday?**

a) Ask and answer questions about the people in the picture. → ○ p. 115

4/6
5/7

have a drink   eat   look at   sit   phone   take a photo

A: <u>What did</u> Henry eat? – B: He ate a sandwich.
B: <u>Did</u> Susan take a photo? – A: No, she …

Who ate my sandwich?

b) Now Partner B closes his or her book. Partner A asks questions. Then take turns.

5/8

A: <u>Did</u> Lisa eat a sandwich? – B: No, she didn't. Henry did.
A: <u>Where did</u> Linda sit? – B: Linda …

9 (YOUR TURN) **New York City sights** → V City guide, p. 183

a) Get into groups of five. Each student chooses a different borough of New York.

b) Find out information about one sight in your borough in the library or on the internet:
   – What is special about it?
   – When was it built? / When did it open?

c) Imagine you are a New York taxi driver and the others are tourists: Present your sight to your group. → M Tip top, p. 173

You can start like this:
We are now in … .
Over there you can see … .
It's … . There is/are … .
It was built in … ./It opened in … .

THE BRONX
The Botanical Garden

MANHATTAN
Rockefeller Center

QUEENS
Citi Field

BROOKLYN
The Brooklyn Bridge

STATEN ISLAND
Postcards
9/11 Memorial

STUDY SKILLS

Wenn du im Internet nach Informationen suchst, gib gezielt mehrere Suchbegriffe ein, um das Ergebnis einzugrenzen, z. B. die Sehenswürdigkeit, den Stadtbezirk und „facts for kids". Kinderseiten sind übersichtlicher und sprachlich einfacher.

Ich kann interessante Orte einer Stadt präsentieren. ✔

Living the dream?

1 (READING) **Read the interview with José Blanco.**

1,4
6/1

1 **Interviewer:** Hello José. Can I ask you a few questions for our magazine, please?
José: Hi. Sure.
Interviewer: You're new on the baseball team.
5 Are you happy?
José: We won the first three matches, so I can't complain.
Interviewer: There are lots of players from Latin America here. When did you immigrate
10 to the United States?
José: That was twelve years ago. I was ten.
Interviewer: That was a big decision for your parents. They left their home and moved to a foreign place.
15 **José:** Yes, but they were very poor in Cuba. My father had been unemployed for a long time. My parents wanted to give me and my sisters the best chances.
Interviewer: What were the first years like?
20 **José:** My parents had problems because they hadn't learned English in school. But there's a strong community of Cubans here in New York. So my parents opened a small shop for other immigrants.
25 **Interviewer:** And how did you feel?
José: At the beginning I was homesick. I missed my friends. But my parents had given up a lot for me and I slowly got used to my new life.

Interviewer: When did you begin your baseball career? 30
José: Before I was 15, I hadn't taken any sports seriously. Then I joined the baseball team in high school and we were very successful. After I had become the star 35 of my team, my baseball career started. I've been very lucky. I can live my dream. For most people it's much harder.
Interviewer: What about your plans for the future? 40
José: I'm a US citizen now and my home is here. But I plan to help people in Cuba.
Interviewer: Thank you for your time.

> **CULTURE**
>
> Der amerikanische Traum besagt, dass jeder Mensch durch harte Arbeit ein erfolgreiches Leben führen kann.
> Ist es bei euch möglich, sich vom Tellerwäscher zum Millionär hochzuarbeiten?

2 (WRITING) **Collect facts about José and his family.** → M Think–pair–share, p. 173

a) Complete the fact card. Take notes. → ◯ p. 115

Name: …   From: …   Plans: …
Job: …   Lives in: …
Age: …   Why they left their country: …

> **STUDY SKILLS**
>
> Halte deine Notizen so kurz wie möglich. Schreibe nur Schlüsselwörter auf, keine ganzen Sätze.

b) Find more facts.

Problems at the beginning: ?   Why he is happy now: ?

3 (LISTENING) **Listen to the interview with Angela.**

1,5

Complete the sentences.
1. Angela was —— when she left the Philippines.
2. She lives with her —— in Brooklyn.
3. She had —— with the language, the culture and her papers.
4. She goes to college now and she has also got a —— .
5. Her —— had an accident, so she helps him now.

6/4 **4** **Imagine you want to leave your country.**

a) Complete the sentences with these phrases. → ○ p. 116

6/2

1. Where could I go? I could immigrate to the USA.

2. It will be hard to —— my old life.

3. I hope I will have many —— in the USA.

4. I hope I won't —— and lonely.

5. I hope I can —— my new life soon.

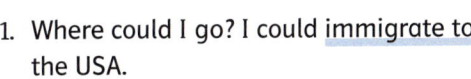

| chances |
| get used to |
| feel foreign |
| immigrate to ✓ |
| give up |

I want to leave this country.

b) Match the sentences with the same meaning. → **V** Going to a new country, p. 180

6/3

1. I want to emigrate from my home country.
2. I can get support from my family.
3. I hope I won't fail.

A I hope I will be successful.
B I want to leave my home country and live in another country.
C My family will help me.

5 (SONG) **Empire State of Mind (Part II) Broken Down**

1,6

Listen to the song. What can you find out about New York?

1 Ooooh, New York!
Ooooh, New York!

Grew up in a town that is famous as a place of movie scenes.
Noise is always loud, there are sirens all around and the streets are mean.
5 If I can make it here, I can make it anywhere, that's what they say.
Seeing my face in lights or my name in marquees found down on Broadway.
Even if it ain't all it seems, I got a pocketful of dreams.

Language detectives → G2, p. 159

Before I was 15, I hadn't taken any sports seriously.
After I had become the star of my team, my baseball career started.

Das simple past und past perfect beschreiben Ereignisse in der Vergangenheit. Das past perfect wird für das Ereignis verwendet, das weiter zurückliegt. Wie bildest du die neue Zeitform?

6 Look at the sentences and say what happened first.

7/5

1. After José's dad had lived in New York for two years, his family joined him.
2. Before José left for the USA, his grandma had died.
3. Before José moved to New York, he hadn't spoken English very often.
4. After José had been in school for a year, he joined the baseball team.
5. After José's dad had opened his own shop, lots of other Cubans came to buy things.

7 Find out about one of Angela's days.

a) Match the sentence parts. The pictures can help you. → ○ p. 116

7/6

A After Pablo had invited Angela to his party, … ✔
B Before Angela ate her pizza, …
C After Angela and Pablo had walked through the park, …
D Before Angela and Pablo went to the stadium, …
E After they had bought tickets, …

… she bought a present.

… they took the subway.

… they visited Ellis Island.

… she had ordered a milkshake.

… they had put on their fan shirts.

b) Complete the sentences about Angela. Use the past perfect.

8/7

Before Angela went to bed, she —— (call) Pablo, she —— (watch) a TV show and she —— (close) the windows.

8/8
52/1

8 (WRITING) Write sentences. Use the past perfect.

a) What <u>had</u> José <u>done</u> before his first important baseball game last summer?
What <u>hadn't</u> he <u>done</u>? → ◯ p. 117

1. played every day ✔
2. bought new sports shoes ✘
3. ordered tickets for my friends ✔
4. watched the other team ✔
5. phoned my dad ✔
6. eaten a big meal ✘

José:
1. Before my first big game I <u>had played</u> every day.
2. I <u>hadn't bought</u> …

b) What <u>had</u> Angela <u>done</u> before she left the Philippines? What <u>hadn't</u> she <u>done</u>?

Before Angela left the Philippines, …

> ask her friends for advice   not organize a party   talk to her uncle on the phone

9 (YOUR TURN) A magazine article → V Presenting personal information, p. 184
→ M Writers' conference, p. 173

8/9
9/1

Collect all the information about José that you can find on page 18.
Use it to write an article about José.

A Cuban–American star

José Blanco is a baseball player with a big future –
that's what people tell us.

José is from … . He immigrated to … when … .
His parents had been … in their home country and José's
dad … .
José lives in … now. He is good at … . He started to take
baseball seriously when … . After he had become … .
Now he … . He wants to … .

Would you like to meet José? Write to us and win a ticket
for his next baseball match.

Einleitung:
das Wichtigste über die Person,
Interesse beim Leser wecken

Hauptteil:
Details zur Person

interessanter Schluss:
z. B. Frage oder Aufforderung
an Leser/Leserin

> Ich kann einen Artikel über eine Person schreiben. ✔

Ellis Island – a symbol of immigration

1 **Why do people leave their home?** → M Think–pair–share, p. 173

2 (READING) **Read the text.**

1,7

1 The United States is a country of immigrants. Between 1892 and 1954 Ellis Island was the most important gateway for twelve million immigrants. In the museum on Ellis Island
5 visitors can look at millions of passenger lists and find out more about their personal family story.

Families often saved money for the father or the oldest son to make the journey alone.
10 They sent for the rest of family when they had a home and a job.
The journey by ship took seven to 21 days. But conditions were very hard on board.

Immigrants were poor, so they traveled third class. It was very crowded and dirty at the 15 bottom of the ship. There was bad food and very little fresh air. Many passengers were sick.
At the end of the long trip, doctors came on board to check the passengers. Then the ship 20 moved slowly into the harbor. The people saw the Statue of Liberty first. "No one spoke a word," said one immigrant. "It was the symbol of the big, powerful country which was our new home." 25
After the ship had arrived in Manhattan, they went to Ellis Island on a small boat. Here they had more checks and personal interviews. About two percent had to go back home because they had diseases or they 30 were too weak to work.
A minority of about 20 percent stayed on the island for days or sometimes weeks for more checks, but the rest could leave after a few hours. 35
The immigrants' journey to the USA was now over. But they still had a long way to go.

3 **Answer the questions about Ellis Island.**

1. How many immigrants arrived from 1892 to 1954?
2. How long was the journey?
3. What were the conditions on the ships like?
   Name three examples.
4. Why did the passengers have to go to Ellis Island?
   Name two reasons.
5. How many immigrants could not stay in the USA?

> **CULTURE**
>
> Jeder, der in den USA geboren wird, hat automatisch die amerikanische Staatsbürgerschaft und einen amerikanischen Pass.
> Wie ist das in deinem Land?

Immigration to the USA

From the 1840s to the 1890s most immigrants to the USA came from Britain, Ireland, Scandinavia and Germany.

Between the 1890s and the 1920s the majority of immigrants came from Italy, Greece, Eastern Europe, Russia and Turkey. Many of them came because they were poor or because there were fights in their home countries. Others came to find work or freedom.

Immigration to the USA today: 2013

- Mexico 135,000
- China 71,800
- India 68,500
- The Philippines 54,500
- The Dominican Republic 41,500
- Cuba 32,000
- Vietnam 27,000
- Others 560,200

Source: Department of Homeland Security

READING SKILLS

Wenn du ein Kreisdiagramm liest, sieh dir die Beschriftungen genau an.

Achte auf die unterschiedlichen Größen der einzelnen Abschnitte innerhalb des Diagramms.

4 Look at the box and find out: Why did people immigrate to the USA?

5 (SPEAKING) Look at the chart and complete the sentences.

This chart shows the countries where the immigrants to the USA came from in … . Most immigrants came from … . The next group came from … . The third group … and … . There were also lots of immigrants from … and lots of other countries.

6 Choose one of these tasks.

OR

a) Work with a partner. Prepare an interview with an immigrant who has just arrived. Here are some questions:

10/1-3

> Where are you from?

> Why did you choose this country?

> What was the journey like?

> What are your plans for the future?

Present your interview to the class.
→ M Dramatic reading, p. 169

b) What is the country of your dreams? What do you like about the country? What don't you like? Give a short presentation to the class.
→ M 1-minute-presentation, p. 168

SPEAKING SKILLS

Interviews und Präsentationen beginnen immer mit einer Begrüßung und enden mit einem Dankeschön.

Ich kann einen Text über die Geschichte der Einwanderung verstehen. ✓

How to become a US citizen

How do I apply for US citizenship?
- be age 18 or older
- be a permanent resident for a certain amount of time (usually 5 years or 3 years)
- be a person of good moral character
- have a basic knowledge of US government
- be able to read, write and speak basic English

Sample test questions:

1. What did the Declaration of Independence do?
2. What is the name of the President of the United States now?
3. In what month do we vote for President?
4. What is one reason colonists came to America?
5. What group of people was taken to America and sold as slaves?
6. There were 13 original states. Name three.
7. Name one Native American tribe in the United States.
8. What ocean is on the West Coast of the United States?
9. Why does the flag have 50 stars?
10. Name two national US holidays.

CULTURE

Um amerikanischer Staatsbürger zu werden, muss man einen Einbürgerungstest machen. Das ist ein mündlicher Test, in dem einem 10 von 100 möglichen Fragen gestellt werden. Von diesen zehn Fragen muss man sechs richtig beantworten. Es gibt auch einen Englischtest. Gibt es so einen Test auch in deinem Land?

Du findest die Lösungen auf S. 282.

11/1-2

1 Fasse die wichtigsten Punkte zusammen.

Was sind die Voraussetzungen, um die amerikanische Staatsbürgerschaft anzunehmen?
- Wie alt muss man sein?
- Was muss man können und wissen? Gib Beispiele.

2 What do you think?

Why do people immigrate to Germany? Give reasons.

Ich kann Informationen über Einbürgerung weitergeben. ✓

New York City, here we come!

1   Talk about New York City.

What do you already know about New York City? Make a mind map of buildings and places.

> the Brooklyn Bridge
>
> **NYC**
>
> buildings   places

CULTURE

Central Park liegt im Herzen Manhattans. Es gibt dort einen Zoo, sieben Seen, eine Eisbahn, Baseballfelder und vieles mehr. Wusstest du, dass der New York Marathon im Central Park endet?
Wo ist der nächste Park bei dir? Was kannst du dort machen?

2   (VIEWING)   Watch the film.

a) Name the sights that Wesley and Jessica show to Ronan. Put them in the right order.

A   B   C   D

b) Match the facts with the pictures.

1. It's between Manhattan and Brooklyn. There were once elephants here.
2. It's not far from Little Italy and there isn't only one of these in NYC.
3. It has names on a 'Wall of Honor'. Maybe Ronan's great-grandparents were here.
4. There are no elevators here. In summer it can get very hot inside.

3   (SPEAKING)   Talk about the film.

Where would you like to go in New York City? Why? Tell your partner.

I would like to go to/see/visit …
because … .
I think … is interesting. I like … .

VIEWING SKILLS

In einem Film sind nicht nur die Personen und die Geschichte wichtig, sondern auch die Orte und das, was man im Hintergrund sehen kann. Suche dir eine Filmsequenz aus und stelle den Ton ab. Was passiert im Hintergrund?

> Ich kann einen Film über Sehenswürdigkeiten in New York verstehen. ✔

Checklist

Ich kann Informationen über New York verstehen. ✔

12

Ich kann interessante Orte einer Stadt präsentieren. ✔

Over there you can see …. • Look at …. • You must visit …. • Around this corner we'll come to …. • Don't miss ….

12

Ich kann einen Artikel über eine Person schreiben. ✔

immigrated to • felt foreign • was homesick • missed • had given up a lot • had many chances • got used to

13

Ich kann einen Text über die Geschichte der Einwanderung verstehen. ✔

13

Ich kann Informationen über Einbürgerung weitergeben. ✔

13

Ich kann einen Film über Sehenswürdigkeiten in New York verstehen. ✔

❀ (TASK) A city profile

Work in groups of three students. Each group chooses an American city and finds out some basic facts about it and its population. Each group makes a poster.

Step 1

Get into groups. Choose an American city.

Choose one of America's big cities like Los Angeles. Look at the map at the back of the book to find an interesting place.

Step 2

Find the basic facts and some photos.

City: Los Angeles
State: California
Sights: Hollywood sign, Venice Beach
One interesting fact about the past:
had a very long Spanish name in 1871
(El Pueblo de la Reina de Los Ángeles)

Step 3

Find the numbers.

Answer these questions with the help of the internet:
1. What's the population of the city?
2. Which ethnic groups are part of the city's population? Name the biggest ones.

STUDY SKILLS

Suche offizielle Webseiten der Regierung, um die korrekten Zahlen herauszufinden. Daten zu Städten in den USA findest du auf der Webseite des US Census Bureau. Du kannst die Angaben dort runden. Finde die größten Volksgruppen heraus und fasse die übrigen Gruppen unter „others" zusammen.

Step 4

Make a chart.

Make a chart. You can make a pie chart (A) or a bar chart (B). Remember that your chart must have a title, labels and a key. Your chart should take up about 30 percent of your poster.

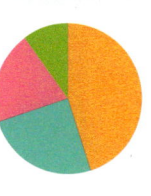

A

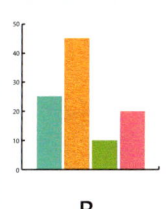

B

STUDY SKILLS

Du kannst Säulen- oder Kreis-diagramme auch mit einem Computerprogramm erstellen. Das ist recht einfach und sieht sauber und ordentlich aus.

Step 5

Write a short text for your chart.

This text should explain the most important information.

most   the next group   the third group   …

Step 6

Finish your poster.

Arrange your photos, chart and texts.
Can you read everything from two metres away?
Don't forget to say where you got your information from.

STUDY SKILLS

Überprüfe, ob dein Poster Aufmerksamkeit auf sich zieht. Ist es gut strukturiert und sieht es gut aus?

Step 7

Put up your poster. → M Tip top, p. 173

0.7 = zero point seven

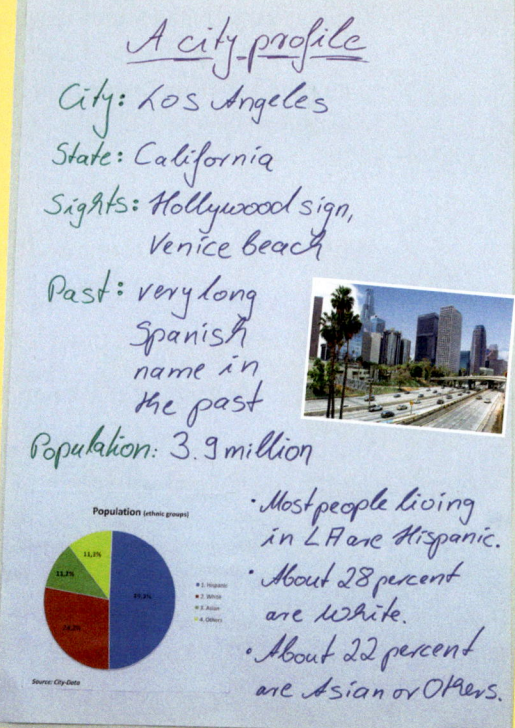

A city profile
City: Los Angeles
State: California
Sights: Hollywood sign, Venice beach
Past: very long Spanish name in the past
Population: 3.9 million

Population (ethnic groups)
1. Hispanic
2. White
3. Asian
4. Other
Source: City-Data

• Most people living in LA are Hispanic.
• About 28 percent are White.
• About 22 percent are Asian or Others.

Make your own street art

Five steps to turn your schoolyard into an American Dream art gallery

You need:

a piece of paper

pens

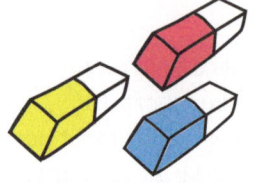

chalk (different colours)

1 **Find out about the American Dream.**

The American Dream

The basic idea of the American Dream is that you can be anything you want – you only have to work hard enough. Typical dreams are, for example, the dream of being happy, rich or famous. Other people dream of a house for their family or want to have a life which is better than their parents' life. Millions of immigrants have come to the United States searching for a country where their dreams can come true. Critics say that the American Dream does not exist in reality because it isn't for everyone.

2 **What do you (not) like about the American Dream?**

3 **Turn your idea into a piece of street art.**

Choose one aspect of the American Dream.

You can write words or sentences and/or draw pictures. Decide the style of your piece of street art.

Vom Tellerwäscher zum Millionär.

Here are some ideas:

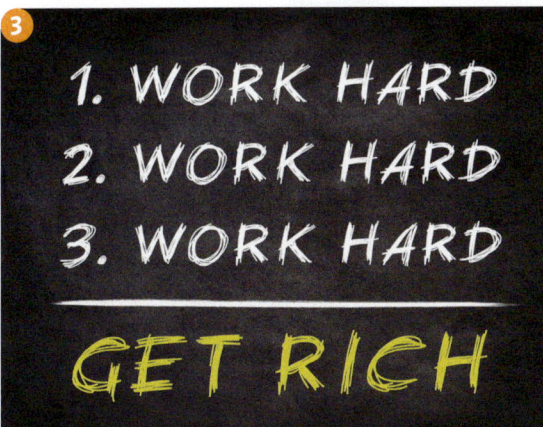

4 Make a draft for your street art on a piece of paper.

5 Draw your street art in the schoolyard with chalk.

Macht Fotos, bevor der Regen eure Kunstwerke wegwischt.

INTERNET

Alaska: Denali National Park
wild and wonderful

🔍 SEARCH   ☰ MENU

Wild and wonderful Alaska is a state full of extremes – freezing winters and warm summers. You can have fantastic adventures and enjoy the amazing wildlife in the USA's most northern state. The park is also the home of Denali, the highest mountain in the United States.

▶ Park history

Ⓐ The life of a Denali husky

The Denali National Park is home to a group of Alaskan huskies. They make travel and transport easier in the park. They travel on paths with the sled where cars and trucks cannot go because of the snow.

▶ Visiting the dogs

Ⓑ Bears in Alaska

One reason tourists come to Alaska is to see the grizzly bears. If you are lucky enough to see them, you will never forget these large, beautiful animals.

▶ What bears eat in the wild

▶ Safety

▶ Bus tours   ▶ Park alerts   ▶ Contact us   ▶ FAQ

Last updated: 02/20/2016
(security information)

1 Find out information.

First look at the website on the left. What could the keywords be to find a website like this? Make a list. Compare it with a partner.

> Je genauer du deine Schlüsselwörter eingibst, desto eindeutiger werden deine Suchergebnisse.
> Wenn du nach Tieren im Denali Nationalpark suchst, beginne mit „animals" und „Denali National Park".
> Benötigst du spezielle Informationen, kannst du in deiner Suchmaschine auch Folgendes eingeben:
> Animal Denali National Park
> Large animals Denali National Park
> What animals are in Denali National Park?

2 Check the information.

Look at the website on the left again. Do you think it is an official website, an ad or a blog? Give reasons.

3 Collect information.

Read text A or B on the left. Write down the most important keywords.

> Es ist wichtig zu wissen, woher die Informationen kommen, die du gefunden hast. Offizielle Webseiten sind verlässlicher als Werbeseiten oder Seiten von Einzelpersonen. Sieh dir immer mehrere Webseiten an.

offizielle Webseite	Werbung	Blog
– Datum, Update – Geschäfts-/Sicherheits-informationen …	– Slogan – kurz, einfach – große Fotos …	– eigene Meinung – wie ein Journal oder Tagebuch …

17/1-3

4 Do a search.

Search for more facts about your topic. Present two interesting things.

1. List keywords.
2. Search the internet.
3. List two to three different websites.
4. Prepare a short presentation.

Here are some ideas:
– Huskies: Training? Typical day? Summer dog sledding?

– Bears: Food? Food cache? Bear spray?

> Benutze deine eigenen Worte, wenn du die Informationen der Webseiten weitergibst. Kopiere nicht einfach den Text. Aber ändere keine Fakten.

⊕ Find more online:
i8ce82

3 ⊟ 1,8 ☞   ## Unit 2

Teens in the Midwest

The American Midwest is famous for its huge areas of farmland and small towns. The summers are very hot and the winters are very cold. In some areas there are terrible storms.

In the 1840s a lot of European settlers moved west. They wanted to find land and gold. The Native Americans had to sell their land and move to reservations.

● 1 (SPEAKING) Talk about the photos.

a) Match the photos with the headings. 18/1-2 ⊡
Which two photos have the same heading?

> Student jobs   The past
>
> Country life   School life

b) Which photo do you like most?
→ M Round robin, p. 172

Photo x looks great. • I like photo x most.
I'm interested in .... • I really like ....

● 2 Read the texts and answer the questions.

1. What is the Midwest famous for?
   The Midwest is famous for its farmland and small towns.
2. Why did European settlers move west?
3. Where can high school students get a job?
4. What's special about the grades at American high schools?
5. When is Homecoming?

3

High school students over 14 often have jobs. They can work in stores, clear the tables or serve in restaurants or cafés.

4

American high schools are usually big. There can be over 2,000 students. They are 15 to 18 years old. They can get grades from A (very good) to F. The schedule is almost the same every day.

5

At the start of the new school year students celebrate Homecoming. There's a football game and a dance. Students vote for a Homecoming King and Queen.

3 (LISTENING) **Listen to a radio report about a tornado.**

1,9

Complete the sentences. Use five of these words:

dangerous	clouds	help
strong	cars	storm
interview		

> tornado [tɔːˈneɪdəʊ] – Tornado, Wirbelsturm
> warning [ˈwɔːnɪŋ] – Warnung
> storm chaser [ˈstɔːm ˌtʃeɪsə] – Sturmjäger/in
> cloud [klaʊd] – Wolke

1. Warren is a —— chaser.
2. The wind is really —— .
3. The —— are moving very fast.
4. The situation is —— .
5. Warren wants to —— some people.

A student exchange

1 What can you see in the photo?

2 (READING) Read Luise's report.

1,10

1 "No! An exchange year in South Dakota? That's in the middle of nowhere," I thought. But after my year there I can say that it was the best time ever.

5 In the beginning it was like in a movie. I had seen it all on TV. My American school was huge. Teachers usually stay in their classrooms, and students go to them for each class. So we had to put our things into our

10 lockers. After two weeks I got used to it, and I could find the way to the classrooms by myself. Every day school started at 8:00 with a morning message from the principal. The

15 first class started at 8:30. I had to take Math, English, Science and History. But I could choose subjects like Astronomy and Journalism, for example. We also had six classes a week in the study hall. There we

20 could do our homework or study. You weren't allowed to talk there.

School rules were strict. Much stricter than at home. Another rule was: You weren't allowed to wear short skirts.

Classes finished at 3:30. After that there were 25 many extracurricular activities. I wanted to join the cheerleaders. There was a lot of competition for places. Exchange students were allowed to try too, so I did. And I got a place! Awesome! 30 My host family was great too. They even took me on a trip to the east coast. My exchange year was fantastic, even in the middle of nowhere.

3 (WRITING) Find out about Luise's exchange year.

a) Make a mind map. → ◯ p.118

b) What did Luise like? What didn't she like? Make a list.

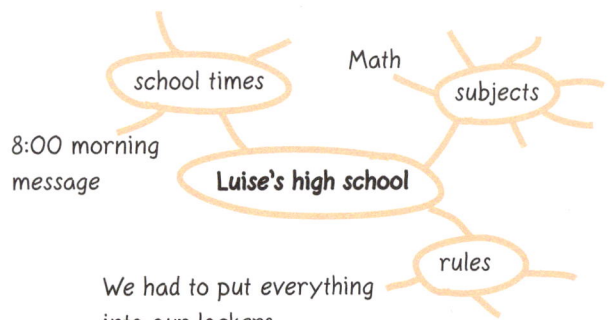

CULTURE

Eltern müssen ihre Kinder nicht in die Schule schicken. Sie dürfen sie auch zu Hause unterrichten. Das tun aber nur sehr wenige (ca. 3%). Gibt es Homeschooling auch in Deutschland?

19/1-2a) **4** **What do these words mean?**

a) Match the words with the definitions. → ○ p. 119

| grade | principal | study hall | locker | exchange year |

1. where students keep their things
2. the leader of a school
3. where you can do your homework or study
4. a number or letter that tells you how well you did in a test
5. a year with a host family in another country

b) Choose the right word. → **V** At American schools, p. 186

19/2b)

1. Math and English are —— .
2. Astronomy and Journalism are —— .
3. When you have to stay at school after classes you have —— .

| electives | detention |
| core subjects |

5 (SPEAKING) **Describe a school day.**

19/3
20/4

a) Describe a day at an American high school. Use the photos for help.

	Monday	Tuesday	Wednesday	Thursday	Friday
1	English	English	English	English	English
2	Math	Math	Math	Math	Math
3	Science	Science	Science	Science	Science
4	History	History	History	History	History
5	Journalism	Journalism	Journalism	Journalism	Journalism
6	Astronomy	Astronomy	Astronomy	Astronomy	Astronomy

(1) In the morning most students go to school by bus. (2) Then students .... (3) At 8:00 there's ....
(4) After that they .... (5) At 1:00 there's .... (6) After school ....

b) Describe a typical day at your school. Use the sentences from a) for help.

6 (SONG) **Cool kids**

1,11

Listen to the song. How does the singer describe the 'cool kids'?

1 She sees them walking in a straight line,
that's not really her style.
And they all got the same heartbeat,
but hers is falling behind.
5 Nothing in this world could
ever bring them down.
Yeah, they're invincible, and she's just in the

background.
And she says,

I wish that I could be like the cool kids,   10
'cause all the cool kids, they seem to fit in.
I wish that I could be like the cool kids,
like the cool kids.

Language detectives → G3, p. 160

I <u>had to</u> take Math, English, Science and History.
I <u>could</u> choose subjects like Astronomy and Journalism.
Exchange students <u>were allowed to</u> try too.

Wie sagt man im simple past,
dass man etwas tun
– konnte?
– durfte?
– musste?

7 (SPEAKING) **Talk about school rules.**

52/2

20/5-6

a) What <u>was</u> Luise <u>allowed to</u> wear at high school? What <u>was</u> she <u>not allowed to</u> wear?

INTERNET

High School Dress Code

Dos

jeans

simple T-shirts

jewellery

Don'ts

jeans with holes

short tops

very short skirts

Luise <u>was allowed to</u> wear jeans. She <u>wasn't allowed to</u> …

21/7 **b)** What are you allowed to do at school? What aren't you allowed to do?
Use different verbs.

We are allowed to <u>wear</u> … . We aren't allowed to <u>wear</u> …

> leave   stay   wear ✓
>
> use   …

8 Complete the sentences.

52/3

a) Write the sentences about Luise and the cheerleaders. → ○ p. 120

21/8a)

1. Before Luise joined the cheerleaders she <u>had to</u> get the right clothes.
2. She was fit, so she —— worry.
3. For the first practice she —— be there 15 minutes early.
4. During her first practice the cheerleaders —— shout really loudly.
5. Luise learned very quickly, so she —— do extra practice.

> had to
>
> didn't have to

b) What did or didn't you have to do on your first day at school after the summer holiday?

21/8b)

> buy exercise books   do homework   get my books   get up early   …

On my first day at school after the summer holiday I had to … but I didn't have to … .

21/9 **9** **Make sentences about Luise's life after her exchange year in the USA.**

a) Say what Luise <u>could</u> (+) or <u>couldn't</u> (−) do after her exchange. → ◯ p. 120

Luise
1. − get used to her old life easily
2. + understand English a lot better
3. + speak English a lot better
4. − keep in touch with all her American friends
5. + help other students with English

1. **Luise** <u>couldn't</u> get used to her old life easily.

b) Interview Luise about the things she could or couldn't do after her exchange.
Use the phrases from part a) and make questions.

1. Interviewer: Could you get used to your old life easily?
   Luise: No, I couldn't. (I missed my host family and my American friends.)

✳**10** (YOUR TURN) **A comparison** → V Comparing schools, p. 190 → M Writers' conference, p. 173

a) Use your notes about American schools from page 34, exercise 3. Make a table:

	American high schools	German schools
school times	8:00 to 3:30	…
…	…	…

b) Compare American and German schools.
Give your opinion: Would you like to go to an American school? Say why (not).

1. You can start like this:
There are many students like Luise who go to an American high school for one year. What is different from schools in Germany?

2. You can go on like this:
In the USA school starts at … and finishes at … . Our school in Germany also starts at …, but we finish at … .

In American high schools students … .
For German schools this is the same/different. We … .

3. You can end like this:
I would (not) like to go to an American school because … .

WRITING SKILLS

So schreibst du einen Vergleich:
1. Stelle dein Thema vor.
2. Nenne im Hauptteil drei Fakten für beide Seiten.
3. Am Ende schreibst du deine eigene Meinung.

Ich kann das Schulleben in den USA und in Deutschland vergleichen.

A lesson outside school

1 **Have you ever tried to earn some extra money? What did you do?** → M Think–pair–share, p. 173

2 (READING) **Read the story.**

1,12
22/1

1 Like a lot of American teenagers Michael
Adams (16) needed to earn some money.
He wanted to get his driver's license soon,
he needed new clothes, and he had a
5 new girlfriend. When he read the advert
for a student job in a sports store, he thought,
"That's the perfect job for me. With all the
customers it'll never be boring." He applied
for the job.
10 The job interview was tough. The manager
asked lots of difficult questions. "What will
you do if somebody steals something?" or
"What will you do if a customer complains?"
Michael answered all the questions and they
15 offered him the job. Ten hours a week and
the minimum wage was OK for him.
His co-workers were very helpful. At the
beginning everything was new and exciting.
After two weeks, however, Michael learned
20 that jobs have their good and bad sides. Some
days were really boring. He didn't have much
to do. On other days he was busy, so he didn't
know what to do first.
One Saturday two students from his school
25 came into the store. They started teasing

INTERNET

Student Jobs

JIMMY'S
SPORTING GOODS   Lincoln, NE

Job title: Sales associate
Job type: Weekends
Education: High school

Bring your love of sports to Jimmy's.

him. "You'll miss all the fun if you work here
every weekend. Just look at you. If you wear
a uniform like that, you won't be one of the
cool kids, ever."
Michael got angry. He got into a big argument 30
with them and in the end he threw them out
of the store.
Later that day his manager called him into
his office. "I can understand you," he said.
"But what will our customers think? Be more 35
responsible. If this happens again, you'll lose
your job."

3 **Find the right order.**

A He throws them out of the store.
B Two students start teasing Michael.
C He gets the job.
D Michael needs money.
E There's a job interview.
F He applies for a job.
G Michael's job has good and bad sides.
H The manager talks to Michael in his office.

4 (SPEAKING) What do you think?

a) What should or shouldn't Michael say to the manager? → ○ p. 120

1. "I'm sorry."
2. "It won't happen again."
3. "But they started it."
4. "It wasn't me."
5. "I don't think you're right."
6. "Next time I'll try to be cooler."

b) Imagine you apply for the job in the sports store. Answer the manager's questions.

1. What will you do if somebody steals something? – I think I'll ... .
2. What will you do if a customer complains? – I think I'll ... .

call ... · talk to ... · say, " ... "

5 (LISTENING) Listen to Marie on her first day at work at Fruit4U.

1,13
52/4

Choose the right answer.

1. Who is Stacey?
   the manager • a co-worker
2. What is Fruit4U famous for?
   the best location and the most friendly waiters •
   the freshest fruit and the lowest prices

3. What are Marie's working hours?
   9:30 a.m. to 3 p.m. • 9 a.m. to 2 p.m.
4. How long is Marie's break?
   30 minutes • 40 minutes
5. How can she get extra money?
   extra hours • good feedback

6 (WRITING) Practise words to describe people at work. → M Peer correction, p. 171

a) Copy and complete the table. → ○ p. 121

22/2

lazy ✓ · hard-working · helpful · responsible · unmotivated · unfriendly

+	–
...	lazy
	...

hard ⚡ working

Welche bekannten Wörter stecken in den neuen Wörtern drin?

b) Find the opposites. → V Describing people, p. 187

22/3

confident · generous · polite · rude · selfish · shy

7 (SPEAKING) Describe the most ... job.

22/4

Think of ten jobs in English. Make a list in two minutes. Then say which job is the ...

most dangerous · most exciting · most boring · best-paying

A: I think a football player has got the most exciting job because he has got a lot of fans.
B: I don't think so. I think an actor has got the most exciting job because ... .

Language → G4, p. 161

If this happens again, you'll lose your job.
If you wear a uniform like that, you won't be one of the cool kids.

Diese Sätze bestehen aus zwei Teilen, dem If-Satz und dem Hauptsatz. In welchem Teil verwendest du das simple present, in welchem Teil das will-future?

8 **What does Marie think after her first day at work? Use the will-future.** → M Bus stop, p. 168

23/5

1. If I watch everything that Linda does, I'll learn quickly. (learn)
2. If the customer feedback is good, I —— extra money. (get)
3. If I have to cut fruit all day, I —— . (not complain)
4. If a customer is unfriendly, I —— polite. (stay)
5. If my friends work every weekend too, we —— time for parties any more. (not have)
6. If I get sick, I —— the manager. (call)

23/6 **9** **Complete the sentences.**

a) Use the simple present. → ○ p. 121

| find a job ✓ | buy two | complain | be late | steal something | need help |

1. If Michael finds a job, he'll earn money.

2. If he ——, he'll ask his co-workers.

3. If he ——, he'll lose his job.

4. If the girl ——, Michael will catch her.

5. If the man ——, he'll get a new sweatshirt.

6. If the woman ——, she'll get one free.

b) What will happen if Michael gets sick? Make a chain of sentences.

If Michael gets sick, he'll stay at home. If he stays at home, he .... If ...

53/5 **10** (SPEAKING) **What will you do if …?**

a) Talk about next weekend. → ◯ p. 121

23/7a)

1. If I get up late,
2. If the weather is fine,
3. If it rains,
4. If I don't have any homework,
5. If my parents are away on Saturday evening,
6. If I'm too busy,

I'll
I won't

watch TV.
have a party.
go cycling.
go to the cinema.
go shopping.
have breakfast.
look for a student job.
…

b) Find a partner. Ask him or her about next weekend.

23/7b)

A: What will you do if you get up late?
B: I'll/I won't …

❀**11** (YOUR TURN) **A job for me** → V Jobs, p. 191

26/1-2

Which student job would you like to do? Choose one and talk about it.

JOBS FOR TEENS

Dog walker
– work near your home
– be outside (also when the weather is bad)
– earn $10 per hour

Babysitter
– look after kids in their homes
– work very often in the evenings
– earn $12 per hour

Paperboy/girl
– work early in the morning
– every day (even on Sundays)
– earn $40 per week

I would like to work as a papergirl because
I like to get up early.
I'm a responsible person,
so this is the perfect job for me.
If I get the job, I'll buy clothes.

dog walker	babysitter	paperboy
I like …	it's the best paying job	…
helpful	hard-working	…
get tickets for …	…

Ich kann über Schülerjobs sprechen. ✔

A first date

1 Which stereotypes of American high school characters do you know from movies and TV shows? → M Placemat, p. 171

2 (READING) Read the comic strip.

1,14

1. Dylan often thought about Abby. He really liked her. But he was too shy to ask her out on a date.

2. One day his books fell out of his locker right when Abby showed up. Scott was with her, of course. How embarrassing.

Forget her. She's not interested in you. She has a boyfriend.

Who's that guy? Look at him!

3. A few days later they had lunch together. Dylan helped Abby with her Science project. They didn't see Scott and his football friends.

4. When Dylan went to the gym, the boys attacked him. Scott pushed him really hard and Dylan couldn't do anything about it.

Isn't she your girlfriend?

Let me explain. It's not that hard!

Stay away from her!

Stop it! You're hurting him!

3 (SPEAKING) Talk about the story.

a) Do you like the story? Why (not)?

I (don't) like the story because ... .

> funny   boring   (not) real life
>
> romance   stereotypes   ...

b) Who is ... ?

A shy
Dylan is shy. That's picture 1.
B proud

C nervous
D unfriendly
E worried

F furious
G brave
H helpful

5. A few days later Dylan asked Abby, "Are you coming to the dance with me?" And she said yes. He was very nervous when he picked her up.

6. The party was great. Everybody enjoyed the music and dancing. There was a big surprise that evening. Dylan and Abby were so proud.

7. At the end of the evening Dylan took Abby home. There it was, the perfect moment. But …

 4 Retell the story.

1. Work in groups of three.
   Each student chooses two pictures.
2. Take notes for your pictures.
3. Tell your part of the story.

> **STUDY SKILLS**
>
> Wenn du einen Comic nacherzählst, benutze auch die Informationen aus den Bildern.

Photo 1
football match – Dylan – his friends – talk about Abby – shy – boyfriend – football player

Dylan and his friends talked about Abby at the football match. Dylan liked Abby but he was too shy to ask her out on a date and she had a boyfriend anyway. He was a very good football player.

 **5 Choose one of these tasks.** → M Tip top, p. 173

P **a)** Do Dylan and Abby stay together? What happens next? Write the last paragraph.

24/1
25/2-3

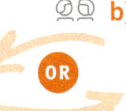 OR

b) Choose one scene. Make a freeze frame. Let other groups guess.

The next day …   Then …   After that …   In the end …

Ich kann einen Comic über das Highschool-Leben verstehen.

How to get your driver's license

Classroom Driver Ed
Length: 9 weeks

Classroom driver education is a course for all students who will be 15 years old before the last day of instruction and who have successfully completed eight out of ten courses in 8th grade. The course introduces students to basic skills of driving.
To take the written and practical driving test, please contact your local driving school.

DRIVER EDUCATION APPROVAL FORM

Name and Address of Driver Training School:

Sally's Driving School Inc., 524 Bird Highway, Park Ridge 60068 IL

Student's Full Name:　(last) Jenkins　(first) Caitlin　(middle) Amy

Street Address:　1815, Baxendale Road

City or Town: Chicago　　**ZIP Code:** 60004 IL

Caitlin A. Jenkins　　12/16/2016
Signature of Student　　**Date**

Steve. M. Jenkins
Signature of Parent

CULTURE

Amerikaner haben keinen Personalausweis. Sie benutzen stattdessen ihren Führerschein. Nach fünf Jahren muss man einen neuen beantragen (aber man muss die Prüfung nicht wiederholen).

1 **Berichte darüber, wie man in den USA den Führerschein macht.**
27/1

2 **Pass on the information in a conversation about how to get a driver's license.**
27/2

A *(from Germany)*: In welchem Alter kann man bei euch in Illinois den Führerschein machen?
You: At what age … ?
B *(from Illinois)*: At the age of 15. And in Germany?
You: …
A: Mit 18. Aber man kann ihn auch schon mit 17 machen, wenn eine weitere Person mit Führerschein im Auto dabei ist.
You: …
B: So, do you need a parent's signature for that too?
You: …
A: Ja, das stimmt. Muss man in den USA auch eine theoretische und eine praktische Prüfung ablegen?
You: …
B: …

Wenn du ein bestimmtes Wort auf Englisch nicht weißt, sage es mit anderen Worten.

Ich kann Informationen über den Führerschein weitergeben.

The new kid at school

new kid: Ronan

buddy: CJ

1 Talk about a new school.

a) What would you show a new kid at your school?

I would show him/her the cafeteria, ...

b) How would you feel if you were the 'new kid' at school?

I would be ... .

nervous   excited   shy   ...

2 (VIEWING) Watch the film.

4

a) Watch the film until 02:48. Right or wrong?
Correct the wrong sentences.

1. A buddy is a teacher's favourite student.
2. CJ and Ronan are in the same homeroom.
3. Ruby has had seven detentions this year.
4. They have Math first period.
5. All students say the Pledge of Allegiance.

b) Watch the film from 02:48 to the end. Name the
places that Ronan and CJ go to. Say one sentence
about what they do there.

CULTURE

In den USA beginnen viele Schulen
jeden Tag mit dem Treueschwur. Die
Schüler stehen auf, legen ihre rechte
Hand aufs Herz, sehen zur amerikanischen Flagge und geloben der Nation
und Gott ihre Treue.
Hältst du einen Treueschwur für eine
gute Idee? Warum? Warum nicht?

3 (WRITING) Write about the film.

Write Ronan's e-mail to Roy, his best friend at his old
school, to tell him about his first day at the new school.

E-MAIL

Hi Roy,
I must tell you about my first day at school. I met CJ.
He's my buddy. He's really ... . We went ... . Then I met
... . Can you believe that ...?
Bye,
Ronan

VIEWING SKILLS

Die meisten Filme beginnen mit einer
Eröffnungsszene. Sie zeigt die Tages-
zeit, den Ort des Geschehens und die
beteiligten Personen etc. an.
Sieh dir die Eröffnungsszene im Film
an. Was erfährst du dort?

Ich kann einen Film über den ersten Tag an einer neuen Schule verstehen. ✔

Checklist

Ich kann Informationen über den Mittleren Westen verstehen. ✔

28

Ich kann das Schulleben in den USA und Deutschland vergleichen. ✔

In American high schools … .
• In German schools … . • In the USA most students go to school by … . • School rules … stricter. • … is the same. • But … is different.

28

Ich kann über Schülerjobs sprechen. ✔

I would like to work as a … . •
I'm very/not so good at … . •
If I earn money, I'll buy … . •
If I work in my free time, I won't have much time for … .

29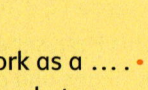

Ich kann einen Comic über das Highschool-Leben verstehen. ✔

29

Ich kann Informationen über den Führerschein weitergeben. ✔

29

Ich kann einen Film über den ersten Tag an einer neuen Schule verstehen. ✔

✿ (TASK) A speech

Every year your class elects a class president. You would like to be the next one. Give a 1-minute speech. Then answer your classmates' questions.

Step 1

Collect ideas.

What's important for you and your class?
(good team, nice teachers, fun …)

What topics interest you?
(school trips, projects, …)

What are you good at?
(listening to …, talking to …, …)

What will you do if your class elects you?
(try to paint the classroom a new colour, have a party every month, …)

Step 2

Structure and write your speech.

→ **M** 1-minute-presentation, p. 168

1. How can you start your speech?
2. Why would you like to be the next class president? Use one paragraph for each topic.
3. How can you finish your speech?

WRITING SKILLS

Eine Rede hat ähnliche Merkmale wie die meisten geschriebenen Texte: Einleitung, Hauptteil, Schluss.

Auf der nächsten Seite findest du eine Vorlage für eine fertige Rede.

Step 3

Practise your speech. → M Read and look up, p. 172

Find different partners.
Practise your speech in front of them.
Read your speech a couple of times.
Then make notes and repeat your speech
again and again.

> **SPEAKING SKILLS**
>
> Um gewählt zu werden, musst du deine Klasse
> überzeugen. Es ist wichtig, dass sie dir zuhört.
> Du kannst z. B. Dinge wiederholen, die dir
> wichtig sind. Sprich nicht zu schnell oder zu
> langsam.

Step 4

Give your speech.

- Stand straight and try to relax.
- Look at your listeners from time to time. Eye contact is important.
- Speak loudly and clearly.

> Dear class,
> Next Friday will be a big day for all of us. We're going to elect our
> class president.
> I think our class is already a really good team. If you elect me,
> I'll … . I'll listen and … . If you have any problems, I'm sure … .
> I promise … because I'm hard-working and motivated.
> You think classes could be more fun? You think we should have …?
> Come and talk to me. I'll try to talk to the teachers and the principal.
> Thanks for listening. I'll be happy to answer your questions now.

Step 5

Answer your listeners' questions.

Answer the questions politely.
If you didn't understand the question, ask the person to repeat it.

High school electives

In American high schools you can choose from a number of electives, depending on your interests. They also look great on your CV. Some courses offer extra credits for your graduation.

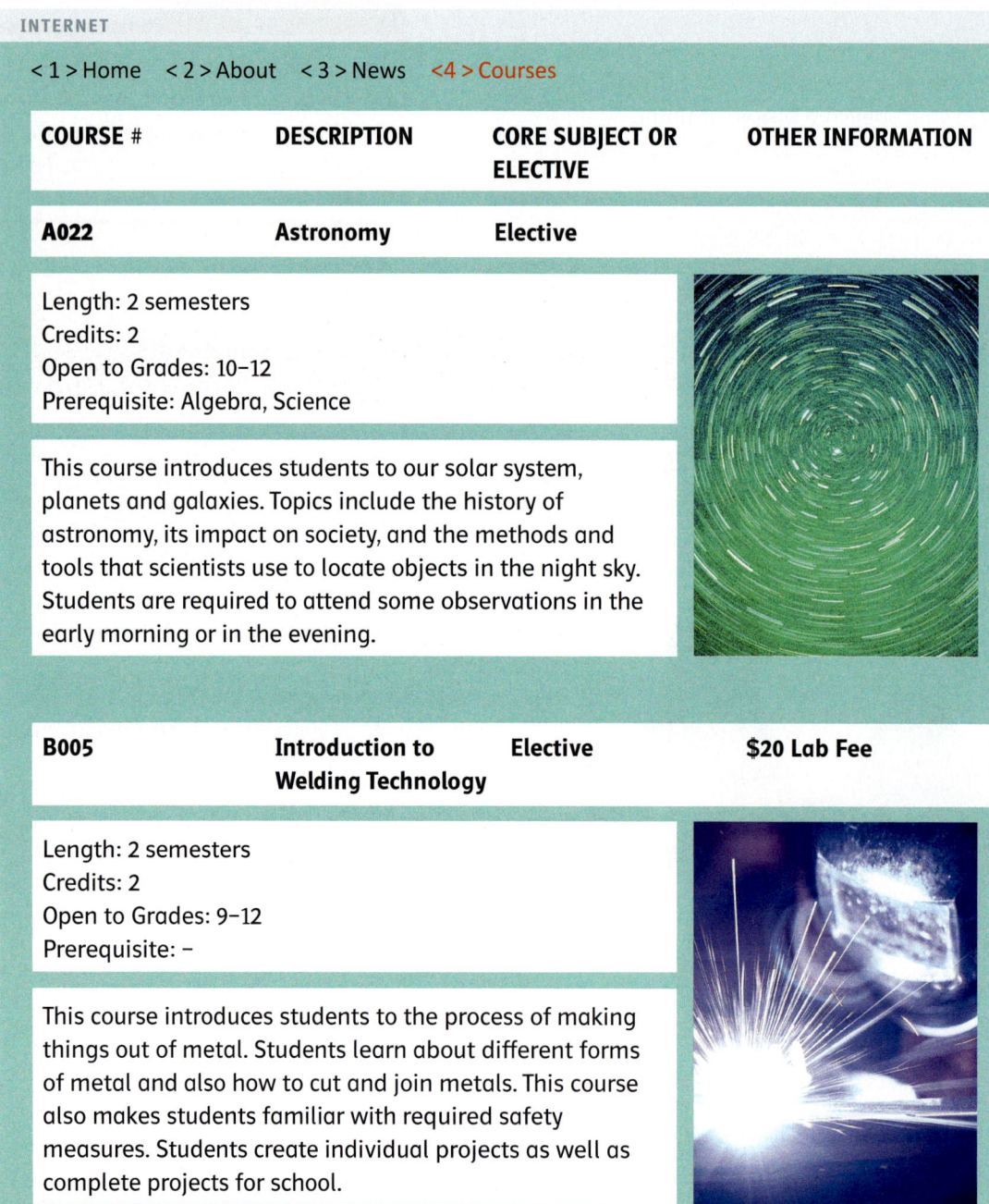

INTERNET

< 1 > Home   < 2 > About   < 3 > News   <4 > Courses

COURSE #	DESCRIPTION	CORE SUBJECT OR ELECTIVE	OTHER INFORMATION
A022	**Astronomy**	**Elective**	

Length: 2 semesters
Credits: 2
Open to Grades: 10–12
Prerequisite: Algebra, Science

This course introduces students to our solar system, planets and galaxies. Topics include the history of astronomy, its impact on society, and the methods and tools that scientists use to locate objects in the night sky. Students are required to attend some observations in the early morning or in the evening.

B005	**Introduction to Welding Technology**	**Elective**	**$20 Lab Fee**

Length: 2 semesters
Credits: 2
Open to Grades: 9–12
Prerequisite: –

This course introduces students to the process of making things out of metal. Students learn about different forms of metal and also how to cut and join metals. This course also makes students familiar with required safety measures. Students create individual projects as well as complete projects for school.

C011	Journalism	Elective

Length: 1 semester
Credits: 1
Open to Grades: 9–12
Prerequisite: –

This course introduces students to the fundamentals of journalism. Topics include writing, editing, layout and graphic design. Students learn different styles of journalistic writing such as news, interviews, features, sports, book and movie reviews, and blogs. They contribute articles to the school's yearbook and online newspaper. Students are required to work in teams, be ready to write articles in their free time and have to meet deadlines.

1 **Which elective would you choose? Say why.**

2 **Think of electives for your school and write a course description.**

Ihr könnt euren Gedanken freien Lauf lassen!

- Collect ideas in groups.
- Write a course description.
  Say what the course is about, what students can learn there and what they have to do.
  Write about 50 words.
- Present your course descriptions in class.
- Vote in class to find the most popular elective.

STUDY SKILLS

Verwende ein Computerprogramm zur Textverarbeitung.
Hier findest du ein paar Anregungen:
- Wähle eine Schriftart und eine Schriftgröße zwischen 10 und 14 aus.
- Hebe die Überschrift fett oder mit Farbe hervor.
- Verwende den Wortzähler und die Rechtschreibprüfung.
- Du kannst Textfelder einfügen, um deine Seite zu strukturieren.
- Du kannst ein Foto im Internet suchen und herunterladen, um deinen Text interessanter zu machen.
- Du kannst eine Seitenfarbe für den Hintergrund auswählen.

American football

A
- Super Bowl: most famous sporting event
- first Sunday in February
- famous sporting event on TV
- like a national holiday
- final match of the season
- game first played in USA in 1869

B

protective pads
helmet
jersey
protective pants
gloves
football
football boots

C
- team of supporters
- motivate players and fans
- today: 95% girls
- dance, jump, shout loudly, do stunts
- 1–3 minutes per performance

D
- pass the ball by throwing and kicking
- allowed: running with the ball, hands
- take the ball as far as possible into the other team's half
- score: touchdown, field goal

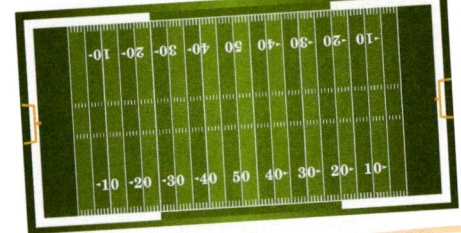

E

F
- team sport
- each team: 11 players on the field
- one game: 60 minutes (plus breaks)
- 4 quarters (one quarter = 15 minutes)

1 Organize the cards on the left.

a) Choose a heading for each card and each photo.

- Equipment
- General facts
- Basic rules
- Cheerleaders
- Move and score
- Performance

b) Put the information cards and the photos in a suitable order.

2 Prepare your presentation about American football.

a) Prepare your poster, transparency or computer presentation.

b) Use the prompt cards from page 50 or prepare your own prompt cards.

3 Practise your presentation.

You can practise your presentation in front of the mirror or with family and friends.

1. Give an introduction.

2. Present the different aspects of your information.

3. End your presentation. Emphasise the most important facts and come to a conclusion.

33/1-3 ## 4 Give your presentation.

Schlage neue Wörter nach. Achte darauf, dass du die richtige Bedeutung auswählst und die Wörter richtig aussprechen kannst. Überlege dir, wie du deiner Klasse unbekannte Wörter erklären kannst. Nutze dazu Fotos oder Skizzen. Du kannst manche Wörter auch umschreiben oder vormachen.

Prüfe, ob deine Präsentation gut ist:
- große Überschrift
- keine Rechtschreibfehler
- Fotos

Das sollte auf deinen Karteikarten stehen:
- nur Stichwörter (keine ganzen Sätze)
- die Erklärung neuer Wörter

Hier sind hilfreiche Redewendungen für den Einstieg:
My presentation is about … .
First, I'd like to talk about … .

So kannst du zum nächsten Punkt deiner Präsentation überleiten:
Now I'm going to talk about … .
My next topic is … .
Finally, I'm going to talk about … .

Bedanke dich bei deinen Zuhörern für ihre Aufmerksamkeit und biete an, Fragen zu beantworten:
That's the end of my presentation.
Thank you for listening. Do you have any questions?

Sieh dein Publikum an, während du sprichst. Sprich langsam, klar und deutlich. Beziehe dein Poster oder deine Folie in deine Präsentation mit ein. Achte auf die Zeit.

Find more online:
i8ce82

5 📖 1,15 ☞ ## Unit 3

In the Northeast

The Northeast of the United States goes from the border with Canada to Washington D.C. Here you can visit the amazing Niagara Falls or enjoy miles of beaches. In the fall you can drive through beautiful red and gold woods.

The USA is a huge country. For example, it's a six and a half hour flight from Boston to Los Angeles. Families often live and work thousands of miles away from each other. So they like to meet for important celebratio

1 (SPEAKING) **Talk about the photos.**

What can you see in the photos? Tell your partner. Can he or she find out which photo it is?

36/1-2 ⬈

A: I can see an old house.
B: That's photo 4.

2 Read the texts and choose the right answer.

1. The Northeast is famous for **beautiful woods • short winters**.
2. It takes six and a half hours to get from Boston to Los Angeles **by car • by plane**.
3. On Thanksgiving most people eat **fish • turkey**.
4. **Most of • Half of** Maine is forest.
5. The Amish **can't choose how they want to live • don't use TVs or phones**.

3
On Thanksgiving almost everyone eats a turkey dinner. The president 'pardons' a turkey in the White House.

4
The state of Maine is a favorite location for creepy movies and books. It's 90 percent forest, not many people live there, and the winters are long and dark.

5
The USA is called the 'land of the free'. People can choose how they want to live. The Amish are an old Christian community who live without modern inventions like TVs or phones.

 3 (LISTENING) **Listen to a story about a Niagara daredevil.**

1,16

Right or wrong?

1. The woman who tells the story was on a boat trip. That's **right.**
2. She saw a boat go over the Niagara Falls.
3. An old man climbed out of it.
4. He was hurt.
5. He wanted to become a stuntman.
6. The second time he had to pay money.

> daredevil [ˈdeəˌdevl] – Draufgänger/in
> close [kləʊs] – nah
> barrel [ˈbærl] – Faß; Tonne
> to sign autographs [ˌsaɪn ˈɔːtəgrɑːfs] –
> Autogramme geben

Ich kann Informationen über den Nordosten der USA verstehen. ✔

A family Thanksgiving

1 What is the biggest celebration that your family has?

2 (READING) Read the dialogue.

1,17

The Millers from Boston are getting ready for Thanksgiving dinner. Julia is in the kitchen. Her husband Mark, their son Jacob and Grandma Brenda are in the living room. Her daughter Lily lives with her boyfriend Evan in Washington D.C. They are not there yet.

1 Grandma: Last year we had a terrible storm. I got stuck in my car for over two hours. Do you remember?

Mark: Yes, that's right. Did you have a hard

5 time again yesterday?

(The doorbell rings. Mark opens the door. It's their neighbor.)

Robert: Happy Thanksgiving, Mark!

Mark: You too, Robert. How are you doing?

10 Robert: Great, thanks. Brr. It's very cold outside.

Mark: Come on in. I'm so glad you could make it. *(They enter the living room.)* Grandma, this is Robert. He's our new neighbor.

15 He doesn't have family here, so we've invited him to join us. Robert, this is Brenda.

Robert: Nice to meet you, Brenda.

Grandma: Nice to meet you too. When did you move here?

20 Mark: *(He shouts across the room)* Jacob, why don't you say hello? You can't spend all your time on your phone.

Jacob: What's up Robert?

Robert: How's it going? Are you enjoying

25 the holiday? Do you like turkey?

Jacob: Not really. I'm a vegetarian, so I won't eat any.

Julia: *(She comes out of the kitchen.)* You always used to eat everything. *(She notices the new guest.)* Oh, hi Robert. 30

Robert: Hey Julia. Thanks so much for inviting me. Here's a little present. You eat chocolates, don't you? *(He gives her a box as a present.)*

(Mark's phone rings.) 35

Mark: That's probably Lily. Hello Lily. … Oh, no! *(to the others)* Their plane from Washington, D.C. had troubles and they had to land in New York. *(to Lily)* So when does your plane arrive? … OK. … Will you call 40 again later?

I promise we'll save some turkey for you!

CULTURE

Small Talk ist in den USA sehr wichtig. Man unterhält sich über sehr einfache, alltägliche Dinge. Was sind für euch alltägliche Dinge?

3 Find out about the Miller family's Thanksgiving. → M Peer correction, p. 171

a) Who is it? → ○ p. 122

1. Who got stuck in her car last year?
   That's **Brenda**.
2. Who is the new neighbor?

3. Who doesn't eat turkey any more?
4. Who gets a present?
5. Who talks to Lily on the phone?

b) Find out three things about Lily.

4 (LISTENING) Listen to the conversation.

1,18 ⏺
37/1 ⎙

a) Choose the right picture.

b) Listen to the conversation again. Who says it?

1. You've finally made it.
   That's Mark.
2. Everything's fine, thanks.
3. Nice to meet you.
4. How was Thanksgiving?
5. Can I help with anything?

5 (WRITING) Collect small talk phrases.

37/2 ⎙

a) Match the sentences. → ○ p. 123

1. How's it going?
2. What's up?
3. Sam, this is Beth.
4. Nice to meet you.
5. Do you like turkey?

A Not really.
B Nice to meet you too.
C Not much.
D Great, thanks.
E Beth, this is Sam.

b) Find answers. → V Small talk, p. 192

1. How are things going?
2. Are you enjoying the holiday?
3. Please have a seat.

6 (SPEAKING) Make small talk. → M Milling around, p. 170

Use the sentences from exercise 5.

7 (SOUNDS) Listen, read and say.

1,19 ⏺

1. Do you like turkey? ↗
2. Yes, I love turkey. ↘
3. I've lived in Boston for five years. ↘

→ **G5**, p. 162

Language

Do you like turkey?
Did you have turkey yesterday?
Will you have turkey later?

Wie bildest du Fragen in der Gegenwart, der Vergangenheit und der Zukunft?

8 Choose the right tense.

38/3-5
53/6

Die Signalwörter helfen dir.

1. **Do** • **Did** • **Will** you usually prefer turkey or ham?
2. **Does** • **Did** • **Will** your dad always watch a football game on Thanksgiving?
3. **Do** • **Did** • **Will** you see the heavy storm on the news yesterday?
4. **Do** • **Did** • **Will** you travel by plane last year?
5. **Do** • **Did** • **Will** you teach me how to make a great cake like this tomorrow, please?
6. **Does** • **Did** • **Will** Grandma stay with you next Thanksgiving?

53/7 **9** (SPEAKING) **Ask questions about holidays.**

a) Choose the right question word. Interview your partner. → ◯ p. 123

39/6a)

Which ✓	Where	Who	How many	What

1. **Which** holidays does your family celebrate?
2. —— do you always eat at Christmas / Easter / Eid / …?
3. —— does your family invite every time?
4. —— guests did your family invite last time?
5. —— will you celebrate next year?

Which holidays does your family celebrate?

We celebrate Christmas and Easter.

b) Look at the picture. Think of more questions that Grandma asks at the family party.

39/6b)

When will you …?

Do you already have a girlfriend?

How old …?

What will you do when you leave school?

…

10 Make a phone call.

a) Complete the phone call between Jacob and his grandma with these questions. → ○ p. 124

39/7a)

Did you have a good trip home? • Will you be there? • Can I bring my new girlfriend? •
What about you? • When will you celebrate? • How are you? ✓ • Where will you celebrate?

Jacob:	Grandma:
Hi, Grandma. This is Jacob. (1) How are you?	Hi, Jacob. I'm fine. (2) —— How nice of you to call me.
(3) ——	Yes, I did. I didn't have any problems with the weather or the traffic. I hope to see you all again on my 65th birthday. I'm planning a big family celebration.
(4) ——	I'll celebrate on May 1. (5) ——
Yes, I think so. (6) ——	Here at my house, in Miami.
That sounds cool. (7) ——	Yes, of course. I'd like to meet her.
I'm sure you'll like her.	…

b) Ask two more questions and finish the phone call. You can use these phrases.

39/7b)

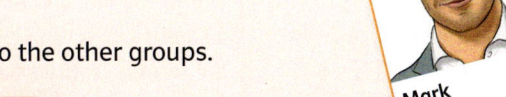

| How old …? | Where … meet her? | I'm sorry I'll have to … now. | Bye. |

✿ 11 (YOUR TURN) A holiday dialogue → M Dramatic reading, p. 169

a) Work in groups of five. Each of you chooses a role from the dialogue on page 54.

b) Listen to the dialogue, then practise and read the dialogue.

c) Give feedback to the other groups.

Grandma
very friendly

Julia
happy to meet
everyone again

Mark
friendly but strict
with his son

Jacob
doesn't enjoy
family parties

Robert
happy to be there

READING SKILLS

Wenn ihr einen Dialog vorlest, achtet auf die richtige
Aussprache und lest den Text so oft, bis ihr ihn ohne
Stocken lesen könnt. Benutzt eure Stimme, um die
Gefühle der Personen gut auszudrücken. Lest z. B.
schneller, wenn es aufgeregt klingen soll.

Ich kann einen Text ausdrucksstark vorlesen. ✓

One country, different worlds

1 **What have you used electricity for today?** → M Round robin, p. 172

This morning I've used the lights, the elevator …

2 (READING) **Read the texts about two American teenagers.**

1,20

1 I live in a small Amish community in
Pennsylvania. Our lives are simple. We don't
have modern devices like a TV, a fridge,
a phone or a computer. That means we can
5 concentrate more on our community life.
I also cover my hair, wear long dresses, and
never use make-up. We grow our own food too.
The people in our community look after each
other. It doesn't matter what you wear or
10 how you look. It's important who you are and
what you do. I really like that.
We don't usually have much contact with
the outside world. But at 16 we're allowed
to go there for some time and do 'forbidden
15 things'. I watched movies, went to parties and
drank alcohol. But I felt lonely.
Now I have to make the most important
decision of my life: Do I join the Amish
community or not?
20 Just think: if I didn't go back, I would really
miss my family and my community. This is
where I belong. I'm sure I'll do the right thing.

I'm an average American girl. I'm interested 1
in fashion and yes … gossip too. I'm always
on the phone. I couldn't live without it.
My friends and I chat a lot about everyone
and everything. 5
My first big decision of the day is: What
am I going to wear? At school we usually
talk about who's wearing what or who's
going out with whom. I often meet my
friends. If I had a car, I would drive around 10
town with them. But I don't have one yet.
Sometimes we go bowling, watch movies or
have something to eat.
Some of my friends go to church, but
I don't. I wouldn't like to change anything 15
about my life.

> **CULTURE**
>
> Die Amischen sind eine religiöse Gruppe, die im
> 18. Jahrhundert aus Europa ausgewandert ist.
> Sie führen in ihren Gemeinschaften ein ein-
> faches Leben und sprechen einen deutschen
> Dialekt. Welche anderen Lebensstile kennst du?

3 (SPEAKING) **Talk to your partner: Which headings would you choose for each text?**

A It's all about fashion and people

B Different from others

C Life in a community

D An average teenager

A: I would choose … for text 1 because …

B: I (don't) agree. I would …

4 Compare the girls' lives.

a) What's important in life?

Look at the texts again and find three things for each girl.

b) Do Ruth and Jennifer like the way they live? Find the information in the text.

Ruth likes the way she lives. The text says in lines 20 to 22, "…". Jennifer …

5 (WRITING) Sort the phrases. → M Peer correction, p. 171

a) Copy and complete the table. → ○ p. 124

40/1a)

I agree 👍	I disagree 👎
Exactly.	…

Exactly. ✓   That's true.   I don't think so.   That's for sure.   Absolutely not.   No way!

b) Put the phrases into the right list. → V Agreeing and disagreeing, p. 193

40/1b)

– I'm sure: …
– I'm not sure: …

As far as I know, …   I guess …   I'm convinced that …   It's clear to me that …

40/2
41/3

6 (SPEAKING) Talk about devices.

a) Make a list. → ○ p. 125

Rank the devices from the most important to the least important. Talk to your partner.

microwave 1   headphones 2   TV 3   phone 4   computer 5

The most important thing for me **is my phone.** • I don't think **phones** are more important than **computers.** • **TVs** come first/second/third. • **Headphones** are next.

b) Which device could you live without? Talk to other students. → V Devices, p. 193

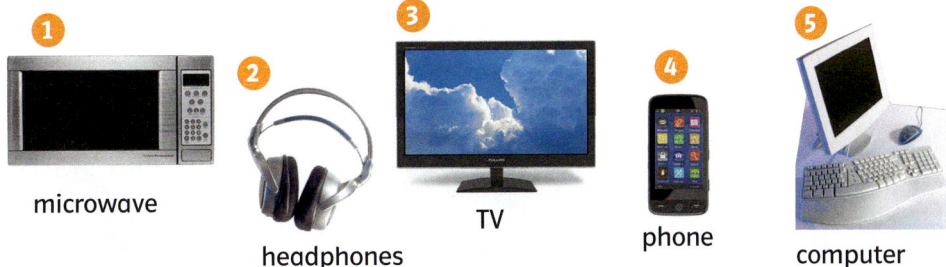

fan   dishwasher   vacuum cleaner   razor   radiator

Language → G6, p. 163

Jennifer: If I had a car, I would drive around town with my friends.
Ruth: If I didn't go back, I would miss my family.

Wie wahrscheinlich ist es, dass die Bedingung (If-Satz) in Erfüllung geht?
In welchem Teil des Satzes verwendest du would und die Grundform des Verbes,
in welchem das simple past?

7 Complete the sentences.

41/4

1. If Jennifer met Ruth, they would compare their different lives. (compare)
2. If Ruth stayed with Jennifer, Jennifer —— bowling with her. (go)
3. If Ruth didn't know how to use a computer, Jennifer —— her. (help)
4. Ruth —— Jennifer how to grow her own food if she visited Ruth's family. (show)
5. Jennifer —— about her clothes if she lived with the Amish. (not worry)
6. Jennifer —— make-up if she stayed with Ruth's family. (not use)

Erinnerst du dich? Die
Verneinung von „would"
ist „wouldn't".

8 What would make Jennifer's life easier?

a) Look at the pictures. Complete the sentences. → ◯ p. 126

41/5

| walk |
| go |
| have |
| not listen |
| choose ✓ |

1. Jennifer would be less worried in the morning if she chose her clothes the evening before.

2. She wouldn't get so tired in the morning if she —— to bed early.

3. She would hear what her dad said if she —— to music.

4. She wouldn't get cold if she —— a warm coat.

5. It would be better if she —— to school.

b) What would make your life easier? Make three sentences.

42/6

My life would be easier if **I had breakfast in the morning**.

42/7

9 (SPEAKING) What would you do if ...? → M Milling around, p. 170

a) Answer the questions. Then ask your partner. → ○ p. 126

What would you do if you …
1. were president of the United States for a day?
2. were a hero?
3. could go back in time?
4. had a million dollars?
5. knew the answers to your next English test before the test?

What would you do if you were president of the United States for a day?

If I were president, I would give all students computers.

That's not a bad idea. But if I were president, everyone would get free food.

b) Make more questions for your partner.

| be a teacher | | meet an alien | | have no brothers/sisters | | … |

If I was a teacher, I would …

✳10 (YOUR TURN) Giving your opinion → V Giving opinions, p. 196

42/8
43/1-2

Could you live without electricity? Why (not)? Write a short text. Give two reasons.

The question is "Could I live without electricity?"
I could live without electricity
because it would be an adventure.
If I had no lights, I could use candles.
I also think that I would have more time
because I couldn't surf the internet.
So my answer is "yes", I could live without electricity.

couldn't

I would …   I couldn't live without …

phone   fridge   …

couldn't …   would …

"no", I couldn't

> **WRITING SKILLS**
>
> 1. Nenne dein Thema. 2. Sage deine Meinung. 3. Begründe deine Aussage.
> 4. Fasse deine Argumente am Schluss kurz zusammen.

Ich kann meine Meinung sagen und begründen. ✔

The Body by Stephen King, 1982

1 What do you do when you meet your friends?

2 (READING) Read the story.

1,21

In The Body, *Gordie Lachance and his three friends hear that a boy from their area, in the state of Maine, has disappeared and is probably dead. They decide to go on a trip to find the boy's body and here they are preparing for the trip.*

1 **The Gun**
My room was on the second floor, and it was really hot up there. I was glad
I wasn't sleeping there that night. I was excited about where we were going.
I grabbed two blankets and all my money, which was less than a dollar.
5 Then I was ready to go.
I went down the back stairs. I didn't want to meet my dad. I was on my way
to the clubhouse when Chris caught up with me. His eyes were shining.
"Gordie! You want to see something?"
"Sure. What?"
10 Chris put his hand into his backpack and took out a big gun.
"Where did you get that?"
"From my dad's desk."
"Man, your dad's going to beat you when he finds out."
Chris's eyes just went on dancing. "He isn't going to find out. He and his
15 friends have got enough wine to keep them drunk for a week.

I'll put it back before then."
Chris hated alcohol – he'd already seen too much of what it can do.

20 "Have you got bullets for it?"
"Nine of them."
"Any in it at the moment?"
"No, of course not. What do you think I am?"

25 I finally took the gun. I liked the heavy way it sat in my hand.
I pointed the gun at a large tin.
KA – BLAM!
The gun jumped in my hand.

30 Fire shot from the end. It felt as if my wrist was broken. My heart was in my mouth. There was a big hole in the tin.
"Wow!" I screamed.
Chris was laughing wildly; I couldn't tell if he was amused or scared.

35 "You did it, you did it! Be careful, everyone! Here comes Gordie!"
"Shut up! Let's go!" I screamed, and grabbed him by the shirt.
I gave the gun to Chris.
"Oh, man, that was really great."
"You knew there was a bullet in it, didn't you? That was a mean trick, Chris,

40 really."
"I didn't know, Gordie, honestly. I just took it out of my dad's desk. He always takes the bullets out of it. I think he was too drunk to remember last time."
Chris looked as innocent as a baby, but when we got to the clubhouse we

45 found Vern and Teddy waiting, and he started to laugh again.
He told them the whole story. Everyone laughed. Teddy asked Chris,
"What do you think we need a gun for?"
"Nothing, really," Chris said. "But maybe we'll see a wild animal.
And anyway, it's scary out in the forest at night." Everyone agreed with that.

50 Chris was the strongest and bravest guy of us all, and he could say things like that.

"Did you put your tent up in the field?" Teddy asked Vern.
"Yeah, and I put two lamps in it and turned them on, so it'll look as if we're there after dark."

55 "So let's go," Teddy said. "It's almost twelve already."
Chris stood up and we gathered round him.
"We'll walk across Beeman's field," he said, "and then we'll get to the railway tracks and just walk across the bridge into Harlow."
"Come on, you guys," Chris said, and picked up his backpack,

60 blankets and water bottle.

CULTURE

In den USA sterben jährlich ungefähr 30.000 Menschen durch Schusswaffen. Das Gesetz besagt, dass jeder Amerikaner das Recht hat, eine Waffe zu besitzen. Viele Amerikaner glauben, dass sie eine Waffe brauchen, um sich selbst zu schützen.
Wer darf in Deutschland eine Waffe tragen? Wie findest du das?

---

3 **Do you like the story? Say why or why not.**

I (don't) like the story because ... .

funny · boring · exciting · creepy · a mystery story · an adventure · crazy · ...

4 **Work with the story.**

a) Put the sentences in the right order.

A The boys tell their friends what happened.
B Gordie takes the gun and shoots.
C They leave before twelve.
D Gordie meets Chris.
E Chris shows Gordie his father's gun.
F Gordie gets ready to leave home.

b) Who tells the story? Choose the right answer.

Chris • Gordie • Vern • Teddy • another person

c) Do you think this chapter is near the beginning or the end of the book?

I think this chapter is near the beginning/the end of the book because ... .

5 Find out about Chris and Gordie.

a) Choose the right adjective.

excited ✓   brave   worried   scared   amused

1. Gordie is <u>excited</u> because he and his friends are going on a trip to find a body.
2. Gordie is —— about what Chris's dad would do if he found out.
3. Gordie is —— after he shot the gun.
4. Chris is —— that Gordie shot the gun.
5. Gordie thinks that Chris is very —— .

b) Talk to your partner:

Do you think Chris knew about the bullet in the gun?

I think he knew/didn't know about the bullet in the gun because … .

6 Choose one of these tasks.

a) Find out on the internet how the story *The Body* by Stephen King goes on. Continue the summary. Add five sentences.
→ M Writers' conference, p. 173

The story *The Body* by Stephen King is about the adventures of Gordie Lachance and his three friends. They hear that a boy from their area has disappeared and is probably dead. They decide to go on a trip to find the boy's body …

44/1-3

b) Work in groups of four. Design a cover for the book. → M Gallery walk, p. 169

Take the roles of the four characters and take a photo. Add the title of the book and the writer. Print it and put up your cover in class. Which cover does your class like most?

STUDY SKILLS

Ein Cover sollte neugierig auf das Buch machen und die Atmosphäre des Buches widerspiegeln. Überlegt euch, wie die Charaktere zueinander stehen sollen. Welcher Hintergrund ist geeignet? Welche Schriftart ist für den Titel geeignet? Wo sollte der Titel platziert werden?

Ich kann eine Geschichte über Freunde verstehen. ✓

From Chicago to Boston

A

OUTGOING TRIP	September 16 (Fri)		Price (USD)
Chicago, IL >	24h 25m >	Boston, MA	Total fare for
08:05 a.m.		09:30 a.m.	1 Adult
		(+ 1 days)	$89
RETURN TRIP	September 18 (Sun)		
Boston, MA >	22h 30m >	Chicago, IL	Total fare for
05:00 p.m.		02:30 p.m.	1 Adult
		(+ 1 days)	$89
		Subtotal	$178
		Taxes and fees	$ 5
		YOUR TOTAL	**$183**

B

Sep 16 (Fri)
1:39 p.m.   5:05 p.m.   2h 26m
Chicago, IL   >   Boston, MA
Sep 18 (Sun)
5:30 p.m.   9:17 p.m.   4h 47m
Boston, MA   >   Chicago, IL   Philadelphia
                                     1 stop

Flight	$141.85
Tax & Fee	$ 47.35
Trip total	**$189.20**
(round trip)	

C

One-way
Time: 14h 46m
Distance: 982 miles
Price of gas:
about $160

---

1 **Beantworte die Fragen.**

45/1-2

Welches Verkehrsmittel ist am billigsten?
Welches am schnellsten? Erstelle ein Ranking.

> **CULTURE**
>
> In den USA gibt es neun Zeitzonen. In Boston ist es immer eine Stunde später als in Chicago. Wie viele Zeitzonen hat Europa?

2 **What do you think?**

If you had to go from Berlin to Frankfurt/Main, how would you get there? By train, plane or bus?
Say why. Find information on the internet.

> Ich kann Informationen über Reisemöglichkeiten weitergeben. ✓

Trouble at Thanksgiving

Jessica's dad

Jessica

1 Look at the photo and guess.

a) What is Jessica making?

b) What could the trouble be? Collect ideas in class and vote on the best idea.

Now watch the beginning of the film.
Were you right?

Ronan

Jessica's mum

2 (VIEWING) Watch the film.

6

a) What else goes wrong that day?

Find out about Amy, Ronan's mum Ella and the turkey.

b) Thanksgiving Day: Which six things do they talk about in the film?

Amy

big parade	balloons	turkey dinner
barbecue party	nice presents	
football game	special songs	pecan pie
president's pardon	volunteer work	
terrible traffic		

CULTURE

Thanksgiving bedeutet „give thanks" (sich bedanken). In den USA kommt an diesem Tag die Familie zusammen. Mit einem Festessen wird die gute Ernte gefeiert und meistens wird dabei ein Dankgebet gesprochen.
Gibt es bei euch so eine ähnliche Tradition?

3 (SPEAKING) Talk about the film.

a) Watch the film from 03:19 again.
What activities do people do at Thanksgiving?

b) Which of these activities are most interesting to you? Say why.

I think ... is really interesting. I love ... .
I like ... because ... .
... is great because ... .

VIEWING SKILLS

Filme beinhalten oft Fotos oder Videos mit zusätzlichen Informationen oder Neben-handlungen.

Ich kann einen Film über Thanksgiving verstehen. ✓

Checklist

Ich kann Informationen über den Nordosten der USA verstehen. ✓

46

Ich kann einen Text ausdrucksstark vorlesen. ✓

What's up? • How's it going? • I'm glad you could make it. • How was …? • Are you enjoying …?

46

Ich kann meine Meinung sagen und begründen. ✓

I really like that. • I wouldn't change … . • I don't think so. • That's for sure. • Absolutely not. • That's true. • I couldn't live without … .

47

Ich kann eine Geschichte über Freunde verstehen. ✓

47

Ich kann Informationen über Reisemöglichkeiten weitergeben. ✓

47

Ich kann einen Film über Thanksgiving verstehen. ✓

✳ (TASK) A talk show

'One day without your phone – piece of cake or total nightmare?' Organize a 5 to 10-minute talk show. At the end make a decision if you want to live without your phone for one day. Do more than one show for practice and for fun.

Collect ideas. → M Think-pair-share, p. 173

Collect arguments for both sides:
What's good about a day without a phone? What isn't?

Step 2

Get into groups: 'piece of cake' or 'total nightmare'.

It's always easier to present your own opinion. However, you sometimes have to take a different perspective. Think of that when you make groups.

Step 3

Prepare for the show.

1. Decide on three to four arguments.
2. Explain your arguments, give reasons and examples.
3. Decide who is going to present which argument in the show.
4. Write your arguments on cards (keywords only).
5. Practise your talk.

> In my opinion one day without my phone is a piece of cake. I think our parents use our phones to check what we are doing. I'm sure you all know situations like this: You're out with your friends and you have fun. Suddenly your phone rings and your mum asks, "Hi, where are you? Why are you not at home yet?" How embarrassing! That's why I think: If we didn't have any phones, our parents couldn't control us.

Step 4

Set the scene and act the show.

1. Prepare the classroom for the show: Arrange the tables and chairs.
2. Decide which groups are going to be in the first show.
3. Your teacher is the host.
4. Act the show.

SPEAKING SKILLS

Sprich das Publikum direkt an, um dessen Aufmerksamkeit zu gewinnen. Sprich flüssig, aber nicht zu schnell.

Step 5

Make a decision.

What does your class think? Should you live without phones for one day?

Step 6

Do more shows for practice and for fun.

The voyage of the Mayflower

The story of the Mayflower

In September 1620, I sailed from Plymouth, in England, to the New World. On board my sailing ship, the Mayflower, were 102 people who were later to be known as the Pilgrims. They left England because they didn't have religious freedom and they wanted to start a new life.

After two months of heavy storms in the Atlantic Ocean, we landed at Cape Cod where we stayed for the winter. Many people died because of the cold, hard winter, diseases and also of hunger. Thank God, we met Indians who gave us food, showed us how to hunt and to catch fish. Later they showed the Pilgrims how to grow corn. The Pilgrims decided to stay at Cape Cod and founded the colony of Plymouth, named after the starting point of their crossing.

My crew and I left the colony in March. I heard that after the first year in the New World, the Pilgrims invited the Indians for a meal. They celebrated a festival to say thanks for the successful harvest – they called it 'Thanksgiving'.

CULTURE

Viele Städtenamen in den USA kommen ursprünglich aus Europa. Manche Namen sind identisch, wie zum Beispiel „Plymouth". Oft stellten die Siedler auch ein „New" vor den ursprünglichen Namen - New York (benannt nach York in England), New Orleans (benannt nach Orléans in Frankreich) ....
Welche deutschen Städtenamen gibt es in den USA?

Build your own Mayflower with recyclable material.

Step 1: Prepare yourself.
You can recycle lots of everyday things to build your own Mayflower: You can choose things from this material list (or your own ideas) in steps 2 to 4 below.

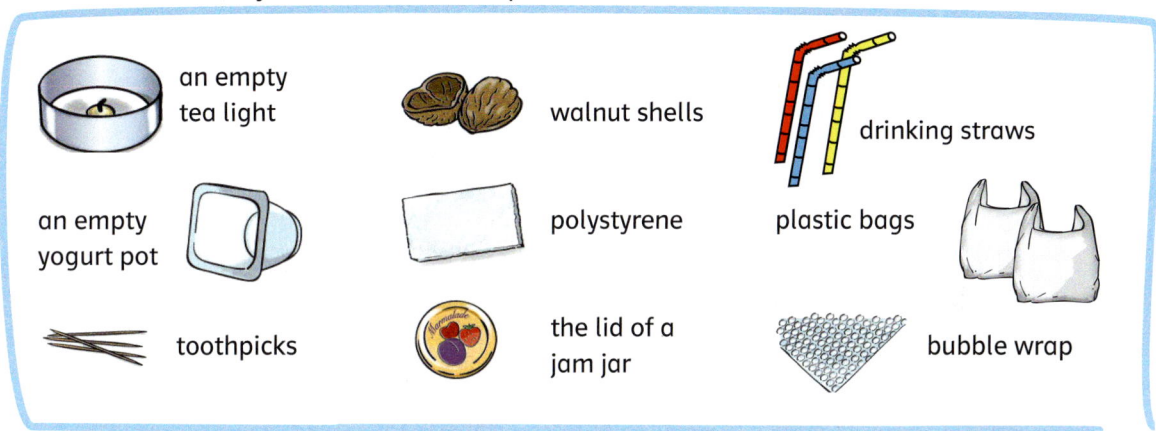

an empty tea light

walnut shells

drinking straws

an empty yogurt pot

polystyrene

plastic bags

toothpicks

the lid of a jam jar

bubble wrap

You also need:

scissors   tape   glue stick   waterproof felt-tips   coloured paper

Step 2: Build and design the body of the ship.
- Choose a material that floats.
- Make the body of the ship.
- Use things like coloured paper and waterproof felt tips to decorate your Mayflower.

Step 3: Make the sails.
- Make the masts and sails and fix them to your Mayflower.

Step 4: Add the crew and passengers.
- Make the Pilgrims, Christopher Jones (Master of the Mayflower) and his crew.
- Put them on your Mayflower.

Welches Schiff kommt zuerst an?

Step 5: Start the journey.
- Fill a big plastic box or a sink with water to make your Atlantic Ocean.
- Put your Mayflower in the water.
- Blow the sails of your Mayflower to make it cross your Atlantic Ocean.

1,22

Healthy and active at Thanksgiving?

> headline

written by Pam Warner
(published 07/12/16 in Health & Style)

> writer, date, source

1 What is your Thanksgiving like? Turkey and pumpkin pie? American
football on the sofa? A new trend has become popular in the USA: More
people like to eat better quality food and live a more active life.

> introduction

Fast food is slowly going out of fashion. A number of people shop for
5 organic food at special supermarkets now. In some states farmers'
markets sell fresh vegetables and fruit from the region. "There are also
other products like bread and meat without chemical additives at these
markets. Organic food is much healthier and it tastes a lot better too,"
explains Emma from Boston. So how about some healthy recipes for
10 Thanksgiving? Pumpkin soup maybe? A roast turkey breast filled with
apples and cranberries is delicious too.

But there's more to a healthy lifestyle than just food. A lot of trend
sports show that you can have fun, spend time with friends and stay
fit at the same time. Have you found the right sport yet? How about
15 standup paddleboarding? If you like water, that's the ideal kind
of sport for you. You stand on the board and you use a paddle
to move through the water. Don't worry, you don't have to travel
to the sea. A lot of clubs offer standup paddleboarding on lakes
and rivers.

> main part

20 Of course living healthy also means no alcohol and no drugs. Finn, a
fitness instructor from Cleveland, says: "Drinking too much alcohol
isn't good for your health. Most alcoholic drinks have a lot of calories
and negative effects on your fitness too. So why not try a smoothie
instead?" Drugs are even worse. You can easily get addicted, and you
25 often get problems with your family or at school.

To sum up, you can say that organic food together with doing sport is a
great way to stay fit. You don't have to do without your favorite meals.
Just changing your lifestyle a bit will make you a much happier person.

> conclusion

1 Read the text and take notes.

Find the most important keywords in each paragraph and make a list. Look at the examples in the introduction and the first paragraph on the left.

> Notiere keine Beispiele, keine Zahlen, keine Vergleiche, keine Zitate oder direkte Rede. Sie sind für eine Zusammenfassung nicht nötig.

2 Write a summary of the text.

Use your notes to write your summary.

> Normalerweise ist eine Zusammenfassung nicht länger als ein Drittel vom Originaltext. Sie kann natürlich auch kürzer sein. Benutze immer deine eigenen Worte.

1. Start with the introduction. Name the title, the writer and where the text comes from. Don't forget to say what the text is about.

> So kannst du deine Zusammenfassung beginnen:
> The text/article/story "…" was written by … on … . The text/article/story is about … .

2. Now summarise each paragraph of the main part in a few sentences. Use your notes to help you.

Here's an example for the first paragraph:

First Pam Warner writes about organic food. You can get it at special markets. It's without chemical additives and it tastes much better. You can use it for healthy Thanksgiving recipes.

> Benutze für die Zusammenfassung das simple present. Verwende verbindende Wörter zwischen den Sätzen oder Abschnitten:
> First … • Then … • After that … • Finally …

3. Write a conclusion.
   Say what you think about the article.

> So kannst du deine Zusammenfassung beenden:
> I think … . • In my opinion … . • To sum up, I can say … .

50/1-2
51/3-5

3 Check your summary.

Read your text again and check:

- Spelling (all words correct?)
- Grammar (correct tense?)
- Style (linking words?)
- Content (the most important information?)

He, she, it – das –s muss mit!

> Wenn du Wörter aus dem Text verwendet hast, kannst du dort nachschauen, ob du sie richtig geschrieben hast. Ansonsten schlag im Wörterbuch nach und kontrolliere deinen Text mit Hilfe der Checkliste auf Seite 175.

Am Ende dieser Unit kann ich . . .
- **Informationen über Kalifornien und den Westen der USA verstehen.**
- **eine Werbeanzeige gestalten.**
- **über Trends sprechen.**
- **einen Text über den Goldrausch verstehen.**
- **Informationen über Kinderarbeit weitergeben.**
- **einen Film über Beruf und Karriere verstehen.**

7 □ 2,1 ☞ Unit 4

California dreams

1

With its 840 miles of coast, California has something for everyone – giant redwood trees in the north and sunny beaches in the south. People live a relaxed lifestyle here. They enjoy surfing and beach volleyball.

2

In San Francisco you can take cable cars which go up and down the hills or visit the largest Chinatown outside of Asia. The Golden Gate Bridge is the city's most famous sight.

1 Look at the photos. → M Think–pair–share, p. 173

a) Use the photos to start a mind map with a partner.

coast   ?   history

CALIFORNIA

people   companies   famous places

b) Now tell the class what you already know about California.

2 Read the texts and add more information about California to your mind map.

54/1-2

3

In 1849 the California Gold Rush started. Hundreds of thousands of people moved to the west. They hoped to find gold there and get rich.

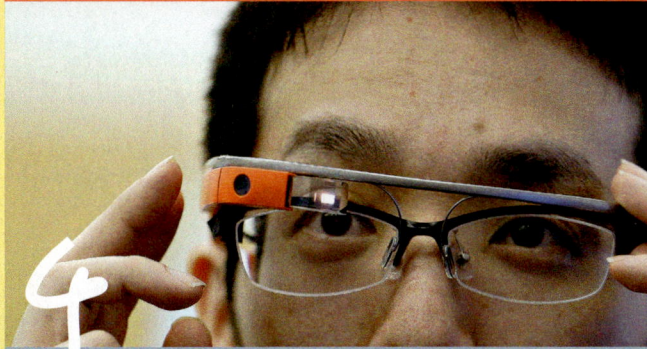

4

There are a great number of modern high-tech companies in Silicon Valley near San Francisco. You can find the world's largest companies there.

5

Hollywood is the capital of the world's movie industry. You can visit the movie studios there and see the Walk of Fame.

---

 3 (LISTENING) **Listen to the information about the Golden Gate Bridge.**

2,2

Complete the notes.

The Golden Gate Bridge

1. almost —— miles long
2. the —— of the bridge: Joseph Strauss
3. opened in ——
4. safety net saved —— workers
5. colour of the bridge: ——
6. —— of San Francisco and California

> bay [beɪ] – Bucht
> architect [ˈɑːkɪtekt] – Architekt/in
> safety net [ˈseɪfti ˌnet] – Sicherheitsnetz

Ich kann Informationen über Kalifornien und den Westen der USA verstehen.

Enjoy the sunny west!

1 Describe the photos in the ads.

55/1 a) Read the description of photo 1.

In photo 1 I can see a beach.
It's a sunny day.
In the background there is the sea.
In the foreground I can see a man and a bus.
The man is standing next to the bus. He is carrying a surfboard.
He has black hair and he is wearing a top and short trousers. He is smiling.

b) Describe photos 2 and 3.

1 Come and chill out in sunny California

2 Book the adventure of a lifetime
Canyon Tours
Phone reservations
8 a.m. to 6 p.m.
702-574-04455

3 If it looks fun, it is fun!
Rock Climbing for kids in Bishop, CA
Click here to learn more.

2,3 **2** (LISTENING) Listen to a conversation about an ad.

a) Answer the questions. → p. 127

    1. Emily, Carol and Daniel are talking about one ad from exercise 1. Which one?

    2. Who doesn't like the ad?

b) What does Daniel dream about?

    Daniel dreams about ... .

86/1

3 (SPEAKING) What do you think of the ads?

55/2a)
a) Use these words to talk about the ads. → ○ p. 127

| simple | informative | special | clear | spectacular | catchy |

I think ad number 1 is/isn't … .

55/2b)
b) Match each word with one of the ads. Does your partner agree? → **V** Adjectives for ads, p. 197

| fascinating | unusual | (un)appealing |

4 (SPEAKING) What makes a good ad?

55/3
56/4
a) Rank ads 1–3 from best to worst.

b) Give reasons for your choice.
Say something about …

The layout:
nice/simple/boring/…

The headline:
funny/catchy/too long/…

Text with a message:
informative/too long/clear/…

> Here we come.
>
> **California Dreaming Tours.**
> *Your experts when planning adventure trips.*

A: I think the best ad is number … . The layout is very nice.
B: Yes, I agree. And the headline is catchy.
C: I don't think so. I think number … is much better.

5 (SONG) Surfin' U.S.A.

2,4
Listen to the song. What does the song sound like? How does it make you feel?

1 If everybody had an ocean
   Across the U.S.A.
   Then everybody'd be surfing
   Like Californ-i-a

5 You'd see 'em wearin' their baggies
   Huarache sandals, too
   A bushy, bushy blond hairdo
   Surfin' U.S.A.

   You'd catch 'em surfin' at Del Mar
10 Ventura County Line
   Santa Cruz and Trestles
   Australia's Narrabeen

   All over Manhattan
   And down Doheny way
15 Everybody's gone surfin'
   Surfin' U.S.A.

Language → **G7**, p. 164

In photo 1 the man is standing next to a bus. He is carrying a surfboard.
He has black hair. The bus looks really old.

Normalerweise verwendest du bei einer Bildbeschreibung das present progressive.
Bei Verben wie have, look (aussehen) und be verwendest du das simple present.
Wie bildest du diese beiden Zeitformen?

6 (WRITING) **What are the people in the ads doing? Write sentences.** → M Peer correction, p. 171

56/5

1. a boy • ride
   A boy is riding a mountain bike.
2. a man • hold
3. a girl and a boy • carry
4. a man and a woman • sit
5. a girl • walk
6. a woman • run

Manche Verben haben eine besondere Schreibweise:
sit → sitting
run → running
ride → riding

57/6 **7** **Look at the ads again.**

a) Complete the sentences. Use the simple present. → ○ p. 128

   1. The mountain bike is $1,500. (be)
   2. The helmet —— cool. (look)
   3. The backpacks —— $99 each. (be)
   4. The camping chairs —— nice. (not look)
   5. The girl —— walking. (like)
   6. The woman —— an umbrella. (not need)

Für die Verneinung im simple present brauchst du „don't" oder „doesn't".

b) Talk to a partner: Which things would you buy? Say why. Use these verbs.

   A: I would buy the helmet. It ... .
   B: I need a new ... . This one ... .

look   like   be   have

86/2 **8** (WRITING) **Simple present or present progressive?**

a) Complete Sandy's e-mail. → ○ p. 128

57/7-8a)

> **E-MAIL**
>
> Hi Becky,
> At the moment I'm sitting (1, sit) in the sun next to the swimming pool. It's always warm here in
> California. It —— (2, not rain) often. We usually —— (3, spend) the weekends at the beach.
> At the moment I —— (4, learn) how to surf. But lots of other things are the same as in the Midwest.
> Every day I —— (5, go) to school, —— (6, do) my homework and —— (7, go) to bed.
> What —— you —— (8, do) right now? I miss you.
> Sandy

b) Complete the sentences in Becky's e-mail.

57/8b)

> **E-MAIL**
>
> Hi Sandy,
> Great to hear from you. I miss you too. (1) Right now I'm waiting for a call from … . (2) We always …
> on Tuesdays. (3) The weather is terrible here. It … now. Lucky you! I hope I can visit you in summer.
> Take care,
> Becky

 9 (YOUR TURN) **Making an ad** → **V** Talking about a region, p. 201

a) Work in groups of four. Make an ad about a state or region in Germany for other students.

1. Decide on a region.
2. Collect ideas. → **M** Placemat, p. 171
3. Make a quick draft of the layout.
4. Work in pairs:
   – Find pictures or draw your own pictures (two students).
   – Write the text (two students).
Use the ads on page 76 as examples.
Don't write too much! Write a headline plus two or three sentences.

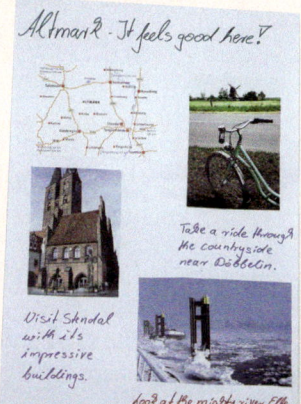

b) Present your work to the class. Which ad is the best? Say why.

> **STUDY SKILLS**
>
> Für welche Zielgruppe ist deine Werbung? Wähle ein Bild aus, das für sich spricht. Der Text sollte kurz und einfach sein und die Botschaft klar.
>
> Sprich die Leser direkt an, benutze Fragen und Aufforderungen. Du kannst im Internet auch einen Slogan Maker nutzen.

Ich kann eine Werbeanzeige gestalten.

Made in California

1 **How often do you go online? Which websites do you use the most?** → M Round robin, p. 172

2 (**READING**) **Read the blog of a Californian teenager.**

2,5

> **BLOG**
>
> ### A quick look back
> Thursday, March 16, 2017
>
>
>
> 1 California has always welcomed new ideas – just think of the high-tech companies in Silicon Valley or the movie industry.
> The internet is one of these ideas. The World Wide Web started in the early 1990s, so it's been around for almost 30 years. And it has really changed
> 5 the world. Today almost everyone uses social media. I've had an account since I was 13. Why have they been so successful? Well, that's easy: you can post your photos, share your thoughts and keep in touch with friends. Most of the time you don't even have to look for information. It'll find you. We should give that a big 'like'.
> 10 Online videos have had a huge impact on our lives too. There are lots of funny videos. I like the tutorials best. You can find anything there from guitar lessons to make-up tips. Nobody watches much TV anymore. People stream their favorite shows instead.
> Smartphones and tablets became the next big thing. Most of my friends go online every day, and half of them are online almost all the time. Most use several different social media sites at the
> 15 same time. Some say it's difficult to stop using social media. They get messages every minute of the day and feel that they have to answer right away. Others are worried about cyberbullying. If somebody writes bad things about you online, a lot of people can read it. We haven't really found any good answers yet.
>
> Posted by Derek Lee   at 8:51 a.m.   2 comments: Links to this post

3 **What does the text say?**

a) **Right or wrong? Correct the wrong sentences.** → ○ p. 129

1. The World Wide Web started about 50 years ago.
   **That's wrong. The World Wide Web started
   . . . .**
2. Social media sites are very popular today.
3. Everyone watches TV.
4. Most people are online almost all the time.
5. There are also problems with the internet.

b) **What examples does Derek give in the text? Complete the list.**

– Social media:
  post photos, …
– Online videos:
  funny videos, …
– Problems:
  too many messages, …

4 (LISTENING) **Listen to the survey. Choose the right phrase.**

2,6
58/1

1. It's **the latest thing** • **something new**.
2. Didn't it become **a big thing** • **popular** in Europe first?
3. It's **fantastic** • **not really my thing**.
4. **Trends** • **Things** like this come and go.
5. I don't think it will be **boring** • **outdated** so soon.

**Jumping Fitness,
the new fun fitness program**

58/3
86/3

5 **Explain the words.**

a) Match the words with the definitions. → ○ p. 130

58/2a)

1. You tell people that you agree with them.
2. You watch a movie online.
3. You move a message from your computer or phone to a social media site.
4. You send a message, a photo or a video that you got to others because you like it.
5. You ask someone to connect with you on social media.

friend

post

like

stream

share

b) Explain these words. → **V** Social media, p. 198

58/2b)

dislike   unfriend   subscribe

1. You tell people ... .   2. You tell someone ... .   3. When you subscribe to ... .

> **CULTURE**
>
> In den USA können sich Kinder ab 13 Jahren in sozialen Netzwerken anmelden, wenn deren Eltern das erlauben. Wie ist das in eurem Land?

6 (SPEAKING) **Say what the cartoon is about.** → **M** Think–pair–share, p. 173

UPDATE MY STATUS

In this cartoon you can see ... .
The man ... .
The cartoon shows ...

Language → **G8**, p. 165

The internet <u>has changed</u> the world.
Online videos <u>have had</u> a huge impact on our lives.
We <u>haven't found</u> answers for these questions yet.

Wie bildest du das present perfect? Welche Signalwörter kennst du für diese Zeitform?

7 **What have or haven't they done?** → **M** Bus stop, p. 168

59/4

1. Derek <u>has</u> just <u>made</u> fresh orange juice. (make)

2. Linda —— already —— her computer. (start)

3. Derek —— already —— his e-mails. (read)

4. Linda —— her blog yet. (not finish)

5. Derek and Linda —— each other yet. (not see)

6. They —— just —— for the first time. (meet)

86/4 **8** **Say <u>for</u> how long or <u>since</u> when.**

a) Choose <u>for</u> or <u>since</u>. → ○ p. 130

59/5

1. I've had my smartphone **for** • **since** three years.
2. I haven't posted a new photo **for** • **since** 10 o'clock.
3. Social media have been popular **for** • **since** 20 years now.
4. Millions of people have seen the cat pictures **for** • **since** Tuesday.
5. More than 5,000 people have watched that tutorial **for** • **since** May.
6. I haven't answered my e-mails **for** • **since** five days.

GRAMMAR	→ **G8**, p. 165
<u>since</u> ten o'clock	– seit zehn Uhr
<u>for</u> an hour	– seit einer Stunde

b) Make sentences with these phrases. Use the present perfect.

59/6

| since 7 o'clock | since Monday | for two hours | for three days |

I have posted five pictures since 7 o'clock. I haven't been online …

60/7 **9** **Complete the survey questions and answers.**

a) Complete the sentences. Use the present perfect. → ○ p. 131

1. Interviewer: —— you —— a book or a magazine this week? (buy)
   Have you bought a book or a magazine this week?
   Jake: I usually read everything online. I —— a book or a magazine for a long time. (not read)
2. Interviewer: —— you ever —— tutorial videos to learn how to do something? (use)
   Sally: Yes, sure. I —— already —— to play the guitar that way. (learn)
3. Interviewer: —— you —— any new music videos that you liked this week? (find)
   Kim: Let me think for a second. Today I —— one that I really enjoyed. (see)

b) Make more sentences from the survey. Use the present perfect.

1. I • buy • a book • this morning
2. I • not see • any tutorials • for months
3. I • not think about • that question • yet

✳**10** (YOUR TURN) **Talking about trends** → V Giving opinions, p. 196

60/8
61/1-2

a) *Hot* or *not?* What do you think? Copy and complete the table.

| selfies | torn jeans | veganism |

hot	not

b) Think of two more trends and put them in the table.

c) Do you agree with your partner?

A: What do you think about selfies:
   Is this trend *hot* or *not?*
B: I think it's hot. / I think it isn't hot.
A: What do you think about this trend?
B: It's cool. / It will be outdated soon. / …
A: Has it had an impact on your life?
B: Yes, (I have lots of funny photos of me and my friends now). /
   No, I don't think so.

Ich kann über Trends sprechen. ✔

Gold rush! → M Jigsaw, p. 170

1 (READING) **Home group: Find two partners. Each of you chooses one of the texts (A, B or C).**

a) Read your text.

b) Complete the summary with words from the text.

2 **Expert group: Find students who have read the same text. Compare your results with them.**

2,7 **Text A: A newspaper report**

California Star
December 6, 1848

GOLD! GOLD! GOLD! Found in California

1 Washington. Yesterday the President of the United States confirmed the discovery of gold in California.

It began in Coloma, a place 40 miles east 5 of Sacramento. In January this year one of Mr. Sutter's workers found gold. Mr. Sutter, a German-Swiss immigrant and businessman, wanted to keep the gold secret. He didn't want to give up his farming plans. He also 10 tried to buy more land and become the official landowner. His workers weren't allowed to talk about the gold, but the news got out slowly. Sutter has to prove now that he officially owns the land.

First, most local people didn't believe it. Then 15 in May people in San Francisco heard the news and half of the city's population decided to look for gold in the American River. Men left everything behind and moved west because they hoped to become rich easily. 20

Summary

Text A is a n——— r——— from 1848. It is about the d——— of g——— in California. W——— on a farm in Coloma found g———. They were not allowed to t——— about it because their boss, Mr S———, wanted to keep it s———. But the n——— got out anyway. Soon a lot of p——— went to the American River to l——— for g———. They hoped to become r———.

2,8

Text B: A letter from a gold hunter

February 15, 1850
San Francisco

1   Dear Maddy,

It's been weeks since I left you, my dear wife. Finally, I've found the time to send you some news.
I arrived safely. There were heavy storms when we crossed the sea to Panama and lots of rain
when we went through the jungle. A lot of men got sick, and some died on the journey. Sometimes
5   I wanted to give up, but then I thought of you and our children. Ninety days after I had left you in
New York, we arrived in San Francisco Bay.

However, it was more than a week before we arrived at our camp in the wilderness. I've made
friends with some of the other men, who came from all over the country. We often sit around the
fire at night, telling stories and singing. We all dream about making a lot of money before we
10   return to our families. Sometimes there are fights in the camps. But don't worry, I'm well.

Finding gold isn't easy. Do you know how happy I was when I found my first little piece of gold?
Some days are better than others, but my love for you keeps me going. One day I got terribly
sick. I hadn't eaten or slept much, and I had worked in very cold water for hours. But I was well
after a week.
15   My thoughts and prayers are with you, Maddy, and our children. Write soon.

Always yours,

Edward

Summary

Text B is a l—— from a g—— h—— to his wife from 1850. His name is E—— . He left his family in
N—— Y—— and went on a long and dangerous j—— to a camp near S—— F—— . There he looks for
g—— . He hopes to become r—— and r—— to his family soon. But f—— g—— is very difficult.

Text C: An encyclopedia entry

A history of California and the Gold Rush

1 The discovery of gold in California in 1848 made people very
   excited, not only in America. Thousands of people came from
   all over the world and in 1849 the Gold Rush started.
   By 1852 it had become more and more difficult and expensive
5 to find gold. But many more immigrants arrived. Before
   the Gold Rush, less than 1,000 non-native people lived in
   California. Ten years later the population was almost 400,000.
   San Francisco went from a small village of 500 people to a
   city of 150,000 in a few years. Many other new towns were
10 also built.
   California quickly became the 31st state of the United States
   in 1850 because of these events. The First Transcontinental
   Railway to San Francisco opened in 1869. It connected
   California with the rest of the country.
15 The impact on the Native American population was terrible.
   The immigrants killed them or made them their slaves. Before
   the Gold Rush, there were about 150,000 Native Americans.
   In 1870 there were only 30,000.
   The gold fever did not last long. When there was no more gold, there was no more work.
20 People moved away and left empty towns behind them. Some of the towns are still there
   today. The town of Bodie, for example, once had 8,000 inhabitants – now it's empty. The
   houses have not changed since then, and visitors can walk through the town.

Summary

Text C is an encyclopedia e⸺ about the history of the G⸺ R⸺ and its impact on C⸺ . In the
middle of the nineteenth century a lot of i⸺ came to C⸺ to find g⸺ . California's p⸺ went
from 1,000 to 400,000 within ten y⸺ . However, the i⸺ killed a lot of N⸺ A⸺ . California
became the 31st s⸺ of the USA in 1850. When there was no more g⸺ people left. Today there
are empty t⸺ like Bodie.

> **CULTURE**
>
> Der Goldrausch wurde zum Symbol des „Kalifornischen Traums".
> Kalifornien wurde ein Ort des Neuanfangs, wo man mit Glück
> sehr schnell sehr reich werden konnte.
> Würdest du so viele Stunden unter schwierigsten Bedingungen
> arbeiten wollen, um reich zu werden?

3 **Meet your home group again.**

a) Read the summary of your text to your group.

b) Write quiz questions: Write one true or false statement about each text. Use your summaries for help.

4 **Do a quiz in class.**

Read the statements to the class.
Are they true or false?

5 **Choose one of these tasks.**

62/1-2

a) Write an interview and act the role play in class. One of you is a reporter for the *California Star* in 1848. Your partner is a gold hunter who has just found a lot of gold.

Reporter: Prepare questions.
1. Where are you from?
2. When did …?
3. Is it …?
4. How much gold …?
5. What will you …?

 **OR**

b) Make a timeline about the history of the Gold Rush. Collect information from text C. Present the timeline to the class.

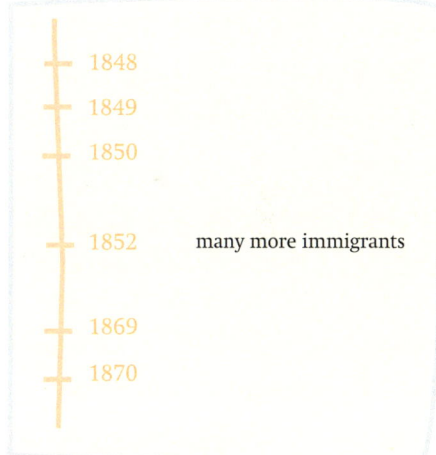

1848
1849
1850

1852   many more immigrants

1869
1870

SPEAKING SKILLS

Wenn du ein Interview vorbereitest, überlege dir, wie du dein Gegenüber begrüßt. Vergiss nicht, ihm oder ihr am Schluss zu danken.

Gold hunter: Prepare your story and your plans for the future. Make notes to answer the reporter's questions.
1. I'm from ….. .
2. I … .
3. Yes/No, … .
4. I found … .
5. I think I'll … .

READING SKILLS

Wenn du nach Einzelheiten in einem Text suchst, musst du nicht den ganzen Text lesen. Du kannst ihn überfliegen und nach Stichwörtern oder Zahlen suchen. Lies dann nur die Sätze, in denen das Stichwort oder die Zahl vorkommt.

Ich kann einen Text über den Goldrausch verstehen. ✓

Too young to work?

Many big farms in California employ children, mostly from Latin America, to pick fruit or vegetables. Migrant parents often don't have enough income, so their children have to help them. Many of them don't have many qualifications or can hardly speak English. Some are even in the USA illegally.

Fresno Weekly Magazine talked to Matteo (12) and his brother Ramon (14) from Sacramento, who have been working on different farms.

Fresno Weekly: What can you tell us about the work in the fields?

Matteo: We have to get up at 4:30 in the morning. Buses drive us to the fields, where we work all day in the heat. We sometimes work more than ten hours a day and only earn the minimum wage or even less.

Fresno Weekly: Ramon, how long have you been working in the fields?

Ramon: Since I was ten, just like my dad.

Fresno Weekly: Do you have any health problems?

Ramon: Yes, I always have difficulties breathing because of the pesticides, and I have a constant headache. But that's not all. Some people get injured working with the large machines.

A federal law from 1938 allows farm owners to employ children from the age of twelve on big farms and even younger children on small farms. Officially, they are only allowed to work outside school hours, but some of them don't even finish high school. People have often tried to change the law, but they have never been successful.

1 Beantworte die Fragen.

63/1

1. In welchem Bereich arbeiten Kinder in Kalifornien?
2. Warum müssen Kinder arbeiten?
3. Was sagen Matteo und Ramon über die Arbeitsbedingungen?
4. Wie sind die gesetzlichen Bestimmungen für Kinderarbeit?

2 Talk to your class.

What jobs are you allowed to do?

> **CULTURE**
>
> Fast die Hälfte des US-amerikanischen Obsts, Gemüses und der Nüsse kommt aus dem Central Valley, Kalifornien. Hohe Temperaturen von 40°C (100°F) und wenig Regen bieten ideale Bedingungen für den Anbau. Aber die Arbeitsbedingungen sind hart.

Ich kann Informationen über Kinderarbeit weitergeben. ✔

Talking about jobs

1 Talk about the ad on the right.

a) Which question in the ad is the most important to you?

b) Would the job interest you? Give reasons.

2 (VIEWING) Watch the film.

8

a) Watch the film until 02:08. Jessica, Wesley or Ronan: Who …

1. helps neighbours in their gardens?
2. walks the neighbours' dogs?
3. works as a waitress?
4. helps students with their homework?
5. puts groceries in bags for customers?

b) Watch the film from 02:08 to the end.

1. What does Wesley want to be?
2. What animals would Jessica like to work with?
3. Where would Ronan like to work?

3 (SPEAKING) Talk about the film.

Choose one of the jobs from the film. Find two or three reasons why you'd like this job.

My big dream is to become a … . / I'd like to work with … .

I love … .
I want to … .
I'm good at … .

Love-4-Animals
Animal Shelter
TWO HELPERS NEEDED
to start as soon as possible.

Both jobs are part-time
with regular working hours.

- Do you love and respect animals?
- Do you enjoy caring for animals?
- Are you energetic & fit?
- Are you a good team player?
- Do you have a practical attitude to work?

If it's yes to all these questions, then what are you waiting for!
E-mail us now at love4animals@shelter.woof

NY Love-4-Animals
254 Olivier Street
New York, NY 11216

CULTURE

Die Rocky Mountains (the Rockies) liegen im Westen Kanadas und der USA. Sie sind beliebt bei Kletterern, Campern, Wanderern und Skifahrern. Teile der Rockies sind in Nationalparks. Finde die Rockies auf der Karte hinten im Buch.
Welche Gebirge kennst du?

VIEWING SKILLS

In einem Film bewegen sich die Menschen oder Dinge – oder die Kamera bewegt sich stattdessen (z. B. durch Schwenken oder Näherkommen). Das kann den Film interessanter machen.
Sieh dir die zweite Hälfte des Films erneut an. Wer oder was bewegt sich – die Schauspieler, die Kamera oder beide?

Ich kann einen Film über Beruf und Karriere verstehen. ✔

Checklist

Ich kann Informationen über Kalifornien und den Westen der USA verstehen. ✔

64

Ich kann eine Werbeanzeige gestalten. ✔

The ad looks spectacular. • The layout is simple and .... • The headline is funny. • In the picture there is ....

64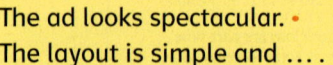

Ich kann über Trends sprechen. ✔

What do you think about this trend? • Almost everyone uses it. • It has had a huge impact. • It's the latest thing/popular. • It's outdated.

65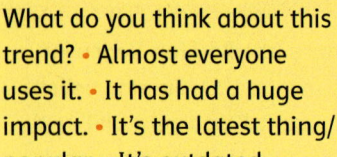

Ich kann einen Text über den Goldrausch verstehen. ✔

65

Ich kann Informationen über Kinderarbeit weitergeben. ✔

65

Ich kann einen Film über Beruf und Karriere verstehen. ✔

✿ (TASK) A blog

Write a blog about a trend that you like. Add pictures.
Share your blog with others. Which trends do you find interesting?
Which ones don't you find interesting? Why?

Step 1

Collect ideas.

Work with a partner.
Make a mind map of trends.

fashion — food

trends

technology — entertainment

Step 2

Choose your topic.

Decide which trend you would like to write about.

Step 3

Collect information.

– Say where you learned about the trend.
– Say what you like about it.
– Say where the trend comes from.
– Talk about the trend. What is it? What's special about it?

WRITING SKILLS

In einem Blog schreibst du deine eigene Meinung.
Vergiss also nicht zu sagen, was du denkst.

Auf der nächsten Seite findest du ein Beispiel. Welche Formulierungen kannst du für deinen Blog übernehmen?

BLOG

Have you ever heard of bento boxes? No? I didn't know about them either until a friend gave me one. He showed me how to make them.

It's fun to organize food that way. You can use bento boxes for parties and they make nice presents too.

Bento comes from Japan and it's a kind of packed lunch. Bentos have been around since the fifth century. They are made from bamboo. Modern bento boxes are made of plastic or metal. In a traditional box you will find rice, fish or meat and vegetables.

You can make your own bento easily. Just follow these steps:
– Choose food that you can eat with your fingers.
– Cut your food into small pieces.
– Make a nice box or buy one.
– Think of a nice way to put your food into the box.

Here's mine.

Step 4

Write your draft and check it.

Check the content and spelling.

WRITING SKILLS

Überprüft gegenseitig eure Entwürfe:
– Enthält der Text alle wichtigen Informationen?
– Ist der Text verständlich?
– Welche Wörter sind schwierig? Sind sie richtig geschrieben? Kontrolliert mit Hilfe eines Wörterbuchs und der Checkliste auf Seite 175.

Step 5

Share your blog with others. → M Gallery walk, p. 169

Read at least two more blogs.

Step 6

Comment on a blog.

Choose one blog. Write a short comment.

`Sounds cool.` `Looks awesome!` `Not bad.` `Sounds boring.` `It's not really my thing.`

`What a great idea!` `I think I'll try it.` `. . .`

Get to the mountain of nuggets

1 **Make a set of cards with your partner.**

You need:

paper

scissors

a pen

1. Fold the sheet of paper in half four times.

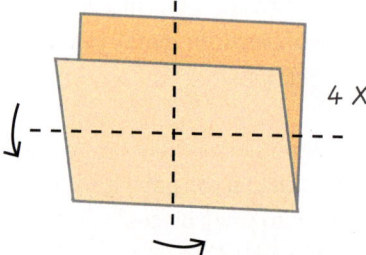

4 X

2. Cut along the lines so you have 16 playing cards.

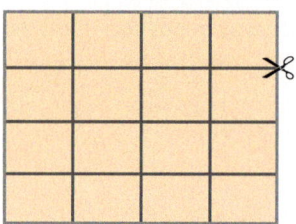

3. Write twelve questions about California on the playing cards. Write the answer in small letters upside down at the bottom of each card.

   Look at Unit 4 for help.

   You need the four empty cards for the next step.

What can you do on the beaches in California?

surf or play volleyball

Where did the Gold Rush start?

in Coloma

What's the English word for 'Entdeckung'?

discovery

2 **Prepare the game.**

1. Swap your set of cards with another pair.
2. Put the cards upside down in the middle of the table.
3. Draw a picture of yourself on an empty playing card.
4. Draw a huge mountain of nuggets on another empty card.
5. Put the two cards on the table in front of you.
6. Put the picture of yourself on the left and the mountain of nuggets on the right. Leave enough space for four more cards in between.

3 Play the game.

1. Pick a card from the pile in the middle of the table and read the question to your partner.
2. If your partner answers the question correctly, he or she can put the card next to his or her picture. If he or she is wrong, put the card to one side. It is now out of the game.
3. Take turns.
4. If you answer four questions correctly and get to your mountain of nuggets card, you win and become the richest boy or girl California has ever seen.

Swap your set of cards with another pair and play another round with their set of cards if you finish your game before others in class.

2,10

A podcast interview

A

B

Wow, that sounds cool!

Isn't that the same every year?

No way!? That's amazing!

That doesn't sound
like much fun.

Tell me more.

Is that really interesting?

Thanks so much.

I can imagine that.

I have to interrupt here.

1 Look at the photos on the left.

a) Talk about the photos with a partner.
Do the people in the photos look interested
or bored? Why?

> Wenn ihr herausfinden wollt, wie
> Menschen sich fühlen, achtet auf den
> Gesichtsausdruck und die Körperhaltung.

I think the man and the woman in photo 1
look interested/bored because ... .

b) Listen to the interviews.
1. Which interview matches which photo?
2. Which interview is the better one?

2 Listen to the interviews again.

Match the sentences from page 94
with the interviews.

> Der Tonfall und die Art, wie Menschen
> reden, können euch viel über die Situation
> verraten.

Interview A
- showing interest
- sounding surprised
- saying thank you

Interview B
- sounding bored
- interrupting

68/1
69/2-4

3 Interview your partner about the last movie he or she saw.

> Beginnt das Interview mit einer Begrüßung:
>
> Hi ... . Nice to meet you. We're talking
> about movies today. What was the last
> movie you saw?

a) Answer these questions:

– What was the last movie you saw?
I saw "..." (title of the movie). It's a(n)
action movie/romance/science fiction
movie/... .

> Wenn ihr das Interview führt, vergesst
> nicht, die Sätze aus Interview A zu
> verwenden.

– What is it about?
– Which actors are in the movie?
– How did you like it?

b) Act the interview with a partner.

> Denkt bei eurem Interview an euren
> Gesichtsausdruck, eure Körperhaltung
> und euren Tonfall.

🌐 Find more online:
i8ce82

Am Ende dieser Unit kann ich ...
- Informationen über die Südstaaten der USA verstehen.
- über Einflüsse verschiedener Kulturen im täglichen Leben sprechen.
- andere über Freizeitaktivitäten informieren.
- einen Bericht über Rassismus verstehen.
- Informationen über Rituale weitergeben.
- einen Film über die Sommerferien verstehen.

9 🔔 2,11 📢 **Unit 5**

Southern life

1

The Southern Appalachian Mountains, the Gulf Coast beaches, the Florida swamps and the Mississippi River – the South has many exciting places for fans of the outdoors.

2

Until the 1950s African Americans in the South did not have the same rights as white Americans. The Civil Rights Movement, a peaceful protest movement, changed that.

1 (SPEAKING) **Talk about the photos.**

Which photo do you like most?
Which photo do you not like? Why?

I like photo 1 most because … .
I don't like photo … because … .

72/1-2 🗗

2 **Read the texts and find the topics.**

a) Which text is it?

A Music is important in the South.
B The nature of the South is great.
C People from Africa had to work as slaves for white people.
D Southern life and culture are different.
E African Americans got more rights.

b) Which topic would you like to know more about?

I'm interested in … . • I like … . •
I'd like to know more about … .

3

In the 18th century, people from France, England, Scotland and Ireland came to the South. Soon they brought in slaves from Africa to work on their plantations.

4

The South has its own lifestyle and culture. People here are proud to be both Americans and Southerners.

5

Some styles of music come from the South like gospel music or rock 'n' roll. New Orleans is the home of jazz, and Nashville is the home of country music.

 3 (LISTENING) **Listen to the online radio broadcast about Taylor Swift.**

2,12

What's special about Taylor Swift? Complete the sentences.

1. She is a —— singer and a popstar.
2. She writes her own —— .
3. Since —— many songs have been at the top of the charts.
4. In 2012 she was the best-paid star under —— .
5. Her —— can see themselves in her songs.

charts [tʃɑːts] – Charts
best-paid [ˈbestˌpeɪd] – höchstbezahlt

Ich kann Informationen über die Südstaaten der USA verstehen.

Living together

1 (READING) **Read the text.**

2,13
73/1

Rich food, rich culture
by Anna Williams

1 Southern food

The South is famous for its great food. And the food shows the history of the South. I went on a trip there, and here's what I found out.

5 In the beginning there was the food of the Native Americans. Then European settlers brought new dishes. The slaves from West Africa had a big influence too.
The delicious southern fried chicken is a good
10 example. This dish came from Scotland and some of the spices came from West Africa. First the spices are mixed with flour. The chicken pieces are washed and dried and then covered in the flour. After that, the chicken
15 is fried in oil until it's golden.

The city of New Orleans

In New Orleans different cultures and traditions meet. The French founded the city in 1718; then it became Spanish. New Orleans
20 was the most important cotton and slave market in the South until the middle of the 19th century. Later it became the country's second biggest gateway for immigrants from Europe. In the late 20th century large
25 numbers of Vietnamese people arrived. When you walk through New Orleans today, you can see that it's a multicultural city. You can be part of it at the famous Mardi Gras carnival and the Jazz Fest.

New Orleans

The Confederate flag

30 But there are also problems with the different groups. The Confederate flag is one example. It flew over the South Carolina State House for years until 2015. For many white people in the South this flag is a symbol of pride. 35
Others just tolerate it. But for most African Americans it is a symbol of racism.
After nine people had been killed in a black church in Charleston, protests started. The state government had to find a solution. In 40
the end they removed the flag.

CULTURE

Die Südstaaten benutzten eine eigene Fahne im amerikanischen Bürgerkrieg (1861–1865).
Der Norden wollte die Sklaverei abschaffen, der Süden nicht. Heute ist die Fahne im Süden immer noch verbreitet, aber bei vielen umstritten.

The Confederate flag

2 Match the sentence parts.

1. The South is famous for
2. Southern fried chicken is
3. In 1718 French settlers founded
4. Later New Orleans was important as
5. Today New Orleans is
6. The Confederate flag is

A New Orleans.
B a symbol of pride and racism.
C a cotton and slave market.
D its food.
E a famous dish from the South.
F a multicultural city.

73/2

3 What's the nationality?

a) Match the nationalities with the flags. → ◯ p. 131

| Chinese | Greek | Italian | Russian | Polish | Turkish |

1. 中国   2. Россия   3. Polska   4. Ελλάδα   5. Türkiye   6. Italia

b) Do you know the colours of these flags? → **V** Nationalities, p. 202

Swiss

Spanish

Japanese

Alle Flaggen haben eine Farbe gemeinsam.

74/4

4 Find the words.

73/3a) a) Find the words with the same meaning. → ◯ p. 131

| disagreed | made a compromise | tolerated | problems |

1. Some people accepted the flag.
2. Others didn't accept it.
3. There were conflicts between the different groups.
4. The different groups found a solution.

STUDY SKILLS

Beim Vokabellernen kann es dir helfen, wenn du Wörter mit gleicher Bedeutung (Synonyme) und Wörter mit gegensätzlicher Bedeutung (Antonyme) zusammen lernst.

73/3b) b) Find the opposites. → **V** Conflicts and solutions, p. 203

| refuse an idea | break a rule | be happy with a situation |

| complain about a situation | respect a rule | accept an idea |

Language detectives → **G9**, p. 166

The spices <u>are mixed</u> with flour. The chicken <u>is fried</u> in oil.
It <u>is eaten</u> with the fingers.

Das Passiv verwendest du, wenn der Handelnde („Täter") unbekannt oder unwichtig ist.
Es kommt häufig in Sachtexten vor. Schau dir die Sätze an: Wie bildest du es?

5 (SPEAKING) **Say how southern fried chicken is cooked.**

Match the sentences with the pictures.

A The spices and flour
   are mixed. ✔

B The chicken is fried
   until it's golden.

C The chicken is
   covered in flour.

D The chicken pieces
   are washed.

E The chicken pieces
   are put in hot oil.

F The chicken pieces
   are dried.

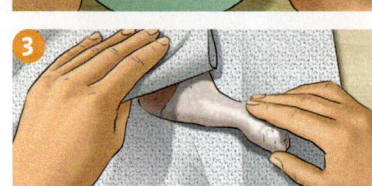

74/5-6 **6 Make passive sentences.** → M Bus stop, p. 168

a) Choose the right form. → ○ p. 132

1. Pork **is** • **are** used in many southern dishes.
2. Southern food **is** • **are** eaten across the USA.
3. Vegetables **is** • **are** kept in the fridge.
4. All these dishes **is** • **are** made with rice.
5. Rice **is** • **are** not grown in many US states.

b) Talk about the food at your school. You can use these words.

sandwiches   cakes   lunch   sold   freshly prepared

drinks   ice cream   . . .   offered   . . .

87/5 **7** **Complete the sentences about multicultural schools.**

75/7 a) Make passive sentences. → ○ p. 132

1. Many languages <u>are spoken</u> at multicultural schools. (speak)
2. Special lessons —— for people who are new. (organize)
3. Lessons —— in different languages at some schools. (give)
4. Multicultural food —— in the cafeteria. (sell)
5. Special days of different cultures —— at school. (celebrate)
6. Racism —— there. (not accept)

Nutze die Liste der unregelmäßigen Verben (3. Spalte) ab S. 210 als Hilfe!

75/8 b) Make passive sentences with these words.

> organize   write   tolerate

1. At multicultural schools different opinions … .
2. Activities against racism … there.
3. Letters to students and parents … in more than one language.

8 (YOUR TURN) **Different cultures where I live** → **V** Talking about culture, p. 206

Ⓟ
⚷
75/9

What is the influence of other cultures where you live? Prepare a short presentation.
→ **M** Tip top, p. 173

- Say where you live.
- Say what multicultural influences you find in:
  - shops
  - restaurants
  - signs
  - music
- How do you like living there?

I live in … .
There are many Turkish/Chinese/… shops.
People like to buy … there.
When you look around, you see … restaurants.
The signs are written in … .
People like to go there because … .
You can listen to … music at/in … .
I (don't) like living there because … .

STUDY SKILLS

Wenn du ein Wort auf Englisch nicht weißt, schlage im Wörterbuch nach. Manche Wörter lassen sich nicht übersetzen. Diese Wörter kannst du umschreiben, in dem du sie auf Englisch erklärst. Manche kannst du auch mit Hilfe eines Fotos erklären.

So kannst du Wörter umschreiben: 'Ajvar' is a kind of sauce. It's made of peppers. You can eat it with meat, vegetables or bread.

A trip to Florida

1 **Look at the websites. Which trip would you like to go on? Why?**

I'd like to go to … because … .

INTERNET

Be there for the most important
NASCAR race!

Our Daytona 500 race packages:
– Daytona 500 race tickets
– hotel
– transfer to the race track
– a booklet with all details

INTERNET

Go into the Florida Everglades!

Airboat rides, alligators, wildlife show
– hotel pick-up
– exciting 30-minute boat tour
– alligator, snake and wildlife show
– jungle trail through the swamps

---

2 (READING) **Read the friends' dialogue.** → M Dramatic reading, p. 169

2,14
76/1

1 **Anna:** My dad can take us to Daytona or
to the Everglades. He says that he needs an
answer today. These are the websites that
he's found.
5 **Matt:** Well, I know. I'd like to go to the race.
It's the biggest NASCAR event of the year.
Anna: That's not my idea of fun. All those
noisy people! I prefer the Everglades. I've
never seen an alligator in the wild.
10 **Matt:** Why do you want to spend the day
walking around in the heat?
Anna: What does Ethan think?
Ethan *is speech impaired. He can hear, but he uses
sign language to speak. Matt understands sign*
15 *language and translates for Anna.*
Matt: Ethan says that he doesn't like crowds
much either.

Anna: There you are. He wants to see the
alligators too.
Ethan *makes more signs.* 20
Matt: I'm sorry, Ethan. Can you repeat it,
please? (**Ethan** *repeats it.*) I see. But he also
says that he has always wanted to watch a
NASCAR race.
Anna: Oh, no! So we'll go to the NASCAR race. 25
Ethan *makes signs.*
Matt: I'm sorry, I didn't get that, Ethan.
(**Ethan** *repeats it.*) Oh, right. He says the jungle
trail sounds really interesting too. He'd like to
see big snakes. He wants to know if your dad 30
can drive us to the Everglades another time.
Maybe next month?
Anna: Yes, I can ask him tonight.

3 (WRITING) **Take notes about the places.**

a) **Where do they want to go?**

Matt: …
Anna: …
Ethan: …

b) **Copy and complete the table.**

	for	against
Daytona	the biggest NASCAR event	
Everglades		

2,15
76/2

4 (LISTENING) **Listen to the text about a visit to an alligator farm.**

a) Correct the notes. → ○ p. 132

> Alligator farm, Florida Everglades
> – a slow boat ride
> – trainer had fight with snake
> – Matt put hand in alligator's mouth
> – photo of Ethan with alligator

LISTENING SKILLS

Keine Sorge, wenn du beim ersten Hören nicht alles verstehst. Achte beim zweiten Hören vor allem auf die Sätze in der Aufgabe.

b) What did Matt like most about the visit to the alligator farm? What did Ethan like most?

1 boat ride   **2** alligator show   **3** snake show

5 (WRITING) **How can you say that you (don't) understand?** → M Peer correction, p. 171

a) Copy and complete the table. → ○ p. 133

76/3

Could you please explain? ✔   I get it.   I know what you mean.   Can you repeat it, please?

Excuse me?   I see.

I understand	I don't understand
…	Could you please explain?

b) Match the phrases with the definitions. → V Understanding things, p. 204

I'm sorry, but I didn't catch that.   Absolutely!   What do you mean by '…'?

1. Ask somebody to explain a word.
2. Ask somebody to say something again.
3. Tell somebody that you agree with them.

SPEAKING SKILLS

Wenn du etwas nicht verstehst, sag nicht einfach „Huh?" oder „What?". Das ist unhöflich.

6 **Use sign language.**

Look at the signs. Then close your books and practise them with a partner.

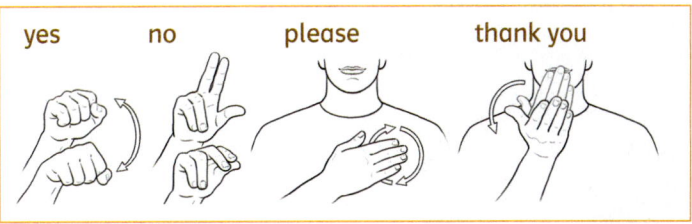

yes   no   please   thank you

Language detectives → G10, p. 167

Dad: "I need an answer today."
→ Dad <u>says he needs</u> an answer today.

Ethan: "I don't like crowds."
→ Ethan <u>says that he doesn't like</u> crowds.

Diese Sätze geben wieder, was der Vater und Ethan sagen. Sieh dir die Sätze an. Welche Wörter kommen in der indirekten Rede (zweite Zeile) hinzu? Was verändert sich noch?

77/4-6

7 Report what other people say.

a) What did Anna write? → ○ p. 133

Report the underlined sentences from Anna's e-mail from Clearwater, Florida.

E-MAIL

Hi Julie,
(1) <u>I'm at Clearwater</u> right now. (2) <u>I love the the warm weather</u> here. (3) <u>We just wear T-shirts and shorts</u> and (4) <u>we often go to the beach.</u> (5) <u>It's awesome!</u> But (6) <u>I hate the insects.</u>
See you soon,
Anna

Das ändert sich in der indirekten Rede:
I love → <u>he/she loves</u>
we love → <u>they love</u>

1. Anna says (that) she is at Clearwater.
2. She writes (that) she ...

b) Play the game.

Your teacher gives a sentence to the first student in your group. He or she whispers the sentence to the next person and so on. Is the sentence still the same at the end?

Play the game with more sentences.

I want to hold a baby alligator.

She says . . . .

8 Complete the sentences.

78/7-8
87/6

Report the sentences in the speech bubbles.

I don't like → he/she <u>doesn't</u> like
we don't like → they don't like

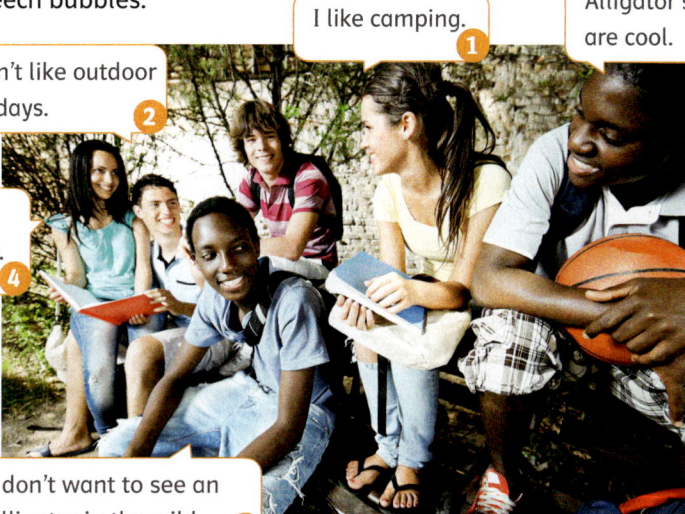

I like camping. **1**

Alligator shows are cool. **3**

I don't like outdoor holidays. **2**

We don't like animal shows. **4**

I don't want to see an alligator in the wild. **5**

1. The girl says (that) she … .
2. The boy says (that) he … .
3. The boy says … .
4. The girl … .
5. …

✳ 9 (YOUR TURN) Information for a day trip → **V** A day trip, p. 207

78/9
79/1-2

Tell an English-speaking friend about Berlin Zoo.

Your friend: Can you tell me where Berlin Zoo is?
You: The website says it's in the centre of Berlin.
Your friend: Which animals can you see there?
You: It says here that you can see … .
Your friend: Which activities can you do there?
You: You can … .
Your friend: When is the zoo open?
You: It's open from … to … .
Your friend: Where can we buy tickets?
You: You can … .

Was heißt „Nachtsafari im Nachttierhaus" auf Englisch? – You can visit the zoo at night and watch the animals that don't sleep at night.

Herzlich willkommen im Zoo Berlin!

Besuchen Sie den ersten Zoo Deutschlands im Zentrum Berlins.
Unter unseren über 17.000 Zoo-Tieren finden Sie Affen, Elefanten, Schlangen, Tiger und viele mehr.

• Erleben Sie die Fütterungen und Tiershows.
• Gehen Sie auf Nachtsafari im Nachttierhaus.
• Feiern Sie Kindergeburtstage bei uns.
• Nehmen Sie am Fotospaziergang teil.

Öffnungszeiten
Heute, 2.6.2018, 9:00 – 18:30 Uhr
Jetzt Online Ticket kaufen!

Ich kann andere über Freizeitaktivitäten informieren. ✔

The girl who fought segregation

1 If you know something is wrong or unfair, what do you do about it?

I talk to … . • I tell … . • I help … . • I don't do anything because … .

2 (READING) Read the report.

2,16

Claudette Colvin, 2016

1 Claudette Colvin was an African-American teenager from Montgomery, Alabama. On March 2, 1955, Claudette was on a bus with three other girls. They were sitting in the middle of the bus. More and more
5 white people got on, and it was soon full. The bus driver told the girls that they had to give up their seats and move to the back. This was the rule. Three of them got up and went to the back. But Claudette didn't move.
10 The bus driver called the police. A police officer got on the bus, but Claudette still didn't move. She said that she paid her fare like other people. It was her right to sit there. In the end, they dragged her off the bus and arrested her.
15 Her parents brought her home later that day. Her father was awake all night with his gun because he was afraid of the Ku Klux Klan.

3 (SPEAKING) Talk to a partner: What is the story about? → M Think–pair–share, p. 173

A Rosa Parks' protest on buses

B the Ku Klux Klan's fight against African Americans

C Claudette Colvin's fight against segregation

I think the story is about … .
The title says '…'. The text says in line(s) … .

READING SKILLS

Die meisten Texte haben ein Hauptthema oder eine Hauptaussage. Es ist wichtig, diese zu finden und zu verstehen. Du findest sie oft in der Überschrift, im ersten Absatz oder am Ende des Textes.

4 Find the information.

1. Where did Claudette sit on the bus?
2. Why did the bus driver tell her to move back?
3. Why was Claudette arrested?
4. Why did Claudette lose a lot of friends?
5. When did segregation on public transport end in Alabama?
6. Why did Claudette move to New York?

The next week Claudette had problems in school too. Some students thought that she was very brave. However, many others thought that she was crazy. They said that she had made

20 things harder for African Americans. Claudette lost a lot of friends.

Claudette's life became very difficult, but her protest was a success. A year later, in 1956, there was a court case and she was the star witness. The case ended segregation on all public transport in Alabama. In that same year Claudette left Montgomery because she couldn't find any work. She moved to New York.

25 Claudette's story has been forgotten by most people. Instead, Rosa Parks became famous for the fight against segregation on buses. She did exactly the same thing nine months later. For Claudette that was OK.

There were hundreds of brave people like Claudette. You never see their names but they played an important role in the long fight against segregation. Their courage will always be remembered.

CULTURE

Der Ku Klux Klan ist eine geheime Organisation weißer Amerikaner, die sich gegen Menschen anderer Kulturen und Religionen richtet. In den 1950er und -60er Jahren griffen sie Afro-Amerikaner und Mitglieder der Bürgerrechtsbewegung an oder brachten sie um.

Gibt es solche Gruppierungen auch in deinem Land?

---

5 **Choose one of these tasks.**

80/1-2

a) Search the internet for information about one of these people:

OR

Rosa Parks • Martin Luther King • Malcolm X • Mahatma Gandhi • Malala Yousafzai

Answer these questions and write four to six sentences about your person:
- Who is he or she?
- Where does/did he or she live?
- When?
- What did he or she do to fight for their rights?

Add pictures.

→ **M** Gallery walk, p. 169

b) Write the court scene with Claudette as the witness.

Here are the questions of the State Attorney:
- What's your name?
- Where are you from?
- Tell the court what happened on the bus on March 2, 1955.
- Do you know the rules on public transport?
- So you broke the rules on purpose. Why did you do that?

Write Claudette's answers. Look at the text for help. Act the scene in class.

→ **M** Dramatic reading, p. 169

Ich kann einen Bericht über Rassismus verstehen.

Going out in style

INTERNET

1   The 'jazz funeral' came from Africa with the slaves about 400 years ago. In the beginning it was called 'funeral with music'. People celebrated the end of slavery for the dead person. It was used mainly for poorer African Americans first and later also for musicians. In the mid 20th century it became an accepted funeral.

5   On the way to the cemetery the brass band plays mostly slow and sad songs. But on the way back you can hear joyful music. One of the most famous songs is 'When the Saints Go Marching In'. At this stage people from the streets are allowed to join in the parade.

One of the biggest jazz funerals in New Orleans took place on August 29, 2006 for
10   the 1,700 victims of Hurricane Katrina. The communities remembered the people who lost their lives the year before. That shows how people here deal with the death of loved ones and still celebrate life.

1 Beantworte die Fragen.

81/1-2

1. Was feierten die Menschen bei einer Jazz-Beerdigung früher?
2. Welche Art Musik wird vor und nach der Beerdigung gespielt?
3. Für wen war die Jazz-Beerdigung am 29. August 2006?

2 Talk to your class.

What do people in your country do after a funeral?

Ich kann Informationen über Rituale weitergeben. ✔

The great outdoors?

1 Talk about the summer holidays.

a) Do you prefer outdoor or indoor activities in your free time?

b) What's your favourite activity? Why?

2 (VIEWING) Watch the film.

10 🎬

a) Match the statements with the right scene.

1. "I got the job interview at Silverley!"
2. "That was last year. I'm 16 now!"
3. "That's for really young kids …"
4. "Very reliable. You can trust her."

b) What are their summer plans? Match each name with the right activity.

Ronan Amy Jessica

work at a summer camp

go to a Science camp

stay at home or with grandma

3 (SPEAKING) Talk about the film.

a) Watch from 01:31 to 01:55. Make notes about five of the activities there.

b) Which activity would you like to try? Why?

I would like to … .
I like … / I'm interested in … .

Ich kann einen Film über die Sommerferien verstehen. ✔

Checklist

Ich kann Informationen über die Südstaaten der USA verstehen. ✔

82

Ich kann über Einflüsse verschiedener Kulturen im täglichen Leben sprechen. ✔

In … different cultures and traditions meet. • … had a big influence on … . • When you look around, you see … . • There are problems/conflicts … .

82

Ich kann andere über Freizeitaktivitäten informieren. ✔

Here it says that … . • You can … . • I'm sorry I didn't get that. • He wants to know if … .

83

Ich kann einen Bericht über Rassismus verstehen. ✔

83

Ich kann Informationen über Rituale weitergeben. ✔

83

Ich kann einen Film über die Sommerferien verstehen. ✔

✲ (TASK) A feature story

Imagine you are a reporter. Choose a place, watch the people there and take notes. Write a feature story. Make a wall newspaper in class.

> Early birds
> (by Mika Hensing)
> May 13, 2016
> — headline, writer, date
>
> It's still dark. There are not many people in the street. However, the smell of fresh bread is in the air. At the baker's stall there's a bright light and I can see a crowd of people.
> — describing the scene
>
> They are all waiting in a long queue. Some are looking at their phones. Some are listening to music; others are talking to each other.
> — describing details
>
> Almost everyone looks tired. I feel … .
> — describing emotions
>
> Bakers usually get up at … .
> — background information
>
> "I come here every day," a woman says … .
> — direct speech

Step 1

Look for an interesting place to go.

You can go to the campus, a bus stop, the park or any other place where you can watch other people. Find other students who chose the same place.

Step 2

Take notes about the scene at your place.

What can you see, hear, smell and feel?
What are the people doing?
What are they saying?
What do you think they are thinking?
What is the weather like?
What time of the day is it?

Take photos too. If you take photos of single people or small groups, you have to ask them if that's OK.

Step 3

Find facts about your place.

You can find facts on location or on the internet. If you choose a bus stop, for example, you can find out how many buses stop there every day and where they go.

Step 4

Use your notes to write a draft.

- Find a catchy headline, an interesting opening and a nice photo.
- Describe the scene, the people and the atmosphere.
- Name the place and give interesting facts and details.
- Say what is special about the place or the people.
- Use a computer programme to format your text. You can find help on page 49.

Beschreibe die Atmosphäre mit treffenden Adjektiven:
lonely, nervous,
in a hurry,
busy, … .

Step 5

Check your draft. → M Writers' conference, p. 173

WRITING SKILLS

Prüft eure Entwürfe in der Klasse gegenseitig:
- Sind folgende Dinge vorhanden: Überschrift, Einleitungssatz, Foto, Namen des Autors/der Autorin, Datum? ✔
- Sind der Ort und die Menschen genau beschrieben? ✔
- Habt ihr schwierige Wörter im Wörterbuch nachgeschlagen und anhand der Checkliste auf Seite 175 geprüft? ✔
- Sind die Zeitformen (present progressive und simple present) richtig verwendet? ✔
- Sind die Zeitformen richtig gebildet? ✔

Der Mustertext hilft dabei.

Step 6

Make a wall newspaper in class. Find the most interesting feature story. → M Gallery walk, p. 169

Read the headlines, the first lines and look at the photos. Vote for the best headline, the most interesting first line and the most interesting photo. Read these three feature stories in class.

Recipes from the South

Po Boy Sandwich (serves 4)

The Po Boy Sandwich is a recipe from New Orleans. It's made with fresh French bread and a wide variety of fillings. You can make a perfect Po Boy Sandwich to your own choice and taste!

You need:
1 fresh French baguette bread
(about 14 ounces or 20 inches long)

Filling of your choice

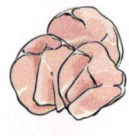    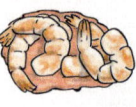 

ham, roast beef or chicken breast, coleslaw

smoked tofu, lettuce and tomatoes, onion rings or coleslaw

shrimps in cocktail sauce and tomatoes, shredded lettuce

Sauce

hot BBQ sauce, salsa or mayonnaise

Extras

gherkins or mixed pickles, grated cheese

Serve with

French fries, crisps or nachos

Preparation:

1. Cut the bread into 4 pieces.
2. Cut each piece in half.
3. Spread the sauce on one half.
4. Next choose the fillings of your choice.
5. Add extras to your taste.
6. Put the two halves together.
7. Serve the sandwich with French fries, crisps or nachos.

Guten Appetit!

> **CULTURE**
>
> In den USA benutzt man andere Maßeinheiten für Gewicht, Länge und Volumen als bei uns:
> 1 ounce = 28,35 g
> 1 inch = 2,54 cm
> 1 cup = 236.6 ml

Louisiana sweet tea (makes 4 glasses)

You need:

4 cups of water

2 breakfast tea bags

1 peppermint tea bag

3–5 tablespoons of sugar

juice of one lemon

crushed ice and slices of lemon

Preparation:

1. Boil the water.

2. Put all the tea bags into the boiling water. Brewing time: 5–6 min.

3. Add the sugar and the juice. Stir it well.

4. Cool it down.

5. You can serve it with crushed ice or slices of lemon.

Diff corner

Unit 1, p.15

○ **4** **Find the words.**   subway   avenue   skyline   playground   rush hour

Choose the right word. The pictures can help you.

1. street · road ·    3. park · lake ·    5. skyscraper · tower ·

2. taxis · bus · U   4. traffic jam · roadwork ·

Unit 1, p.15

○ **5** (SPEAKING) **Act as a guide.**

Present what is on the map. Look at the numbers for help.

1 Over there you can see ...   2 Don't miss ...

3 You must visit ...   4 Around the corner you can see ...

5 Look, there's ...

Unit 1, p.16

○ **7** (WRITING) **Tell the taxi driver's story.**

Sieh in der Liste auf S. 210 nach, ob das Verb in Klammern unregelmäßig ist!

Make sentences. Use the simple past.

1. Last winter I **was** (be) at the airport.
   A woman —— (get) in my taxi.

2. It —— (be) cold and there —— (be) heavy snow.

3. Then there —— (be) a traffic jam. I —— (talk) to the woman.

4. When we —— (arrive) at the hotel, she —— (forget) her saxophone.

5. I —— (run) to the hotel and I —— (look) for her.

6. When I —— (give) the saxophone back, she was very happy.

Unit 1, p.17

8 (SPEAKING) What did they do at One World Trade Center yesterday?

Look at the people in the picture. Match the questions with the answers.

1. What did Henry eat?
2. Did Susan take a photo?
3. What did Lisa do?
4. What did Frank look at?
5. Where did Linda sit?
6. Did Nancy eat a sandwich?

A He looked at the view.
B She sat next to the window.
C No, she had a drink.
D No, she phoned somebody.
E He ate a sandwich.
F She took a photo of herself.

Unit 1, p.18

2 (WRITING) Collect facts about José and his family. → M Think–pair–share, p.173

Complete the fact card.

1 Interviewer: Hello José. Can I ask you a few questions for our magazine, please?
José: Hi. Sure.
Interviewer: You're new on the baseball team.
5 Are you happy?
José: We won the first three matches, so I can't complain.
Interviewer: There are lots of players from Latin America here. When did you immigrate
10 to the United States?
José: That was twelve years ago. I was ten.
Interviewer: That was a big decision for your parents. They left their home and moved to a foreign place.
15 José: Yes, but they were very poor in Cuba. My father had been unemployed for a long time. My parents wanted to give me and my sisters the best chances. …

Interviewer: What about your plans for the future?
José: I'm a US citizen now and my home is here. But I plan to help people in Cuba.
Interviewer: Thank you for your time.

20

Name: J—— (line 1)
Job: b—— p—— (lines 4 and 8)
Age: —— (line 11)
From: C—— (line 15)
Lives in: the U—— (lines 9 to 10)
Why they left their country:
p——, u——, get best c—— (lines 15 to 18)
Plans: h—— p—— in C—— (line 22)

Unit 1, p. 19

○ **4 Imagine you want to leave your country.**

Complete the sentences with these phrases.

| chances | get used to | feel foreign | immigrate to ✔ | give up |

1. Where could I go? I could <u>immigrate to</u> the USA.

2. It will be hard to g—— my old life.

3. I hope I will have many c—— in the USA.

4. I hope I won't f—— and lonely.

5. I hope I can g—— my new life soon.

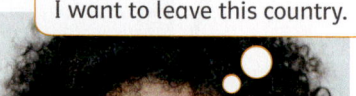

I want to leave this country.

Unit 1, p. 20

○ **7 Find out about one of Angela's days.**

Welche Puzzleteile gehören zusammen?

Match the sentence parts. The pictures can help you.

After Pablo had invited Angela to his party, . . .

. . . she bought a present.

After Angela and Pablo had walked through the park, . . .

. . . she had ordered a milkshake.

After they had bought tickets, …

… they took the subway.

Before Angela ate her pizza, …

… they had put on their fan shirts.

Before Angela and Pablo went to the stadium, …

… they visited Ellis Island.

Unit 1, p. 21

○ **8** (WRITING) **Write sentences. Use the past perfect.**

What <u>had</u> José <u>done</u> before his first important baseball game last summer?
What <u>hadn't</u> he <u>done</u>? Look at José's list. Then choose the right word.

José:
1. Before my first big game I **had** • **hadn't** played every day.
2. I **had** • **hadn't** bought new sports shoes.
3. I **had** • **hadn't** ordered tickets for my friends.
4. I **had** • **hadn't** watched the other team.
5. I **had** • **hadn't** phoned my dad.
6. I **had** • **hadn't** eaten a big meal.

1. played every day ✔
2. bought new sports shoes ✖
3. ordered tickets for my friends ✔
4. watched the other team ✔
5. phoned my dad ✔
6. eaten a big meal ✖

○ **3** (WRITING) **Find out about Luise's exchange year.**

1,10 ⌖

1 "No! An exchange year in South Dakota? That's in the middle of nowhere," I thought. But after my year there I can say that it was the best time ever.

5 In the beginning it was like in a movie. I had seen it all on TV. My American school was huge. Teachers usually stay in their classrooms, and students go to them for each class. So we had to put our things into our
10 lockers. After two weeks I got used to it, and I could find the way to the classrooms by myself.
Every day school started at 8:00 with a morning message from the principal. The
15 first class started at 8:30. I had to take Math, English, Science and History. But I could choose subjects like Astronomy and Journalism, for example. We also had six classes a week in the study hall. There we
20 could do our homework or study. You weren't allowed to talk there.

School rules were strict. Much stricter than at home. Another rule was: You weren't allowed to wear short skirts.
Classes finished at 3:30. After that there were 25 many extracurricular activities. I wanted to join the cheerleaders. There was a lot of competition for places. Exchange students were allowed to try too, so I did. And I got a place! Awesome! 30
My host family was great too. They even took me on a trip to the east coast. My exchange year was fantastic, even in the middle of nowhere.

Make a mind map. Use the underlined phrases from the text for help.

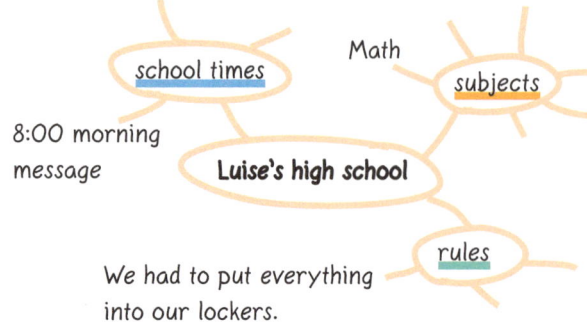

Math

school times   subjects

8:00 morning message

Luise's high school

rules

We had to put everything into our lockers.

Unit 2, p. 35

4 What do these words mean?

Match the words with the definitions. The pictures can help you.

1. where students keep their things

2. the leader of a school

3. where you can do your homework or study

4. a number or letter that tells you how well you did in a test

5. a year with a host family in another country

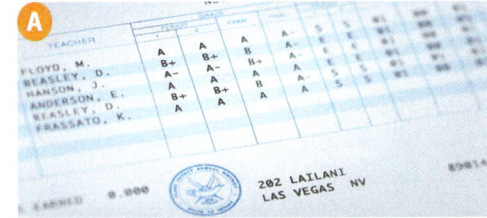

grade

exchange year

locker

study hall

principal

Unit 2, p. 36

○ **8 Complete the sentences.**

Complete the sentences about Luise and the cheerleaders with these words.

| had to | musste(n) | didn't have to | brauchte(n) nicht |

1. Before Luise joined the cheerleaders she **(+)** get the right clothes.
   Before Luise joined the cheerleaders she <u>had to</u> get the right clothes.
2. She was fit, so she **(–)** worry.
3. For the first practice she **(+)** be there 15 minutes early.
4. During her first practice the cheerleaders **(+)** shout really loudly.
5. Luise learned very quickly, so she **(–)** do extra practice.

Ob die Aussage stimmt oder nicht, siehst du an den Symbolen (+) und (–).

Unit 2, p. 37

○ **9 Make sentences about Luise's life after her exchange year in the USA.**

Say what Luise <u>could</u> **(+)** or <u>couldn't</u> **(–)** do after her exchange.

1. Luise **(–)** get used to her old life easily.
   Luise <u>couldn't</u> get used to her old life easily.
2. She **(+)** understand English a lot better.
3. She **(+)** speak English a lot better.
4. She **(–)** keep in touch with all her American friends.
5. She **(+)** help other students with English.

Die Verneinung von „could" (konnte) heißt „could not" oder „couldn't".

Unit 2, p. 39

○ **4** (SPEAKING) **What do you think?**

What should or shouldn't Michael say to the manager?

1. "I'm sorry."
2. "It won't happen again."
3. "But they started it."
4. "It wasn't me."
5. "I don't think you're right."
6. "Next time I'll try to be cooler."

Welche Sätze zeigen, dass er seinen Fehler einsieht? Mit welchen Sätzen gibt er die Schuld anderen?

Unit 2, p. 39

○ **6** (WRITING) **Practise words to describe people at work.** → M Peer correction, p. 171

Copy and complete the table.

+	–
—— ing	lazy
—— ful	un ——
—— ible	un ——

lazy ✔ hard-working

helpful responsible

unmotivated unfriendly

Welche bekannten Wörter stecken in den neuen Wörtern drin?

hard working

Unit 2, p. 40

○ **9** **Complete the sentences.**

Use the simple present.

He, she, it – das -s muss mit!

1. If Michael finds a job, he'll earn money. (find a job)

2. If he —— , he'll ask his co-workers. (need help)

3. If he —— , he'll lose his job. (be late)

4. If the girl —— , Michael will catch her. (steal something)

5. If the man —— , he'll get a new pullover. (complain)

6. If the woman —— , she'll get one free. (buy two)

Unit 2, p. 41

○ **10** (SPEAKING) **What will you do if . . . ?**

Talk about next weekend. Complete the sentences with these words. I'll   I won't

1. If I get up late, I won't have breakfast.
2. If the weather is fine, —— go to the cinema.
3. If it rains, —— go cycling.

4. If I don't have any homework, —— watch TV.
5. If my parents are away on Saturday evening, —— have a party.
6. If I'm too busy, —— go shopping.

3 Find out about the Miller family's Thanksgiving. → M Peer correction, p. 171

The Millers from Boston are getting ready for Thanksgiving dinner. Julia is in the kitchen. Her husband Mark, their son Jacob and Grandma Brenda are in the living room. Her daughter Lily lives with her boyfriend Evan in Washington D.C. They are not there yet.

1 **Grandma:** Last year we had a terrible storm. I got stuck in my car for over two hours. Do you remember?

Mark: Yes, that's right. Did you have a hard
5 time again yesterday?

(The doorbell rings. Mark opens the door. It's their neighbor.)

Robert: Happy Thanksgiving, Mark!

Mark: You too, Robert. How are you doing?

10 **Robert:** Great, thanks. Brr. It's very cold outside.

Mark: Come on in. I'm so glad you could make it. *(They enter the living room.)* Grandma, this is Robert. He's our new neighbor.
15 He doesn't have family here, so we've invited him to join us. Robert, this is Brenda.

Robert: Nice to meet you, Brenda.

Grandma: Nice to meet you too. When did you move here?

20 **Mark:** *(He shouts across the room)* Jacob, why don't you say hello? You can't spend all your time on your phone.

Jacob: What's up Robert?

Robert: How's it going? Are you enjoying the holiday? Do you like turkey? 25

Jacob: Not really. I'm a vegetarian, so I won't eat any.

Julia: *(She comes out of the kitchen.)* You always used to eat everything. *(She notices the new guest.)* Oh, hi Robert. 30

Robert: Hey Julia. Thanks so much for inviting me. Here's a little present. You eat chocolates, don't you? *(He gives her a box as a present.)*

(Mark's phone rings.) 35

Mark: That's probably Lily. Hello Lily. … Oh, no! *(to the others)* Their plane from Washington, D.C. had troubles and they had to land in New York. *(to Lily)* So when does your plane arrive? … OK. … Will you call 40 again later?
I promise we'll save some turkey for you!

Mark   Grandma

Julia

Jacob

Robert

Who is it?

1. Who got stuck in her car last year?
   That's **Brenda**.
2. Who is the new neighbor?

3. Who doesn't eat turkey any more?
4. Who gets a present?
5. Who talks to Lily on the phone?

D

Unit 3, p. 55

○ **5** (WRITING) **Collect small talk phrases.**

Choose the right answer.

1. How's it going? – <u>Great, thanks.</u> • Not much.
2. What's up? – Nice to meet you too. • Not much.
3. Sam, this is Beth. – Great, thanks. • Beth, this is Sam.
4. Nice to meet you. – Nice to meet you too. • Not really.
5. Do you like turkey? – Not really. • Great, thanks.

Unit 3, p. 56

○ **9** (SPEAKING) **Ask questions about holidays.**

Choose the right question word. Interview your partner.

| What | Where | Who |
| How many | Which ✓ |

Mit „who" fragt man nach Personen. Es kann „wer" oder „wen" heißen.

Partner A:

1. **(Welche)** holidays does your family celebrate?
Which holidays does your family celebrate?

2. **(Was)** do you always eat at Christmas / Easter / Eid / ...?

3. **(Wen)** does your family invite every time?

4. **(Wie viele)** guests did your family invite last time?

5. **(Wo)** will you celebrate next year?

Partner B:

1. We celebrate Christmas / Easter / Eid / ... .

2. We always eat ... at Christmas / Easter / Eid / ... .

3. My family invites my grandparents / uncles / aunts / cousins ... every time.

4. Last time my family invited ... guests.

5. Next year we'll celebrate at our home / at my ...'s home / at a restaurant / ... .

Unit 3, p. 57

○ 10 Make a phone call.

Complete the phone call between Jacob and his grandma with these questions.

Did you have a good trip home? • Will you be there? • Can I bring my new girlfriend? •
What about you? • When will you celebrate? • How are you? ✔ • Where will you celebrate?

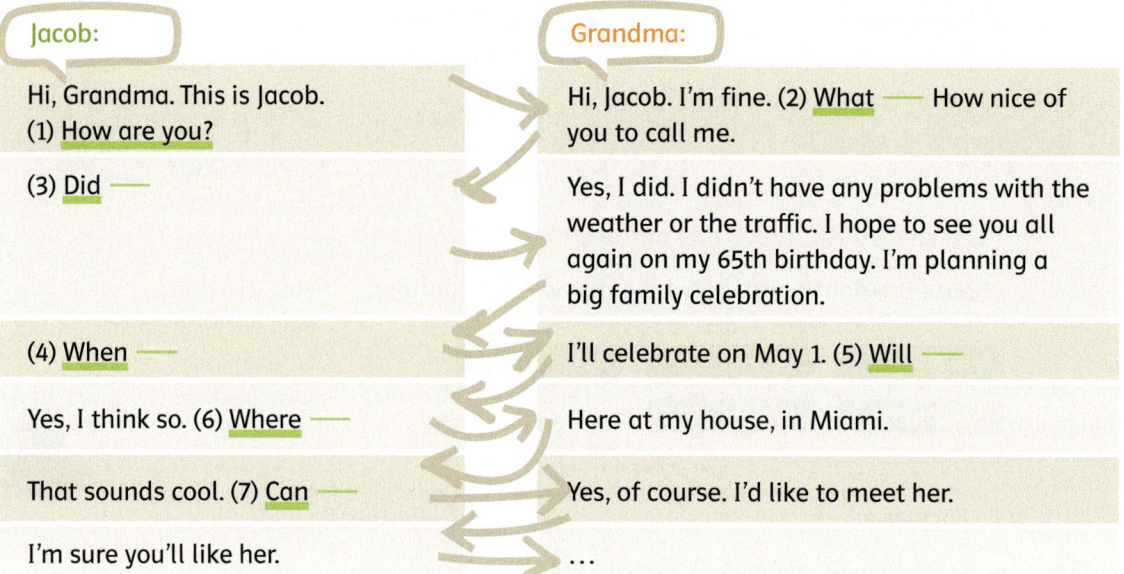

Jacob:

Hi, Grandma. This is Jacob.
(1) How are you?

(3) Did —

(4) When —

Yes, I think so. (6) Where —

That sounds cool. (7) Can —

I'm sure you'll like her.

Grandma:

Hi, Jacob. I'm fine. (2) What —— How nice of
you to call me.

Yes, I did. I didn't have any problems with the
weather or the traffic. I hope to see you all
again on my 65th birthday. I'm planning a
big family celebration.

I'll celebrate on May 1. (5) Will —

Here at my house, in Miami.

Yes, of course. I'd like to meet her.

…

Unit 3, p. 59

○ 5 (WRITING) Sort the phrases. → M Peer correction, p. 171

Copy and complete the table.

I agree 👍	I disagree 👎
Exactly.	— not.
That's —	I —
That's —	No —

Exactly. ✔   That's true.   I don't think so.

That's for sure.   Absolutely not.   No way!

○ **6** (SPEAKING) **Talk about devices.**

Make a list. Rank the devices from the most important to the least important.
Talk to your partner.

microwave **headphones** **TV** **phone** **computer**

Partner A:

The most important thing
for me is my <u>phone</u>.

Headphones are second.

——s are third. ——s are next.
——s come last.

Partner B:

I agree.

I don't think so.

I think ——s are more
important than ——s.

Achtung, "headphones" ist immer in
der Mehrzahl: The most important
thing for me <u>are</u> my headphones.

○ **8** **What would make Jennifer's life easier?**

Look at the pictures. Complete the sentences. Use the simple past.

Sieh in der Liste ab S. 210 nach, ob das Verb in Klammern unregelmäßig ist!

1. Jennifer would be less worried in the morning if she <u>chose</u> her clothes the evening before. (choose)

2. She wouldn't feel so tired in the morning if she — to bed early. (go)

3. She would hear what her dad said if she — to music. (not listen)

4. She wouldn't get cold if she — a warm coat. (have)

5. It would be better if she — to school. (walk)

○ **9** (**SPEAKING**) **What would you do if ...?** → M Milling around, p. 170

Complete the sentences.

1. If I were president of the United States for a day, I would ... .
2. If I were a superhero, I would ... .
3. If I could go back in time, I would ... .
4. If I had a million dollars, I would ... .
5. If I knew the answers to my next English test before the test, I would ... .

Here are some ideas:

- be the best student in class
- buy a big house with a swimming pool
- give all students computers
- always have holidays
- jump from the tallest building
- ...

Now ask your partner. What would you do if you ...

1. were president of the United States for a day?
2. were a superhero?
3. could go back in time?
4. had a million dollars?
5. knew the answers to your next English test before the test?

Unit 4, p. 76

○ **2** (LISTENING) **Listen to a conversation about an ad.**
2,3

Choose the right answer.

1

Come and chill out in sunny California

2

Book the adventure of a lifetime

Canyon Tours

Phone reservations
8 a.m. to 6 p.m.
(Pacific Time Zone):
702-574-04455

3

If it looks fun, it is fun!

Rock Climbing for Kids
in Bishop, CA

Click here to learn more

1. Emily, Carol and Daniel are talking about
   one ad from exercise one. Which one? **1 • 2 • 3**
2. Who doesn't like the ad? **Emily • Carol • Daniel**

Worüber reden die Jugendlichen?
Zu welcher Werbung passt das?

Unit 4, p. 77

○ **3** (SPEAKING) **What do you think of the ads?**

Talk about the ads from exercise 2.

A: I think ad number 1 is spectacular.
   I like ... .
B: I agree.

| 2 | 3 | isn't |

| simple | informative | special | clear | catchy |

| I don't think so. I think ... . |

Unit 4, p.78

7 Look at the ads.

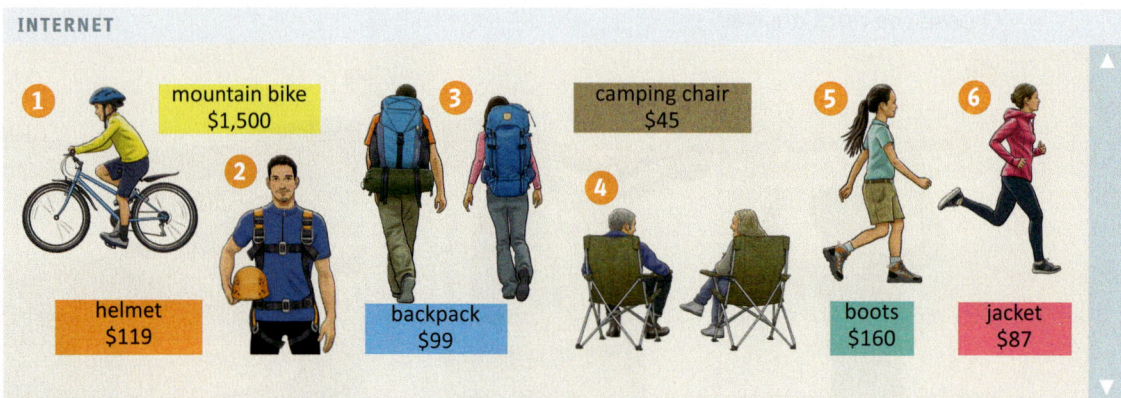

Complete the sentences. Use the simple present.

1. The mountain bike **is** • **are** $1,500.
2. The helmet **looks** • **look** cool.
3. The backpacks **is** • **are** $99 each.
4. The camping chairs **doesn't look** • **don't look** nice.
5. The girl **likes** • **like** walking.
6. The woman **doesn't need** • **don't need** an umbrella.

Unit 4, p.79

8 (WRITING) Simple present or present progressive?

Choose the right tense. Look at the signal words for help.

> **E-MAIL**
>
> Hi Becky,
> At the moment (1) **I sit** • **I'm sitting** in the sun next to the swimming pool. It's always warm here in California. (2) **It doesn't rain** • **It isn't raining** often. (3) We usually **spend** • **are spending** the weekends at the beach. (4) At the moment **I learn** • **I'm learning** how to surf. But lots of other things are the same as in the Midwest. (5) Every day **I go** • **I'm going** to school, (6) **I do** • **I'm doing** my homework and (7) **I go** • **I'm going** to bed.
> (8) What **do you do** • **are you doing** right now? I miss you.
> Sandy

○ **3 What does the text say?**

2,5

BLOG

A quick look back

Thursday, March 16, 2017

1 California has always welcomed new ideas – just think of the high-tech companies in Silicon Valley or the movie industry.
The internet is one of these ideas. The World Wide Web started in the early 1990s, so it's been around for almost 30 years. And it has really changed
5 the world. Today almost everyone uses social media. I've had an account since I was 13. Why have they been so successful? Well, that's easy: you can post your photos, share your thoughts and keep in touch with friends. Most of the time you don't even have to look for information. It'll find you. We should give that a big 'like'.
10 Online videos have had a huge impact on our lives too. There are lots of funny videos. I like the tutorials best. You can find anything there from guitar lessons to make-up tips. Nobody watches much TV anymore. People stream their favorite shows instead.
Smartphones and tablets became the next big thing. Most of my friends go online every day, and half of them are online almost all the time. Most use several different social media sites at the
15 same time. Some say it's difficult to stop using social media. They get messages every minute of the day and feel that they have to answer right away. Others are worried about cyberbullying.
If somebody writes bad things about you online, a lot of people can read it. We haven't really found any good answers yet.

Posted by Derek Lee   at 8:51 a.m.   2 comments: Links to this post

Right or wrong? Correct the wrong sentences.

1. The World Wide Web started about 50 years ago. (lines 3 to 4)
   That's wrong. The World Wide Web started almost 30 years ago.
2. Social media sites are very popular today. (line 5)
3. Everyone watches TV. (line 13)
4. Most people are online almost all the time. (lines 14 to 15)
5. There are also problems with the internet. (lines 16 to 17)

Prüfe, ob die unterstrichenen Satzteile richtig oder falsch sind. Schau im Text in den angegebenen Zeilen nach. Achtung: Die Sätze sind anders formuliert.

Unit 4, p. 81

○ **5 Explain the words.**

Find the definitions for these words.

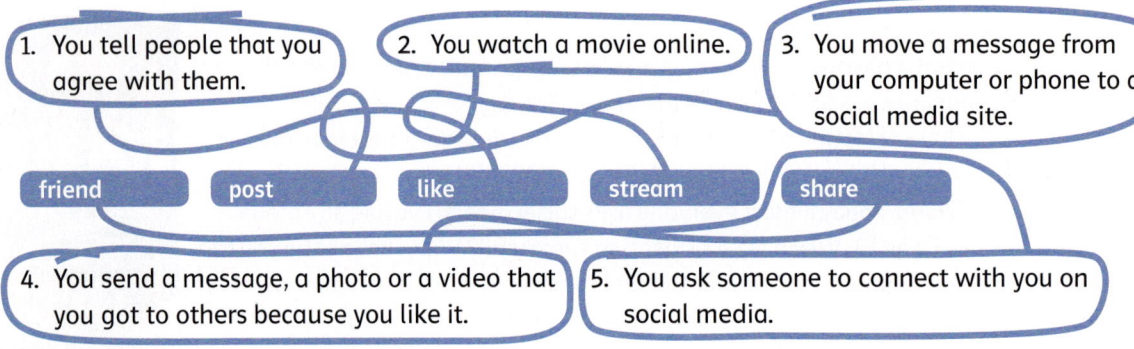

1. You tell people that you agree with them.
2. You watch a movie online.
3. You move a message from your computer or phone to a social media site.

friend · post · like · stream · share

4. You send a message, a photo or a video that you got to others because you like it.
5. You ask someone to connect with you on social media.

Unit 4, p. 82

○ **8 Say for how long or since when.**

Zeitpunkt

Zeitraum

GRAMMAR → G8, p. 165

since ten o'clock – seit zehn Uhr
for an hour – seit einer Stunde

Choose **for** or **since**.

1. I've had my smartphone
   for · **since** three years.

2. I haven't posted a new photo
   for · **since** ten o'clock.

3. Social media have been popular
   for · **since** 20 years now.

4. Millions of people have seen the cat pictures
   for · **since** Tuesday.

5. More than 5,000 people have watched that
   tutorial **for** · **since** May.

6. I haven't answered my e-mails
   for · **since** five days.

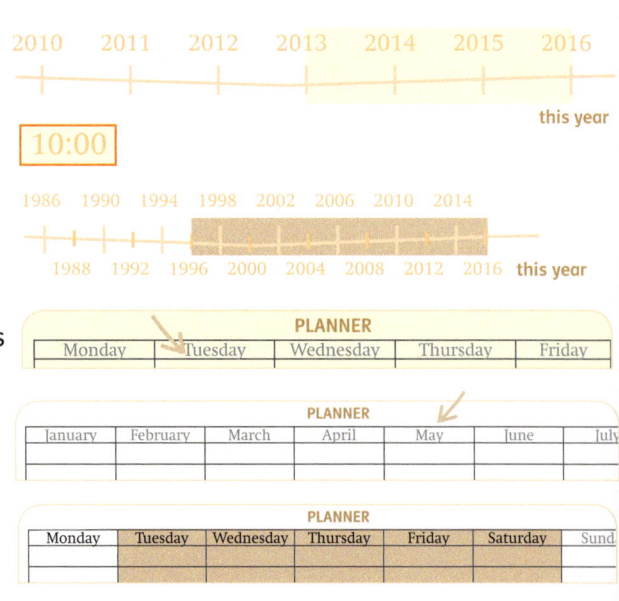

Unit 4, p.83

○ 9 Complete the survey questions and answers.

Match the questions with the answers.

1. **Interviewer:** Have you bought a book or a magazine this week?
2. **Interviewer:** Have you ever used tutorial videos to learn how to do something?
3. **Interviewer:** Have you found any new music videos that you liked this week?

Kim: Let me think for a second. Today I've seen one that I really enjoyed.
Jake: I usually read everything online. I haven't read a book or a magazine for a long time.
Sally: Yes, sure. I've already learned to play the guitar that way.

Unit 5, p.99

○ 3 What's the nationality?

Match the nationalities with the flags.

| Chinese | Greek | Italian | Russian | Polish | Turkish |

1. 中国 (China)
2. Россия (Russia)
3. Polska (Poland)
4. Ελλάδα (Greece)
5. Türkiye (Turkey)
6. Italia (Italy)

Unit 5, p.99

○ 4 Find the words.

Match the sentences with the same meaning.

1. Some people accepted the flag.
2. Others didn't accept it.
3. There were conflicts between the different groups.
4. The different groups found a solution.

A Others disagreed.
B There were problems between the different groups.
C The different groups made a compromise.
D Some people tolerated the flag.

Unit 5, p.100

○ **6 Make passive sentences.** → M Bus stop, p.168

Choose the right form.

1. Pork **is** • **are** used in many southern dishes.
2. Southern food **is** • **are** eaten across the USA.
3. Vegetables **is** • **are** kept in the fridge.
4. All these dishes **is** • **are** made with rice.
5. Rice **is** • **are** not grown in many US states.

Sieh dir die unterstrichenen Subjekte an:
Einzahl (oder nicht zählbar) → „is"
Mehrzahl (endet meistens auf –s) → „are"

Unit 5, p.101

○ **7 Complete the sentences about multicultural schools.**

Make passive sentences.

1. Many languages are spoken at multicultural schools. (speak)
2. Special lessons are —— for people who are new. (organize)
3. Lessons are —— in different languages at some schools. (give)
4. Multicultural food is —— in the cafeteria. (sell)
5. Special days of different cultures are —— at school. (celebrate)
6. Racism isn't —— there. (accept)

„Organize", „celebrate" und „accept"
sind regelmäßig. Die anderen Verben
kannst du in der Liste der unregel-
mäßigen Verben (3. Spalte) ab S. 210
nachschauen.

Unit 5, p.103

○ **4 (LISTENING) Listen to the text about a visit to an alligator farm.**

2,15

Choose the right word.

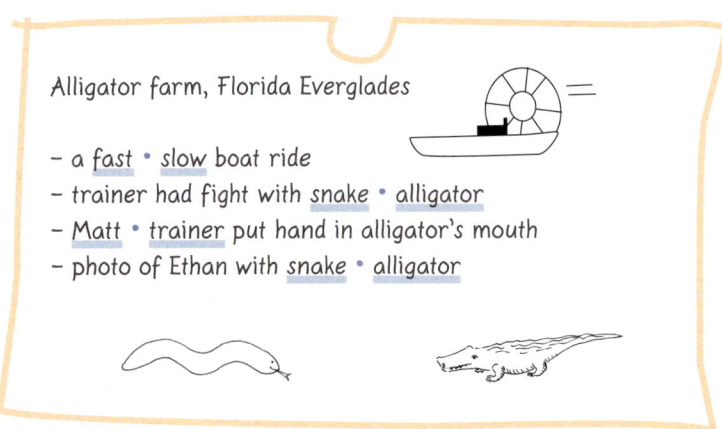

Alligator farm, Florida Everglades

– a fast • slow boat ride
– trainer had fight with snake • alligator
– Matt • trainer put hand in alligator's mouth
– photo of Ethan with snake • alligator

○ **5** (WRITING) **How can you say that you (don't) understand?** → M Peer correction, p. 171

Copy and complete the table.

Could you please explain? ✔	I get it.	I know what you mean.
Can you repeat it, please?	Excuse me?	I see.

I understand	I don't understand
I ——	Could you please explain?
I ——	C ——
I ——	E ——

○ **7** **Report what other people say.**

What did Anna write? Read Anna's e-mail from Clearwater, Florida. Then complete the sentences with the right pronoun.

E-MAIL

Hi Julie,
(1) I'm at Clearwater right now. (2) I love the the warm weather here. (3) We just wear T-shirts and shorts and (4) we often go to the beach. (5) It's awesome! But (6) I hate the insects.
See you soon,
Anna

Das ändert sich in der indirekten Rede:
I → he/she
we → they
Diese Pronomen ändern sich nicht: it, they

Here's an e-mail from Anna.

1. Anna says (that) she is at Clearwater.
2. She writes (that) —— loves the warm weather.
3. She writes (that) —— just wear T-shirts and shorts.
4. She says (that) —— often go to the beach.
5. She says (that) —— is awesome.
6. She says (that) —— hates the insects.

2,17 Art and culture in NYC

Big city lights

1

New York City has great museums, lots of movie theaters, the finest restaurants, street markets, parades, festivals with free events …
Walk down Broadway at night, and you'll see the lights of 40 theaters. Watch popular actors in world-class shows, plays and musicals.
There's a great number of things to see and do here …

Hip hop culture

2

It's the end of the 1960s in the Bronx, at the time a poor part of the city. Here African-American teenagers start a new cultural movement, hip hop.
Rap, DJing, breakdancing and graffiti were the main parts of hip hop culture. DJs took parts of older songs to create a new style of music.

Rappers often rapped about life in street gangs and about social questions. Breakdancers became famous for their robotic moves. Graffiti artists used subway trains and buildings as their canvas. Hip hop has now gone global.

D

Street art

3

In the past street art meant large murals, often in poorer parts of the city. Today you can go on guided tours to see the best murals. Some think it's art, some don't.

The city in comics

4

Spiderman lives in Queens, Iron Man's company is in Long Island, and Batman's Gotham City is a fictional version of New York. And there are lots of other examples – the city is the home of superheroes.

Comics are an art form that comes from the United States. You can find the biggest comic book companies in New York City, and famous writers too.

1 What's new to you? Tell your partner three things.

I didn't know that ... .
It's new to me that ... .
I'm surprised to read that ... .

movie theater *(AE)* – *Kino*; event – *Ereignis, Veranstaltung*; cultural movement – *kulturelle Bewegung*; social – *gesellschaftlich*; artist – *Künstler/in*; canvas – *Leinwand*; global – *weltweit*; guided tour – *Führung*; fictional – *erfunden*

2,18 Native Americans then and now

Christopher Columbus didn't discover America!

The history of Native Americans in our country is fascinating and tragic. When Europeans made first contact with them around 1500, about ten million Native American people lived in North America. They had come from Siberia to Alaska in about 10,000 BC. They spoke different languages and had many different lifestyles. They were hunters, fishermen, farmers and traders. They lived in houses made of wood and built canoes or they moved from place to place and lived in tepees.

The Europeans arrive

From the 17th century a large number of European settlers arrived. They brought illnesses which killed thousands of Native Americans. When more people arrived, they wanted land, and the tribes had to leave their traditional farming and hunting lands. The settlers pushed them further away from the coast, until in the 1830s a lot of tribes had to move west of the Mississippi River. On this terrible journey hundreds died of cold, hunger and illness.

Bloody battles

On the Great Plains, however, life was different. The tribes had got horses from the Europeans, so they could hunt buffalo more easily. They didn't want to give up their freedom and their hunting lands, and they often attacked settlers who crossed the plains. Many bloody battles followed. By 1900 most tribes had to go and live on reservations.

"I was born on the prairie where the wind blew free [...] I want to die there and not within walls. I know every stream and every wood between the Rio Grande and the Arkansas. [...] So, why do you ask us to leave the rivers and the sun and the wind and live in houses?"

Chief Ten Bears in 1867

Native Americans today

Today Native Americans are full American citizens. Only a minority of the five million Native Americans live on reservations. Some make money from the casino business, but most of them are poor, and they are unemployed. There's a new interest in the Native American culture among younger people today.

"The government took my grandad away from his parents and sent him to boarding school, together with thousands of others. They didn't let him learn about his language or culture there. So my dad never learned anything either. We lost a lot of things.
Even in school today nobody teaches us about the thousands of years of our history before the Europeans arrived. But many of us want to change this situation. My history is part of me. I feel like we Native Americans are picking up the pieces of our culture and moving forward. I want to help rebuild things."
Alaqua, 16, Oklahoma

By Pat Smith
September 15, 2016
Junior History Magazine

1 **Choose one paragraph. What did you already know about Native Americans? What didn't you know? Talk in groups.**

I already knew that … .
I didn't know that … .
It's new to me that … .

---

tragic – *tragisch*; BC (= before Christ) – *vor Christus*; hunter – *Jäger/in*;
fisherman – *Fischer*; trader – *Händler/in*; illness – *Krankheit*; tribe – *(Volks-)Stamm*;
hunting land – *Jagdgebiet*; bloody – *blutig*; Great Plains – *Flachland in den USA*;
to attack – *angreifen*; casino business – *Casino-Geschäft*; boarding school – *Internat*;
to rebuild – *wiederaufbauen*

2,19 ☞ # Holidays in the USA

JANUARY Martin Luther King Day

1

I have a dream

This day is the birthday of Martin Luther King. He lived at a time when African Americans did not have the same rights as white Americans. He used peaceful ways to protest against this and to change it. His 'I have a dream' speech is famous. Martin Luther King was assassinated in 1968.

FEBRUARY Presidents' Day

2

This holiday celebrates the birthdays of two great presidents – George Washington and Abraham Lincoln. Washington led the American army which defeated Great Britain. He became the first American president in 1789. In 1865, after the terrible Civil War, Lincoln ended slavery in the United States. He was assassinated in the same year.

JULY Independence Day

3

The Fourth of July celebrates the USA's independence from Great Britain. That is the day in 1776 when the 13 American states signed the Declaration of Independence, now a famous document. People dress in red, white and blue – the color of the flag. They have picnics or barbecues and there are fantastic fireworks across the country.

OCTOBER Columbus Day

4

Christopher Columbus first saw America on October 12, 1492. Today there are parades and dinners to celebrate him. However, some people don't like this holiday because Columbus didn't actually discover America. But the day also remembers a man of ideas, dreams and great ambition. That is something most Americans understand very well.

NOVEMBER Thanksgiving

5

The history of Thanksgiving began in 1621 when the Pilgrim settlers celebrated their first year in their new country. They invited some local Native Americans to share their meal. Thanksgiving is a family day. A traditional Thanksgiving dinner has turkey, cranberry sauce, and pumpkin pie for dessert. Football games are usually a big part of the day too.

1 **What celebration would you like to take part in? Why? Talk with a partner.**

A: I'd like to take part in Independence Day because fireworks are great.
B: I'd like to take part in Independence Day too because I love picnics and barbecues.

> rights – *Rechte*; peaceful – *friedlich*; was assassinated – *wurde ermordet*;
> to defeat – *schlagen, besiegen*; civil war – *Bürgerkrieg*; slavery – *Sklaverei*;
> to sign – *unterschreiben*; actually – *wirklich*; ambition – *Ehrgeiz*;
> pumpkin pie – *Kürbiskuchen*

2,20 🔊 # Hollywood

The movie industry

1

Since the silent movies of the early 20th century, Hollywood has been the center of the movie industry. The sign was originally an ad from 1923 which read HOLLYWOODLAND. They changed it to HOLLYWOOD in 1949. Today the sign is famous all over the world.

"And the Oscar goes to ..."

Hollywood Walk of Fame

2

The highest honor in the movie business is an Oscar or Academy Award. Millions of people around the world watch the stars arrive and walk along the Red Carpet. There are many different categories of awards, but the most famous are Best Picture, Best Actor and Best Director.

3

The Walk of Fame remembers famous or important people in the entertainment industry. The names of more than 2,500 actors, musicians, directors, writers and many others from the past and present are written on pink stars. Every year they add new names.

Movie studio tours

4

From the very beginning, big movie companies have had their own production sets and studios. Most of the studios offer tours. At Universal Studios, for example, you can experience a fight between King Kong and a dinosaur.

Hollywood or Bollywood

5

Hollywood may be famous, but the biggest film industry in the world is actually in India. 'Bollywood' is its nickname. Here's the difference:

Bollywood movies	Hollywood movies
- action, drama, romance and comedy all in one movie	- action, drama, romance and comedy in four different movies
- music and dance in every movie	- music and dance in musicals only
- three hours long with a short break in the middle	- usually two hours long

1 **What did you find interesting? What did you already know?**

I already knew about (the Oscar).
I didn't know about (Bollywood).
It's interesting that . . . .

silent movie – *Stummfilm*; originally – *ursprünglich*; honor *(AE)* – *Ehre*;
movie business – *Filmgeschäft*; the Red Carpet – *der Rote Teppich*; award – *Preis*;
fame – *Ruhm*; entertainment – *Unterhaltung*; star – *Stern, Star*; set – *Kulisse*;
experience – *erleben*; nickname – *Spitzname*

2.21 🔊 Life in the South

Plantation houses

1

In 1803 the United States bought Louisiana and other territories from the French. Rich Anglo-American landowners moved there. They built large houses on their plantations to show their wealth. Many of these houses were destroyed after the American Civil War (1861 – 1865), but some are still there. Oak Alley Plantation was built by slaves on a sugar plantation. It was completed in 1839. Today the house is open to visitors. It's a popular location for movies and for weddings.

Paddle steamers

2

The Mississippi is almost 4,000 miles long. It's one of the longest rivers in the USA. In the 19th century paddle steamers took people and goods up and down the river. Because of their paddlewheels, they could go far up the river, even when the water level was very low. Today there are many modern riverboats for tourists on the Mississippi.

Fishing in the Florida Keys

3

In the Florida Keys you can find all kinds of fishing. From fishing for beginners to fishing for experts. If you love the sea and fishing, there's no better place. When you go back to the harbor, take your fish back to one of the local restaurants. They will prepare a great meal for you.

Line dance

4

What is line dance? A group of people who dance in one or more lines. They all face the same direction and they all do the same steps at the same time. Each dance has its own style. People can dance to country and western music but also to rock and pop. Even the internet sensation video 'Gangnam Style' had elements of line dancing in it.

1 Choose one paragraph and tell your group three facts about your topic.

My text is about … • It says that … • Today … • You can also … • However, …

> territory – *Gebiet*; Anglo-American – *anglo-amerikanisch (bezieht sich auf Amerikaner mit englischen Wurzeln)*; wealth – *Reichtum*; to destroy – *zerstören*; paddle steamer – *Raddampfer*; fishing – *Angeln*; line – *Reihe*; to face the same direction – *in die gleiche Richtung blicken*

Extra

When the earth shakes

1 What's an earthquake?

Every day there are minor or major earthquakes[1] around the world. The ground shakes for seconds or sometimes even minutes. Earthquakes can occur at any time, and we don't notice most of them. You can't tell when or where they will happen. In the USA the West Coast is most at risk[2] because of its special geological structure. However, there can be earthquakes in the Midwest or on the East Coast too.

2 What causes an earthquake?

The earth's crust consists[3] of about 20 different (tectonic) plates which slowly move. The place where two plates meet is called a fault line[4]. One plate rubs[5] against another. This puts both plates under stress. When the force[6] gets too strong, it comes apart with a jerk[7]. The released energy makes the earth move in waves.

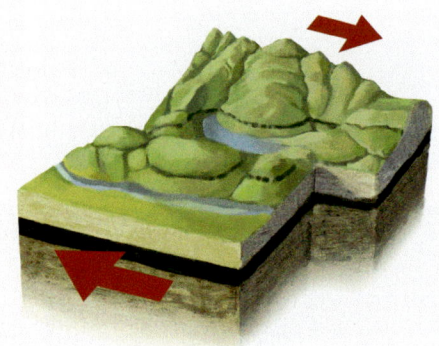

3 What can earthquakes do?

Major earthquakes can cause many problems. Buildings or bridges can collapse[8] or pipelines burst[9]. There can be mudslides[10], fires or tsunamis too. A large number of people can be hurt or even die during an earthquake.

---

1 earthquake ['ɜːθkweɪk] – *Erdbeben;* 2 be at risk [rɪsk] – *einem Risiko ausgesetzt sein;* 3 consist of [kənˈsɪstˌəv] – *bestehen aus;* 4 fault line [ˈfɔːltˌlaɪn] – *Verwerfungs-, Bruchlinie;* 5 rub [rʌb] – *reiben;* 6 force [fɔːs] – *Kraft, Stärke;* 7 jerk [dʒɜːk] – *Ruck;* 8 collapse [kəˈlæps] – *zusammenbrechen;* 9 burst [bɜːst] – *platzen;* 10 mudslide [ˈmʌdslaɪd] – *Schlammlawine*

4 How are earthquakes measured?

Scientists[1] record earthquakes with the help of a special instrument – the seismograph. It measures[2] the magnitude of an earthquake.
The Richter scale shows how destructive[3] earthquakes can be:

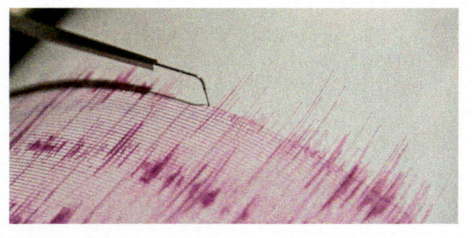

The Richter scale

0 – 1.9	only recorded by seismograph; not felt
2.0 – 2.9	objects may swing; hardly any damage
3.0 – 3.9	comparable to a passing truck
4.0 – 4.9	may break windows; smaller objects may fall
5.0 – 5.9	loose objects may fall from walls; furniture moves
6.0 – 6.9	damage to buildings
7.0 – 7.9	major ground breaks; buildings destroyed in large numbers
8.0 – 8.9	bridges and most houses destroyed
9.0 and over	total devastation

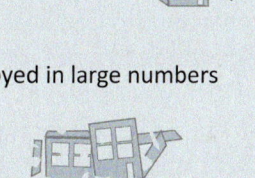

5 Find out about recent earthquakes worldwide.

Search the internet for a 'map of latest earthquakes'. Where did the last earthquakes happen?

6 Earthquake facts – What do you find most interesting?

Animals seem to sense[4] an earthquake is going to happen. No one knows how they do it.

An earthquake on the moon is called a moonquake. But they happen less often and are smaller than earthquakes on earth.

There are about 500,000 earthquakes in the world each year. 100 of them cause heavy damage[5].

Because of the earth's movements, San Francisco and Los Angeles will meet in a few million years.

In Japanese mythology, a giant fish makes the earth move.

1 scientist ['saɪəntɪst] – *Wissenschaftler/-in*; 2 measure ['meʒə] – *messen*; 3 destructive [dɪˈstrʌktɪv] – *zerstörerisch*;
4 sense [sens] – *spüren, fühlen*; 5 damage ['dæmɪdʒ] – *Schaden*

Static electricity

1 Are you 'electrified'?

Have you ever …

☐ … rubbed[1] a balloon on your hair and made it stand on end[2]?

☐ … touched a person or a metal object and felt an electric shock[3]?

☐ … taken off a pullover which made your hair crackle[4]?

☐ … felt like your clothes were clinging[5] to you?

All of these situations happen because of static[6] electricity. Sometimes your hair does funny things. Sometimes you may feel a small electric shock. It doesn't hurt badly, but it's a strange feeling. The most spectacular example of static electricity is lightning[7].

2 Why does static electricity happen?

Static electricity happens because everything is made of atoms. Atoms are tiny particles that are so small we can't see them. Inside of atoms are protons, neutrons and electrons. Protons, neutrons and electrons are very different from each other. Protons have a positive charge[8] (+). Neutrons have no charge. Electrons have a negative charge (-). Protons and neutrons make the center of the atom, the nucleus. The electrons move around this center.

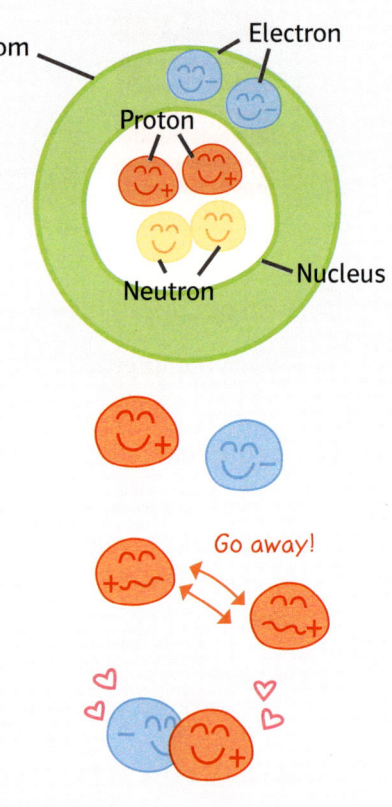

Usually atoms have no charge because there are as many electrons as protons. But some electrons can move between atoms. This happens when two atoms come in contact or rub against each other. If electrons move from one atom to another, the charge of the atom changes. If there are more protons than electrons in an atom, the atom has a positive charge. If there are more electrons than protons, it has a negative charge.

If two atoms meet and they have the same charge, they move away from each other. If two atoms have different charges, they move towards each other.

1 rub [rʌb] – *reiben*; 2 stand on end [stænd ˌɒnˈend] – *zu Berge stehen lassen*; 3 electric shock [ɪˈlektrɪk ʃɒk] – *elektrischer Schock*; 4 crackle [ˈkrækl] – *knistern*; 5 cling [klɪŋ] – *sich festhalten, klammern, hängenbleiben*; 6 static [ˈstætɪk] – *statisch*; 7 lightning [ˈlaɪtnɪŋ] – *Blitz*; 8 charge [tʃɑːdʒ] – *Ladung*

3 Why does your hair stand on end?

When two objects with different charges touch[1] or rub against each other, the charges react and we sometimes see sparks[2] or feel an electric shock. When you rub a balloon on your hair, for example, electrons move from your hair to the balloon. The balloon then has more negative charge and the tips[3] of your hair have more positive charge. That's why your hair moves towards the negative charge of the balloon and away from all the other positively charged hair – suddenly your hair stands on end!

4 Some experiments

a) You need these materials:

| balloons | a wool scarf | pieces of paper | an empty can[4] | a string[5] |

b) Try these experiments and write what happens.

1. Rub a balloon on a wool scarf. Hold it against a wall and let go[6].

2. Rub a balloon on a wool scarf. Hold the balloon over some small pieces of paper (e.g. confetti).

3. Put an empty can on the floor or a table. Rub a balloon with a wool scarf. Hold the balloon in front of the can without touching it.

4. Cut a piece of string (~70 cm). Tie a balloon to each end of the string. Rub both balloons with a wool scarf and then hold up the middle of the string so that the balloons hang down.

1 touch [tʌtʃ] – *berühren, antippen*; 2 spark [spɑːk] – *Funke*; 3 tip [tɪp] – *Spitze*; 4 can [kæn] – *Dose, Getränkedose*; 5 string [strɪŋ] – *Schnur, Bindfaden*; 6 let go [let 'gəʊ] – *loslassen*

The Absolutely True Diary of a Part-Time Indian by S. Alexie (2007)

1 *This is the diary of Arnold 'Junior' Spirit. He is small, very skinny[1], wears big glasses and has a stutter[2] and a lisp[3]. He is also really intelligent, and he loves to draw cartoons. This is a cartoon Arnold 'Junior' drew of himself:*

Arnold 'Junior' Spirit is a Spokane[4] Indian. He lives in Wellpinit, a small town on
5 *an Indian reservation. He calls it the 'rez'. A lot of people there are very poor and never leave the rez.*
One day Arnold 'Junior' decides that he has to change his life. He doesn't want to be poor all his life, and he wants to see the world. So Arnold 'Junior' decides to go to school in Reardan, a little town outside the reservation. At Reardan High School,
10 *all the kids are white, rich and amazing. Arnold is scared because he will be the only Indian at the school. But he also knows that it is his only chance to make his life better.*
That's how Arnold 'Junior' becomes a part-time[5] Indian: He goes to school in Reardan where everyone calls him Arnold, but he lives on the reservation with
15 *his family where everyone calls him Junior.*
This is his diary entry from his first day at the new school:

The next morning, Dad drove me the twenty-two miles to Reardan.
"I'm scared," I said.
"I'm scared, too," Dad said.
20 He hugged[6] me. "You don't have to do this," he said. "You can always go back to the rez school."
"No," I said. "I have to do this."

---

1 skinny [ˈskɪni] – *dünn, mager*; 2 stutter [ˈstʌtə] – *Stottern*; 3 lisp [lɪsp] – *Lispeln*; 4 Spokane [spəʊˈkan] – „Kinder der Sonne" oder „Sonnenvolk", *ein Indianerstamm im Nordwesten der USA (Bundesstaat Washington)*; 5 part-time [ˌpɑːtˈtaɪm] – *Teilzeit-*; 6 hug sb [hʌg] – *jmd. umarmen*

"Just remember this," my father said. "Those white people aren't better than you."
But he was so wrong. And he knew he was wrong. He was the loser Indian father

25 of a loser Indian son living in a world built for winners.
But he loved me so much. He hugged me again.
"This is a great thing," he said. "You're so brave. You're a warrior[1]."
It was the best thing he could have said.
"Hey, here's some lunch money," he said and gave me a dollar.

30 We were poor enough to get free lunch, but I didn't want to be the only Indian
and the only one who needed charity[2].
"Thanks, Dad," I said.
"I love you," he said.
"I love you, too."

35 I felt stronger so I stepped out of the car and walked to the door. It was closed.
I watched my father drive away.

2,23 I stood at the door for a few very long minutes. It was still early.
Then the white kids arrived for school. They surrounded[3] me.
Most of the kids were my size or smaller, but there were ten or twelve monster

40 dudes[4]. Giant white guys. They looked like men, not boys. Some of them looked
like they had to shave[5] two or three times a day.
They stared[6] at me, the Indian boy. Those white kids couldn't believe their eyes. They
stared at me like I was a UFO. What was I doing at Reardan, whose mascot[7] was an
Indian, thereby making me the only other Indian in town?

REARDAN'S
INSPIRING
MASCOT.

bright
red

45 So what was I doing in racist[8] Reardan, where more than half of every graduating[9]
class went to college? Nobody in my family had ever gone near a college.
Reardan was the opposite of the rez. It was the opposite of my family. It was the
opposite of me. I didn't deserve to be there. I knew it; all of those kids knew it.
Indians don't deserve anything.

50 So, feeling worthless[10] and stupid[11], I just waited. And pretty soon, a janitor[12]
opened the door and all of the other kids strolled inside.
"Okay," I said to myself. "Here I go."

---

1 warrior ['wɒriə] – *Krieger/-in*; 2 charity ['tʃærɪti] – *Almosen, Wohltätigkeit*; 3 surround [sə'raʊnd] – *umgeben, umringen*;
4 dude [duːd] – *Mann (ugs.)*; 5 shave [ʃeɪv] – *sich rasieren*; 6 stare [steə] – *starren*; 7 mascot ['mæskɒt] – *Maskottchen*;
8 racist ['reɪsɪst] – *rassistisch*; 9 graduating ['græʤueɪtɪŋ] – *Abschluss-*; 10 worthless ['wɜːθləs] – *wertlos*;
11 stupid ['stjuːpɪd] – *blöd, dumm*; 12 janitor ['ʤænɪtə] – *Hausmeister/-in*

WHITE | INDIAN

A BRIGHT FUTURE

Ralph Lauren shirt

Ergonomic backpack (with cell phone)

POSITIVE ROLE MODELS

Timex wristwatch

Tommy Hilfiger khakis

HOPE

the latest Air Jordans

A VANISHING PAST

Kmart T-shirt

A FAMILY HISTORY OF DIABETES AND CANCER

Sears blue jeans (2 pairs for $19.99!)

no watch ("It's skin-thirty!")

Glad garbage book bag

BONE-CRUSHING REALITY

canvas tennis shoes (purchased in aisle 7 of Safeway supermarket)

I walked into the school, made my way to the office, and told them who I was. 55

"Oh, you're the one from the reservation," the secretary said.

"Yeah," I said.

I couldn't tell if she thought the reservation was a good or bad thing. 60

"My name is Melinda," she said. "Welcome to Reardan High School. Here's your schedule and a Student ID. We've got you in Mr. Grant's homeroom[1]. You better walk there 65 quickly. You're late."

"Ah, where is that?" I asked.

"We've only got one hallway[2] here," she said. She had red hair and green eyes. "It's all the way down on the 70 left."

I put the paperwork into my backpack and walked to my homeroom.

I waited a second at the door and then walked inside.

2,24 Everybody, all of the students and the teacher, stopped to stare at me.

75 They stared hard.

Like I was bad weather.

"Take your seat," the teacher said. He was a muscular[3] guy. He had to be a football coach.

I sat down in the back and tried to ignore[4] all the stares and whispers[5],

80 until a blond girl leaned[6] over toward me.

Penelope!

Yes, there are places left in the world where people are named Penelope!

"What's your name?" Penelope asked.

85 "Junior," I said.

She laughed and told her girlfriend at the next desk that my name was Junior. They both[7] laughed. Word spread[8] around the

My name is Penelope.

Totally, absolutely gorgeous!

---

1 homeroom ['həʊmruːm] – *Zimmer des/der Klassenlehrers/-in*; 2 hallway ['hɔːlweɪ] – *Flur*; 3 muscular ['mʌskjələ] – *muskulär*;
4 ignore [ɪgˈnɔː] – *ignorieren*; 5 whisper ['wɪspə] – *Geflüster*; 6 lean over toward sb [liːnˈəʊvə] – *sich zu jmd. rüberbeugen*;
7 both [bəʊθ] – *beide, beides*; 8 word spread ['wɜːd ˌspred] – *es sprach sich herum*

room and pretty soon everybody was laughing. They were laughing at *my name*.
90 I had no idea that Junior was a weird[1] name. It's a normal name on my rez,
on any rez. You walk into any trading post[2] on any rez in the United States and
shout, "Hey, Junior!" and seventeen guys will turn around. And three women.
But there were no other people named Junior in Reardan, so I was being laughed
at because I was the only one who had that silly name.
95 And then I felt smaller because the teacher was taking roll[3] and he called out my
name name.
"Arnold Spirit," the teacher said. No, he yelled[4] it.
"Here," I said as quietly as possible.
"Speak up," the teacher said.
100 "Here," I said.
"My name is Mr. Grant," he said.
"I'm here, Mr. Grant."
He moved on to other students, but Penelope leaned over toward me again, but
she wasn't laughing at all. She was very angry now.
105 "I thought you said your name was Junior," Penelope said.
She *accused*[5] me of telling her my *real* name. Well, okay, it wasn't completely my real
name. My full name is Arnold Spirit Jr. But nobody calls me that. Everybody
calls me Junior. Well, every other *Indian* calls me Junior.
"My name is Junior," I said. "And my name is Arnold. It's Junior and Arnold. I'm
110 both."
I felt like two people inside of one body. No, I felt like a magician[6] cutting myself
in half, with Junior living on the north side of the Spokane River[7] and Arnold living
on the south.
"Where are you from?" she asked.
115 She was so pretty and her eyes were so blue. She was the prettiest girl I had ever
seen. She was movie star pretty.
"Hey," she said. "I asked you where you're from."
Wow, she was tough.
"Wellpinit," I said. "Up on the rez, I mean, the reservation."
120 "Oh," she said. "That's why you talk so funny."
And yes, I had that stutter and lisp, but I also had that singsong reservation accent
that made everything I said sound like a bad poem.
Man, I was scared. I didn't say another word for six days.

---

1 weird [wɪəd] – *komisch*; 2 trading post ['treɪdɪŋ pəʊst] – *Laden, Handelsposten*; 3 take roll [teɪk 'rəʊl] – *die Anwesenheitsliste durchgehen*; 4 yell [jel] – *brüllen, schreien*; 5 accuse sb of sth [əˈkjuːz] – *jmd. beschuldigen*; 6 magician [məˈdʒɪʃn] – *Magier, Zauberer*; 7 Spokane River [spəʊˌkæn ˈrɪvə] – *Flussname*

Deep water by C. Gardiner (2009)

1 *Henry Jackson is sixteen years old, and he lives with his grandmother in a small town in Nebraska. Their house is outside of town; near a dam[1] and a lake that were built some years ago. Every day when Henry comes home, his grandmother tells him to not go to The Lake. It is dangerous and people die there. That's why Henry is afraid of deep[2] water,*

5 *and he still cannot swim. Henry's best friend is Alice. She is a great swimmer, and Henry likes her a lot.*

One day Alice tells him that she is going to have a picnic and go swimming with some friends. Henry doesn't go because he hates swimming. But later in the evening he realizes[3] that Alice and the other kids from his class probably went to The Lake. Some

10 *strange things have been happening at The Lake and Henry is afraid that something bad will happen, so he quickly leaves the house to go find Alice …*

Henry ran into the woods at the back of the house. It was nearly night and the moon was just rising. Now Henry was glad that he was a good runner. No other kid in the school could have got through the woods so fast.

15 He wished he had Alice's cell phone number. Then he could call her and warn her. But then what could he say – 'don't swim in The Lake! There's something evil[4] there'? She wouldn't believe him and he would just look stupid[5].

He had to go to The Lake. Grandma's worries[6] weren't important. His friend Alice, the girl he liked more than anyone else in the whole school, was in

20 danger[7]. He had to help her.

The moon was up as Henry burst[8] out of the woods. He heard kids laughing. He could see the dam wall not far away. The surface[9] of The Lake was shining in the moonlight. Everything looked calm[10].

The whole class was there with their picnic baskets. But they were over on the

25 other side of The Lake. Henry shouted, "Alice!" She looked up and saw him. She waved to him and shouted something. But she was too far away so he couldn't hear her. He shouted again, "Don't go swimming, it's dangerous!" Alice shook[11] her head to show that she didn't understand what he was saying.

Henry looked around quickly. There was a path all along The Lake. But it was a

30 long way to the other side. Even at his fastest, it'd take time to get to Alice. He was tired from his run through the woods but he had to try.

"Oh, Alice – please, please don't go swimming before I get there," Henry said softly to himself.

---

1 dam [dæm] – *Damm, Staumauer*; 2 deep [diːp] – *tief*; 3 realize [ˈrɪəlaɪz] – *erkennen, realisieren*; 4 evil [ˈiːvl] – *böse, schlecht*; 5 stupid [ˈstjuːpɪd] – *dumm, blöd*; 6 worry [ˈwʌri] – *Sorge*; 7 danger [ˈdeɪndʒə] – *Gefahr*; 8 burst out of [bɜːst] – *herausstürzen*; 9 surface [ˈsɜːfɪs] – *Oberfläche*; 10 calm [kɑːm] – *ruhig, friedlich*; 11 shake [ʃeɪk] – *schütteln*

Then Matt jumped. Henry heard the splash as Matt went under the water.

35 Henry ran faster. He was afraid that Matt would just disappear, that something would grab his foot and pull him down.

But then Matt's head came up again. He was laughing as he shook the water out of his hair. Henry shouted but the kids paid no attention[1]. He was still a long way away. Most of the other kids followed Matt into the water. Henry could see their heads as

40 they splashed each other. Alice stood at the waterside. She didn't go in right away. She was watching Henry racing[2] round the path.

Henry ran on although it was getting hard to breathe. He waved and waved, trying to get the kids' attention. Then Alice went into the water. Henry almost fell to the ground. "Alice! No!" Henry was shouting as loudly as he could.

45 Suddenly something started moving towards the swimmers. It was big and black, like a shadow[3], moving smoothly[4] just under the surface of the water. The kids couldn't see it. They were busy with their game. They were playing with a ball, throwing it and trying to catch[5] it before it hit the water.

---

1 pay no attention [ˌpeɪ nəʊ əˈtenʃn] – *nicht beachten*; 2 race [reɪs] – *(sehr schnell) rennen*; 3 shadow [ˈʃædəʊ] – *Schatten*;
4 smooth [smuːð] – *geschmeidig, gleichmäßig*; 5 catch [kætʃ] – *fangen*

Alice started to swim towards Henry and away from the other kids. Henry
50 could not run another step. He could hardly get his breath.
He fell down onto his knees.
2,26 Then Chet threw the ball up high into the air instead of throwing it to
the next kid. He laughed loudly and he looked over at Henry. So Henry
could see how surprised Chet was as something pulled him under the water.
55 His head went down so fast that he didn't even have time to shout.
His mouth was wide open as he went under.
The ball that Chet had thrown was still up in the air. At that same moment
every other kid disappeared under the water. Every head just went down
without making any waves in the water. Except Alice. She was quite a bit away.
60 She was moving fast towards Henry and didn't notice anything behind her.

The surface of the water was smooth again. The Lake was quiet. The black
shadow was gone and the kids were gone. It all happened in just a few seconds.
The ball landed back on the surface of the water with a splash.
Alice heard the splash. She looked back. The ball floated[1] on the water. There was
65   nothing else, no kids anywhere. She turned round and started to swim faster and
faster towards Henry.
Henry stood up again. The dark water of The Lake came right up to the path.
He wanted to save Alice. But he was afraid of the black shadow in the water.
She was still swimming fast towards him.
70   Something moved on the other side of The Lake, where the picnic baskets were.
Henry didn't want to look but he could not control his eyes. He saw a tall, thin[2] man
standing there.
"Henry!" Alice screamed, and he tore[3] his eyes away from the man. She was much
nearer Henry now but still too far for him to reach[4] her. He put one foot into the
75   water. It was very cold. It was like putting his foot into ice. He stepped in a bit
deeper. Alice swam closer[5]. Behind her Henry saw the black shadow in the water
again. It was coming very close to her. Henry went into the water as fast as he could.
The water was up to his knees. The black shadow was right at Alice's feet. Her hand
came towards him, her fingers just touched[6] his fingers – then a shout came from
80   the other side of The Lake.
"Henry! Henry!" That was Grandma's voice!
Henry automatically looked up towards her.
And then suddenly he couldn't feel Alice's hand any more.
He looked back at the Lake.
85   Alice was gone.

What happened? Will Henry be able to save Alice?

1 float [fləʊt] – *gleiten, treiben*; 2 thin [θɪn] – *dünn*; 3 tear one's eyes away [teə] – *die Augen losreißen*;
4 reach [riːtʃ] – *erreichen, greifen*; 5 close [kləʊs] – *nah*; 6 touch [tʌtʃ] – *berühren, antippen*

Grammar

G2

Mit **G** sind die Grammatikkapitel gekennzeichnet und der Reihe nach durchnummeriert. Eine Übersicht über alle Themen in diesem Band findest du auf der nächsten Seite.

Hier stehen Besonderheiten und Tipps.

(**TEST YOURSELF**)

Hier kannst du üben.
Die Lösungen findest du auf S. 282.

(**FÜR PROFIS**)

Hier findest du knifflige Extras zum Thema.

R = Revision (Wiederholung)

Unit 1

G1 R: Die einfache Vergangenheit
Revision: The simple past

Um über Dinge zu sprechen, die in der Vergangenheit passiert und vorbei sind, verwendest du die einfache Vergangenheit (**simple past**).

Signalwörter	
yesterday	gestern
last year	letztes Jahr
a week ago	vor einer Woche
in 2015	(im Jahr) 2015

Das **simple past** bildest du so:
Hänge die Endung **–ed** an das Verb.
Achte auf unregelmäßige Verben, z. B. have → **had**; do → **did**; get → **got**; build → **built**; go → **went** etc.

Eine Liste der unregelmäßigen Verben findest du ab Seite 210.

They **started** roadwork last Monday.	Sie begannen am letzten Montag mit Straßenarbeiten.
Two years ago they **had** a lot of snow in New York.	Vor zwei Jahren hatten sie in New York viel Schnee.

Um zu sagen, was in der Vergangenheit nicht passiert ist, setzt du **didn't** (= did not) vor das Verb.

David **didn't get** into the city.	David kam nicht in die Stadt.

Und so kannst du im **simple past** Fragen stellen:

Did you **have** a good time in New York?	Yes, I **did**.	No, I **didn't**.
When **did** your friend **visit** Manhattan?	Last weekend.	

Aussagen und Verneinungen mit **be** bildest du so:

I **was** in New York.	Ich war in New York.
I **wasn't** in Washington.	Ich war nicht in Washington.
The Statue of Liberty **was** a present from France. It **wasn't** a present from Germany.	Die Freiheitsstatue war ein Geschenk von Frankreich. Sie war kein Geschenk von Deutschland.
We **were** in New York, but we **weren't** in Brooklyn.	Wir waren in New York, aber wir waren nicht in Brooklyn.

Fragen mit **be** bildest du so:

Were you at the zoo in Central Park?	Yes, I **was**.	No, I **wasn't**.
What **was** special in New York?	The Brooklyn Bridge.	

(TEST YOURSELF) **Put the verbs in the simple past.**

1. Tom —— (have) a great time in NYC last summer.
2. He —— (like) the New York skyline.
3. We —— (not take) a taxi.
4. What —— you —— (do) in Manhattan?
5. —— (be) you in the USA last year?
6. I —— (not be) in Chicago.

G2 Die Vorvergangenheit

The past perfect

After I had built my new house, I felt much better.

Um über Ereignisse zu sprechen, die noch **vor** einem vergangenen Ereignis stattfanden, verwendest du die Vorvergangenheit, das **past perfect**: **had / hadn't + 3. Form** des Verbs (past participle).

Signalwörter	
after	nachdem
before	bevor

Bei den meisten Verben hängst du für die 3. Form ein **-ed** an das Verb: visit → visit**ed**
Achte auf unregelmäßige Verben, z.B. go → **gone**; see → **seen**; be → **been** etc.

Eine Liste der unregelmäßigen Verben findest du ab Seite 210.

 Was in der Vergangenheit weiter zurückliegt, wird mit dem **past perfect** ausgedrückt!

She wasn't at home. She **had gone** to Tim's (house).	Sie war nicht zu Hause. Sie war zu Tim gegangen.
After I **had been** in NYC for two months, I moved to Chicago.	Nachdem ich zwei Monate in NYC gewesen war, zog ich nach Chicago um.
I **hadn't seen** skyscrapers before I went to New York.	Ich hatte noch keine Wolkenkratzer gesehen, bevor ich nach New York ging.

 Aufgepasst! Im Nebensatz mit **after** steht **past perfect**, dann folgt **simple past**.
Im Nebensatz mit **before** steht **simple past**, dann folgt **past perfect**.

(TEST YOURSELF) Put the verbs in the past perfect.

1. After I —— (leave) the shop, I lost my shopping bag.
2. I couldn't go to the swimming pool because I —— (not do) my homework.
3. When I arrived, the concert —— already —— (start).
4. I —— (watch) a TV show before you phoned me.
5. My grandad didn't want to move because he —— (live) in Cuba all his life.
6. Yesterday I saw an animal which I —— (not see) before.

Unit 2

G3 Modale Hilfsverben und ihre Ersatzformen

Modal auxiliaries and their substitutes

*I'm lucky. I didn't have to book a holiday.
I only had to swim to this lovely rock.*

Modale Hilfsverben kannst du nur im **simple present** verwenden. Für alle anderen Zeiten benötigst du **Ersatzformen**. Ausnahme **can**: Für **can** kannst du im **simple past** auch **could** verwenden.

Mit **can** und **could** sagst du, was du tun **kannst** (Fähigkeit).

Simple present	Simple past
Kim **can** speak English.	Kim **could** understand it.
Kim **kann** Englisch sprechen.	Kim **konnte** es verstehen.
Can your friend speak English?	**Could** he speak English?
Kann dein Freund Englisch sprechen?	**Konnte** er Englisch sprechen?

Mit **can/could** und der Ersatzform **be allowed to** sagst du, was du tun **darfst** (Erlaubnis).

She **can't/isn't allowed to** use her phone.	She **couldn't/wasn't allowed to** use it.
Sie **darf** ihr Handy **nicht** benutzen.	Sie **durfte** es **nicht** benutzen.
Can you/**Are** you **allowed to** wear jeans?	**Could** you/**Were** you **allowed to** wear jeans?
Darfst du Jeans tragen?	**Durftest** du Jeans tragen?

Mit **must** und der Ersatzform **have to** sagst du, was du tun **musst** (Verpflichtung).

Sarah **must** take English and History.	Sarah **had to** take Biology too.
Sarah **muss** Englisch und Geschichte nehmen.	Sarah **musste** auch Biologie nehmen.
We **don't have to** worry.	We **didn't have to** worry.
Wir **müssen** uns **keine** Sorgen machen.	Wir **mussten** uns **keine** Sorgen machen.
Must you help your parents?	**Did** you **have to** help in the house?
Musst du deinen Eltern helfen?	**Musstest** du im Haus helfen?

 Bei **must** musst du die Ersatzform schon in **verneinten Sätzen** im **simple present** benutzen!

(TEST YOURSELF) Use the correct forms in the simple past.

1. When Luise was in the USA, she —— (not can) keep her things in the classrooms.
2. She —— (must) put her books into lockers.
3. She —— (can) travel around the USA.
4. She —— (not must) take lessons in basketball.
5. The students —— (can) wear jeans.
6. When she was ten, she —— (not can) dance like she dances today.

G4 R: Bedingungssätze Typ I

Revision: If-clauses type I

Um Bedingungen und Folgen auszudrücken, benutzt man **if**-Sätze.
Dabei steht im **if**-Satz das **simple present**, im Hauptsatz das **will-future**.
Geht der **if**-Satz voran, steht am Ende des **if**-Satzes ein Komma.

Bedingung (condition)	Folge (consequence)	
If Michael **finds** a job,	he **will earn** some money.	Wenn Michael einen Job findet, wird er etwas Geld verdienen.
If you **don't work** well,	you **won't get** extra money.	Wenn du nicht gut arbeitest, bekommst du nicht mehr Geld.

Bedingungssätze können auch mit dem Hauptsatz beginnen. Dann entfällt das Komma.

Folge (consequence)	Bedingung (condition)	
You **will be** late	if you **walk**.	Du wirst zu spät kommen, wenn du zu Fuß gehst.
You **won't be** successful	if you **don't work** more carefully.	Du wirst nicht erfolgreich sein, wenn du nicht sorgfältiger arbeitest.

Das **will-future** drückt allgemein Zukünftiges aus. Im **if**-Satz steht nie **will** oder **won't**!

Für das **will-future** kannst du im Deutschen die Zukunft oder die Gegenwart benutzen. Beides ist richtig. Vergleiche:

He will earn some money.	Er wird etwas Geld verdienen. Er verdient etwas Geld.

(TEST YOURSELF) **Complete the sentences.**

1. If you need me, I —— (help) you.
2. If you don't phone me, I —— (be) sad.
3. If she —— (not come) on time, she will lose her job.

4. Matt —— (not find) a job if he doesn't read the adverts.
5. I will talk to Sue if I —— (meet) her.
6. You won't sleep well if you always —— (read) scary stories.

(FÜR PROFIS)

Im Deutschen können **if** (falls, wenn) und **when** (dann, wenn) mit **wenn** übersetzt werden.
Im Englischen kommt es darauf an, welche **Absicht** du ausdrücken möchtest.

If I go shopping, I'll get you a T-shirt.
(Ich weiß noch nicht, **ob** ich einkaufen gehe. Aber **falls** ich gehe, dann kaufe ich dir ein T-Shirt. Es ist nicht sicher und nur eine Möglichkeit.)

When I go shopping, I'll get you a T-shirt.
(Ich gehe auf jeden Fall einkaufen. Das weiß ich schon sicher. Ich weiß nur noch nicht, **wann**. Aber dann kaufe ich dir ein T-Shirt. Es ist sicher und nur eine Frage des Zeitpunkts.)

Unit 3

G5 R: Fragen

Revision: Questions / questions with who

So bildest du unterschiedliche Fragen mit Vollverben, z. B. like, go etc.:

Fragen, auf die man mit <u>yes</u> oder <u>no</u> antwortet (Ja/Nein-Fragen)
– Fragen im **simple present** beginnst du mit **do** oder **does** (he, she, it).

Do you **like** turkey?	Magst du Truthahn?
Does Jacob **like** chocolate?	Mag Jacob Schokolade?

– Fragen im **simple past** beginnst du mit **did** für alle Personen.

Did you **travel** by car last year?	Bist du letztes Jahr mit dem Auto verreist?
Did it **rain** last December?	Hat es im letzten Dezember geregnet?

– Fragen im **will-future** beginnst du mit **will** für alle Personen.

Will you **call** us again tomorrow?	Wirst du uns morgen nochmal anrufen?

Fragen mit Fragewörtern

What do you **like**?	Was magst du gerne?
Where did you **spend** your summer?	Wo hast du deinen Sommer verbracht?
When will you **go** to Boston?	Wann wirst du nach Boston fahren?

Fragen mit who
– Das Fragewort **who?** kann **verschiedene Bedeutungen haben**:
– Heißt es **Wer?** wird **keine Form von do** verwendet.
– Heißt es **Wen?** oder **Wem?** muss **eine Form von do** verwendet werden.

<u>**Who**</u> **lives** in Boston?	**Wer** lebt in Boston?
Who do you **like**?	**Wen** magst du?
<u>**Who did**</u> you **help** last week?	**Wem** hast du letzte Woche geholfen?

(TEST YOURSELF) **Put in <u>do</u>, <u>does</u>, <u>did</u>, <u>will</u> – if necessary.**

1. —— you often have a turkey dinner?
2. Where —— your uncle live?
3. Who —— you invite next Friday?
4. —— you see the heavy storm on TV last Sunday?
5. Who —— got stuck in his car last night?
6. Who —— Mark meet yesterday?

G6 R: Bedingungssätze Typ II

Revision: If-clauses type II

Bei den Bedingungssätzen Typ II ist eine Bedingung unwahrscheinlich oder nicht erfüllbar. Du verwendest im **if**-Satz **simple past**. Im Hauptsatz steht **would / wouldn't + Grundform des Verbs**.

Bedingung (condition)	Folge (consequence)	
If it **rained**,	I **would stay** at home.	Wenn es regnen würde, würde ich zu Hause bleiben (aber es regnet nicht).
If you **didn't call**,	I **would be** very sad.	Wenn du nicht anrufen würdest, wäre ich sehr traurig (aber du rufst bestimmt an).

Bedingungssätze können auch mit dem Hauptsatz beginnen. Dann entfällt das Komma.

Folge (consequence)	Bedingung (condition)	
I **would buy** new clothes	if I **had** more money.	Ich würde mir neue Kleidung kaufen, wenn ich genug Geld hätte (aber ich habe nicht genug Geld).
I **wouldn't have** problems with my clothes	if I **lived** in the Amish community.	Ich hätte keine Kleidungsprobleme, wenn ich in der Gemeinschaft der Amish leben würde (aber ich lebe dort nicht).

 Statt **If I was** … wird oft **If I were** … gebraucht.

If I **were** a film star,	I **would live** in Beverly Hills.	Wenn ich ein Filmstar wäre, würde ich in Beverly Hills wohnen.

 Im **if**-Satz steht nie **would / wouldn't**!

 Im Deutschen verwendet man in beiden Satzteilen **würde**, **wäre** oder **hätte (Konjunktiv)**.

(TEST YOURSELF) **Complete the sentences.**

1. If you visited your grandma on Sundays, she —— (be) very glad.
2. If she had less time, she —— (not meet) her friends every week.
3. If I —— (be) in Pennsylvania, I would like to see the Amish community.
4. I would really miss you if you —— (not come) back.
5. Jennifer —— (not worry) about clothes if she lived with the Amish community.
6. Maybe it —— (be) better if you didn't phone me every day.

Unit 4

G7 R: Gegenüberstellung: Simple present – present progressive

Revision: Simple present – present progressive

Du kennst schon die Zeiten **simple present** und **present progressive**. Hier findest du noch einmal die Situationen, in denen du sie benutzen kannst und siehst, wie sie gebildet werden.

Simple present

Das **simple present** verwendest du, wenn du sagen willst, dass jemand etwas häufig oder regelmäßig tut.

Signalwörter: always, never, sometimes, often, usually, every …

Aussagen bildest du mit der Grundform des Verbs.

> I **work** every day. You never **listen**.

Achtung: **He**, **she**, **it** – das **s** muss mit:
He work**s**. She talk**s**. It rain**s**. Aber: He go**es**.

Sätze mit Vollverben verneinst du mit **don't** und **doesn't**:

> I **don't play** football.

Bei Fragen mit Vollverben musst du mit **do** oder **does** beginnen:

> **Do** you **eat** fish? **Does** he **like** games?

Present progressive

Mit dem **present progressive** kannst du sagen, was jemand gerade tut oder was im Augenblick passiert.

Signalwörter: now, at the moment

Aussagen bildest du so:
am / are / is + Verb + **-ing**

> I'm **working** at the moment. It **is raining** now.

Achtung Schreibweise: make → mak**ing**; write → writ**ing**; run → runn**ing**; sit → sitt**ing**

So verneinst du Sätze:
am / are / is <u>not</u> + Verb + **-ing**:

> He **isn't eating** at the moment.

Bei Fragen stellst du **am / are / is** an den Satzanfang:

> **Are** you **listening**? **Is** she **dancing**?

Simple present und present progressive kannst du auch einsetzen, um ein **Bild** zu beschreiben. Zunächst sagst du, wen oder was du siehst. Dann beschreibst du, was jemand tut.

Simple present

Du benutzt es, um zu sagen, wer oder was auf dem Bild zu sehen ist, oder in welchem Zustand etwas ist.

> **There is** a boy in the picture.
> **There are** a man and a woman.
> She **looks** happy.
> She **has** two dogs.
> The weather **is** nice. It **is** warm.

Present progressive

Du benutzt es für alle Handlungen, die im Bild zu sehen sind und für alles, was jemand tut.

> The boy **is riding** a mountain bike.
> They**'re sitting** in camping chairs.
> She**'s wearing** boots.
> They **are playing** with a ball.
> The sun **is shining**. It **isn't raining**.

(TEST YOURSELF) **Use present progressive or simple present.**

1. Sandy often —— (go) surfing.
2. But at the moment she —— (not surf).
3. "—— you really —— (listen), Sandy?"
4. Students —— (not like) tests.
5. What —— you usually —— (do) after school?
6. We sometimes —— (meet) some friends.

G8 R: Das Perfekt

Revision: The present perfect

Wenn eine Handlung in der Vergangenheit beginnt und in der Gegenwart zu einem Ergebnis führt, verwendest du das **present perfect**:
have/has + 3. Form des Verbs (past participle). Bei den meisten Verben hängst du ein **-ed** an das Verb: help → help**ed**

Eine Liste der unregelmäßigen Verben findest du ab Seite 210.

Signalwörter	
already	schon
just	gerade
not … yet	noch … nicht
never	noch nie
ever (in Fragen)	jemals (in Fragen)
since	seit (Zeitpunkt)
for	seit (Zeitspanne)

 Einige Verben haben unregelmäßige 3. Formen: z. B. be → **been**; write → **written**

I **have** just **posted** a photo.	Ich habe gerade ein Foto verschickt.
She **has** already **written** ten text messages.	Sie hat schon zehn SMS geschrieben.

Um Sätze zu verneinen, benutzt du **haven't** oder **hasn't** (bei he, she, it):

I **haven't been** to California yet.	Ich bin noch nicht in Kalifornien gewesen.
She **hasn't seen** Los Angeles yet.	Sie hat Los Angeles noch nicht gesehen.

Fragen und Kurzantworten bildest du so:

Have you ever **been** to San Francisco?	Yes, I **have**.	No, I **haven't**.
Has your sister ever **met** a famous star?	Yes, she **has**.	No, she **hasn't**.

Present perfect mit **for** und **since**
since (seit) verwendest du vor einem **Zeitpunkt**, z. B. **since** 5 o'clock, **since** July, **since** 2013.
for (seit) verwendest du vor einer **Zeitspanne**, z. B. **for** five hours, **for** three years, **for** a long time.

I haven't seen Lara **since** Monday.	Ich habe Lara **seit** Montag nicht gesehen.
I haven't seen Lara **for** a week.	Ich habe Lara **seit** einer Woche nicht gesehen.

 Im Deutschen verwendet man oft die **Gegenwart**, wenn man sagen will, seit wann oder wie lange etwas schon andauert. Vergleiche:

I **have lived** in Los Angeles **for** two years.	Ich **lebe seit** zwei Jahren in Los Angeles.
She **has had** a smartphone **since** last year.	Sie **hat seit** letztem Jahr ein Smartphone.

(TEST YOURSELF) **Put the verbs in the present perfect.**

1. Linda —— never —— (meet) a Hollywood star.
2. I —— (not see) you for two months.
3. Why —— your sister —— (not call) yet?
4. —— you —— (forget) your homework again?
5. We —— (not be) on holiday since 2010.
6. —— you ever —— (watch) funny videos?

Unit 5

G9 Das Passiv

Passive voice (simple present)

*English is important.
It is spoken all over the world.*

Mit dem Passiv kannst du über eine Handlung Auskunft geben, ohne zu sagen, wer die Handlung ausführt. Im Vordergrund steht die Handlung.

So bildest du das **Passiv** im **simple present: am / are / is + 3. Form des Verbs** (past participle)

English **is spoken** in a lot of countries.	Englisch **wird** in vielen Ländern **gesprochen**.
Racism **isn't accepted**.	Rassismus **wird nicht akzeptiert**.
Spices and flour **are mixed**.	Gewürze und Mehl **werden gemischt**.
Tickets **aren't sold** here.	Karten **werden** hier **nicht verkauft**.

(**TEST YOURSELF**) **Use the passive voice.**

1. Southern fried chicken —— (cook) all over the USA.
2. This dish —— (make) with flour and spices.
3. The chicken and the rice —— (not cook) for a long time.
4. Language courses —— (organize) for people who are new.
5. Chewing gum —— (not accept) at school.
6. Bananas and pineapples —— (not grow) in Germany.

G10 Indirekte Rede (ohne Zeitverschiebung)

Reported speech (without backshift)

Oh no!
Dad says we have to take a shower now.

Mit der indirekten Rede kannst du über das berichten, was jemand anderes **gerade gesagt hat**. Du beginnst mit **He says that ...** / **She says that ...** usw. Das Wort **that** kann man auch weglassen.

Positive Aussagen und verneinte Sätze in der indirekten Rede bildest du so:

Direkte Rede	Indirekte Rede
Anna says, "**I like** Florida."	Anna says (that) **she likes** Florida.
Anna says, "**We want** to see the alligators."	Anna says (that) **they want** to see the alligators.
Anna says, "**I don't need** a hotel."	Anna says (that) **she doesn't need** a hotel.
Anna says, "**We don't need** a sweatshirt."	Anna says (that) **they don't need** a sweatshirt.
Anna says, "**I can see** a snake over there."	Anna says (that) **she can see** a snake over there.
Anna says, "**We can't visit** the animal show."	Anna says (that) **they can't visit** the animal show.

Beachte die Änderungen:

I	→ **he/she**	my	→ **his/her**
we	→ **they**	our	→ **their**
(I) like	→ (he/she) **likes**		
(I) don't ...	→ (he/she) **doesn't** ...		

(TEST YOURSELF) Report what Anna says.

1. "We prefer the Everglades."
2. "I want to go on a boat tour."
3. "I don't like all those crowds."
4. "I don't want to feed the alligators."
5. "I know Florida."
6. "We can't visit the zoo at night."

Methods

1-minute-presentation

Step 1
Nimm ein Blatt DIN A4-Papier quer und falte es so, dass das untere Drittel nach hinten wegknickt.

Step 2
Schreibe den Vortragstext auf die oberen zwei Drittel.

Step 3
Streiche nun die wichtigsten Stichpunkte im Text an. Notiere sie noch einmal auf dem unteren Drittel. Das ist dein Spickzettel.

Step 4
In deiner Präsentation verwendest du nur den Spickzettel. Wenn du steckenbleibst, darfst du ihn umknicken und kurz auf den Text oben schauen.

Bus stop
(Lerntempoduett)

Step 1
Bearbeite die Aufgabe zunächst allein. Schreibe deine Lösungen auf.

Step 2
Wenn du fertig bist, gehe zum „bus stop". Warte dort auf die nächste Person bzw. triff die Person, die dort schon wartet. Vergleicht und korrigiert eure Ergebnisse.

Step 3
Gehe danach wieder zu deinem Platz zurück. Bearbeite die nächste Aufgabe.

Dramatic reading
(Szenisches Lesen)

Step 1
Verteilt die Rollen innerhalb eurer Gruppe.

Step 2
Lies dir deinen Text lautlos oder ganz leise immer wieder vor, bis du ihn gut kennst.

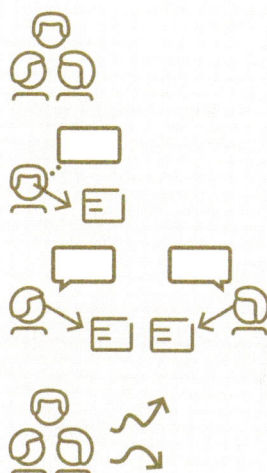

Step 3
Übt euren Text in der Gruppe mit der Methode „Read and look up" (Seite 172).

Step 4
Überlegt euch, wie ihr euch in der Rolle fühlt und wie ihr euch bewegen würdet. Tragt euren Text so frei wie möglich vor.

Gallery walk

Step 1
Hängt nach eurer Gruppenarbeit euer Produkt gut sichtbar im Klassenzimmer auf.

Step 2
Einer von euch, der „Experte", bleibt bei eurem Produkt stehen und erklärt es den anderen. Die anderen gehen herum. Nach jedem Durchgang wechselt der Experte.

Step 3
Seht euch die Produkte der anderen an und bewertet sie.

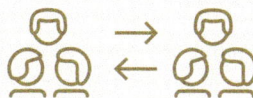

Step 4
Wertet im Anschluss eure Ergebnisse in der Klasse aus.

Jigsaw
(Gruppenpuzzle)

Step 1
Bildet Stammgruppen („home groups").
Jedes Gruppenmitglied wählt einen Text aus, liest
ihn und bearbeitet ihn. Macht euch Notizen dazu.

Step 2
Trefft euch in Expertengruppen („expert groups") mit
den Mitgliedern der anderen Stammgruppen, die
denselben Text wie ihr bearbeitet haben. Vergleicht eure
Notizen, besprecht sie gemeinsam und ergänzt sie.

Step 3
Geht zurück in eure Stammgruppe. Präsentiert dort die
Informationen aus eurem Text. Macht euch Notizen zu
den Texten der anderen, so dass am Ende jeder die
Informationen aus allen Texten hat.

Milling around
(Marktplatz)

Step 1
Bearbeite die Aufgabe zunächst allein.
Auf ein Zeichen vom Lehrer oder der Lehrerin
steht ihr auf und geht durch den Raum.
Nimm die Aufgabe und einen Stift mit.

Step 2
Wenn ein Signal ertönt, bleibt ihr stehen.
Besprecht mit der Person die Aufgabe,
die euch am nächsten steht.

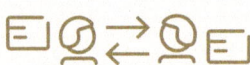

Step 3
Beim nächsten Signal trennt ihr euch und geht
weiter durch den Raum. Wiederholt den Vorgang.

Peer correction

(Partnerkontrolle)

Step 1
Bearbeite die Aufgabe zunächst selbstständig.

Step 2
Tausche deine Lösungen mit einem Partner/einer Partnerin. Kontrolliere seine oder ihre Lösungen.

Step 3
Tauscht euch danach zu der Aufgabe aus und korrigiert den Text.

Placemat

(Platzdeckchen)

Step 1
Bildet Vierergruppen.

Step 2
Teilt ein großes Blatt Papier in fünf Bereiche ein.

Step 3
Setzt euch so hin, dass alle in eine Ecke des Blattes schreiben können.

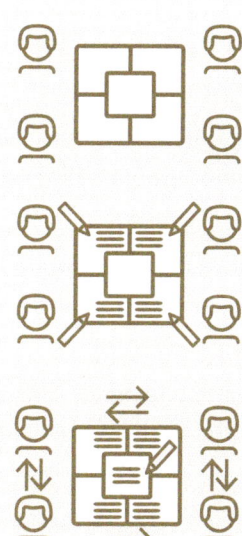

Step 4
Jedes Gruppenmitglied denkt allein über das Thema nach und schreibt Ideen auf seinen Teil des Blattes.

Step 5
Tauscht euch über die Ideen aus. Einigt euch auf die besten Ideen und schreibt diese in die Mitte des Blattes.

Read and look up

(Lesen und Aufschauen)

Step 1

Schaue auf deinen Text und präge dir die erste Zeile oder den ersten Satz ein. Schaue hoch und sprich deine Zeile/ deinen Satz lautlos oder leise vor dich hin. Nimm dir die nächste Zeile/den nächsten Satz vor.

Step 2

Übe nun mit einer Partnerin/einem Partner. Erzähle deinen Text, Zeile für Zeile oder Satz für Satz. Dazwischen schaust du immer wieder nach unten auf deinen Text.

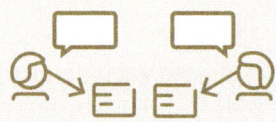

Step 3

Wiederhole alles, bis es gut klappt. Überlege dir, wo du stehen und wie du dich bewegen willst.

Round robin

(Blitzlicht)

Step 1

Bildet Gruppen und setzt euch in einen Kreis.

Step 2

Jedes Gruppenmitglied überlegt sich kurz einen Satz, der seine persönliche Meinung zum Thema ausdrückt.

Step 3

Wenn alle bereit sind, sagen die Gruppenmitglieder der Reihe nach ihre Meinung.

Step 4

Die anderen Gruppenmitglieder dürfen die Sätze nicht kommentieren.

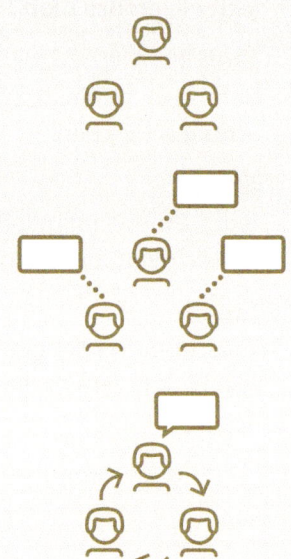

Think – pair – share

Step 1
Schreibe deine Ideen, Gedanken oder Lösungen zur Aufgabe auf.

Step 2
Tauscht eure Notizen zu zweit aus und besprecht sie.

Step 3
Präsentiert euer Ergebnis anderen Paaren oder der gesamten Klasse.

Tip top

Step 1
Sage zunächst, was dir gut gefallen hat – was „top" war.

Step 2
Sage nun, was noch nicht so gut war, und gib einen Tipp, was man noch verbessern könnte.

Writers' conference
(Schreibwerkstatt)

Step 1
Bildet Vierergruppen.

Step 2
Lest euch eure Sätze/Texte gegenseitig vor.

Step 3
Die anderen sagen, was ihnen gefallen hat.

Step 4
Die Zuhörer machen Verbesserungsvorschläge.

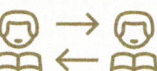

Step 5
Jede Gruppe wählt den besten Text aus und liest ihn der Klasse vor.

Du kennst schon einige Tipps und
Tricks zum Vokabellernen.
Erinnerst du dich?
Hier gibt es weitere Tipps.

Vocabulary

Vocabulary tips

Lerntipp: Englisch im Alltag

Achte während des Tages auf alle englischen Wörter, die dir begegnen. Ob im Supermarkt, im Fernsehen, in Büchern, auf Werbeplakaten oder Schildern am Bahnhof, Flughafen etc.: Du wirst erstaunt sein, wie oft man im Alltag auf die englische Sprache stößt. Das ist ein gutes Training, um auf noch unbekannte Vokabeln aufmerksam zu werden. Deinen Sprachschatz erweiterst du ganz leicht, indem du dir ein schönes Heft oder Notizbuch kaufst, das speziell für solche Vokabeln da ist. Nimm es so oft wie möglich mit, vor allem, wenn du verreist! Die noch unbekannten Wörter kannst du dann zu Hause in einem Wörterbuch nachschlagen. Da du mit jedem Wort eine kleine Geschichte oder bestimmte besondere Umstände verbindest (zum Beispiel: „Ach ja! Dieses Wort habe ich am Bahnhof gesehen, im Kino gehört" etc.), wirst du es dir sehr leicht merken können!

Wortbildung

Es gibt verschiedene Möglichkeiten, um aus einem Verb ein Nomen abzuleiten.

1. Du kannst die Endung *-ing* anhängen:
   to build → a building
   to meet → a meeting

2. Manche Nomen werden mit der Endung *-er* oder *-or* gebildet.
   Solche Nomen bezeichnen meistens eine Person:
   to ride → a rider
   to visit → a visitor

3. Es gibt auch die Endung *-ion:*
   to define → a definition
   to invent → an invention

4. Sehr oft haben auch Verb und Nomen dieselbe Form:
   to call → a call
   to dream → a dream

Diese Checkliste kann dir helfen, Fehler zu vermeiden und deine Rechtschreibung zu verbessern. Prüfe alle deine Texte damit.

- **Schreibung:**
  - ☐ *gh* wird meist nicht gesprochen. Vergiss es beim Schreiben nicht.
  - ☐ *k* kommt vor *t* so gut wie nie vor, z. B. action – Aktion, October – Oktober

- **Gleiche Aussprache, unterschiedliche Schreibung:**
  - ☐ [i:] z. B. teacher, meeting, media, magazine, people, field
  - ☐ [u:] z. B. food, route, to do, swimsuit, supermarket, true, crew

- **Gleiche Aussprache, unterschiedliche Schreibung und Bedeutung:**
  - ☐ [i:] z. B. see – sehen, sea – Meer; meet – treffen, meat – Fleisch
  - ☐ [u:] z. B. two – zwei, too – auch

- **Verdoppelung der Endkonsonanten:**
  - ☐ to stop – stopping, stopped
  - ☐ to plan – planning, planned

- **y wird zu *ie*:**
  - ☐ in der 3. Person Singular: z. B. to carry – he carries; aber: to buy – she buys
  - ☐ im Plural: z. B. city – cities, party – parties; aber: boy – boys
  - ☐ bei der Steigerung von Adjektiven: z. B. happy – happier – (the) happiest; easy – easier – (the) easiest

- **Ähnlich und doch anders:**
  - ☐ Wortendung *le:* z. B. engl. title – dt. Titel; engl. middle – dt. Mittel
  - ☐ *ph* statt *f:* z. B. engl. phone – dt. Telefon; engl. photo – dt. Foto

- **Großschreibung:**
  - ☐ Monatsnamen: z. B. January, July, December
  - ☐ Wochentage: z. B. Monday, Wednesday, Saturday
  - ☐ Eigennamen: z. B. Tom, Lisa, the Brooks, the London Eye, the Thames
  - ☐ geografische Namen: Bristol, Greenwich, Germany, Italy

- **Plural:**
  - ☐ Der Plural bekommt normalerweise ein *-s:* z. B. friend – friends, chair – chairs, film – films
  - ☐ Endet ein Wort auf *s* oder *x*, wird *-es* angehängt: z. B. bus – buses, box – boxes
  - ☐ Manche Wörter haben einen unregelmäßigen Plural: z. B. man – men, child – children, shelf – shelves, mouse – mice

- **Apostroph:**
  - ☐ bei Kurzformen: z. B. she is → she's; they are → they're
  - ☐ beim Genitiv-s: z. B. Sam's bike, Emma's family, the Jacksons' house, the children's games

- **Wörterbuch:**
  - ☐ Prüfe die Schreibung aller Wörter, bei denen du dir nicht ganz sicher bist, indem du sie im Wörterbuch nachschlägst.

Vocabulary

Das Vocabulary enthält alle neuen Wörter und Wendungen. Sie stehen in der Reihenfolge, wie sie im Buch vorkommen.

Die Wortliste ist in drei Spalten aufgeteilt:

Links findest du das englische Wort mit der Lautschrift in Klammern. (Die Lautschrift wird ganz unten auf jeder Seite im *Dictionary* erklärt.)

In der mittleren Spalte steht die deutsche Übersetzung.

Rechts findest du Beispielsätze, Hinweise und Tipps, die dir beim Lernen helfen.

Die **fett** gedruckten Wörter musst du lernen.
Die blau gedruckten Wörter kannst du lernen, musst du aber nicht.
Die Wörter aus den Checkpoints musst du nicht lernen.

Symbole und Abkürzungen:

⇔	Achte auf die Aussprache!	=	entspricht
✎	Achte auf die Schreibung!	*(sg)*	Einzahl (Singular)
↔	ist das Gegenteil von	*(pl)*	Mehrzahl (Plural)
→	ist verwandt mit	Ⓡ	ähnlich wie im Russischen
sth	something	Ⓣ	ähnlich wie im Türkischen
sb	somebody		

Die *Word bank*-Seiten helfen dir, die *Your turn*-Aufgaben in den *Units* zu bearbeiten.
Du findest dort nützlichen individuellen Wortschatz zum Thema der *Unit*, der dir hilft, über deine eigene Situation zu sprechen oder zu schreiben. Diese Wörter findest du auch im *Dictionary*.

Wenn du ein Wort nicht weißt und im Wörterbuch nachschlagen willst, schau auf den *Dictionary*-Seiten ab S. 213 nach. Oder bei den *Instructions* auf S. 208.

Zoom in – The USA

p. 8	**fall** *(AE)* [fɔːl]	Herbst	AE: **fall** BE: autumn
	state [steɪt]	Staat; Bundesstaat; Land	There are 50 **states** in the USA.
	to **shine** [ʃaɪn], **shone** [ʃɒn], **shone** [ʃɒn]	scheinen; glänzen	The sun is **shining** today.
	bright [braɪt]	hell; leuchtend; strahlend	**bright** ↔ dark
	color *(AE)* [ˈkʌlə]	Farbe	AE: **color** BE: colour
p. 9	**huge** [hjuːdʒ]	riesig; riesengroß	**huge** = very big
	area [ˈeəriə]	Fläche; Gegend; Gebiet; Areal	The USA has an **area** of over 9,000,000 km².
	corn [kɔːn]	Korn; Mais; Getreide	

soy bean [ˈsɔɪˌbiːn]	Sojabohne	You can see **soy beans** in the Midwest.	
field [fiːld]	Feld; Wiese; Weide	There are corn **fields** in the Midwest.	
surfer [ˈsɜːfə]	Wellenreiter; Wellenreiterin; Surfer; Surferin	T sörfçü	
paradise [ˈpærədaɪs]	Paradies	Hawaii is a surfer's **paradise**.	
perfect [ˈpɜːfɪkt]	perfekt; vollkommen	Today is the **perfect** weather for a picnic.	
wave [weɪv]	Welle		
p. 8 **North America** [ˌnɔːθ əˈmerɪkə]	Nordamerika	Denali is the highest mountain in **North America**.	
p. 9 **landscape** [ˈlændskeɪp]	Landschaft	Tourists enjoy the beautiful **landscape**.	
American [əˈmerɪkən]	amerikanisch; Amerikanisch; aus Amerika; Amerikaner; Amerikanerin	**American** → America	
swamp [swɒmp]	Sumpf	There are **swamps** in the American south.	
alligator [ˈælɪɡeɪtə]	Alligator	R аллигатор T alligator	
p. 8 **rose** [rəʊz]	Rose	R роза	
bald eagle [ˌbɔːld ˈiːɡl]	Weißkopfseeadler	The **bald eagle** is an American symbol.	
population [ˌpɒpjəˈleɪʃn]	Einwohner; Einwohnerzahl; Bevölkerung	What's the **population** of the United States?	
total [ˈtəʊtl]	Gesamt-; gesamt	The **total** area is all of the area.	
square mile (= sq. mi.) [ˌskweə ˈmaɪl]	Quadratmeile	The United States' total area is about 3,600,000 **square miles**.	
currency [ˈkʌrnsi]	Währung	The **currency** in Germany is the euro.	
dollar [ˈdɒlə]	Dollar *(amer. Währungseinheit)*	R доллар T dolar	
time zone [ˈtaɪmˌzəʊn]	Zeitzone	There are nine **time zones** in the USA.	
major [ˈmeɪdʒə]	Haupt-; wichtig; bedeutend	There are three **major** rivers in the USA.	
p. 9 **to name** [neɪm]	benennen	to **name** → name	
north of [ˈnɔːθˌəv]	nördlich von	Denmark is **north of** Germany.	
south of [ˈsaʊθˌəv]	südlich von	Italy is **south of** Germany.	
ocean [ˈəʊʃn]	Ozean; Meer	R океан T okyanus	
east of [ˈiːstˌəv]	östlich von	Poland is **east of** Germany.	
west of [ˈwestˌəv]	westlich von	France is **west of** Germany.	
distance [ˈdɪstns]	Entfernung; Distanz	Find out the **distance** from A to B.	

Unit 1 Gateway NYC

| p. 12 | **gateway** [ˈɡeɪtweɪ] | Tor; Eingangstor | NYC is the **gateway** to America. |

Way in

	over [ˈəʊvə]	über	**Over** eight million people live in NYC.
	borough [ˈbʌrə]	Stadtteil; Bezirk	NYC has five **boroughs**.
	skyline [ˈskaɪlaɪn]	Skyline	
	to replace [rɪˈpleɪs]	ersetzen	I **replaced** my old car.
	attack [əˈtæk]	Angriff; Attacke	There were **attacks** on September 11, 2001.
p. 13	**baseball** [ˈbeɪsbɔːl]	Baseball	R бейсбол T beyzbol
	New Yorker [ˌnjuːˈjɔːkə]	New Yorker; New Yorkerin	**New Yorkers** live in New York City.
	center *(AE)* [ˈsentə]	Zentrum; Mitte; Center	AE: **center** BE: centre
	culture [ˈkʌltʃə]	Kultur	It is a center for American **culture**.
	theater *(AE)* [ˈθɪətə]	Theater	AE: **theater** BE: theatre
	street art [ˈstriːt ɑːt]	Straßenkunst	**Street art** started in New York.
	independence [ˌɪndɪˈpendəns]	Unabhängigkeit	They celebrated 100 years of **independence**.
	immigrant [ˈɪmɪɡrənt]	Immigrant; Immigrantin; Einwanderer; Einwandererin	A lot of **immigrants** went to America.
	symbol [ˈsɪmbl]	Symbol	R символ T sembol
	hope [həʊp]	Hoffnung	**hope** → to hope
	on TV [ɒn ˌtiːˈviː]	im Fernsehen	You could see everything **on TV**.
	billion [ˈbɪliən]	Milliarde	R биллион
	top [tɒp]	Spitze	It took 30 seconds to travel to the **top**.
	elevator *(AE)* [ˈelɪveɪtə]	Aufzug; Lift	AE: **elevator** BE: lift
	light [laɪt]	Licht	

Station 1

City words

traffic jam ['træfɪk ˌdʒæm]	Stau
rush hour ['rʌʃ ˌaʊə]	Hauptverkehrszeit
roadwork *(AE)* ['rəʊdwɜ:k]	Straßenbauarbeiten
downtown *(AE)* [ˌdaʊn'taʊn]	im Stadtzentrum
skyscraper ['skaɪskreɪpə]	Wolkenkratzer
subway *(AE)* ['sʌbweɪ]	U-Bahn
avenue ['ævənju:]	Allee; Boulevard
lights [laɪts]	Ampel
sidewalk *(AE)* ['saɪdwɔ:k]	Gehweg; Bürgersteig
suburb ['sʌbɜ:b]	Vorort
construction site [kən'strʌkʃn ˌsaɪt]	Baustelle
parking lot *(AE)* ['pɑ:kɪŋ ˌlɒt]	Parkplatz

p. 14	**ride** [raɪd]	Fahrt; Ritt	A taxi **ride** in NYC is very interesting.
	snow [snəʊ]	Schnee	
	to **get into** [ˌget‿'ɪntə]	hineingelangen; hineinkommen	I usually **get into** town by bus.
	look [lʊk]	Blick; Anblick; Sicht	**look** → to look
	to **get tired of sth** [ˌget 'taɪəd‿əv]	etw. sattbekommen; etw. satthaben	I never **get tired of** it.
	financial [faɪ'nænʃl]	finanziell; Finanz-	Where is the **financial** centre of the world?
	view [vju:]	Aussicht; Sicht; Ausblick; Blick	The **view** from the top is amazing.
	anyway ['eniweɪ]	eigentlich	How long are you here for, **anyway**?
	around [ə'raʊnd]	um … herum	The café is **around** the corner.
	hot dog ['hɒt ˌdɒg]	Hot Dog *(Würstchen im Brötchen)*	R хот-дог T hot dog 
p. 15	in the distance [ˌɪn ðə 'dɪstns]	in der Ferne	I can see the bridge **in the distance**.
	right ahead [ˌraɪt ə'hed]	geradeaus	Look, the museum is **right ahead**.

Station 2

Going to a new country

to **immigrate** [ˈɪmɪgreɪt]	einwandern; immigrieren		**career** [kəˈrɪə]	Beruf; Laufbahn; Karriere
decision [dɪˈsɪʒn]	Entscheidung		**citizen** [ˈsɪtɪzn]	Staatsbürger; Staats-bürgerin; Staats-angehöriger; Staats-angehörige
foreign [ˈfɒrɪn]	fremd; ausländisch			
unemployed [ˌʌnɪmˈplɔɪd]	arbeitslos			
chance [tʃɑːns]	Möglichkeit		**papers** *(pl)* [ˌpeɪpəz]	Unterlagen; Papiere
community [kəˈmjuːnəti]	Gemeinde; Gemeinschaft		to **emigrate** [ˈemɪgreɪt]	auswandern; emigrieren
to **get used to (sth)** [ˌget ˈjuːzd tə]	sich an (etw.) ge-wöhnen		**support** [səˈpɔːt]	Unterstützung; Hilfe
			to **fail (at)** [feɪl (ət)]	versagen (in/bei); aus-fallen; fehlschlagen

p. 18	**interviewer** [ˈɪntəvjuːə]	Interviewer; Interviewerin; Be-frager; Befragerin	**interviewer** → interview → to interview
	to **complain** [kəmˈpleɪn]	sich beschweren; sich beklagen	Don't **complain** and think positive.
	Latin America [ˌlætɪn əˈmerɪkə]	Lateinamerika	In **Latin America** the first language isn't English.
	poor [pɔː]	arm	**poor** ↔ rich
	Cuba [ˈkjuːbə]	Kuba	Ⓡ Куба Ⓣ Küba
	Cuban [ˈkjuːbən]	kubanisch; aus Kuba; Kubaner; Kubanerin	**Cuban** → Cuba
	to **give up** [ˌgɪvˈʌp]	aufgeben	The spider never **gives up**.
	to **begin** [bɪˈgɪn], **began** [bɪˈgæn], **begun** [bɪˈgʌn]	beginnen; anfangen	**to begin** ↔ to finish
	to **take sth seriously** [ˌteɪk ˈsɪəriəsli]	etw. ernst nehmen	I don't **take sport seriously**, I do it for fun.
	high school [ˈhaɪ ˌskuːl]	Highschool *(weiterführende Schule, Oberstufe)*	I worked hard at **high school**.
	future [ˈfjuːtʃə]	Zukunft	I had a better **future** in the USA.
	US [juːˈes]	US-amerikanisch	It is a **US** school, not a British one.
p. 19	**The Philippines** [ˌðə ˈfɪlɪpiːnz]	die Philippinen	Angela is from **the Philippines**.
	college [ˈkɒlɪdʒ]	College; Institut	Angela goes to **college** too.

Reading corner

p. 22	**immigration** [ˌɪmɪˈɡreɪʃn]	Immigration; Zuwanderung	**immigration** → to immigrate → immigrant
	condition [kənˈdɪʃn]	Bedingung; Zustand	The **conditions** were very hard.
	crowded [ˈkraʊdɪd]	überfüllt	**crowded** → crowd
	air [eə]	Luft	You have to put **air** in the tyres.
	to move [muːv]	(sich) bewegen	I **moved** slowly around the ship.
	harbor (AE) [ˈhɑːbə]	Hafen	AE: **harbor** BE: harbour
	powerful [ˈpaʊfl]	stark; mächtig; bedeutend; beeindruckend	America is a **powerful** country.
	check [tʃek]	Kontrolle	**check** → to check
	disease [dɪˈziːz]	Krankheit	Doctors checked for **diseases**.
	minority [maɪˈnɒrəti]	Minderheit	The **minority** of the people were OK.
p. 23	**percent (%)** [pəˈsent]	Prozent	50 **percent** of ten is five.
	the rest [ðə ˈrest]	der Rest	**The rest** of us left for our new life.
	Ireland [ˈaɪələnd]	Irland	Immigrants came from **Ireland**.
	Scandinavia [ˌskændɪˈneɪviə]	Skandinavien	Denmark is in **Scandinavia**.
	majority [məˈdʒɒrəti]	Mehrheit	**majority** ↔ minority
	Greece [griːs]	Griechenland	**Greece** is in the south of Europe.
	Eastern Europe [ˈiːstn ˌjʊərəp]	Osteuropa	Poland is in **Eastern Europe**.
	Russia [ˈrʌʃə]	Russland	**Russia** is to the east of Germany.
	freedom (no pl) [ˈfriːdəm]	Freiheit; Unabhängigkeit	**Freedom** hat keine Mehrzahl.
	Mexico [ˈmeksɪkəʊ]	Mexiko	Ⓡ Мексика Ⓣ Meksika
	China [ˈtʃaɪnə]	China	👄 Achtung Aussprache!
	The Dominican Republic [ðə dəˌmɪnɪkn rɪˈpʌblɪk]	Dominikanische Republik	**The Dominican Republic** is to the east of Cuba.
	Vietnam [ˌvjetˈnæm]	Vietnam	**Vietnam** is south of China.

Film corner

p. 25	**once** [wʌns]	einst; einmal	at a time in the past
	honor (AE) [ˈɒnə]	Ehre	There's a Wall of **Honor** on Ellis Island.
	great-grandparents [ˌɡreɪtˈɡrænˌpeərənts]	Urgroßeltern	My **great-grandparents** are my grandparents' parents.
	inside [ɪnˈsaɪd]	innen; drinnen	In summer it can get hot **inside**.

Checkpoint

Spanish [ˈspænɪʃ]	spanisch; Spanisch; aus Spanien	ethnic [ˈeθnɪk]	ethnisch; Volks-

---

Word bank: City Guide

skyscraper

cathedral

tower

museum

gallery

station

bridge

building

monument

Over there you can see …
Don't miss …
Around this corner we'll come to …
Right/Straight ahead are …
You must visit …
In the distance you can see …
Have a look at/Look at …

Make sure you visit …
I'd like to point out …
Down there / Over there is …
From here …
… built it in …
It opened in …
It is special because …

Word bank: **Presenting personal information**

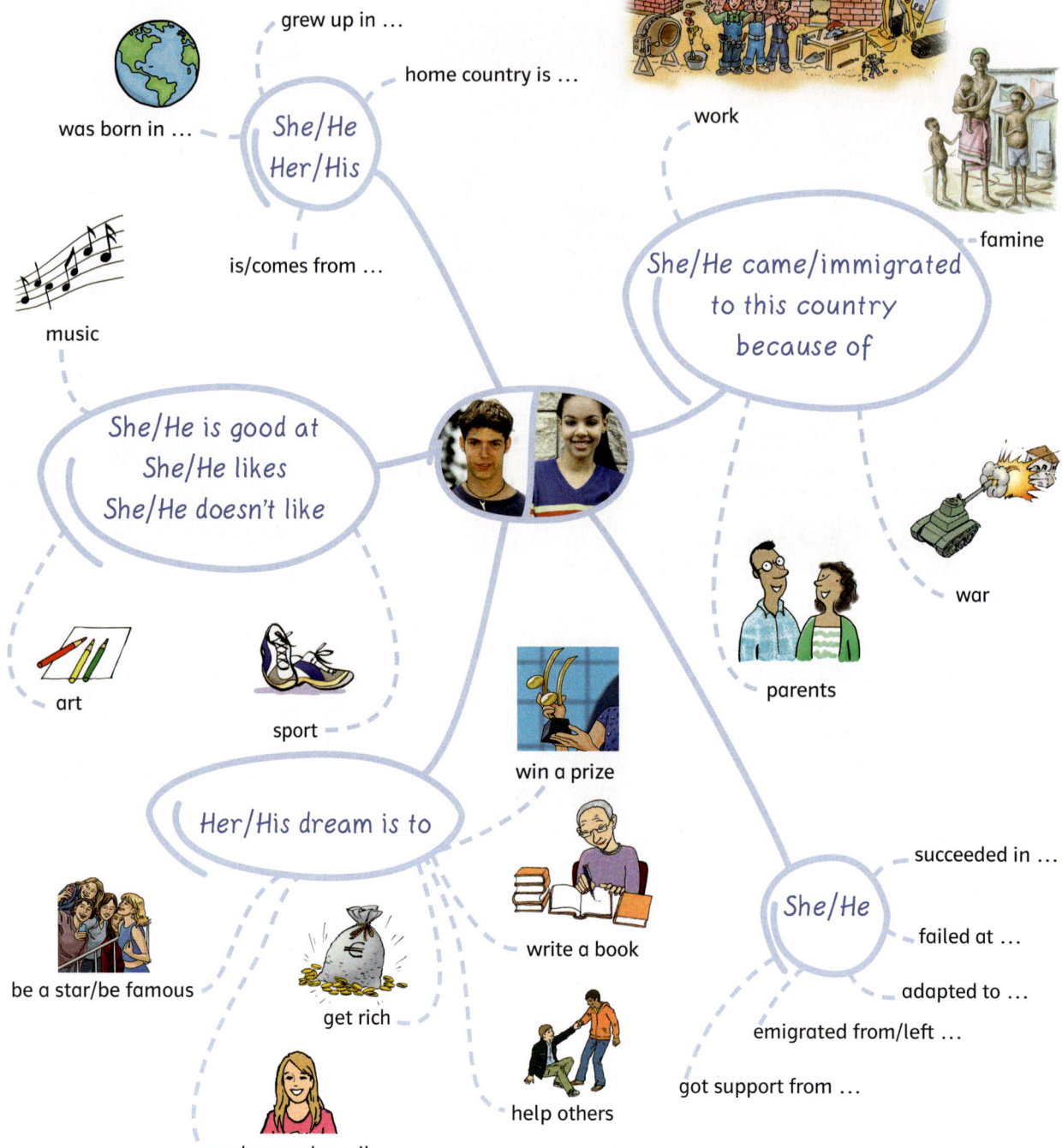

grew up in …

home country is …

was born in …

She/He
Her/His

work

is/comes from …

music

She/He came/immigrated
to this country
because of

famine

She/He is good at
She/He likes
She/He doesn't like

war

art

parents

sport

win a prize

Her/His dream is to

write a book

She/He

succeeded in …

failed at …

adapted to …

emigrated from/left …

got support from …

be a star/be famous

get rich

help others

make people smile

Unit 2 Teens in the Midwest

Way in

p. 32	**farmland** [ˈfɑːmlænd]	Ackerland; Ackerboden; Landwirtschaftsflächen	You can see corn on **farmland** in the Midwest.
	storm [stɔːm]	Sturm	The **storm** was awful. I was sick.
	European [ˌjʊərəˈpiːən]	europäisch; Europäisch; aus Europa; Europäer; Europäerin	T Avrupalı
	settler [ˈsetlə]	Siedler; Siedlerin	Thousands of **settlers** came to the West.
	Native American [ˌneɪtɪv əˈmerɪkən]	Ureinwohner Amerikas; Ureinwohnerin Amerikas; Indianer; Indianerin; indianisch	**Native Americans** live in the USA.
	reservation [ˌrezəˈveɪʃn]	Reservat	We had to live on **reservations**.
p. 33	**store** (AE) [stɔː]	Laden; Geschäft	AE: **store** BE: shop
	to **clear** [klɪə]	abräumen; ausräumen	I **clear** the tables in a café on Fridays.
	to **serve** [sɜːv]	servieren	Sarah **serves** ice cream in the new café.
	grade (AE) [greɪd]	Note; Klasse	AE: **grade** BE: mark; class
	schedule (AE) [ˈskedʒuːl]	Stundenplan; Fahrplan	AE: **schedule** BE: timetable
	Homecoming (AE) [ˈhəʊmˌkʌmɪŋ]	Ehemaligentreffen	The **Homecoming** Dance is always fun.
	to **vote for** [ˈvəʊt fə]	abstimmen über; wählen	
	tornado [tɔːˈneɪdəʊ]	Tornado; Wirbelsturm	R торнадо
	cloud [klaʊd]	Wolke	
	chaser [ˈtʃeɪsə]	Jäger; Jägerin; Verfolger; Verfolgerin	Warren is a storm **chaser**.
	warning [ˈwɔːnɪŋ]	Warnung	There was a **warning** on the radio.

Station 1

At American schools

locker [ˈlɒkə]	Schließfach; Spind	**cheerleader** [ˈtʃɪəˌliːdə]	Cheerleader (*Mädchen, das in einer Gruppe eine Sportmannschaft anfeuert*)
morning message [ˈmɔːnɪŋ ˌmesɪdʒ]	morgendliche Ansprache		
principal *(AE)* [ˈprɪnsɪpl]	Schulleiter; Schulleiterin	**elective** [ɪˈlektɪv]	Wahlfach
		detention [dɪˈtenʃn]	Nachsitzen
class [klɑːs]	Unterrichtsstunde; Kurs	**core subject** [ˌkɔː ˈsʌbdʒɪkt]	Pflichtfach
Math *(AE)* [mæθ]	Mathematik; Mathe	**dress code** [ˈdres ˌkəʊd]	Kleiderordnung; Bekleidungsvorschriften
study hall period [ˈstʌdi hɔːl ˌpɪəriəd]	Freistunde		
extracurricular [ˌekstrəkəˈrɪkjələ]	außerhalb des Lehrplans; außerunterrichtlich (*Zusatzunterricht*)		

p. 34	**exchange** [ɪksˈtʃeɪndʒ]	Austausch	Luise did a student **exchange** in the USA.
	nowhere [ˈnəʊweə]	nirgendwo; nirgendwohin	We live in the middle of **nowhere**.
	way [weɪ]	Weg	I couldn't find the **way** to school.
	astronomy [əˈstrɒnəmi]	Astronomie	R астрономия T astronomi
	journalism [ˈdʒɜːnlɪzm]	Journalistik; Journalismus	R журналистика
	for example [fər ɪgˈzɑːmpl]	zum Beispiel	I like fruit, **for example** apples.
	to **be allowed to (do sth)** [biː əˈlaʊd tə]	(etw.) dürfen	We **were allowed to** talk in class.
	strict [strɪkt]	streng; strikt	The school rules are very **strict**.
	competition [ˌkɒmpəˈtɪʃn]	Konkurrenz	There was lots of **competition** for places.
	awesome [ˈɔːsəm]	super; spitze	**awesome** = amazing, great
	host family [ˈhəʊst ˌfæmli]	Gastfamilie	I really liked my **host family**.

Station 2

Describing people

helpful ['helpfl]	hilfsbereit		**generous** ['dʒenrəs]	großzügig
responsible [rɪs'pɒnsəbl]	verantwortlich; verantwortungsvoll		**rude** [ruːd]	unhöflich; unverschämt
hard-working [ˌhɑːd'wɜːkɪŋ]	fleißig		**selfish** ['selfɪʃ]	selbstsüchtig
			shy [ʃaɪ]	schüchtern
unmotivated [ˌʌn'məʊtɪveɪtɪd]	unmotiviert			

p. 38	**outside** [ˌaʊt'saɪd]	außerhalb	Extracurricular activites are **outside** school.
	to earn [ɜːn]	verdienen	I have a job and **earn** money.
	driver's license (AE) ['draɪvəz ˌlaɪsns]	Führerschein	AE: **driver's license** BE: driving licence
	girlfriend ['gɜːlfrend]	Freundin (in einer Paarbeziehung)	Sarah is Michael's **girlfriend**.
	job title ['dʒɒb ˌtaɪtl]	Stellenbezeichnung; Berufsbezeichnung	What is the **job title** of your new job?
	sales associate (AE) [ˌseɪlz ə'səʊʃiət]	Verkäufer; Verkäuferin	AE: **sales associate** BE: sales assistant
	education [ˌedʒʊ'keɪʃn]	Ausbildung; Erziehung; Bildung	My **education** was at the local school.
	to apply (for) [ə'plaɪ (fə)]	sich bewerben (für/um)	He **applied for** the student job.
	interview ['ɪntəvjuː]	Vorstellungsgespräch	He had an **interview** on Thursday.
	manager ['mænɪdʒə]	Manager; Managerin; Geschäftsführer; Geschäftsführerin	Ⓡ менеджер
	somebody ['sʌmbədi]	jemand	**somebody** ↔ nobody
	to steal [stiːl], **stole** [stəʊl], **stolen** ['stəʊlən]	stehlen	I saw the boy **steal** a T-shirt.
	to offer ['ɒfə]	anbieten	The manager **offered** Michael the job.
	minimum ['mɪnɪməm]	Minimum; minimal; Mindest-	Ⓣ minimum
	wage [weɪdʒ]	Lohn	He earned the minimum **wage**.
	co-worker ['kəʊˌwɜːkə]	Arbeitskollege; Arbeitskollegin	My **co-workers** are friendly.
	to tease [tiːz]	hänseln; sticheln; reizen	People came in and **teased** Michael.
	to throw [θrəʊ], **threw** [θruː], **thrown** [θrəʊn]	werfen	He **threw** them out of the store.
p. 39	**working hours** (pl) ['wɜːkɪŋ ˌaʊəz]	Arbeitszeit	9:00 to 5:00 are my **working hours**.

feedback ['fiːdbæk]	Feedback; Rückmeldung	She got good **feedback**.	
best-paying [ˌbestˈpeɪɪŋ]	bestbezahlt	This is the **best-paying** job I've ever had.	
p. 41	**dog walker** ['dɒɡ ˌwɔːkə]	Hundeausführer; Hundeausführerin	a person who takes dogs for a walk
per [pɜː]	pro	I earn $40 **per** week.	
babysitter ['beɪbɪˌsɪtə]	Babysitter; Babysitterin	a person who looks after children	
paperboy ['peɪpəˌbɔɪ]	Zeitungsausträger	I'm Dave, I'm a **paperboy**.	
papergirl ['peɪpəˌɡɜːl]	Zeitungsausträgerin	A paperboy or **papergirl** works every day.	

Reading corner

p. 42	**date** [deɪt]	Verabredung; Date	They went on their first **date**.
boyfriend ['bɔɪfrend]	Freund (in einer Paarbeziehung)	**boyfriend** ↔ girlfriend	
shy [ʃaɪ]	schüchtern	I like her, but I'm too **shy** to tell her.	
to ask sb out [ˌaːsk … ˈaʊt]	sich mit jmdm. verabreden	Dylan **asked Abby out** on a date.	
guy [ɡaɪ]	Typ; Kerl	Who is the **guy** in the hall?	
to fall out of [fɔːl ˈaʊt əv]	herausfallen aus	All my books **fell out of** my locker.	
right [raɪt]	gerade; genau; in dem Moment als	It happened **right** when he walked past.	
to show up [ˌʃəʊˈʌp]	auftauchen; erscheinen	He **showed up** late for school.	
embarrassing [ɪmˈbærəsɪŋ]	peinlich	It was so **embarrassing**, I went red.	
gym(nasium) [dʒɪm (dʒɪmˈneɪziəm)]	Turnhalle	the room in a school where PE lessons are	
to attack [əˈtæk]	angreifen	The boys **attacked** him in the gym.	
p. 43	**to pick up** [pɪkˈʌp]	abholen	Dylan **picked** Abby **up** at seven o'clock.
everybody ['evribɒdi]	jeder; alle	**everybody** = everyone	
dancing ['daːnsɪŋ]	Tanzen; Tanz-	T dans	
to take [teɪk]	bringen; hinbringen	Dylan **took** Abby home.	
stereotype ['steriəʊtaɪp]	Stereotyp; Klischee	Which **stereotypes** do you know from movies?	

Film corner

p. 45	**buddy** (infml) ['bʌdi]	Kumpel	David is my best **buddy**.
homeroom ['həʊmruːm]	erste Stunde (in der Schule)	We are in the same **homeroom**.	
detention [dɪˈtenʃn]	Nachsitzen	I haven't had **detention** this year.	

pledge of allegiance [ˌpledʒ əv ˌəˈliːdʒns]	Treueeid	We say the **pledge of allegiance** every morning.

─── Checkpoint ───

to **interest** [ˈɪntrəst]	interessieren	to **elect** [ɪˈlekt]	wählen

Presentation skills

p. 51	**presentation** [ˌprezn'teɪʃn]	Präsentation; Vortrag	My **presentation** is about cats.
	topic [ˈtɒpɪk]	Thema	My next **topic** is the rules of the game.

Word bank: **Comparing schools**

dress code

cheerleading

marching band

pledge of allegiance

school bus

locker

Homecoming Dance

schedule

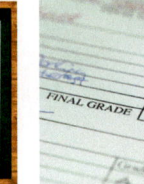

grade

hall pass

class

I would like to compare …
In/At American high schools …
In/At German schools …
Both countries have detention/principals/…

In America there is … but not in Germany.
… is the same.
… is different.

Word bank: Jobs

waitress

waiter

serve ice cream

work on a market stall

shop assistant

wash up in a café/ restaurant

babysitter

dog walker

paperboy/girl

help in the garden/ mow the lawn

do the shopping for people

I earn …
I work inside/outside.
I work every day/at the weekends/in the holidays/on …
I work in the mornings/afternoons/evenings.
I start work at …

I like it/don't like it because …
I'm a … person.
It's hard/easy work.
It's fun/boring.
I work with nice/interesting/fun/strange/ quiet/… people.

Unit 3 In the Northeast

Way in

p. 52	**border** ['bɔ:də]	Grenze	There is a **border** between two countries.
	to **drive** [draɪv], **drove** [drəʊv], **driven** ['drɪvn]	fahren; treiben	You can **drive** through the beautiful woods.
	celebration [ˌselə'breɪʃn]	Feier	**celebration** → to celebrate
p. 53	**Thanksgiving** [ˌθæŋks'gɪvɪŋ]	Erntedankfest	**Thanksgiving** is the 4th Thursday in November.
	turkey ['tɜ:ki]	Truthahn; Pute	
	dinner ['dɪnə]	Essen	meals: breakfast, lunch, **dinner**
	president ['prezɪdnt]	Präsident; Präsidentin	R президент
	to **pardon** ['pɑ:dn]	begnadigen; entschuldigen; verzeihen	The President **pardons** a turkey.
	favorite *(AE)* ['feɪvrɪt]	Lieblings-	AE: **favorite** BE: favourite
	creepy ['kri:pi]	gruselig	**Creepy** films are often made in Maine.
	forest ['fɒrɪst]	Wald	
	land of the free [ˌlænd ˌəv ðə 'fri:]	Land der Freien	The USA is called the **land of the free**.
	the Amish [ði 'ɑ:mɪʃ]	die Amischen	**The Amish** don't have mobile phones.
	Christian ['krɪstʃn]	christlich	T Hıristiyan
	daredevil ['deəˌdevl]	Draufgänger; Draufgängerin	The **daredevil** did dangerous tricks.
	stuntman ['stʌntmæn]	Stuntman	**Stuntmen** work in films.
	close [kləʊs]	in der Nähe; nahe	It's **close**, not far from here.
	barrel ['bærl]	Fass; Tonne	
	to **sign autographs** [ˌsaɪn 'ɔ:təgrɑ:fs]	Autogramme geben	The actor **signed autographs** for us.

Station 1

Small talk

What's up? [ˌwɒts ˌʌp]	Wie geht's?	**How are things going?** [ˌhaʊ ɑ: θɪŋz 'gəʊɪŋ]	Wie läuft's?; Wie geht's?
How's it going? [ˌhaʊz ɪt 'gəʊɪŋ]	Wie geht's?; Wie läuft's?		

p. 54	to **get ready** [ˌget ˈredi]	sich vorbereiten; sich fertig machen	We have to **get ready** for the party.
	husband [ˈhʌzbənd]	Ehemann	My **husband** is in the kitchen.
	to **get stuck** [ˌget ˈstʌk]	stecken bleiben	I **got stuck** in the snow for two hours.
	doorbell [ˈdɔːbel]	Türklingel	
	neighbor (AE) [ˈneibə]	Nachbar; Nachbarin	AE: **neighbor** BE: neighbour
	glad [glæd]	froh	We were **glad** you liked the flowers.
	make it [ˈmeikˌit]	es schaffen	I'm glad you could **make it**.
	to **enter** [ˈentə]	hineingehen; hereinkommen; betreten; eintreten	to **enter** ↔ to leave
	across [əˈkrɒs]	über; hinüber; herüber; quer durch	He looked **across** the room at me.
	chocolate [ˈtʃɒklət]	Praline	T çikolata
	to **land** [lænd]	landen	Our plane **lands** at seven o'clock.
	to **promise** [ˈprɒmis]	versprechen	I **promise** we will wait for you.
	to **save** [seiv]	aufheben	We will **save** you some turkey.
p. 55	**Please have a seat.** [ˌpliːz hæv ə ˈsiːt]	Bitte Platz nehmen.	Come in. **Please have a seat.**

Station 2

Agreeing and disagreeing

Exactly. [igˈzæktli]	Genau.	**I guess ...** [ai ˈges]	Ich nehme an, dass ...
Absolutely not. [ˌæbsəˈluːtli nɒt]	Ganz und gar nicht.; Auf keinen Fall!	**I'm convinced that ...** [ˌaim kənˈvinst ðət]	Ich bin überzeugt, dass ...
As far as I know, ... [ˌəz ˈfaːrˌəzˌai nəʊ]	Soweit ich weiß, ...	**It's clear to me that ...** [its ˈkliə tə ˌmiː ðæt]	Mir ist klar, dass ...

Devices

device [diˈvais]	Gerät; Vorrichtung	**dishwasher** [ˈdiʃwɒʃə]	Spülmaschine
microwave [ˈmaikrəweiv]	Mikrowelle	**vacuum cleaner** [ˈvækjuːm ˌkliːnə]	Staubsauger
headphones (pl) [ˈhedfəʊnz]	Kopfhörer	**razor** [ˈreizə]	Rasierer; Rasierapparat
fan [fæn]	Ventilator	**radiator** [ˈreidieitə]	Heizkörper

p. 58	**Amish** [ˈɑːmɪʃ]	amisch	We live in an **Amish** community.
	to **concentrate** [ˈkɒnsntreɪt]	(sich) konzentrieren	This is hard. I have to **concentrate**.
	to **cover** [ˈkʌvə]	bedecken; abdecken	Amish girls often **cover** their hair.
	make-up [ˈmeɪkʌp]	Make-up; Schminke	T makyaj
	to **grow** [grəʊ], **grew** [gruː], **grown** [grəʊn]	anbauen; züchten; ziehen; wachsen	We **grow** our own vegetables.
	forbidden [fəˈbɪdn]	verboten	I never do **forbidden** things.
	alcohol (no pl) [ˈælkəhɒl]	Alkohol	R алкоголь T alkol
	average [ˈævrɪdʒ]	durchschnittlich	I'm an **average** American teenager.
	fashion (no pl) [ˈfæʃn]	Mode	I love clothes and the newest **fashion**.
	gossip [ˈgɒsɪp]	Klatsch; Tratsch; Gerede	I read the **gossip** about the stars too.
	to **go out with** [ˌgəʊˈaʊt wɪð]	(aus)gehen mit	She's **going out with** him.
	whom [huːm]	wem; wen	They ask who has a date with **whom**.
	bowling [ˈbəʊlɪŋ]	Bowlen	R боулинг T bowling
p. 59	**electric** [ɪˈlektrɪk]	elektrisch	T elektrik
p. 61	**before** [bɪˈfɔː]	vor	**before** ↔ after
	alien [ˈeɪliən]	Außerirdischer; Außerirdische	

Reading corner

p. 62	**body** [ˈbɒdi]	Leiche	There was a man's **body** on the beach.
	to **disappear** [ˌdɪsəˈpɪə]	verschwinden	The man **disappeared** two weeks ago.
	gun [gʌn]	Schusswaffe	He had a **gun** in his hand.
	blanket [ˈblæŋkɪt]	Decke; Bettdecke; Wolldecke	
	back [bæk]	Hinter-	We went in the **back** door.
	clubhouse [ˈklʌbhaʊs]	Klubhaus; Vereinsheim	We meet at the **clubhouse** on Tuesdays.
	backpack [ˈbækpæk]	Rucksack	
	desk [desk]	Schreibtisch	
	wine [waɪn]	Wein	
	drunk [drʌŋk]	betrunken	After one glass of wine he was **drunk**.
p. 63	**bullet** [ˈbʊlɪt]	Kugel; Geschoss	There are no **bullets** in the gun.
	sat [sæt]	simple past, past participle von *to sit* (sitzen)	I **sat** = ich saß/ich habe gesessen

tin [tɪn]	Dose; Büchse; *hier:* Mülleimer	
to **jump** [dʒʌmp]	springen	
to **shoot (at)** [ʃuːt (ət)], **shot (at)** [ʃɒt (ət)], **shot (at)** [ʃɒt (ət)]	schießen (auf)	He **shot** at the bottles on the wall.
wrist [rɪst]	Handgelenk	It is between your hand and your arm.
to **scream** [skriːm]	schreien; kreischen	Don't **scream**. I can hear you.
wild [waɪld]	wild	There are **wild** animals at the zoo.
amused [əˈmjuːzd]	amüsiert; vergnügt	Was Chris **amused** or scared?
to **shut up** [ʃʌtˈʌp]	die Klappe halten	**Shut up** and listen to me!
by [baɪ]	an	He grabbed me **by** the shirt.
mean [miːn]	gemein	He was really **mean** to us.
honestly [ˈɒnɪstli]	ehrlich	**Honestly**, I didn't know it was broken.
innocent [ˈɪnəsnt]	unschuldig	He didn't do it, he is **innocent**.
whole [həʊl]	ganz	We spent the **whole** week there.
nothing [ˈnʌθɪŋ]	nichts	**nothing** ↔ something
to **stand up** [ˌstændˈʌp]	aufstehen; stehen	He **stood up** and left the room.
p. 64 to **gather** [ˈɡæðə]	(sich) sammeln	We **gathered** round him and listened.
railway track [ˈreɪlweɪ ˌtræk]	Gleis	We went across the bridge on the **railway tracks**.
scared [skeəd]	verängstigt	I was **scared** in the dark.

Film corner

p. 67 pecan [ˈpiːkæn]	Pekannuss	**Pecan** pie is my favourite pie.
pardon [ˈpɑːdn]	Begnadigung; Entschuldigung; Verzeihung	The President's **pardon** is for a turkey.

--- Checkpoint ---

out [aʊt]	aus; draußen; außerhalb	to **control** [kənˈtrəʊl]	kontrollieren

Writing skills

p. 73 to **sum up** [ˌsʌmˈʌp]	zusammenfassen	To **sum up** you can say this food is better.

Word bank: **Giving opinions**

I agree with the statement …

I agree with you.

I think you're right (there).

That's true.

I think so because …

In my opinion …

I think …

I also think that … because …

So my answer is …

I tried it when I was …

One reason is …

Another reason is …

To conclude I would like to say …

It had an impact on my life because …

I don't agree/disagree with the statement …

I don't agree/disagree with you.

That's false.

I don't think so because …

In my opinion …

I think …

You can't be serious!

I think you're wrong (there).

I tried it when I was …

Another reason is …

One reason is …

To conclude I would like to say …

It had an impact/influence on my life because …

Unit 4 California dreams

Way in

p. 74	**giant** [dʒaɪənt]	Riesen-; riesig	Look at the **giant** sandwiches.
	redwood (tree) [ˈredwʊd (triː)]	Mammutbaum	
	relaxed [rɪˈlækst]	entspannt; locker; gelassen	People are very **relaxed** in California.
	lifestyle [ˈlaɪfstaɪl]	Lebensart; Lifestyle	the way you live your life
	surfing [ˈsɜːfɪŋ]	Wellenreiten; Surfen	I love **surfing** in the summer.
	volleyball [ˈvɒlibɔːl]	Volleyball	Ⓡ волейбол Ⓣ voleybol
	cable car [ˈkeɪbl ˌkaː]	Seilbahn	
	hill [hɪl]	Berg; Hügel	
	Asia [ˈeɪʒə]	Asien	Ⓡ азия Ⓣ Asya
p. 75	**number** [ˈnʌmbə]	Anzahl	There are a **number** of big museums.
	high-tech [ˌhaɪˈtek]	Hightech-	I work for a **high-tech** company.
	studio [ˈstjuːdiəʊ]	Studio	They make movies in **studios**.
	safety net [ˈseɪfti ˌnet]	Sicherheitsnetz	There's a **safety net** to catch you.
	bay [beɪ]	Bucht	
	architect [ˈaːkɪtekt]	Architekt; Architektin	Ⓡ архитектор

Station 1

Adjectives for ads

informative [ɪnˈfɔːmətɪv]	informativ	**fascinating** [ˈfæsɪneɪtɪŋ]	faszinierend
clear [klɪə]	klar; eindeutig; deutlich	**unusual** [ʌnˈjuːʒl]	ungewöhnlich; außergewöhnlich
spectacular [spekˈtækjələ]	spektakulär	**appealing** [əˈpiːlɪŋ]	ansprechend
catchy [ˈkætʃi]	eingängig; einprägsam	**unappealing** [ˌʌnəˈpiːlɪŋ]	uninteressant

p. 76	**ad(vert) (advertisement)** [ˈæd(vɜːt) (ədˈvɜːtɪsmənt)]	Annonce; Werbespot	I saw an **advert** for a student job.
	surfboard [ˈsɜːfbɔːd]	Surfbrett	I have a new **surfboard**. Let's go surfing!
	to **chill out** [ˌtʃɪlˈaʊt]	chillen; sich entspannen	**Chill out** in sunny California.

reservation [ˌrezəˈveɪʃn]	Reservierung	T rezervasyon
to **book** [bʊk]	buchen; reservieren	We booked our **flights** yesterday.
lifetime [ˈlaɪftaɪm]	Leben; Lebenszeit	It will be the holiday of a **lifetime**.
tour [tʊə]	Tour; Fahrt; Reise	We went on the Grand Canyon **tour**.
p. 77 **layout** [ˈleɪaʊt]	Layout; Anordnung	Look at the **layout** of this ad.
headline [ˈhedlaɪn]	Überschrift; Schlagzeile	We need a good **headline** for our ad.

Station 2

Social media

social media [ˌsəʊʃl ˈmiːdiə]	soziale Medien	to **dislike** [dɪˈslaɪk]	nicht mögen
account [əˈkaʊnt]	Konto	to **friend** [frend]	befreunden (*jmdn. zu seiner Freundesliste hinzufügen*)
to **post** [pəʊst]	online stellen; posten		
video [ˈvɪdiəʊ]	Video		
tutorial [tjuːˈtɔːriəl]	Anleitung; Tutorial	to **unfriend** [ʌnˈfrend]	entfreunden (*jmdn. von seiner Freundesliste streichen*)
to **stream** [striːm]	*hier:* streamen (*im Internet*)		
smartphone [ˈsmɑːtˌfəʊn]	Smartphone	to **subscribe** [səbˈskraɪb]	abonnieren
site [saɪt]	*hier:* Seite (*im Internet*)	to **update** [ˈʌpdeɪt]	updaten; auf den neuesten Stand bringen
		status [ˈsteɪtəs]	Status
cyberbullying [ˈsaɪbəˌbʊliɪŋ]	Cyber-Mobbing	**selfie** [ˈselfi]	Selfie (*Schnappschuss von sich selbst*)

p. 80 to **welcome** [ˈwelkəm]	willkommen heißen	California **welcomes** new ideas.
for [fɔː]	seit	I have lived here **for** two months.
to **be around** [bi: əˈraʊnd]	geben; existieren	The WWW has **been around** for 30 years.
since [sɪns]	seit; seitdem	I have lived here **since** March.
trend [trend]	Trend; Entwicklung; Richtung	There are always new **trends** to follow.
impact [ˈɪmpækt]	Einfluss; Auswirkung	Social media had a big **impact** on us.
instead [ɪnˈsted]	stattdessen; anstelle von	I don't like ham, let's have cheese **instead**.
half (*sg*) [hɑːf], **halves** (*pl*) [hɑːvz]	(die) Hälfte	**half** a lemon
several [ˈsevrl]	einige; mehrere; verschiedene	**several** = three or more, but not many
right away [ˌraɪt əˈweɪ]	sofort; gleich	I answer my messages **right away**.

p. 81	**jumping fitness** [ˈdʒʌmpɪŋ ˌfɪtnəs]	Jumping Fitness *(Trendsportart)*	**Jumping fitness** is a new sport.
	outdated [ˌaʊtˈdeɪtɪd]	veraltet	Listening to CDs is very **outdated**.
	cartoon [kɑːˈtuːn]	Cartoon; Zeichentrickfilm	The **cartoon** was so funny, wasn't it?
p. 83	**torn** [tɔːn]	zerrissen; aufgerissen	The jeans are **torn**.
	veganism *(no pl)* [ˈviːgənɪzm]	Veganismus	T veganizm

Reading corner

p. 84	**gold rush** [ˈgəʊld ˌrʌʃ]	Goldrausch	Everyone wanted gold in the **gold rush**.
	report [rɪˈpɔːt]	Bericht	T rapor
	to **confirm** [kənˈfɜːm]	bestätigen; bekräftigen	Can you **confirm** when you arrive?
	discovery [dɪˈskʌvri]	Entdeckung	I made an awesome **discovery** – gold!
	Swiss [swɪs]	schweizerisch; aus der Schweiz; Schweizer; Schweizerin	He was a **Swiss** immigrant.
	businessman [ˈbɪznɪsmæn]	Geschäftsmann	R бизнесмен
	official [əˈfɪʃl]	offiziell	It was his **official** name.
	landowner [ˈlændˌəʊnə]	Grundbesitzer; Grundbesitzerin	He owns the land, he's the **landowner**.
	to **allow** [əˈlaʊ]	erlauben; gestatten	He didn't **allow** us to say anything.
	to **prove** [pruːv]	beweisen	He has to **prove** he owns the land.
p. 85	**hunter** [ˈhʌntə]	Jäger; Jägerin	Gold **hunters** came to California.
	rain [reɪn]	Regen	**rain** → to rain
	jungle [ˈdʒʌŋgl]	Dschungel	
	wilderness [ˈwɪldənəs]	Wildnis	Our camp was in the **wilderness**.
	all over [ˌɔːlˈəʊvə]	überall	There's food **all over** the floor.
	to **return** [rɪˈtɜːn]	zurückkehren	My friends had to **return** home.
	love [lʌv]	Liebe	**love** → to love
	to **keep going** [kiːp ˈgəʊɪŋ]	weitergehen; weitermachen	I will **keep going** until I find more gold.
	prayer [preə]	Gebet	Say a **prayer** for me on Sunday.
	wife *(sg)* [waɪf], **wives** *(pl)* [waɪvz]	Ehefrau	**wife** ↔ husband
p. 86	**encyclopedia** *(AE)* [ɪnˌsaɪkləˈpiːdiə]	Enzyklopädie; Lexikon	✐ Achtung Schreibweise! en**cyc**lop**ed**ia
	entry [ˈentri]	Eintrag	What does the **entry** for Gold Rush say?
	event [ɪˈvent]	Ereignis; Veranstaltung	Many people watched the **events**.

transcontinental [ˌtræns͵kɒntɪ'nentl]	transkontinental (über den Kontinent hinweg)	**Transcontinental** trains make long journeys.
railway ['reɪlweɪ]	Eisenbahn	
slave [sleɪv]	Sklave; Sklavin	There were **slaves** before the Civil War.
fever ['fi:və]	Fieber	The gold rush is also called gold **fever**.
to last [lɑːst]	dauern; andauern; anhalten	My headache **lasted** for hours.
empty ['emti]	leer	**empty** ↔ full

Film corner

p. 89	helper ['helpə]	Helfer; Helferin	**helper** → to help → help
	as soon as [əz 'su:n͜əz]	sobald	**as soon as** → soon
	regular ['regjələ]	regelmäßig; normal; üblich; gleichmäßig	I work **regular** hours in my job.
	to **respect** [rɪ'spekt]	respektieren	I love and **respect** animals.
	energetic [͵enə'dʒetɪk]	tatkräftig	I am **energetic** and fit for the job.
	practical ['præktɪkl]	praktisch	I like making things, I'm **practical**.
	attitude ['ætɪtjuːd]	Einstellung; Haltung	I have a practical **attitude** to work.
	waitress ['weɪtrəs]	Kellnerin; Bedienung	She is a **waitress** in the new café.
	groceries (pl) ['grəʊsriz]	Lebensmittel	We buy our **groceries** at the supermarket.

Checkpoint

| technology [tek'nɒlədʒi] | Technologie | Japan [dʒə'pæn] | Japan |
| entertainment (no pl) [͵entə'teɪnmənt] | Unterhaltung | bamboo [͵bæm'bu:] | Bambus |

Communication skills

p. 94	podcast ['pɒdkɑːst]	Podcast	I got the new **podcast** last night.
	Thanks so much. [͵θæŋk͜səʊ 'mʌtʃ]	Vielen Dank.; Herzlichen Dank.	**Thanks so much** for your help!
	to **interrupt** [͵ɪntə'rʌpt]	unterbrechen	I have to **interrupt** here.

Word bank: Talking about a region

Which region?

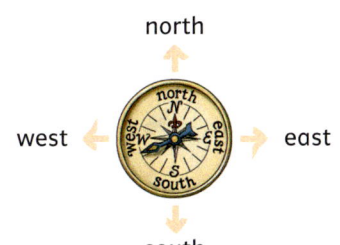

north

west ← → east

south

How many people live in the region/visit the region?

thousands   millions   billions

What does it look like?

mountains

beach

countryside

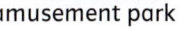

town

city

coastline

What can you do there?

museum

amusement park

zoo

church

skiing

shopping

hiking

sightseeing

It's in the … of …   … people live in the region/visit the region.
It's near the …   I like it because …
There are …   It's nice/quiet/busy/beautiful/…
There is …

Unit 5 Southern Life

p. 96	**southern** [ˈsʌðən]	südlich	**northern** ↔ southern

Way in

	African American [ˌæfrɪkən əˈmerɪkən]	Afroamerikaner; Afroamerika-nerin	There were lots of **African Americans** in the South.
	right [raɪt]	Recht	African Americans wanted the same **rights**.
	civil rights *(pl)* [ˌsɪvl ˈraɪts]	Bürgerrechte	They fought for **civil rights** in the 1950s.
	movement [ˈmuːvmənt]	Bewegung	The Civil Rights **Movement** changed people's rights.
	peaceful [ˈpiːsfl]	friedlich	Protests aren't always **peaceful**.
	protest [ˈprəʊtest]	Protest; Demonstration	Ⓡ протест
p. 97	**plantation** [plænˈteɪʃn]	Plantage	People had to work on the **plantations**.
	Southerner [ˈsʌðənə]	Südstaatler; Südstaatlerin	**Southern** → south → southern
	charts *(pl only)* [tʃɑːts]	*hier:* Hitparade	There are **charts** for different types of music.
	best-paid [ˈbestˌpeɪd]	bestbezahlt	He is the **best-paid** actor.

Station 1

Nationalities

the **French** *(pl)* [ðə ˈfrenʃ]	die Franzosen
Spanish [ˈspænɪʃ]	spanisch; Spanisch; aus Spanien
Vietnamese [ˌvjetnəˈmiːz]	vietnamesisch; Vietnamesisch; aus Vietnam; Vietnamese; Vietnamesin
Chinese [tʃaɪˈniːz]	chinesisch; Chine-sisch; aus China; Chinese; Chinesin
Greek [griːk]	griechisch; Griechisch; aus Griechenland
Russian [ˈrʌʃn]	russisch; Russisch; aus Russland; Russe; Russin
Polish [ˈpəʊlɪʃ]	polnisch; Polnisch; aus Polen
Turkish [ˈtɜːkɪʃ]	türkisch; Türkisch; aus der Türkei
Japanese [ˌdʒæpənˈiːz]	japanisch; Japanisch; aus Japan; Japaner; Japanerin

Conflicts and solutions

to **tolerate** ['tɒlreɪt]	tolerieren; dulden	to **accept** [ək'sept]	akzeptieren; annehmen; hinnehmen
solution [sə'luːʃn]	Lösung	**conflict** ['kɒnflɪkt]	Konflikt; Auseinandersetzung
compromise ['kɒmprəmaɪz]	Kompromiss	to **refuse** [rɪ'fjuːz]	ablehnen; sich weigern

p. 98	**influence** ['ɪnfluəns]	Einfluss	He is a bad **influence** on her.
	example [ɪg'zaːmpl]	Beispiel	Give me an **example** of a good book.
	to **mix** [mɪks]	mischen; vermischen; mixen	If you **mix** blue and yellow, you get green.
	to **dry** [draɪ]	trocknen	**to dry** → dry
	to **cover in flour** [ˌkʌvər ɪn 'flaʊə]	in Mehl wenden	First **cover** the chicken **in flour**.
	to **fry** [fraɪ]	braten; frittieren	
	oil [ɔɪl]	Öl	
	golden ['gəʊldn]	golden; Gold-	California is called 'The **Golden** State'.
	to **found** [faʊnd]	gründen	They **founded** the city in 1718.
	multicultural [ˌmʌltiˈkʌltʃrl]	multikulturell	The south is a **multicultural** area.
	carnival ['kaːnɪvl]	Karneval; Fasching	R карнавал T karnaval
	State House (AE) ['steɪt ˌhaʊs]	Regierungsgebäude	The US flag flies over the **State House**.
	pride [praɪd]	Stolz	This flag is a symbol of **pride**.
	racism ['reɪsɪzm]	Rassismus	Some say the flag is a symbol of **racism**.
	state government ['steɪt ˌgʌvnmənt]	Landesregierung	Protesters confronted the **state government**.
	to **remove** [rɪ'muːv]	entfernen	I **removed** the plaster from my knee.

Station 2

Understanding things

I didn't get that. [aɪ ˌdɪdnt 'get ðæt]	Ich habe es nicht verstanden.	**I didn't catch that.** [aɪ ˌdɪdnt 'kætʃ ðæt]	Das habe ich nicht verstanden.; Das habe ich nicht gehört.
I know what you mean. [aɪ ˌnəʊ wɒt jə 'miːn]	Ich verstehe, was du meinst.	**Absolutely!** [ˌæbsə'luːtli]	Auf jeden Fall!
I see. [aɪ 'siː]	Ich verstehe.		

p. 102	**package** ['pækɪdʒ]	Paket	T paket
	transfer [træns'fɜː]	Transport; Transfer	There is a free **transfer** by bus.
	track [træk]	Strecke	The race **track** isn't far away.
	booklet ['bʊklət]	Broschüre; Heft	
	detail ['diːteɪl]	Detail; Einzelheit	T detay
	airboat ['eəbəʊt]	Propellerboot	We can go on an **airboat** there.
	wildlife ['waɪldlaɪf]	Tierwelt *(in freier Wildbahn)*	There is lots of **wildlife** in Florida.
	show [ʃəʊ]	Show; Schau; Aufführung	There is a **show** every 30 minutes.
	pick-up ['pɪkʌp]	Abholung; Pick-up	Look, there is a free hotel **pick-up** too.
	trail [treɪl]	Wanderweg; Spur	There is a **trail** through the swamps.
	the wild [ðə 'waɪld]	Wildnis; freie Wildbahn	I've never seen a cat in **the wild**.
	heat [hiːt]	Hitze	This **heat** is too much for me.
	speech impaired ['spiːtʃ ɪmˌpeəd]	sprachbehindert	He can't speak, he's **speech impaired**.
	to translate [trænz'leɪt]	übersetzen	I can **translate** the text for you.
p. 103	**trainer** ['treɪnə]	Trainer; Trainerin	The **trainer** fed the alligators.

Reading corner

p. 106	**segregation** [ˌsegrɪ'geɪʃn]	Rassentrennung; Trennung	Not everyone believed in **segregation**.
	African-American [ˌæfrɪkənə'merɪkən]	afroamerikanisch	Obama was the first **African-American** president of the USA.
	to get on (the bus) [ˌget 'ɒn]	einsteigen (in den Bus)	A police officer **got on** the bus.
	full [fʊl]	voll	**full** ↔ empty
	seat [siːt]	Sitz; Sitzplatz	If we book early, we'll get good seats.
	back [bæk]	Hinterteil	We moved to the **back** of the bus.

p. 107	to drag [dræg]	schleppen; schleifen; ziehen	They **dragged** him away from the dog.
	off [ɒf]	von … weg	They pulled the dog **off** the man.
	to **arrest** [əˈrest]	festnehmen; verhaften	She was **arrested** by the police.
	success [səkˈses]	Erfolg	**success** → successful
	court case [ˈkɔːt ˌkeɪs]	Gerichtsverhandlung; Rechtsfall	The **court case** ended segregation.
	witness [ˈwɪtnəs]	Zeuge; Zeugin	She saw it, she was a **witness**.
	to **end** [end]	enden	The court case **ended** segregation.
	role [rəʊl]	Rolle	I played an important **role** in the fight.
	courage [ˈkʌrɪdʒ]	Mut; Tapferkeit; Courage	She showed a lot of **courage** on the bus.

Film corner

p. 109	**reliable** [rɪˈlaɪəbl]	verlässlich; zuverlässig; vertrauenswürdig	She's very **reliable**. She's always on time.
	to **trust** [trʌst]	vertrauen	She's reliable and you can **trust** her.

Checkpoint

feature story [ˈfiːtʃə ˌstɔːri]	Leitartikel; Sonderbericht

Word bank: **Talking about culture**

influences

Jewish

Christian

Catholic

Protestant

Islam

Muslim

music

traditional music

rock

techno

pop

hip hop

RnB

country music

jazz

kebab

sushi

paella

fish `n` chips

food

sweet and
sour with rice

sausages and
potato salad

culture

pasta

moussaka

cevapcici

language/
nationality

English

French

Greek

Polish

Arabic

Japanese

German

Italian

Russian

Vietnamese

Romanian

Chinese

Spanish

Swiss

Croatian

Serbian

Turkish

Syrian

Word bank: **A day trip**

opening times

all day   half day
from 9:00 a.m. until 5:00 p.m.
weekends only
last entry one hour before closing time
afternoons/morning only
closed on Mondays

tickets

adults   £ 10.00
children (under 14)   £ 5.00
senior citizens/OAPs   £ 5.00
students   £ 5.00
family (2 adults + 2 children) £ 17.50

places

museum

zoo

amusement/
theme park

city

beach

transport

coach

train

tram

car

bike

boat

activities

hiking

sightseeing

fishing

a guided tour

cycling

Instructions

Act the dialogue • the role play.	**Spielt** den Dialog • das Rollenspiel.
Add more words.	**Ergänze** mehr Wörter.
Answer the questions.	**Beantworte** die Fragen.
Ask a partner.	**Frage** eine Partnerin / einen Partner.
Check the sentences.	**Überprüfe** die Sätze.
Choose one of the tasks • the right answer.	**Wähle** eine der Aufgaben • die richtige Antwort **aus**.
Collect ideas.	**Sammle** Ideen.
Compare with your partner.	**Vergleicht** zu zweit.
Complete the sentences • the dialogue.	**Vervollständige** die Sätze • den Dialog.
Copy the list.	**Schreibe** die Liste **ab**.
Correct the wrong sentences.	**Verbessere** die falschen Sätze.
Decide on the best order.	**Entscheide dich für** die beste Reihenfolge.
Describe the picture.	**Beschreibe** das Bild.
Discuss in groups.	**Besprecht euch** in Gruppen.
Draw a picture.	**Zeichne** ein Bild.
Exchange your lists.	**Tauscht** eure Listen **aus**.
Explain the rules.	**Erkläre** die Regeln.
Finish the sentences.	**Vervollständige** die Sätze.
Give feedback.	**Gib** Rückmeldung.
Give reasons.	**Gib** Gründe **an**.
Guess.	**Überlege.**
Interview your partner.	**Interviewe** deine Partnerin / deinen Partner.
Label the picture.	**Beschrifte** das Bild.
Listen to the dialogue.	**Höre** dir den Dialog **an**.
Look at the photos • pictures (again).	**Schau** dir die Fotos • Bilder (noch einmal) **an**.
Make a list • a chart • a mind map.	**Erstelle** eine Liste • eine Tabelle • ein Wörternetz.
Make notes.	**Mache** dir **Stichpunkte**.
Make up more verses.	**Denke dir** weitere Strophen **aus**.
Match the sentences with the pictures.	**Ordne** den Bildern die richtigen Sätze **zu**.
Name the place.	**Nenne** den Ort.
Plan your role play.	**Plant** euer Rollenspiel.
Practise with a partner.	**Übe** mit einer Partnerin / einem Partner.
Present your profile to the class.	**Stelle** dein Profil deiner Klasse **vor**.
Put in the right verbs.	**Setze** die richtigen Verben **ein**.
Put the words **in the right order**.	**Bringe** die Wörter **in die richtige Reihenfolge**.
Read the story **again**.	**Lies** die Geschichte **noch einmal**.
Record your dialogue.	**Nehmt** euren Dialog **auf**.

Rewrite the sentences.	**Schreibe** die Sätze **um**.
Say how you feel.	**Sage**, wie du dich fühlst.
Show your text to a partner.	**Zeige** deinen Text einer Partnerin / einem Partner.
Sort the words **into groups**.	**Sortiere** die Wörter **in Gruppen**.
Take notes.	**Mache dir Notizen**.
Talk about the photos.	**Rede** über die Fotos.
Tell the class.	**Erzähle** es der Klasse.
Think about the story.	**Denke über** die Geschichte **nach**.
Think of a number.	**Denke** dir eine Nummer **aus**.
Use your own ideas.	**Benutze** deine eigenen Ideen.
Watch the film.	**Schau** den Film **an**.
Write a poem • a heading • a draft.	**Schreibe** ein Gedicht • einen Titel • einen Entwurf.

Classroom phrases

You and your teacher

I'm sorry I'm late.	Tut mir leid, dass ich mich verspätet habe.
I'm sorry I don't have my exercise book.	Tut mir leid, ich habe mein Heft nicht dabei.
What's the homework?	Was haben wir als Hausaufgabe auf?
Can you help me, please?	Können Sie / Kannst du mir bitte helfen?
Can you say that again, please?	Können Sie / Kannst du das bitte wiederholen?
Can I go to the toilet, please?	Kann ich bitte auf Toilette gehen?
Mr / Mrs / Miss …, I don't feel well.	Herr / Frau …, mir geht es nicht gut.
What page is it, please?	Auf welcher Seite ist das?
What's the German / English word for …?	Was ist das deutsche / englische Wort für …?
How do you spell …?	Wie schreibt man …?
What does that mean?	Was heißt / bedeutet das?
Sorry, I don't understand / I don't know.	Tut mir leid, ich verstehe das nicht / ich weiß es nicht.

Working together

Can we work in pairs / groups?	Können wir zu zweit / in Gruppen arbeiten?
Do you want to work with me / us?	Willst du / Wollt ihr mit mir / uns arbeiten?
Let's make a / draw a …	Lass(t) uns ein … machen / zeichnen.
Whose turn is it? – It's my / your turn.	Wer ist dran? – Ich bin dran. / Du bist dran.

Your teacher can say …

Turn to page …	Schlagt Seite … auf.
Look at the board.	Schaut an die Tafel.
Put your hands up, please!	Meldet euch, bitte!
Try again!	Versuche es noch einmal.

List of irregular verbs

Hier findest du alle unregelmäßigen Verben, die im Buch vorkommen. Die Liste enthält jeweils alle drei Formen, auch wenn sie noch nicht alle in den Units vorgekommen sind.

infinitive	simple past	past participle	German
be [biː]	was, were [wɒz, wɜː]	been [biːn]	sein
beat [biːt]	beat [biːt]	beaten [ˈbiːtn]	schlagen; besiegen
become [bɪˈkʌm]	became [bɪˈkeɪm]	become [bɪˈkʌm]	werden
begin [bɪˈgɪn]	began [bɪˈgæn]	begun [bɪˈgʌn]	beginnen; anfangen
bleed [bliːd]	bled [bled]	bled [bled]	bluten
break [breɪk]	broke [brəʊk]	broken [ˈbrəʊkn]	brechen
bring [brɪŋ]	brought [brɔːt]	brought [brɔːt]	bringen; mitbringen
build [bɪld]	built [bɪlt]	built [bɪlt]	bauen
burn [bɜːn]	burned/burnt [bɜːnt]	burned/burnt [bɜːnt]	brennen
buy [baɪ]	bought [bɔːt]	bought [bɔːt]	kaufen
choose [tʃuːz]	chose [tʃəʊz]	chosen [ˈtʃəʊzn]	auswählen; wählen
come [kʌm]	came [keɪm]	come [kʌm]	kommen
cost [kɒst]	cost [kɒst]	cost [kɒst]	kosten
cut [kʌt]	cut [kʌt]	cut [kʌt]	(sich) schneiden
do [duː]	did [dɪd]	done [dʌn]	machen; tun
draw [drɔː]	drew [druː]	drawn [drɔːn]	zeichnen
dream [driːm]	dreamed/dreamt [dremt]	dreamed/dreamt [dremt]	träumen
drink [drɪŋk]	drank [dræŋk]	drunk [drʌŋk]	trinken
drive [draɪv]	drove [drəʊv]	driven [ˈdrɪvn]	fahren; treiben
eat [iːt]	ate [eɪt]	eaten [ˈiːtn]	essen
fall [fɔːl]	fell [fel]	fallen [ˈfɔːln]	fallen; hinfallen
feed [fiːd]	fed [fed]	fed [fed]	füttern; ernähren
feel [fiːl]	felt [felt]	felt [felt]	(sich) fühlen
fight [faɪt]	fought [fɔːt]	fought [fɔːt]	kämpfen; streiten
find [faɪnd]	found [faʊnd]	found [faʊnd]	finden
fly [flaɪ]	flew [fluː]	flown [fləʊn]	fliegen
forget [fəˈget]	forgot [fəˈgɒt]	forgotten [fəˈgɒtn]	vergessen
freeze [friːz]	froze [frəʊz]	frozen [ˈfrəʊzn]	frieren; gefrieren
get [get]	got [gɒt]	got [gɒt]	bekommen; werden
give [gɪv]	gave [geɪv]	given [ˈgɪvn]	geben
go [gəʊ]	went [went]	gone [gɒn]	gehen; fahren
grow [grəʊ]	grew [gruː]	grown [grəʊn]	anbauen; züchten; ziehen; wachsen
grow up [ˌgrəʊ ˈʌp]	grew up [ˌgruː ˈʌp]	grown up [ˌgrəʊn ˈʌp]	aufwachsen
hang [hæŋ]	hung [hʌŋ]	hung [hʌŋ]	hängen
have [hæv]	had [hæd]	had [hæd]	haben; besitzen
hear [hɪə]	heard [hɜːd]	heard [hɜːd]	hören
hide [haɪd]	hid [hɪd]	hidden [ˈhɪdn]	verstecken

infinitive	simple past	past participle	German
hit [hɪt]	hit [hɪt]	hit [hɪt]	schlagen; treffen
hold [həʊld]	held [held]	held [held]	halten; festhalten
hurt [hɜːt]	hurt [hɜːt]	hurt [hɜːt]	verletzen; weh tun
keep [kiːp]	kept [kept]	kept [kept]	halten
know [nəʊ]	knew [njuː]	known [nəʊn]	wissen; kennen
know [nəʊ]	knew [njuː]	known [nəʊn]	wissen; kennen
lay [leɪ]	laid [leɪd]	laid [leɪd]	legen; (den Tisch) decken
leave [liːv]	left [left]	left [left]	verlassen; lassen; abfahren
lend [lend]	lent [lent]	lent [lent]	leihen; verleihen
lose [luːz]	lost [lɒst]	lost [lɒst]	verlieren
make [meɪk]	made [meɪd]	made [meɪd]	machen; tun; bilden
mean [miːn]	meant [ment]	meant [ment]	bedeuten; meinen
meet [miːt]	met [met]	met [met]	kennen lernen; (sich) treffen
pay [peɪ]	paid [peɪd]	paid [peɪd]	bezahlen
put [pʊt]	put [pʊt]	put [pʊt]	setzen; legen; stellen
read [riːd]	read [red]	read [red]	lesen
ride [raɪd]	rode [rəʊd]	ridden ['rɪdn]	fahren; reiten
ring [rɪŋ]	rang [ræŋ]	rung [rʌŋ]	klingeln; läuten
run [rʌn]	ran [ræn]	run [rʌn]	laufen; rennen
say [seɪ]	said [sed]	said [sed]	sagen; sprechen
see [siː]	saw [sɔː]	seen [siːn]	sehen
sell [sel]	sold [səʊld]	sold [səʊld]	verkaufen
send [send]	sent [sent]	sent [sent]	schicken; senden
shine [ʃaɪn]	shone [ʃɒn]	shone [ʃɒn]	glänzen; scheinen
shoot [ʃuːt]	shot [ʃɒt]	shot [ʃɒt]	schießen
show [ʃəʊ]	showed [ʃəʊd]	shown [ʃəʊn]	zeigen
sing [sɪŋ]	sang [sæŋ]	sung [sʌŋ]	singen
sink [sɪŋk]	sank [sæŋk]	sunk [sʌŋk]	untergehen; sinken
sit [sɪt]	sat [sæt]	sat [sæt]	sitzen
sleep [sliːp]	slept [slept]	slept [slept]	schlafen
smell [smel]	smelled/smelt [smelt]	smelled/smelt [smelt]	riechen
speak [spiːk]	spoke [spəʊk]	spoken ['spəʊkn]	sprechen
spell [spel]	spelled/spelt [spelt]	spelled/spelt [spelt]	buchstabieren
spend [spend]	spent [spent]	spent [spent]	ausgeben; verbringen
stand [stænd]	stood [stʊd]	stood [stʊd]	stehen
steal [stiːl]	stole [stəʊl]	stolen ['stəʊlən]	stehlen
sweep [swiːp]	swept [swept]	swept [swept]	fegen
swim [swɪm]	swam [swæm]	swum [swʌm]	schwimmen

infinitive	simple past	past participle	German
take [teɪk]	took [tʊk]	taken ['teɪkn]	nehmen; mitnehmen
tell [tel]	told [təʊld]	told [təʊld]	erzählen; sagen
think [θɪŋk]	thought [θɔːt]	thought [θɔːt]	denken; glauben
throw [θrəʊ]	threw [θruː]	thrown [θrəʊn]	werfen
understand [ˌʌndəˈstænd]	understood [ˌʌndəˈstʊd]	understood [ˌʌndəˈstʊd]	verstehen
wake up [weɪkˈʌp]	woke up [wəʊkˈʌp]	woken up [ˌwəʊknˈʌp]	aufwachen
wear [weə]	wore [wɔː]	worn [wɔːn]	tragen
win [wɪn]	won [wʌn]	won [wʌn]	gewinnen; siegen
write [raɪt]	wrote [rəʊt]	written [ˈrɪtn]	schreiben

Dictionary

Im Dictionary kannst du Wörter nachschlagen!

Im *Dictionary* sind alle wichtigen Wörter aus deinem Buch enthalten. Die Wörter stehen in alphabetischer Reihenfolge. Englische Wörter schlägst du ab S. 213 nach, deutsche Wörter ab S. 257.

Die Abkürzungen geben an, wo das Wort zum ersten Mal im Buch erscheint.

account	[əˈkaʊnt]	Konto	IV	U4	80
englisches Wort	Aussprache	deutsche Übersetzung	Band 4	Unit 4	Seite 80

Die mit einem Sternchen (*) gekennzeichneten Verben sind unregelmäßige Verben (→ *List of irregular verbs*, S. 210 – 212).

Manche Wörter haben verschiedene Bedeutungen. Am besten liest du alle, bevor du dich für eine entscheidest.

practice [ˈpræktɪs] Training; Übung I[1]
addicted [əˈdɪktɪd] süchtig <IV U3, 73>[3]

*to **spend** [spend] ausgeben *(Geld)*; verbringen *(Zeit)* II[1]
accident [ˈæksɪdnt] Unfall III[1]

appealing [əˈpiːlɪŋ] ansprechend IV U4, 77[2]
address [əˈdres] Adresse II[2]

1 Lernwortschatz für alle: schwarz; 2 Differenzierungswortschatz: blau; 3 kein Lernwortschatz: < >

A

a [ə] ein, eine I
  a bit [ə ˈbɪt] ein bisschen; ein wenig II
  a few [ə ˈfjuː] ein paar; wenige; einige III
  a five minute walk [ə ˈfaɪv mɪnɪt ˌwɔːk] fünf Minuten zu Fuß III
  a little [ə ˈlɪtl] ein bisschen II
  a lot [ə ˈlɒt] viel I; sehr II
  a lot of [ə ˈlɒt ˌəv] viel(e); eine Menge I
  a pair of [ə ˈpeər ˌəv] ein Paar II
  a/one hundred [ˈhʌndrəd] einhundert; hundert I
  a/one thousand [ə/wʌn ˈθaʊznd] eintausend; tausend II
a.m. [ˌeɪˈem] vormittags *(Uhrzeit)* II
*to be **able** [bi: ˈeɪbl] fähig sein; können; dürfen <IV U1, 24>

about [əˈbaʊt] über I; ungefähr; circa; etwa II
  to be about [bi: əˈbaʊt] gehen um; handeln von III
  out and about [ˌaʊt ˌən əˈbaʊt] unterwegs I
to **abseil** [ˈæbseɪl] sich abseilen II
absolutely [ˌæbsəˈluːtli] absolut; völlig IV U3, 59
to **accept** [əkˈsept] akzeptieren; annehmen; hinnehmen IV U5, 99
accident [ˈæksɪdnt] Unfall III
account [əˈkaʊnt] Konto IV U4, 80
stomach **ache** [ˈstʌmək ˌeɪk] Bauchweh; Bauchschmerzen II
across [əˈkrɒs] über; hinüber; herüber; quer durch IV U3, 54
to **act** [ækt] spielen II
acting [ˈæktɪŋ] Schauspielen; Schauspielerei III
  acting workshop [ˈæktɪŋ ˌwɜːkʃɒp] Schauspielworkshop II

Action! [ˈækʃn] Achtung, Aufnahme <III>
active [ˈæktɪv] aktiv <IV U3, 72>
activity [ækˈtɪvəti] Aktivität I
  activity centre [ækˈtɪvəti ˌsentə] Jugendzentrum III
actor [ˈæktə] Schauspieler; Schauspielerin II
actually [ˈæktʃuəli] tatsächlich; wirklich; eigentlich III
adaptor [əˈdæptə] Adapter III
to **add** [æd] hinzufügen II
addicted [əˈdɪktɪd] süchtig <IV U3, 72>
chemical **additive** [ˌkemɪkl ˈædətɪv] chemischer Zusatzstoff <IV U3, 72>
address [əˈdres] Adresse II
adjective [ˈædʒɪktɪv] Adjektiv; Eigenschaftswort III
adult [ˈædʌlt] Erwachsene; Erwachsener III
adventure [ədˈventʃə] Abenteuer I
adverb [ˈædvɜːb] Adverb <III>

adverb

ad(vert)

ad(vert) (= advertisement) [ˈæd(vɜːt) (ədˈvɜːtɪsmənt) Annonce; Werbespot IV U4, 76

advertisement [ədˈvɜːtɪsmənt] Anzeige; Werbespot II

advice [ədˈvaɪs] Rat; Ratschlag III

afraid [əˈfreɪd] ängstlich II
to be afraid [biː əˈfreɪd] sich fürchten; Angst haben II

African American [ˌæfrɪkən əˈmerɪkən] Afroamerikaner; Afroamerikanerin IV U5, 96

African-American [ˌæfrɪkənəˈmerɪkən] afroamerikanisch IV U5, 106

after [ˈɑːftə] nach I; danach; später III
after that [ˈɑːftə ðət] danach I

afternoon [ˌɑːftəˈnuːn] Nachmittag I
in the afternoon [ˌɪn ði ˌɑːftəˈnuːn] nachmittags I

again [əˈgen] wieder; noch einmal II

against [əˈgenst] gegen II

age [eɪdʒ] Alter I

ago [əˈgəʊ] vor II

to **agree** [əˈgriː] zustimmen II
to agree (on) [əˈgriː (ɒn)] sich einigen (auf) <III>
to agree (with) [əˈgriː (wɪð)] einer Meinung sein (mit); zustimmen III

right **ahead** [ˌraɪt əˈhed] geradeaus IV U1, 15

ain't (= isn't/aren't) [eɪnt] ist nicht; sind nicht <IV U1, 19>

air [eə] Luft IV U1, 22

airboat [ˈeəbəʊt] Propellerboot IV U5, 102

airport [ˈeəpɔːt] Flughafen II

alarm clock [əˈlɑːm ˌklɒk] Wecker I

Alaskan [əˈlæskən] Alaska-; alaskisch <IV U1, 30>

alcohol (no pl) [ˈælkəhɒl] Alkohol IV U3, 58

alcoholic [ˌælkəˈhɒlɪk] alkoholisch; Alkohol- <IV U3, 72>

alert [əˈlɜːt] Alarm <IV U1, 30>

algebra [ˈældʒɪbrə] Algebra <IV U2, 48>

alien [ˈeɪliən] Außerirdischer; Außerirdische I

alive [əˈlaɪv] am Leben III

all [ɔːl] alle I; ganz II
all alone [ˌɔːl əˈləʊn] ganz allein I
all day [ˌɔːl ˈdeɪ] den ganzen Tag III
all over [ˌɔːl ˈəʊvə] überall IV U4, 85
all right [ˌɔːl ˈraɪt] in Ordnung; alles klar II

allegiance [əˈliːdʒns] Treue IV U2, 45
pledge of allegiance [ˌpledʒ əv əˈliːdʒns] Treueeid IV U2, 45

allergic to [əˈlɜːdʒɪk tə] allergisch gegen II

allergy [ˈælədʒi] Allergie II

alligator [ˈælɪgeɪtə] Alligator IV ZI, 9

to **allow** [əˈlaʊ] erlauben; gestatten IV U4, 84
to be allowed to (do sth) [biː əˈlaʊd tə] (etw.) dürfen IV U2, 34

almost [ˈɔːlməʊst] fast; beinahe III

alone [əˈləʊn] allein I
all alone [ˌɔːl əˈləʊn] ganz allein I

along [əˈlɒŋ] entlang I

alphabet [ˈælfəbet] Alphabet I

already [ɔːlˈredi] schon; bereits II

also [ˈɔːlsəʊ] auch I

always [ˈɔːlweɪz] immer I

amazing [əˈmeɪzɪŋ] unglaublich; toll; erstaunlich II

ambition [æmˈbɪʃn] Ziel II; Ehrgeiz; Streben; Ambitionen <IV U3, 139>

ambulance [ˈæmbjələns] Krankenwagen III

American [əˈmerɪkən] amerikanisch; Amerikanisch; aus Amerika; Amerikaner; Amerikanerin IV ZI, 9
Native American [ˌneɪtɪv əˈmerɪkən] Ureinwohner Amerikas; Ureinwohnerin Amerikas; Indianer; Indianerin; indianisch IV U2, 32

the **Amish** [ði ˈɑːmɪʃ] die Amischen IV U3, 53

Amish [ˈɑːmɪʃ] amisch IV U3, 58

amount (of) [əˈmaʊnt (əv)] Menge; Summe <IV U1, 24>

amused [əˈmjuːzd] amüsiert; vergnügt IV U3, 63

amusement park [əˈmjuːzmənt ˌpɑːk] Freizeitpark <IV U4, 201>

an [ən] ein, eine I

and [ænd] und I

Anglo-American [ˌæŋgləʊəˈmerɪkən] anglo-amerikanisch <IV U5, 142>

angry [ˈæŋgri] wütend; zornig; verärgert; böse II

animal [ˈænɪml] Tier I
animal rescue shelter [ˌænɪml ˈreskjuː ˌʃeltə] Tierheim I

ankle [ˈæŋkl] Fußgelenk; Fußknöchel II

announcement [əˈnaʊnsmənt] Durchsage; Ankündigung II

annoyed [əˈnɔɪd] verärgert III

another [əˈnʌðə] ein anderer; noch ein II

answer [ˈɑːnsə] Antwort II

to **answer** [ˈɑːnsə] antworten; beantworten I
to answer the phone [ˈɑːnsə ðə ˈfəʊn] ans Telefon gehen III

antenna [ænˈtenə] Antenne III

any [ˈeni] irgendein; irgendwelche II
not … any [ˌnɒt … eni] kein II

anything [ˈeniθɪŋ] irgendetwas II
Anything else? [ˈeniθɪŋ els] Darf es sonst noch etwas sein? I
anything to drink [ˈeniθɪŋ tə ˈdrɪŋk] etwas zu trinken II

anyway [ˈeniweɪ] eigentlich IV U1, 14

anywhere [ˈeniweə] überall; irgendwo <IV U1, 19>

appealing [əˈpiːlɪŋ] ansprechend IV U4, 77

apple crumble [ˌæpl ˈkrʌmbl] Apfelauflauf (mit Streuseln bedeckt) II

to **apply** (for) [əˈplaɪ (fə)] sich bewerben (für/um) IV U2, 38

approval form [əˈpruːvl ˌfɔːm] Einverständnisformular <IV U2, 44>

April [ˈeɪprl] April I

Arabic [ˈærəbɪk] arabisch; Arabisch <IV U5, 206>

architect [ˈɑːkɪtekt] Architekt; Architektin IV U4, 75

archive [ˈɑːkaɪv] Archiv II

are [ɑː] bist; sind I

are required [rɪˈkwaɪəd] werden gebeten <IV U2, 48>

Are you serious? [ˌɑː ju ˈsɪərɪəs] Im Ernst? III

… are 99p. [ˌɑː ˈnaɪntnaɪn ˌpens] … kosten 99 Pence. I

area [ˈeəriə] Fläche; Gegend; Gebiet; Areal IV ZI, 9

argument [ˈɑːgjəmənt] Auseinandersetzung; Streit II; Argument <IV U3, 68>

arm [ɑːm] Arm I

armour [ˈɑːmə] Rüstung III

army [ˈɑːmi] Armee; Heer III

around [əˈraʊnd] herum; umher I; gegen; ungefähr um III; um … herum IV U1, 14

around the house [əˈraʊnd ðə haʊs] im Haus I

to be around [bi: əˈraʊnd] geben; existieren IV U4, 80

to get around [ˌget əˈraʊnd] herumkommen III

to **arrange** [əˈreɪndʒ] ausmachen; arrangieren <IV U1, 27>

to **arrest** [əˈrest] festnehmen; verhaften IV U5, 107

to **arrive** [əˈraɪv] ankommen II

Art [ɑːt] Kunst I

street art [ˈstriːt ɑːt] Straßenkunst IV U1, 13

article [ˈɑːtɪkl] Artikel; Bericht (in einer Zeitung) <IV U1, 21>

artist [ˈɑːtɪst] Künstler; Künstlerin <IV U1, 134>

as [æz] als II; wie II

as … as [əz … əz] so … wie II

as far as [ˌəz ˈfɑːr ˌəz] soweit IV U3, 59

as soon as [əz ˈsuːn ˌəz] sobald IV U4, 89

to **ask** [ɑːsk] fragen I

to ask about [ˈɑːsk əˌbaʊt] sich erkundigen nach; fragen nach II

to ask for [ˈɑːsk fɔː] bitten um II

to ask sb out [ˌɑːsk … ˈaʊt] sich mit jmdm. verabreden IV U2, 42

---

asking the way [ˈɑːskɪŋ ðə ˌweɪ] nach dem Weg fragen I

*to be **asleep** [bi: əˈsliːp] schlafen III

to fall asleep [ˌfɔːl əˈsliːp] einschlafen III

aspect [ˈæspekt] Aspekt; Gesichtspunkt; Blickwinkel <IV U1, 29>

to **assassinate** [əˈsæsɪneɪt] ermorden <IV U3, 138>

assistant [əˈsɪstnt] Verkäufer; Verkäuferin III

shop assistant [ˈʃɒp əˌsɪstnt] Verkäufer; Verkäuferin II

sales **associate** (AE) [ˌseɪlz əˈsəʊʃiət] Verkäufer; Verkäuferin IV U2, 38

astronomy [əˈstrɒnəmi] Astronomie IV U2, 34

at [æt] an; in; um; bei; auf I

at break [ət ˈbreɪk] in der Pause I

at home [ət ˈhəʊm] zu Hause I

at last [ət ˈlɑːst] endlich; zu guter Letzt II

at school [ət ˈskuːl] in der Schule I

at the back [ət ðə ˈbæk] hinten; am Ende; im hinteren Teil <IV ZI, 9>

at the front of [ət ðə ˈfrʌnt ˌəv] an der Spitze (von); im vorderen Bereich II

at the seaside [ət ðə ˈsiːsaɪd] am Meer I

at the weekend [ət ðə ˈwiːkend] am Wochenende I

at this stage [æt ðɪs ˈsteɪdʒ] zu diesem Zeitpunkt <IV U5, 108>

ate [eɪt] simple past von to eat II

atmosphere [ˈætməsfɪə] Atmosphäre; Stimmung <IV U5, 111>

to **attach** [əˈtætʃ] verbinden III

attack [əˈtæk] Angriff; Attacke IV U1, 12

to **attack** [əˈtæk] angreifen IV U2, 42

to **attend** [əˈtend] teilnehmen; anwesend sein; besuchen <IV U2, 48>

attic [ˈætɪk] Dachboden I

attitude [ˈætɪtjuːd] Einstellung; Haltung IV U4, 89

---

attorney [əˈtɜːni] Anwalt; Anwältin; Staatsanwalt; Staatsanwältin <IV U5, 108>

audition [ɔːˈdɪʃn] Vorspielen; Vorsprechen; Vorsingen; Vortanzen II

August [ˈɔːgəst] August I

in August [in ˈɔːgəst] im August I

aunt [ɑːnt] Tante II

autograph [ˈɔːtəgrɑːf] Autogramm IV U3, 53

to sign autographs [ˌsaɪn ˈɔːtəgrɑːfs] Autogramme geben IV U3, 53

avenue [ˈævənjuː] Allee; Boulevard IV U1, 14

average [ˈævrɪdʒ] durchschnittlich IV U3, 58

awake [əˈweɪk] bei Bewusstsein; wach III

away [əˈweɪ] weg; entfernt II

right away [ˌraɪt əˈweɪ] sofort; gleich IV U4, 80

awesome [ˈɔːsəm] super; spitze IV U2, 34

awful [ˈɔːfl] schrecklich; furchtbar I

B

baby [ˈbeɪbi] Baby II

babysitter [ˈbeɪbɪˌsɪtə] Babysitter; Babysitterin IV U2, 41

back [bæk] Rückseite <III>; Hinterteil IV U5, 106

at the back [ət ðə ˈbæk] hinten; am Ende; im hinteren Teil <IV ZI, 9>

back [bæk] Hinter- IV U3, 62

back [bæk] zurück I

back home [bæk ˈhəʊm] zu Hause II

background [ˈbækgraʊnd] Hintergrund III

in the background [in ðə ˈbækgraʊnd] im Hintergrund III

backpack [ˈbækpæk] Rucksack IV U3, 62

bad [bæd] schlecht I

bag [bæg] Tasche; Tüte; Sack I

bag

tea bag [ˈtiː ˌbæg] Teebeutel <IV U5, 113>

baggies (pl) (coll) [ˈbægiz] kurze Hosen (ugs.) <IV U4, 77>

bagpipes (pl) [ˈbægpaɪps] Dudelsack III

baguette [bægˈet] **Baguette** (Stangenweißbrot) <IV U5, 112>

pasta **bake** [ˌpæstə ˈbeɪk] Nudelauflauf II

baker [ˈbeɪkə] Bäcker; Bäckerin III
baker's [ˈbeɪkəz] Bäckerei III

bald eagle [ˌbɔːld ˈiːgl] Weißkopfseeadler IV ZI, 8

ball [bɔːl] Ball II
cannon ball [ˈkænən ˌbɔːl] Kanonenkugel II

balloon [bəˈluːn] Luftballon I

bamboo [bæmˈbuː] Bambus <IV U4, 90>

banana [bəˈnɑːnə] Banane I

band [bænd] Band; Musikgruppe II
brass band [ˌbrɑːs ˈbænd] Blaskapelle; Blasensemble <IV U5, 108>
marching band [ˈmɑːtʃɪŋ ˌbænd] Marschkapelle <IV U2, 190>
to start a band [ˌstɑːt ə ˈbænd] eine Band gründen II

bandage [ˈbændɪdʒ] Verband III

bar chart [ˈbɑː ˌtʃɑːt] Balkendiagramm; Säulendiagramm <IV U1, 27>

bar of chocolate [bɑːr əv ˈtʃɒklət] Tafel Schokolade I

barbecue [ˈbɑːbɪkjuː] Grill; Grillparty I

bargain [ˈbɑːgɪn] Schnäppchen II

barrel [ˈbærl] Fass; Tonne IV U3, 53

baseball [ˈbeɪsbɔːl] Baseball IV U1, 13

basic [ˈbeɪsɪk] grundlegend; einfach <IV U1, 24>

basketball [ˈbɑːskɪtbɔːl] Basketball II

bat [bæt] Fledermaus I

bathroom [ˈbɑːθrʊm] Badezimmer; Bad I

battle [ˈbætl] Kampf; Schlacht III

bay [beɪ] Bucht IV U4, 75

BC (= before Christ) [biːˈsiː] vor Christus <IV U2, 136>

*to **be** [biː] sein I

to be **able** [biː ˈeɪbl] fähig sein; können; dürfen <IV U1, 24>

to be **about** [biː əˈbaʊt] gehen um; handeln von III

to be **afraid** [biː əˈfreɪd] sich fürchten; Angst haben II

to be **allowed** to (do sth) [biː əˈlaʊd tə] (etw.) dürfen IV U2, 34

to be **around** [biː əˈraʊnd] geben; existieren IV U4, 80

to be **asleep** [biː əˈsliːp] schlafen III

to be **born** [biː ˈbɔːn] geboren werden III

to be **called** [biː ˈkɔːld] heißen; genannt werden II

to be **fed** up (with) [biː fed ˈʌp (wɪð)] die Nase voll haben (von); sauer sein III

to be **good** at [biː ˈgʊd ət] gut sein in/bei I

to be **homesick** [biː ˈhəʊmsɪk] Heimweh haben III

to be **interested** in [biː ˈɪntrəstɪd ɪn] sich interessieren für; interessiert sein an III

to be **known** as [biː ˈnəʊn əz] bekannt sein als <IV U3, 70>

to be **lucky** [biː ˈlʌki] Glück haben III

to be **made** of [biː ˈmeɪd əv] hergestellt sein aus III

to be **on** fire [biː ɒn ˈfaɪə] brennen II

to be **right** [biː ˈraɪt] recht haben II

to be **scared** [biː ˈskeəd] Angst haben; erschrocken sein II

to be **sick** [biː ˈsɪk] sich übergeben I

to be **sorry** [biː ˈsɒri] leidtun III

to be **stuck** [biː ˈstʌk] feststecken; nicht weg können I

to be **up** to [biː ˈʌp tə] vorhaben III
Be careful! [biː ˈkeəfl] Sei vorsichtig! I

beach [biːtʃ] Strand I
to go beach combing [gəʊ ˈbiːtʃ ˌkəʊmɪŋ] den Strand nach Strandgut absuchen II

kidney **bean** [ˈkɪdni ˌbiːn] Kidneybohne II

soy **bean** [ˈsɔɪ ˌbiːn] Sojabohne IV ZI, 9

bear [beə] Bär I
grizzly bear [ˈgrɪzli ˌbeə] Grizzlybär <IV U1, 30>

*to **beat** [biːt] besiegen; schlagen III

beat [biːt] simple past von to beat III

beaten [ˈbiːtn] past participle von to beat III

beautiful [ˈbjuːtɪfl] schön; hübsch I

became [bɪˈkeɪm] simple past von to become II

because [bɪˈkɒz] weil; da I
because of [bɪˈkɒz əv] wegen III

*to **become** [bɪˈkʌm] werden II

become [bɪˈkʌm] past participle von to become II

bed [bed] Bett I
bed and breakfast (B & B) [ˌbed ən ˈbrekfəst] Frühstückspension III
to go to bed [ˌgəʊ tə ˈbed] ins Bett gehen I

bedroom [ˈbedrʊm] Schlafzimmer; Kinderzimmer I

beef [biːf] Rindfleisch II
roast beef [ˌrəʊst ˈbiːf] Roastbeef; Rinderbraten <IV U5, 112>

been [biːn] past particple von to be II

before [bɪˈfɔː] vorher; zuvor II; bevor; bis zu II; vor IV U3, 61

began [bɪˈgæn] simple past von to begin IV U1, 18

*to **begin** [bɪˈgɪn] beginnen; anfangen IV U1, 18

beginner [bɪˈgɪnə] Anfänger; Anfängerin <IV U5, 143>

beginning [bɪˈgɪnɪŋ] Anfang; Beginn III

begun [bɪˈgʌn] past participle von to begin IV U1, 18

behind [bɪˈhaɪnd] hinter II
from behind [ˌfrəm bɪˈhaɪnd] von hinten I

to **believe** [bɪˈliːv] glauben II

bell [bel] Glocke II

bench [bentʃ] Bank; Sitzbank III

best [best] beste II

to like … best [ˌlaɪk 'best] am meisten mögen; am liebsten mögen I

Best wishes, [ˌbest 'wɪʃɪz] Viele Grüße, I

the best [ðə 'best] die besten II

best-paid ['best.peɪd] bestbezahlt IV U5, 97

best-paying [ˌbest'peɪɪŋ] bestbezahlt IV U2, 39

better ['betə] besser I

better quality food [betə 'kwɒləti ˌfuːd] qualitativ besseres Essen <IV U3, 72>

between [bɪ'twiːn] zwischen II

in between [ˌɪn bɪ'twiːn] dazwischen <IV U4, 92>

big [bɪɡ] groß I

big wheel [ˌbɪɡ 'wiːl] Riesenrad II

bike [baɪk] Fahrrad I

bill [bɪl] Rechnung III

to pay the bill [ˌpeɪ ðə 'bɪl] die Rechnung bezahlen III

billion ['bɪlɪən] Milliarde IV U1, 13

biography [baɪ'ɒɡrəfi] Biografie <III>

Biology [baɪ'ɒlədʒi] Biologie I

bird [bɜːd] Vogel I

bird watching ['bɜːd ˌwɒtʃɪŋ] Vogelbeobachtung III

birthday ['bɜːθdeɪ] Geburtstag I

Happy birthday! [ˌhæpi 'bɜːθdeɪ] Alles Gute zum Geburtstag! I

biscuit ['bɪskɪt] Keks II

dog biscuit ['dɒɡ ˌbɪskɪt] Hundekeks II

a bit [ə 'bɪt] ein bisschen; ein wenig II

black [blæk] schwarz I

blanket ['blæŋkɪt] Decke; Bettdecke; Wolldecke IV U3, 62

bled [bled] simple past, past participle von *to bleed* III

***to bleed** [bliːd] bluten III

blog [blɒɡ] Blog; Internettagebuch II

blond [blɒnd] blond <IV U4, 77>

bloody ['blʌdi] blutig <IV U2, 136>

blouse [blaʊz] Bluse I

***to blow** [bləʊ] wehen; blasen; pusten <IV U3, 71>

blue [bluː] blau I

blue cheese [ˌbluː 'tʃiːz] Schimmelkäse II

board [bɔːd] Tafel I; Brett <IV U3, 72>

on board ['ɒn bɔːd] an Bord III

boarding school ['bɔːdɪŋ ˌskuːl] Internat <IV U2, 137>

boat [bəʊt] Boot II

boat trip ['bəʊt ˌtrɪp] Bootsfahrt; Schiffsfahrt II

body ['bɒdi] Körper III; Leiche IV U3, 62

body lotion ['bɒdi ˌləʊʃn] Körperlotion III

to boil [bɔɪl] kochen <IV U5, 113>

boiling ['bɔɪlɪŋ] kochend <IV U5, 113>

book [bʊk] Buch; Heft I

exercise book ['eksəsaɪz ˌbʊk] Übungsheft I

to book [bʊk] buchen; reservieren IV U4, 76

booklet ['bʊklət] Broschüre; Heft IV U5, 102

to bookmark ['bʊkmaːk] zu … hinzufügen II

boot [buːt] Stiefel II; Schuh <IV U2, 50>

border ['bɔːdə] Grenze IV U3, 52

boring ['bɔːrɪŋ] langweilig I

***to be born** [bi: 'bɔːn] geboren werden III

borough ['bʌrə] Stadtteil; Bezirk IV U1, 12

to borrow ['bɒrəʊ] ausleihen II

boss [bɒs] Boss; Chef; Chefin II

both [bəʊθ] beide <IV U3, 68>

bottle ['bɒtl] Flasche I

bottle bank ['bɒtl bæŋk] Altglascontainer II

bought [bɔːt] simple past von *to buy* I; past participle von *to buy* II

bowl [bəʊl] Schale; Schälchen; Schüssel II

bowling ['bəʊlɪŋ] Bowlen IV U3, 58

box [bɒks] Box; Kiste; Schachtel I

telephone box ['telɪfəʊn ˌbɒks] Telefonzelle II

boy [bɔɪ] Junge I

boyfriend ['bɔɪfrend] Freund *(in einer Paarbeziehung)* IV U2, 42

brand [brænd] Marke III

brass band [ˌbraːs 'bænd] Blaskapelle; Blasensemble <IV U5, 108>

brave [breɪv] tapfer; mutig III

bread [bred] Brot II

sliced bread [ˌslaɪst 'bred] in Scheiben geschnittenes Brot III

break [breɪk] Pause I

at break [ət 'breɪk] in der Pause I

to take a break [ˌteɪk ə 'breɪk] Pause machen II

***to break** [breɪk] brechen; zerbrechen II

breakdancing ['breɪkdaːnsɪŋ] Breakdance <IV U1, 134>

breakfast ['brekfəst] Frühstück I

bed and breakfast (B & B) [ˌbed ən 'brekfəst] Frühstückspension III

to have breakfast [ˌhæv 'brekfəst] frühstücken I

breast [brest] Brust <IV U3, 72>

to breathe [briːð] atmen III

breathing ['briːðɪŋ] Atmung <IV U4, 88>

brewing time ['bruːɪŋ ˌtaɪm] Brühzeit <IV U5, 113>

brick [brɪk] Stein; Ziegelstein II

bridge [brɪdʒ] Brücke II

briefcase ['briːfkeɪs] Aktenkoffer; Aktentasche III

bright [braɪt] hell; leuchtend; strahlend IV ZI, 8

brilliant ['brɪlɪənt] toll I

***to bring** [brɪŋ] bringen; mitbringen II

to bring down [ˌbrɪŋ 'daʊn] herunterbringen <IV U2, 35>

British ['brɪtɪʃ] britisch II

broadcast ['brɔːdkaːst] Sendung; Ausstrahlung; Übertragung <IV U5, 97>

brochure ['brəʊʃə] Broschüre; Prospekt III

broke [brəʊk] simple past von *to break* II

broken ['brəʊkn] past participle von *to break* II

broken

brother ['brʌðə] Bruder I

brought [brɔːt] simple past von *to bring* II

brown [braʊn] braun I

bubble wrap ['bʌbl ˌræp] Luftpolsterfolie <IV U3, 71>

speech **bubble** ['spiːtʃ ˌbʌbl] Sprechblase <III>

bucket of water ['bʌkɪt əv ˌwɔːtə] Eimer Wasser I

buddy *(infml)* ['bʌdi] Kumpel IV U2, 45

buffalo ['bʌfləʊ] Büffel <IV U2, 136>

buffet ['bʊfeɪ] Büfett III

*to **build** [bɪld] bauen II

builder ['bɪldə] Bauarbeiter; Bauarbeiterin II

ship builder ['ʃɪp ˌbɪldə] Schiffsbauer; Schiffsbauerin III

building ['bɪldɪŋ] Gebäude II

built [bɪlt] simple past, past participle von *to build* II

light **bulb** ['laɪt ˌbʌlb] Glühbirne III

bullet ['bʊlɪt] Kugel; Geschoss IV U3, 63

burger ['bɜːgə] Hamburger II

burglar ['bɜːglə] Einbrecher; Einbrecherin I

*to **burn** [bɜːn] verbrennen; brennen III

to burn down [bɜːn 'daʊn] niederbrennen; verbrennen II

burnt [bɜːnt] simple past, past participle von *to burn* III

bus [bʌs] Bus I

bus stop ['bʌs ˌstɒp] Bushaltestelle II

on the bus [ɒn ðə 'bʌs] im Bus II

bushy ['bʊʃi] buschig <IV U4, 77>

business ['bɪznɪs] Geschäft; Branche <IV U2, 137>

businessman ['bɪznɪsmæn] Geschäftsmann IV U4, 84

busy ['bɪzi] beschäftigt; arbeitsreich I

a busy day [ə ˌbɪzi 'deɪ] ein ausgefüllter Tag I

but [bʌt] aber I

butcher's ['bʊtʃəz] Metzgerei III

butter ['bʌtə] Butter I

peanut butter [ˌpiːnʌt 'bʌtə] Erdnussbutter III

*to **buy** [baɪ] kaufen I

by [baɪ] von II; bis (spätestens) III; an IV U3, 63

by *(train)* [baɪ] mit *(dem Zug)* I

by the end [ˌbaɪ ðɪ 'end] am Schluss II

by yourself [baɪ 'jɔːself] allein II

Bye. [baɪ] Tschüss. I

C

cabbage ['kæbɪdʒ] Kohl; Kraut II

cable car ['keɪbl ˌkaː] Seilbahn IV U4, 74

café ['kæfeɪ] Café I

cafeteria [kæfə'tɪəriə] Cafeteria; Mensa I

cage [keɪdʒ] Käfig I

cake [keɪk] Kuchen I

to make a cake [ˌmeɪk ə 'keɪk] einen Kuchen backen I

piece of cake ['piːs əv keɪk] einfach <IV U3, 68>

calculator ['kælkjəleɪtə] Rechner; Taschenrechner I

call [kɔːl] Anruf; Ruf III

phone call ['fəʊn ˌkɔːl] Telefonanruf I

to **call** [kɔːl] rufen; anrufen I

to be called [bi 'kɔːld] heißen; genannt werden II

caller ['kɔːlə] Anrufer; Anruferin II

calorie ['kælri] Kalorie <IV U3, 72>

came [keɪm] simple past von *to come* I

camel ['kæml] Kamel I

camera ['kæmrə] Fotoapparat; Kamera <III>

camp [kæmp] Camp; Lager II

camping ['kæmpɪŋ] Camping; Zelten III

to go camping [ˌgəʊ 'kæmpɪŋ] campen gehen; zelten II

campsite ['kæmpsaɪt] Campingplatz; Zeltplatz III

campus ['kæmpəs] Campus; Hochschulgelände <IV U5, 110>

can [kæn] Dose I

can [kæn; kən] können I

can't [kaːnt] nicht können I

canary [kə'neəri] Kanarienvogel III

candle ['kændl] Kerze I

cannon ['kænən] Kanone II

cannon ball ['kænən ˌbɔːl] Kanonenkugel II

cannot ['kænɒt] nicht können III

canoe [kə'nuː] Kanu <IV U2, 136>

canoeing [kə'nuːɪŋ] Kanufahren I

canvas ['kænvəs] Leinwand <IV U1, 134>

cap [kæp] Kappe; Mütze I

capital (city) ['kæpɪtl (ˌsɪti)] Hauptstadt III

captain ['kæptɪn] Kapitän; Kapitänin I

caption ['kæpʃn] Untertitel; Bildunterschrift <II>

car [kaː] Auto I

caravan ['kærəvæn] Wohnwagen III

card [kaːd] Karte; Spielkarte I

playing card ['pleɪɪŋ ˌkaːd] Spielkarte <IV U4, 92>

prompt card ['prɒmt ˌkaːd] Stichwortkarte <IV U2, 51>

cardboard ['kaːdbɔːd] Pappe; Karton III

to **care** (for) ['keə (fə)] sich kümmern (um) III

career [kə'rɪə] Beruf; Laufbahn; Karriere IV U1, 18

careful ['keəfl] vorsichtig; sorgfältig II

Be careful! [bi 'keəfl] Sei vorsichtig! I

caretaker ['keəˌteɪkə] Hausmeister; Hausmeisterin I

carnival ['kaːnɪvl] Karneval; Fasching IV U5, 98

carpenter ['kaːpəntə] Zimmermann; Zimmerin; Tischler; Tischlerin II

carpet ['kaːpɪt] Teppich I

carrot ['kærət] Karotte II

to **carry** ['kæri] tragen; befördern II

cartoon [kɑːˈtuːn] Cartoon; Zeichen-trickfilm IV U4, 81

case [keɪs] Fall IV U5, 107

   court case [ˈkɔːt ˌkeɪs] Gerichtsver-handlung; Rechtsfall IV U5, 107

   pencil case [ˈpensl ˌkeɪs] Feder-mäppchen I

cash [kæʃ] (mit) Bargeld II

casino [kəˈsiːnəʊ] Kasino; Spielkasino <IV U2, 137>

cast [kɑːst] Gips III

castle [ˈkɑːsl] Schloss; Burg II

cat [kæt] Katze I

*to catch [kætʃ] fangen II; finden <IV U4, 77>

catchy [ˈkætʃi] eingängig; einpräg-sam IV U4, 77

category [ˈkætəgri] Kategorie <IV U4, 140>

catering college [ˈkeɪtərɪŋ ˌkɒlɪdʒ] Hotelfachschule II

cathedral [kəˈθiːdrl] Dom; Kathedrale <IV U1, 183>

Catholic [ˈkæθlɪk] Katholik; Katholi-kin; katholisch III

caught [kɔːt] simple past, past parti-ciple von to catch II

'cause (= because) [kɒz] weil <IV U2, 35>

cave [keɪv] Höhle II

ceiling [ˈsiːlɪŋ] Zimmerdecke I

to celebrate [ˈseləbreɪt] feiern I

celebration [ˌseləˈbreɪʃn] Feier IV U3, 52

cemetery [ˈsemətri] Friedhof <IV U5, 108>

center (AE) [ˈsentə] Zentrum; Mitte; Center IV U1, 13

centimetre (cm) [ˈsentɪˌmiːtə] Zenti-meter (cm) I

centre [ˈsentə] Zentrum; Mitte; Center III

   activity centre [ækˈtɪvəti ˌsentə] Jugendzentrum III

   city centre [ˌsɪti ˈsentə] Stadtzent-rum; Stadtmitte III

   shopping centre [ˈʃɒpɪŋ ˌsentə] Einkaufszentrum I

town centre [ˌtaʊn ˈsentə] Stadt-zentrum; Stadtmitte <IV U1, 15>

   in the centre of [ˌɪn ðə ˈsentər ˌəv] in der Mitte III

century [ˈsenʃri] Jahrhundert III

cereal [ˈsɪəriəl] Müsli; Cornflakes III

certain [ˈsɜːtn] bestimmte <IV U1, 24>

cevapcici [səˈvæpˈtʃətʃi] Cevapcici <IV U5, 206>

chair [tʃeə] Stuhl I

chalk [tʃɔːk] Kreide <IV U1, 28>

chance [tʃɑːns] Chance; Gelegenheit II; Möglichkeit IV U1, 18

change [tʃeɪndʒ] Münzgeld; Wech-selgeld II

to change [tʃeɪndʒ] wechseln II; ver-ändern; (sich) ändern; umsteigen III

   to change one's mind [tʃeɪndʒ wʌnz ˈmaɪnd] seine Meinung ändern III

chant [tʃɑːnt] Sprechgesang <I>

character [ˈkærəktə] Charakter; Figur <IV U1, 24>

charades [ʃəˈrɑːdz] Scharaden <II>

charger [ˈtʃɑːdʒə] Ladegerät III

chart [tʃɑːt] Diagramm; Tabelle <I>

   bar chart [ˈbɑː ˌtʃɑːt] Balken-diagramm; Säulendiagramm <IV U1, 27>

   pie chart [ˈpaɪ ˌtʃɑːt] Kuchen-diagramm; Tortendiagramm <IV U1, 26>

charts (pl only) [tʃɑːts] Hitparade IV U5, 97

chaser [ˈtʃeɪsə] Jäger; Jägerin; Verfol-ger; Verfolgerin IV U2, 33

video chat [ˈvɪdiəʊ ˌtʃæt] Video-Chat III

to chat [tʃæt] chatten; plaudern II

cheap [tʃiːp] billig II

check [tʃek] Kontrolle IV U1, 22

to check [tʃek] überprüfen; kontrol-lieren III

   to check in [ˌtʃek ˈɪn] einchecken III

   to check out [ˌtʃek ˈaʊt] auschecken III

checklist [ˈtʃeklɪst] Checkliste <I>

cheeky [ˈtʃiːki] frech III

to cheer sb up [ˌtʃɪər ˈʌp] jmdn. auf-heitern; jmdn. aufmuntern III

cheerleader [ˈtʃɪəˌliːdə] Cheerleader (Mädchen, das in einer Gruppe eine Sportmannschaft anfeuert) IV U2, 34

cheese [tʃiːz] Käse I

   blue cheese [ˌbluː ˈtʃiːs] Schimmel-käse II

cheesecake [ˈtʃiːskeɪk] Käsekuchen II

chef [ʃef] Koch; Köchin II

   head chef [ˈhed ˌʃef] Chefkoch; Chefköchin II

chemical additive [ˌkemɪkl ˈædətɪv] chemischer Zusatzstoff <IV U3, 72>

chewing gum [ˈtʃuːɪŋ ˌgʌm] Kau-gummi I

chic [ʃik] schick; elegant I

chicken [ˈtʃɪkɪn] Huhn I

child [tʃaɪld] Kind II

children (pl) [ˈtʃɪldrn] Kinder II

to chill out [ˌtʃɪl ˈaʊt] chillen; sich entspannen IV U4, 76

chilli [ˈtʃɪli] Chili II

Chinese [tʃaɪˈniːz] chinesisch; Chine-sisch; aus China; Chinese; Chinesin IV U5, 99

chips (pl) [tʃɪps] Pommes frites I

chocolate [ˈtʃɒklət] Schokolade I; Praline IV U3, 54

choice [tʃɔɪs] Auswahl; Wahl <IV U4, 77>

*to choose [tʃuːz] auswählen; wählen II

chorus [ˈkɔːrəs] Refrain <I>

chose [tʃəʊz] simple past von to choose II

chosen [ˈtʃəʊzn] past participle von to choose II

Christian [ˈkrɪstʃn] christlich IV U3, 53

Christmas [ˈkrɪsməs] Weihnachten I

church [tʃɜːtʃ] Kirche II

cinema [ˈsɪnəmə] Kino I

circle [ˈsɜːkl] Kreis; Ring III

citizen [ˈsɪtɪzn] Staatsbürger; Staats-bürgerin; Staatsangehöriger; Staatsangehörige IV U1, 18

citizenship [ˈsɪtɪznʃɪp]
Staatsangehörigkeit;
Staatsbürgerschaft <IV U1, 24>
city [ˈsɪti] Stadt; Großstadt II
city centre [ˌsɪti ˈsentə]
Stadtzentrum; Stadtmitte III
civil rights (pl) [ˌsɪvl ˈraɪts]
Bürgerrechte IV U5, 96
Civil War [ˌsɪvl ˈwɔː] Bürgerkrieg
<IV U3, 138>
to **clap** [klæp] klatschen <I>
class [klɑːs] Unterricht I; Klasse III;
Unterrichtsstunde; Kurs IV U2, 34
classmate [ˈklɑːsmeɪt]
Klassenkamerad;
Klassenkameradin; Mitschüler;
Mitschülerin <II>
classroom [ˈklɑːsrʊm]
Klassenzimmer I
to **clean** [kliːn] sauber machen;
putzen I
clean [kliːn] sauber I
vacuum **cleaner** [ˈvækjuːm ˌkliːnə]
Staubsauger IV U3, 59
to **clear** [klɪə] abräumen; ausräumen
IV U2, 33
to clear the table [ˌklɪə ðə ˈteɪbl]
den Tisch abräumen II
clear [klɪə] klar; eindeutig; deutlich
IV U4, 77
clever [ˈklevə] schlau; klug;
intelligent I
to **click** [klɪk] klicken I
to **climb** [klaɪm] besteigen; steigen;
klettern III
rock **climbing** [ˈrɒk ˌklaɪmɪŋ]
Klettern I
clock [klɒk] Uhr II
alarm clock [əˈlɑːm ˌklɒk] Wecker I
clock tower [ˈklɒk ˌtaʊə] Uhrenturm
II
o'clock [əˈklɒk] Uhr (Zeitangabe bei
vollen Stunden) I
to **close** [kləʊz] schließen;
zumachen I
close [kləʊs] in der Nähe; nahe
IV U3, 53

clothes (pl) [kləʊðz] Kleider (Pl.);
Kleidung I
cloud [klaʊd] Wolke IV U2, 33
cloudy [ˈklaʊdi] wolkig I
club [klʌb] Klub; Verein II
clubhouse [ˈklʌbhaʊs] Klubhaus;
Vereinsheim IV U3, 62
clue [kluː] Hinweis; Spur I
coach [kəʊtʃ] Trainer; Trainerin <III>;
Reisebus <IV U5, 207>
coal [kəʊl] Kohle III
coast [kəʊst] Küste III
on the coast [ˌɒn ðə ˈkəʊst] an der
Küste III
roller **coaster** [ˈrəʊlə ˌkəʊstə]
Achterbahn II
coastline [ˈkəʊstlaɪn] Küste <IV U4, 201>
coat [kəʊt] Jacke I
cocktail sauce [ˈkɒkteɪl ˌsɔːs]
Cocktailsoße <IV U5, 112>
coconut [ˈkəʊkənʌt] Kokosnuss II
dress **code** [ˈdres ˌkəʊd]
Kleiderordnung;
Bekleidungsvorschriften IV U2, 36
coin [kɔɪn] Münze III
coke [kəʊk] Cola I
cold [kəʊld] Kälte <IV U2, 136>
cold [kəʊld] kalt I
to get cold [ˌget ˈkəʊld] frieren III
coleslaw [ˈkəʊlslɔː] Krautsalat
<IV U5, 112>
collar [ˈkɒlə] Halsband I
to **collect** [kəˈlekt] sammeln I
college [ˈkɒlɪdʒ] College; Institut
IV U1, 19
catering college [ˈkeɪtərɪŋ ˌkɒlɪdʒ]
Hotelfachschule II
colonist [ˈkɒlənɪst] Kolonist;
Kolonistin; Siedler; Siedlerin
<IV U1, 24>
colony [ˈkɒləni] Kolonie <IV U3, 70>
color (AE) [ˈkʌlə] Farbe IV ZI, 8
colour [ˈkʌlə] Farbe I
coloured [ˈkʌləd] buntes <IV U3, 71>
colourful [ˈkʌləfl] bunt II
comb [ˈkəʊm] Kamm III
combination [ˌkɒmbɪˈneɪʃn]
Kombination II

*to **come** [kʌm] kommen I
Come on! [ˌkʌm ˈɒn] Komm jetzt! I
comedy [ˈkɒmədi] Komödie III
comfortable [ˈkʌmftəbl] bequem;
angenehm II
comic [ˈkɒmɪk] Comic(heft) II
comic strip [ˈkɒmɪk strɪp]
Comicstrip <IV U2, 42>
comment [ˈkɒment] Kommentar
IV U4, 80
to put a comment [ˌpʊt ə ˈkɒment]
einen Kommentar schreiben <I>
community [kəˈmjuːnəti] Gemeinde;
Gemeinschaft IV U1, 18
company [ˈkʌmpəni] Gesellschaft;
Firma II
to **compare** [kəmˈpeə] vergleichen I
comparison [kəmˈpærɪsn] Vergleich
<IV U2, 37>
competition [ˌkɒmpəˈtɪʃn]
Wettbewerb II; Konkurrenz
IV U2, 34
to **complain** [kəmˈpleɪn] sich
beschweren; sich beklagen
IV U1, 18
to **complete** [kəmˈpliːt]
vervollständigen I; absolvieren;
abschließen <IV U2, 44>
complete [kəmˈpliːt] vollständig
<IV U2, 48>
compromise [ˈkɒmprəmaɪz]
Kompromiss IV U5, 99
computer [ˌkəmˈpjuːtə] Computer I
to **concentrate** [ˈkɒnsntreɪt] (sich)
konzentrieren IV U3, 58
concert [ˈkɒnsət] Konzert II
to **conclude** [kənˈkluːd] schließen;
zusammenfassen <IV U3, 196>
conclusion [kənˈkluːʒn]
Schlussfolgerung; Schluss III
concrete [ˈkɒŋkriːt] Beton III
condition [kənˈdɪʃn] Bedingung;
Zustand IV U1, 22
confident [ˈkɒnfɪdnt] selbstsicher;
selbstbewusst III
to **confirm** [kənˈfɜːm] bestätigen;
bekräftigen IV U4, 84

conflict [ˈkɒnflɪkt] Konflikt;
Auseinandersetzung IV U5, 99

confused [kənˈfjuːzd] verwirrt; wirr III

Congratulations! [ˌkɒŋgrætjʊˈleɪʃnz]
Glückwunsch! II

to **connect** [kəˈnekt] verbinden III

connecting [kəˈnektɪŋ] verbindend
<II>

constant [ˈkɒnstənt] ständig;
konstant <IV U4, 88>

construction site [kənˈstrʌkʃn ˌsaɪt]
Baustelle IV U1, 15

contact [ˈkɒntækt] Kontakt
<IV U2, 136>
eye contact [aɪ ˈkɒntækt]
Augenkontakt <IV U2, 47>

to **contact** [ˈkɒntækt] sich in
Verbindung setzen; kontaktieren
<IV U2, 44>

content [ˈkɒntent] Inhalt III

to **continue** [kənˈtɪnjuː]
weitermachen <IV U3, 65>

to **contribute** [kənˈtrɪbjuːt] beitragen;
mitwirken <IV U2, 49>

to **control** [kənˈtrəʊl] kontrollieren
<IV U3, 68>

conversation [ˌkɒnvəˈseɪʃn]
Konversation; Gespräch;
Unterhaltung <IV U3, 55>

convinced [kənˈvɪnst] überzeugt
IV U3, 59

to **cook** [kʊk] kochen II

cooking [ˈkʊkɪŋ] Kochen II

to **cool** [kuːl] kühlen III; abkühlen
lassen <IV U5, 113>

cool [kuːl] cool; super; kühl I
to keep cool [ˌkiːp ˈkuːl] Ruhe
bewahren <III>

copy [ˈkɒpi] Kopie II; Abschrift <III>

to **copy** [ˈkɒpi] kopieren II;
abschreiben <III>

core subject [kɔː ˈsʌbdʒɪkt]
Pflichtfach IV U2, 35

corn [kɔːn] Korn; Mais; Getreide
IV ZI, 9

corner [ˈkɔːnə] Ecke III
corner shop [ˈkɔːnə ˌʃɒp] Tante-
Emma-Laden I

Cornish [ˈkɔːnɪʃ] Cornish; aus
Cornwall II

to **correct** [kəˈrekt] verbessern I

correct [kəˈrekt] richtig; korrekt <III>

corridor [ˈkɒrɪdɔː] Gang; Flur II

*to **cost** [kɒst] kosten III

cost [kɒst] simple past, past
participle von to cost III

costume [ˈkɒstjuːm] Kostüm I

cosy [ˈkəʊzi] gemütlich III

cottage [ˈkɒtɪdʒ] Häuschen III

cotton [ˈkɒtn] Baumwolle III

to **cough** [kɒf] husten III

could [kʊd] konnte; könnte III

countdown [ˈkaʊntdaʊn] Countdown
<I>

country [ˈkʌntri] ländliche Gegend;
Land I; Country (Musikrichtung)
IV U5, 97
country and western music [ˌkʌntri
ənd ˈwestən ˌmjuːzɪk] Countrymusik <IV U5, 143>
in the country [ɪn ðə ˈkʌntri] auf
dem Land I

countryside [ˈkʌntrisaɪd] Landschaft;
Land III

a **couple** of [ə ˈkʌpl əv] ein paar Mal
<IV U2, 47>

courage [ˈkʌrɪdʒ] Mut; Tapferkeit;
Courage IV U5, 107

course [kɔːs] Kurs III
main course [ˌmeɪn ˈkɔːs]
Hauptgericht II

of **course** [əv ˈkɔːs] natürlich;
selbstverständlich I

court [kɔːt] Spielfeld III; Gericht
IV U5, 107
court case [ˈkɔːt ˌkeɪs]
Gerichtsverhandlung; Rechtsfall
IV U5, 107

cousin [ˈkʌzn] Cousin; Cousine II

cover [ˈkʌvə] Cover; Titelblatt
<IV U3, 65>

to **cover** [ˈkʌvə] bedecken; abdecken
IV U3, 58
to cover in flour [ˌkʌvər ɪn ˈflaʊə] in
Mehl wenden IV U5, 98

cow [kaʊ] Kuh III

co-worker [ˈkəʊˌwɜːkə]
Arbeitskollege; Arbeitskollegin
IV U2, 38

cranberry [ˈkrænbri] Cranberry;
Preiselbeer- <IV U3, 72>

crazy [ˈkreɪzi] verrückt I
to drive sb crazy [draɪv … ˈkreɪzi]
jmdn. verrückt machen III

ice cream [aɪs ˈkriːm] Eiscreme; Eis I

to **create** [kriˈeɪt] machen <IV U2, 48>

credit [ˈkredɪt] Schein <IV U2, 48>

creepy [ˈkriːpi] gruselig IV U3, 53

crew [kruː] Crew; Besatzung;
Mannschaft III

cricket [ˈkrɪkɪt] Kricket II

crisp [krɪsp] Kartoffelchip I

critic [ˈkrɪtɪk] Kritiker; Kritikerin
<IV U1, 28>

Croatian [krəʊˈeɪʃn] kroatisch;
Kroatisch; aus Kroatien; Kroate;
Kroatin <IV U5, 206>

crocodile [ˈkrɒkədaɪl] Krokodil I

to **cross** [krɒs] überqueren III

crowd [kraʊd] Menschenmenge II

crowded [ˈkraʊdɪd] überfüllt IV U1, 22

crushed ice [ˈkrʌʃt ˌaɪs] zerstoßenes
Eis <IV U5, 113>

Cuban [ˈkjuːbən] kubanisch; aus
Kuba; Kubaner; Kubanerin IV U1, 18

cuddly [ˈkʌdli] knuddelig III
cuddly toy [ˈkʌdli ˌtɔɪ] Kuscheltier
III

cultural [ˈkʌltʃrl] kulturell <IV U1, 134>

culture [ˈkʌltʃə] Kultur IV U1, 13

cup [kʌp] Tasse II

cupboard [ˈkʌbəd] Schrank III

currency [ˈkʌrnsi] Währung IV ZI, 8

curry [ˈkʌri] Curry II

custard [ˈkʌstəd] Vanillesauce II

customer [ˈkʌstəmə] Kunde; Kundin
III

*to **cut** [kʌt] (sich) schneiden II

cut [kʌt] simple past, past participle
von to cut II

cute [kjuːt] niedlich; süß I

CV (= Curriculum Vitae) [ˌsiːˈviː]
Lebenslauf <IV U2, 48>

CV

cyberbullying ['saɪbəˌbʊliɪŋ] Cyber-Mobbing IV U4, 80

cycling ['saɪklɪŋ] Radfahren III

D

dad [dæd] Papa I

daily ['deɪli] täglich III

dance [dɑːns] Tanz III

   line dance ['laɪn ˌdɑːns] Line Dance *(alle tanzen zusammen in einer Reihe)* <IV U5, 143>

to dance [dɑːns] tanzen I

dancer ['dɑːnsə] Tänzer; Tänzerin I

dancing ['dɑːnsɪŋ] Tanzen; Tanz- IV U2, 43

dangerous ['deɪndʒrəs] gefährlich III

daredevil ['deəˌdevl] Draufgänger; Draufgängerin IV U3, 53

the dark [ðə 'dɑːk] Dunkelheit III

dark [dɑːk] dunkel I

date [deɪt] Datum I; Verabredung; Date IV U2, 42

daughter ['dɔːtə] Tochter I

day [deɪ] Tag I

   all day [ɔːl 'deɪ] den ganzen Tag III

   lucky day [ˌlʌki 'deɪ] Glückstag II

   one day [wʌn 'deɪ] eines Tages III

   a busy day [ə ˌbɪzi 'deɪ] ein ausgefüllter Tag I

   four hours a day [ˌaʊəz ə 'deɪ] vier Stunden täglich I

dead [ded] tot III

deadline ['dedlaɪn] Termin; Abgabetermin <IV U2, 49>

deadly ['dedli] tod-; tödlich III

deaf [def] gehörlos; schwerhörig; taub III

Dear …, [dɪə] Liebe/Lieber …, *(Anrede in Briefen)* I

death [deθ] Tod <IV U5, 108>

December [dɪ'sembə] Dezember I

to decide [dɪ'saɪd] (sich) entscheiden III

decision [dɪ'sɪʒn] Entscheidung IV U1, 18

to decorate ['dekreɪt] dekorieren; verzieren; schmücken <IV U3, 71>

to defeat [dɪ'fiːt] besiegen <IV U3, 138>

definition [ˌdefɪ'nɪʃn] Definition <III>

delicious [dɪ'lɪʃəs] köstlich II

department [dɪ'pɑːtmənt] Abteilung II

   department store [dɪ'pɑːtmənt ˌstɔː] Kaufhaus II

to depend (on) [dɪ'pend (ɒn)] abhängen (von) <IV U2, 48>

to describe [dɪ'skraɪb] beschreiben <I>

description [dɪ'skrɪpʃn] Beschreibung <IV U2, 49>

Design Technology (DT) [dɪˌzaɪn tek'nɒlədʒi, ˌdiː'tiː] Technik I

graphic design [ˌgræfɪk dɪ'zaɪn] Grafikdesign; grafische Gestaltung <IV U2, 49>

to design [dɪ'zaɪn] entwerfen; gestalten <III>

desk [desk] Schreibtisch IV U3, 62

   information desk [ɪnfə'meɪʃn ˌdesk] Information II

dessert [dɪ'zɜːt] Nachspeise II

to destroy [dɪ'strɔɪ] zerstören <IV U5, 142>

detail ['diːteɪl] Detail; Einzelheit IV U5, 102

language detectives ['læŋgwɪdʒ ˌdɪtektɪvz] Sprachdetektive <I>

detention [dɪ'tenʃn] Nachsitzen IV U2, 45

device [dɪ'vaɪs] Gerät; Vorrichtung IV U3, 58

dialogue ['daɪəlɒg] Dialog; Gespräch <III>

diamond ['daɪəmənd] Diamant <II>

diary ['daɪəri] Tagebuch I

dictionary ['dɪkʃnri] Wörterbuch <III>

did [dɪd] simple past von *to do* I

to die [daɪ] sterben III

difference ['dɪfrns] Unterschied <IV U4, 141>

different ['dɪfrnt] anders; unterschiedlich I

difficult ['dɪfɪklt] schwierig III

difficulty ['dɪfɪklti] Schwierigkeit <IV U4, 88>

dining room ['daɪnɪŋ ˌrʊm] Esszimmer I

dinner ['dɪnə] Abendessen II; Essen IV U3, 53

dinosaur ['daɪnəsɔː] Dinosaurier <IV U4, 141>

direct speech [dɪˌrekt 'spiːtʃ] direkte Rede <IV U5, 110>

direction [dɪ'rekʃn] Richtung <IV U5, 143>

directions [dɪ'rekʃnz] Anweisungen; Wegbeschreibung <III>

director [dɪ'rektə] Regisseur; Regisseurin II

dirty ['dɜːti] dreckig; schmutzig I

to disagree [ˌdɪsə'griː] anderer Meinung sein; nicht einverstanden sein II

to disappear [ˌdɪsə'pɪə] verschwinden IV U3, 62

disaster [dɪ'zɑːstə] Katastrophe; Desaster; Unglück III

to discover [dɪ'skʌvə] entdecken <IV U2, 136>

discovery [dɪ'skʌvri] Entdeckung IV U4, 84

disease [dɪ'ziːz] Krankheit IV U1, 22

dish [dɪʃ] Gericht; Speise II

dishwasher ['dɪʃwɒʃə] Spülmaschine IV U3, 59

to dislike [dɪ'slaɪk] nicht mögen IV U4, 81

distance ['dɪstns] Entfernung; Distanz IV ZI, 9

   in the distance [ˌɪn ðə 'dɪstns] in der Ferne IV U1, 15

DJing [ˌdiː'dʒeɪɪŋ] Musikauflegen <IV U1, 134>

*to do [duː] machen; tun I

   to do homework [ˌduː 'həʊmwɜːk] Hausaufgabe(n) machen I

   to do the right thing [ˌduː ðə 'raɪt θɪŋ] das Richtige tun III

   to do the shopping [ˌduː ðə 'ʃɒpɪŋ] Einkäufe machen; Besorgungen machen II

   to do the washing up [ˌduː ðə 'wɒʃɪŋ ʌp] abspülen II

doctor [ˈdɒktə] Arzt; Ärztin II
document [ˈdɒkjəmənt] Dokument
    <IV U3, 138>
dog [dɒg] Hund I
    dog biscuit [ˈdɒg ˌbɪskɪt]
    Hundekeks II
    dog walker [ˈdɒg ˌwɔːkə]
    Hundeausführer;
    Hundeausführerin IV U2, 41
dollar [ˈdɒlə] Dollar (amer.
    Währungseinheit) IV ZI, 8
dome [dəʊm] Kuppel II
done [dʌn] past participle von to
    do II
door [dɔː] Tür I
doorbell [ˈdɔːbel] Türklingel IV U3, 54
down [daʊn] entlang; herunter;
    hinunter; deprimiert III
    down there [ˌdaʊn ˈðeə] dahin; da
    unten <IV U1, 183>
to download [ˌdaʊnˈləʊd]
    herunterladen II
downtown (AE) [ˌdaʊnˈtaʊn] im
    Stadtzentrum IV U1, 14
Dr [ˈdɒktə] Dr. (Anrede) III
draft [drɑːft] Entwurf <II>
to drag [dræg] schleppen; schleifen;
    ziehen IV U5, 107
drama [ˈdrɑːmə] Theater II; Drama III
drank [dræŋk] simple past von to
    drink II
to draw [drɔː] zeichnen II
drawn [drɔːn] past participle von to
    draw II
dreadful [ˈdredfl] furchtbar III
dream [driːm] Traum I
to dream [driːm] träumen III
dreamt [dremt] simple past, past
    participle von to dream III
dress [dres] Kleid I
    dress code [ˈdres
    ˌkəʊd] Kleiderordnung;
    Bekleidungsvorschriften IV U2, 36
    fancy dress [ˌfænsi ˈdres]
    Verkleidung; Kostüm I
dressed [drest] angezogen (wie);
    verkleidet (als) III

to get dressed [ˌget ˈdrest] sich
    anziehen II
drew [druː] simple past von to draw
    II
drink [drɪŋk] Getränk II
to drink [drɪŋk] trinken II
    anything to drink [ˈeniθɪŋ tə ˈdrɪŋk]
    etwas zu trinken II
drinking straw [ˈdrɪŋkɪŋ ˌstrɔː]
    Trinkhalm <IV U3, 71>
drive [draɪv] Fahrt; Autofahrt III
to drive [draɪv] fahren; treiben
    IV U3, 52
    to drive sb crazy [draɪv … ˈkreɪzi]
    jmdn. verrückt machen III
driven [ˈdrɪvn] past participle von to
    drive IV U3, 52
driver [ˈdraɪvə] Fahrer; Fahrerin III
    driver's license (AE) [ˈdraɪvəz
    ˌlaɪsns] Führerschein IV U2, 38
    lorry driver [ˈlɒri ˌdraɪvə] LKW-
    Fahrer; LKW-Fahrerin II
driving [ˈdraɪvɪŋ] Fahren; Fahr-
    <IV U2, 44>
    driving school [ˈdraɪvɪŋ ˌskuːl]
    Fahrschule <IV U2, 44>
drove [drəʊv] past simple von to
    drive IV U3, 52
drug [drʌg] Droge <IV U3, 72>
drumming [ˈdrʌmɪŋ] Trommel- III
drunk [drʌŋk] past participle von to
    drink II; betrunken IV U3, 62
to dry [draɪ] trocknen IV U5, 98
dry [draɪ] trocken III
dumpling [ˈdʌmplɪŋ] Kloß II
during [ˈdjʊərɪŋ] während III

E

each [iːtʃ] jeder <I>
    each other [iːtʃ ˈʌðə] einander;
    sich; sich gegenseitig III
each [iːtʃ] pro Stück II
bald eagle [ˌbɔːld ˈiːgl]
    Weißkopfseeadler IV ZI, 8
ear [ɪə] Ohr II
early [ˈɜːli] früh I
    earlier [ˈɜːliə] früher I

to earn [ɜːn] verdienen IV U2, 38
east [iːst] Osten III
    east of [ˈiːst ˌəv] östlich von IV ZI, 9
easy [ˈiːzi] einfach; leicht I
to eat [iːt] essen I
eaten [ˈiːtn] past participle von to
    eat II
editing [ˈedɪtɪŋ] Bearbeitung;
    Redaktion <IV U2, 49>
education [edʒʊˈkeɪʃn] Ausbildung;
    Erziehung; Bildung IV U2, 38
effect [ɪˈfekt] Effekt; Wirkung
    <IV U3, 72>
egg [eg] Ei I
    scrambled egg [ˌskræmbld ˈeg]
    Rührei II
eight [eɪt] acht I
eighteen [ˌeɪˈtiːn] achtzehn I
eighty [ˈeɪti] achtzig I
not … either [nɒt … ˈaɪðə] auch
    nicht III
to elect [ɪˈlekt] wählen <IV U2, 46>
elective [ɪˈlektɪv] Wahlfach IV U2, 34
electric [ɪˈlektrɪk] elektrisch IV U3, 59
electricity [elɪkˈtrɪsəti] Strom; Elek-
    trizität III
element [ˈelɪmənt] Element
    <IV U5, 139>
elephant [ˈelɪfənt] Elefant I
elevator (AE) [ˈelɪveɪtə] Aufzug; Lift
    IV U1, 13
eleven [ɪˈlevn] elf I
e-mail [ˈiːmeɪl] E-Mail I
embarrassed [ɪmˈbærəst] verlegen II
embarrassing [ɪmˈbærəsɪŋ] peinlich
    IV U2, 42
emergency [ɪˈmɜːdʒənsi] Notfall III
    emergency call [ɪˈmɜːdʒənsi ˌkɔːl]
    Notruf III
    emergency service [ɪˈmɜːdʒənsi
    ˌsɜːvɪs] Notdienst; Rettungsdienst
    III
to emigrate [ˈemɪgreɪt] auswandern;
    emigrieren IV U1, 19
to emphasize [ˈemfəsaɪz] betonen
    <IV U2, 51>
to employ [ɪmˈplɔɪ] einstellen;
    anstellen; beschäftigen <IV U4, 88>

employ

empty ['emti] leer IV U4, 86

encyclopedia [ɪnˌsaɪklə'piːdiə] Enzy-klopädie; Lexikon IV U4, 86

end [end] Ende; Schluss II

    by the end [ˌbaɪ ði 'end] am Schluss II

    in the end [ɪn ði 'end] schließlich; zum Schluss II

to end [end] enden IV U5, 107

ending ['endɪŋ] Schluss; Ende III

enemy ['enəmi] Feind; Feindin III

energetic [ˌenə'dʒetɪk] tatkräftig IV U4, 89

fire engine ['faɪəˌendʒɪn] Feuerwehrauto II

steam engine ['stiːmˌendʒɪn] Dampfmaschine III

engineer [ˌendʒɪ'nɪə] Ingenieur; Ingenieurin; Techniker; Technikerin II

English ['ɪŋglɪʃ] englisch; Englisch; aus England I

the English [ði 'ɪŋglɪʃ] die Engländer III

to enjoy [ɪn'dʒɔɪ] genießen II; mögen III

enough [ɪ'nʌf] genug; genügend III

to enter ['entə] hineingehen; hereinkommen; betreten; eintreten IV U3, 54

entertainment (no pl) [ˌentə'teɪnmənt] Unterhaltung <IV U4, 90>

entry ['entri] Eintrag IV U4, 86; Einlass <IV U5, 207>

    entry form ['entri ˌfɔːm] Anmeldeformular II

equipment [ɪ'kwɪpmənt] Ausrüstung III

Victorian era [vɪkˌtɔːriən 'ɪərə] viktorianisches Zeitalter III

eraser [ɪ'reɪzə] Radiergummi I

escalator ['eskəleɪtə] Rolltreppe II

especially [ɪ'speʃli] besonders; vor allem II

ethnic ['eθnɪk] ethnisch; Volks- <IV U1, 26>

euro ['jʊərəʊ] Euro (Währung) III

European [jʊərə'piːən] europäisch; Europäisch; aus Europa; Europäer; Europäerin IV U2, 32

even ['iːvn] noch; sogar II

evening ['iːvnɪŋ] Abend I

in the evenings [ɪn ði 'iːvnɪŋz] abends III

event [ɪ'vent] Ereignis; Veranstaltung IV U4, 86

    sporting event ['spɔːtɪŋ ɪˌvent] Sportereignis; Sportveranstaltung <IV U2, 50>

ever ['evə] jemals II

every ['evri] jeder I; alle III

everybody ['evribɒdi] jeder; alle IV U2, 43

everyone ['evriwʌn] jeder I; zusammen; alle II

everything ['evriθɪŋ] alles II

exact [ɪg'zækt] exakt; genau III

Exactly. [ɪg'zæktli] Genau. IV U3, 59

example [ɪg'zaːmpl] Beispiel IV U5, 98

    for example [fər ɪg'zaːmpl] zum Beispiel IV U2, 34

except [ɪk'sept] außer III

exchange [ɪks'tʃeɪndʒ] Austausch IV U2, 34

to exchange [ɪks'tʃeɪndʒ] tauschen; austauschen <III>

excited [ɪk'saɪtɪd] aufgeregt; begeistert II

exciting [ɪk'saɪtɪŋ] spannend; aufregend I

Excuse me! [ɪk'skjuːz mi] Entschuldigung! I

exercise ['eksəsaɪz] Übung I

    exercise book ['eksəsaɪz ˌbʊk] Übungsheft I

exhausted [ɪg'zɔːstɪd] erschöpft III

to exist [ɪg'zɪst] existieren; bestehen <IV U1, 28>

to expect [ɪk'spekt] erwarten III

expensive [ɪk'spensɪv] teuer II

to experience [ɪk'spɪəriəns] erleben; erfahren <IV U4, 141>

experiment [ɪk'sperɪmənt] Versuch II

expert ['ekspɜːt] Experte; Expertin <IV U4, 80>

to explain [ɪk'spleɪn] erklären III

to explode [ɪk'spləʊd] explodieren III

to explore [ɪk'splɔː] erkunden; erforschen II

explosion [ɪk'spləʊʒn] Explosion III

extra ['ekstrə] Extra; Zusatz <IV U5, 112>

extra ['ekstrə] zusätzlich; Zusatz- II

    extra activities ['ekstrə æk'tɪvətiz] Zusatzaktivitäten <I>

extracurricular [ˌekstrəkə'rɪkjələ] außerhalb des Lehrplans; außer-unterrichtlich (Zusatzunterricht) IV U2, 34

extreme [ɪk'striːm] Extreme <IV U1, 30>

eye [aɪ] Auge II

    eye contact [aɪ 'kɒntækt] Augenkontakt <IV U2, 47>

F

fable ['feɪbl] Fabel; Märchen III

to face [feɪs] schauen <IV U5, 143>

fact [fækt] Fakt; Tatsache II

factory ['fæktri] Fabrik; Werk III

to fail (at) [feɪl (ət)] versagen (in/ bei); ausfallen; fehlschlagen IV U1, 19

fall (AE) [fɔːl] Herbst IV ZI, 8

***to fall** [fɔːl] fallen I

    to fall (over) [fɔːl 'əʊvə] fallen; hinfallen; umfallen III

    to fall asleep [fɔːl ə'sliːp] einschlafen III

    to fall behind [ˌfɔːl bɪ'haɪnd] zurückfallen <IV U2, 35>

    to fall in love (with) [ˌfɔːl ɪn 'lʌv] sich verlieben (in) III

    to fall out of [fɔːl 'aʊt ˌəv] herausfallen aus IV U2, 42

false [fɔːls] falsch <II>

family ['fæmli] Familie I

    host family ['həʊst ˌfæmli] Gastfamilie IV U2, 34

famine ['fæmɪn] Hungersnot <IV U1, 184>

famous ['feɪməs] berühmt I

fan [fæn] Fan I; Ventilator IV U3, 59

fancy dress [ˌfænsi ˈdres] Verkleidung; Kostüm I

fantastic [fænˈtæstɪk] fantastisch; großartig II

fantasy [ˈfæntəsi] Fantasie; Fantasy II

FAQ (= frequently asked questions) [ˌefeɪˈkjuː (ˌfriːkwəntli ˌɑːskt ˈkwestʃənz)] häufig gestellte Fragen <IV U1, 30>

far [fɑː] weit III
as far as [əz ˈfɑːr̬əz] soweit IV U3, 59

fare [feə] Fahrpreis III

farewell speech [feəˈwel spiːtʃ] Abschiedsrede II

farm [fɑːm] Bauernhof I
wind farm [ˈwɪnd fɑːm] Windpark III

farmer [ˈfɑːmə] Landwirt; Landwirtin; Bauer; Bäuerin I
farmers' market [ˌfɑːməz ˈmɑːkɪt] Bauernmarkt <IV U3, 72>

farming [ˈfɑːmɪŋ] Landwirtschaft; Ackerbau <IV U2, 136>

farmland [ˈfɑːmlænd] Ackerland; Ackerboden; Landwirtschaftsflächen IV U2, 32

fascinating [ˈfæsɪneɪtɪŋ] faszinierend IV U4, 77

fashion (no pl) [ˈfæʃn] Mode IV U3, 58
out of fashion [ˌaʊt̬əv ˈfæʃn] altmodisch; nicht mehr aktuell <IV U3, 72>

fashionable [ˈfæʃnəbl] modisch II

fast [fɑːst] schnell II
fast food [ˌfɑːst ˈfuːd] Fastfood I
fast food restaurant [ˌfɑːst fuːd ˈrestrɒnt] Fastfood-Restaurant I
the fastest [ðə ˈfɑːstɪst] der/die/das schnellste I

father [ˈfɑːðə] Vater I

favorite (AE) [ˈfeɪvrɪt] Lieblings- IV U3, 53

favourite [ˈfeɪvrɪt] Lieblings- I

feature [ˈfiːtʃə] Merkmal <III>; Feature; Artikel <IV U2, 49>

feature story [ˈfiːtʃə ˌstɔːri] Leitartikel; Sonderbericht <IV U5, 110>

February [ˈfebruri] Februar I

fed [fed] simple past von *to feed* I; past participle von *to feed* II

***to be fed up (with)** [bi: fed ˈʌp (wɪð)] die Nase voll haben (von); sauer sein III

federal [ˈfedrl] Bundes-; föderalistisch <IV U4, 88>

fee [fiː] Gebühr <IV U3, 66>

***to feed** [fiːd] füttern I

feedback [ˈfiːdbæk] Feedback; Rückmeldung IV U2, 39

***to feel** [fiːl] (sich) fühlen II
to feel sorry for [ˌfiːl ˈsɒri] Mitleid haben mit; bedauern III
to make sb feel like sth [ˌmeɪk … ˈfiːl laɪk] jmdm. das Gefühl geben, etw. zu sein III

feeling [ˈfiːlɪŋ] Gefühl <III>

fell [fel] simple past von *to fall* I

felt [felt] simple past von *to feel* II

felt-tip [ˌfelt'tɪp] Filzstift I

fever [ˈfiːvə] Fieber IV U4, 86

a few [ə ˈfjuː] ein paar; wenige; einige III

science fiction [ˌsaɪəns ˈfɪkʃn] Science-Fiction I

fictional [ˈfɪkʃnl] fiktiv <IV U1, 135>

field [fiːld] Feld; Wiese; Weide IV ZI, 9
field goal [ˈfiːld ˌɡəʊl] Feldtor <IV U2, 50>

fifteen [ˌfɪfˈtiːn] fünfzehn I

fifty [ˈfɪfti] fünfzig I

fight [faɪt] Kampf; Streit III

***to fight** [faɪt] kämpfen; (sich) streiten III

file [faɪl] Datei II

to fill [fɪl] befüllen <IV U3, 71>
filled with [ˈfɪld ˌwɪð] gefüllt mit <IV U3, 72>

filling [ˈfɪlɪŋ] Füllung <IV U5, 112>

film [fɪlm] Film I
film maker [ˈfɪlm ˌmeɪkə] Filmemacher; Filmemacherin <III>
to film [fɪlm] filmen; drehen <III>

final match [ˌfaɪnl ˈmætʃ] Endspiel <IV U2, 50>

finally [ˈfaɪnli] schließlich; zum Schluss II

financial [faɪˈnænʃl] finanziell; Finanz- IV U1, 14

***to find** [faɪnd] finden; herausfinden I
to find out [ˌfaɪnd ˈaʊt] herausfinden I

fine [faɪn] schön; gut; in Ordnung II

finger [ˈfɪŋɡə] Finger III

fingerprint [ˈfɪŋɡəprɪnt] Fingerabdruck II

to finish [ˈfɪnɪʃ] beenden; enden; aufhören; fertigstellen; vervollständigen II

fire [faɪə] Feuer I
to be on fire [bi: ɒn ˈfaɪə] brennen II
fire engine [ˈfaɪər̬ˌendʒɪn] Feuerwehrauto II

firework [ˈfaɪəwɜːk] Feuerwerk <IV U3, 138>

first [fɜːst] zuerst; als Erstes; erste I

fish (sg) [fɪʃ], **fish** (pl) [fɪʃ] Fisch I

fisherman [ˈfɪʃəmən] Fischer <IV U2, 136>

fishing [ˈfɪʃɪŋ] Angeln; Fischen <IV U5, 143>

to fit [fɪt] passen II
to fit (in) [fɪt (ɪn)] hineinpassen (in) <IV U2, 35>

fit [fɪt] fit; in Form III

fitness [ˈfɪtnəs] Fitness <IV U3, 72>
fitness instructor [ˈfɪtnəs ɪnˌstrʌktə] Fitnesstrainer; Fitnesstrainerin <IV U3, 72>
jumping fitness [ˈdʒʌmpɪŋ ˌfɪtnəs] Jumping Fitness (Trendsportart) IV U4, 81

five [faɪv] fünf I

to fix [fɪks] fixieren; befestigen <IV U3, 71>

flag [flæɡ] Flagge; Fahne II

flamingo [fləˈmɪŋɡəʊ] Flamingo I

flat [flæt] Wohnung I

flew [fluː] simple past von *to fly* II

flew

flight [flaɪt] Flug II

to **float** [fləʊt] treiben <IV U3, 71>

floor [flɔ:] Fußboden I; Stockwerk II

flour [flaʊə] Mehl II

   to cover in flour [ˌkʌvər ɪn ˈflaʊə] in Mehl wenden IV U5, 98

flower [ˈflaʊə] Blume III

flown [fləʊn] past participle von *to fly* II

fluent [ˈflu:ənt] fließend; flüssig III

*to **fly** [flaɪ] fliegen II

flyer [ˈflaɪə] Flyer; Faltblatt II

foggy [ˈfɒgi] neblig I

to **fold in half** [ˌfəʊld ɪn ˈha:f] in der Mitte falten <IV U4, 92>

to **follow** [ˈfɒləʊ] befolgen; folgen III

food [fu:d] Essen; Nahrung; Lebensmittel I

   food stall [ˈfu:d ˌstɔ:l] Essensstand II

   better quality food [ˌbetə ˈkwɒləti ˌfu:d] qualitativ besseres Essen <IV U3, 72>

foot *(sg)* [fʊt], **feet** *(pl)* [fi:t] Fuß I

   on foot [ɒn ˈfʊt] zu Fuß I

football [ˈfʊtbɔ:l] Fußball I

for [fɔ:] für I; seit IV U4, 80

   for five months [fə ˈfaɪv ˌmʌnθs] fünf Monate lang I

   for fun [fə ˈfʌn] zum Spaß III

forbidden [fəˈbɪdn] verboten IV U3, 58

foreground [ˈfɔ:graʊnd] Vordergrund III

   in the foreground [ɪn ðə ˈfɔ:graʊnd] im Vordergrund III

foreign [ˈfɒrɪn] fremd; ausländisch IV U1, 18

forest [ˈfɒrɪst] Wald IV U3, 53

*to **foretell** [fɔ:ˈtel] vorhersagen III

forever [fəˈrevə] für immer; ewig II

*to **forget** [fəˈget] vergessen I

forgot [fəˈgɒt] simple past von *to forget* I

forgotten [fəˈgɒtn] past participle von *to forget* II

fork [fɔ:k] Gabel II

form [fɔ:m] Form <III>; Art <IV U2, 48>

approval form [əˈpru:vl ˌfɔ:m] Einverständnisformular <IV U2, 44>

   entry form [ˈentri ˌfɔ:m] Anmeldeformular II

forty [ˈfɔ:ti] vierzig I

forward [ˈfɔ:wəd] vorwärts <IV U2, 137>

fought [fɔ:t] simple past, past participle von *to fight* III

to **found** [faʊnd] gründen IV U5, 98

found [faʊnd] simple past von *to find* I

four [fɔ:] vier I

fourteen [ˌfɔ:ˈti:n] vierzehn I

fourth [fɔ:θ] vierte I

land of the free [ˌlænd ˌəv ðə ˈfri:] Land der Freien IV U3, 53

free [fri:] kostenlos III

   free range [ˌfri: ˈreɪndʒ] Freiland- II

   free time [ˌfri: ˈtaɪm] Freizeit I

freedom *(no pl)* [ˈfri:dəm] Freiheit; Unabhängigkeit IV U1, 23

   religious freedom [ˌrɪlɪdʒəs ˈfri:dəm] Religionsfreiheit <IV U3, 70>

*to **freeze** [fri:z] frieren; gefrieren III

   freeze frame [ˈfri:z ˌfreɪm] Standbild <I>

freezing [ˈfri:zɪŋ] eiskalt; gefrierend <IV U1, 30>

French [frentʃ] Französisch I

the French *(pl)* [ðə ˈfrenʃ] die Franzosen IV U5, 98

fresh [freʃ] frisch II

Friday [ˈfraɪdeɪ] Freitag I

fridge [frɪdʒ] Kühlschrank III

fried [fraɪd] (in der Pfanne) gebraten II

friend [frend] Freund; Freundin I

   to make friends [ˌmeɪk ˈfrendz] Freundschaften schließen I

   to see friends [si: ˈfrendz] Freunde treffen I

to **friend** [frend] befreunden *(jmdn. zu seiner Freundesliste hinzufügen)* IV U4, 81

friendly [ˈfrendli] freundlich; nett III

frisbee [ˈfrɪzbi] Frisbee; Frisbeescheibe I

from [frɒm] aus; von I

   from behind [ˌfrəm bɪˈhaɪnd] von hinten I

front [frʌnt] Vorderseite; Front-; Vorder- <IV U1,

   at the front of [ət ðə ˈfrʌnt ˌəv] an der Spitze (von); im vorderen Bereich II

   in front of [ɪn ˈfrʌnt ˌəv] vor; davor II

froze [frəʊz] simple past von *to freeze* III

frozen [ˈfrəʊzn] past participle von *to freeze* III

fruit [fru:t] Frucht; Obst I

to **fry** [fraɪ] braten; frittieren IV U5, 98

full [fʊl] vollwertig <IV U2, 137>; voll IV U5, 106

fun [fʌn] Freude; Spaß I

   for fun [fə ˈfʌn] zum Spaß III

fundamental [ˌfʌndəˈmentl] Grundlage <IV U2, 49>

funeral [ˈfju:nrəl] Beerdigung; Begräbnis <IV U5, 108>

funny [ˈfʌni] lustig; witzig I; merkwürdig; seltsam II

furious [ˈfjʊəriəs] wütend III

further [ˈfɜ:ðə] weiter <IV U2, 136>

future [ˈfju:tʃə] Zukunft IV U1, 18

G

galaxy [ˈgæləksi] Galaxie; Galaxis <IV U2, 48>

gallery [ˈgælri] Galerie <IV U1, 28>

game [geɪm] Spiel I

gamer [ˈgeɪmə] Spieler *(Computer)*; Spielerin *(Computer)* II

street gang [ˈstri:t ˌgæŋ] Straßengang <IV U1, 134>

garden [ˈga:dn] Garten I

garlic [ˈga:lɪk] Knoblauch II

gas [gæs] Gas III

gas *(AE)* [gæs] Benzin <IV U3, 66>

gateway [ˈgeɪtweɪ] Tor; Eingangstor IV U1, 12

to **gather** [ˈgæðə] (sich) sammeln IV U3, 64

p pen • b bed • t ten • d dad • k cat • g grey • tʃ chair • dʒ joke • f fan • v very • θ three • ð the

gave [geɪv] simple past von *to give* II

gel [dʒel] Gel III

   hair gel [ˈheə ˌdʒel] Haargel III

   shower gel [ˈʃaʊə ˌdʒel] Duschgel III

generous [ˈdʒenrəs] großzügig IV U2, 39

geocaching [ˈdʒiəʊkæʃɪŋ] Geocaching I

Geography [dʒiˈɒgrəfi] Geografie; Erdkunde I

German [ˈdʒɜːmən] Deutsch I; deutsch; aus Deutschland III

*to get [get] bekommen; werden I; holen II; verstehen III

   to get around [ˌget əˈraʊnd] herumkommen III

   to get cold [ˌget ˈkəʊld] frieren III

   to get dressed [ˌget ˈdrest] sich anziehen II

   to get in [ˈget ˌɪn] hereinkommen I

   to get into [ˌget ˈɪntə] hineingelangen; hineinkommen IV U1, 14

   to get lost [ˌget lɒst] sich verirren I

   to get married [ˌget ˈmærɪd] heiraten II

   to get off [ˌget ˈɒf] aussteigen II

   to get on (the bus) [ˌget ˈɒn] einsteigen (in den Bus) IV U5, 106

   to get out [ˌget ˈaʊt] herauskommen III

   to get ready [ˌget ˈredi] sich vorbereiten; sich fertig machen IV U3, 54

   to get started [ˌget ˈstɑːtɪd] anfangen <III>

   to get sth [get] etw. verstehen IV U5, 102

   to get stuck [ˌget ˈstʌk] stecken bleiben IV U3, 54

   to get tired of sth [ˌget ˈtaɪəd ˌəv] etw. sattbekommen; etw. satthaben IV U1, 14

   to get to know [ˌget tə ˈnəʊ] kennen lernen II

   to get up [ˌget ˈʌp] aufstehen I

   to get used to (sth) [ˌget ˈjuːzd tə] sich an (etw.) gewöhnen IV U1, 18

gherkin [ˈgɜːkɪn] Essiggurke <IV U5, 112>

ghost [gəʊst] Geist II

giant [dʒaɪənt] Riese III

giant [dʒaɪənt] Riesen-; riesig IV U4, 74

giraffe [dʒɪˈrɑːf] Giraffe I

girl [gɜːl] Mädchen I

girlfriend [ˈgɜːlfrend] Freundin *(in einer Paarbeziehung)* IV U2, 38

*to give [gɪv] geben I

   to give a talk [ˌgɪv ə ˈtɔːk] einen Vortrag halten <III>

   to give reasons [ˌgɪv ˈriːznz] Gründe nennen; Gründe angeben III

   to give sth a miss [ˌgɪv sʌmθɪŋ ə ˈmɪs] auf etw. verzichten; etw. bleiben lassen III

   to give up [ˌgɪv ˈʌp] aufgeben IV U1, 18

glad [glæd] froh IV U3, 54

glass [glɑːs] Glas II

global [ˈgləʊbl] global; weltweit <IV U1, 134>

glove [glʌv] Handschuh <IV U2, 50>

glue [gluː] Klebstoff I

   glue stick [ˈgluː ˌstɪk] Klebestift <IV U3, 71>

*to go [gəʊ] gehen; fahren I

   to go beach combing [ˌgəʊ ˈbiːtʃ ˌkəʊmɪŋ] den Strand nach Strandgut absuchen II

   to go camping [ˌgəʊ ˈkæmpɪŋ] campen gehen; zelten II

   to go on [ˌgəʊ ˈɒn] hineingehen II; weitermachen <IV U2, 37>

   to go out with [ˌgəʊ ˈaʊt wɪð] (aus)gehen mit IV U3, 58

   to go shopping [ˌgəʊ ˈʃɒpɪŋ] einkaufen gehen II

   to go sightseeing [ˌgəʊ ˈsaɪtsiːɪŋ] eine Besichtigungstour machen II

   to go swimming [ˌgəʊ ˈswɪmɪŋ] schwimmen gehen I

   to go to bed [ˌgəʊ tə ˈbed] ins Bett gehen I

field goal [ˈfiːld ˌgəʊl] Feldtor <IV U2, 50>

goat [gəʊt] Ziege III

thank God [ˌθæŋk ˈgɒd] Gott sei Dank <IV U3, 70>

gold [gəʊld] Gold III

gold [gəʊld] golden; Gold- III

   gold rush [ˈgəʊld ˌrʌʃ] Goldrausch IV U4, 84

golden [ˈgəʊldn] golden; Gold- IV U5, 98

gone [gɒn] past participle von *to go* II

good [gʊd] gut I

   to be good at [biː ˈgʊd ˌət] gut sein in/bei I

   Good morning. [ˌgʊd ˈmɔːnɪŋ] Guten Morgen. II

   good luck [ˌgʊd ˈlʌk] viel Glück II

Goodbye. [gʊdˈbaɪ] Auf Wiedersehen. I

gospel [ˈgɒspl] Gospel *(Musikrichtung)* IV U5, 97

gossip [ˈgɒsɪp] Klatsch; Tratsch; Gerede IV U3, 58

got [gɒt] simple past von *to get* I

government [ˈgʌvnmənt] Regierung <IV U1, 24>

   state government [ˈsteɪt ˌgʌvnmənt] Landesregierung IV U5, 98

GPS *(Global Positioning System)* [ˌdʒiːpiːˈes] GPS I

to grab [græb] schnappen; greifen; ergreifen III

grade *(AE)* [greɪd] Note; Klasse IV U2, 33

graduation [ˌgrædʒuˈeɪʃn] Schulabschluss <IV U2, 48>

graffiti [grəˈfiːti] Graffiti <IV U1, 134>

grammar [ˈgræmə] Grammatik <I>

grandad [ˈgrændæd] Opa III

   great-great-grandad [ˌgreɪtgreɪt ˈgrændæd] Ururopa I

grandfather [ˈgrænˌfɑːðə] Großvater II

grandma [ˈgrænmɑː] Oma II

grandmother [ˈgrænˌmʌðə] Großmutter III

grandparents *(pl)* ['grænˌpeərənts] Großeltern II

graphic design [ˌgræfɪk dɪ'zaɪn] Grafikdesign; grafische Gestaltung <IV U2, 49>

grass [grɑ:s] Gras I

grated ['greɪtɪd] gerieben <IV U5, 112>

grave [greɪv] Grab III

great [greɪt] großartig; toll I

great-grandparents [ˌgreɪt'grænˌpeərənts] Urgroßeltern IV U1, 25

Greek [gri:k] griechisch; Griechisch; aus Griechenland IV U5, 99

green [gri:n] grün I

greengrocer's ['gri:nˌgrəʊsəz] Obst- und Gemüseladen III

grew [gru:] simple past von *to grow* IV U3, 58

grey [greɪ] grau I

grizzly bear ['grɪzli ˌbeə] Grizzlybär <IV U1, 30>

groceries *(pl)* ['grəʊsriz] Lebensmittel IV U4, 89

ground [graʊnd] Boden; Erdboden III

group [gru:p] Gruppe I

tutor group ['tju:tə ˌgru:p] Klasse *(in einer englischen Schule)* I

*to **grow** [grəʊ] anbauen; züchten; ziehen; wachsen IV U3, 58

to grow up [ˌgrəʊ 'ʌp] aufwachsen III

grown [grəʊn] past participle von *to grow* IV U3, 58

to **guess** [ges] erraten; raten; überlegen II; schätzen; vermuten IV U3, 59

guest [gest] Gast III

guestbook ['gestbʊk] Gästebuch <I>

guide [gaɪd] Führer; Führerin II

guided tour ['gaɪdɪd ˌtɔ:] Führung <IV U1, 13>

guinea pig ['gɪni ˌpɪg] Meerschweinchen I

guitar [gɪ'tɑ:] Gitarre III

gun [gʌn] Schusswaffe IV U3, 62

guy [gaɪ] Typ; Kerl IV U2, 42

guys *(pl)* [gaɪz] Leute II

gym(nasium) [dʒɪm (dʒɪm'neɪziəm)] Turnhalle IV U2, 42

gymnasium [dʒɪm'neɪziəm] Fitnessraum III

H

had [hæd] simple past von *to have* I; past participle von *to have* II

haggis ['hægɪs] Haggis *(schottisches Gericht aus Schafsinnereien)* III

hair [heə] Haar; Haare III

hair gel ['heə ˌdʒel] Haargel III

hair straightener ['heə ˌstreɪtnə] Haarglätter I

haircut ['heəkʌt] Haarschnitt II

to have a haircut ['heəkʌt] sich die Haare schneiden lassen II

hairdo ['heədu:] Frisur <IV U4, 77>

hairdresser ['heəˌdresə] Friseur; Friseurin II

hairdryer ['heəˌdraɪə] Fön III

half *(sg)* [hɑ:f], **halves** *(pl)* [hɑ:vz] (die) Hälfte IV U4, 80

to fold in half [ˌfəʊld ɪn 'hɑ:f] in der Mitte falten <IV U4, 92>

half [hɑ:f] halb III

half a million [ˌhɑ:f ə 'mɪljən] eine halbe Million III

half past (two) [ˌhɑ:f 'pɑ:st] halb (drei) I

hall [hɔ:l] Flur; Diele; Korridor II

town hall [ˌtaʊn 'hɔ:l] Rathaus II

ham [hæm] Schinken II

hand [hænd] Hand I

*to **hang** [hæŋ] hängen II

to **happen** ['hæpn] geschehen; passieren II

That's what happened. [ˌðæts wɒt 'hæpnd] Das ist passiert. II

happy ['hæpi] glücklich I

Happy birthday! [ˌhæpi 'bɜ:θdeɪ] Alles Gute zum Geburtstag! I

harbor *(AE)* ['hɑ:bə] Hafen IV U1, 22

harbour ['hɑ:bə] Hafen II

hard [hɑ:d] hart; schwer; schwierig II

hardly ['hɑ:dli] kaum <IV U4, 88>

hard-working [ˌhɑ:d'wɜ:kɪŋ] fleißig IV U2, 39

harvest ['hɑ:vɪst] Ernte <IV U3, 70>

hat [hæt] Hut II

to **hate** [heɪt] hassen; nicht mögen I

*to **have** [hæv] haben I; essen II

to have a haircut ['heəkʌt] sich die Haare schneiden lassen II

to have a look [ˌhæv ə 'lʊk] anschauen II

to have breakfast [ˌhæv 'brekfəst] frühstücken I

to have got [ˌhæv 'gɒt] besitzen; haben II

to have to ['hæv tə] müssen II

Please have a seat. [ˌpli:z hæv ə 'si:t] Bitte Platz nehmen. IV U3, 55

he [hi:] er I

head [hed] Kopf II

head chef ['hed ʃef] Chefkoch; Chefköchin II

head first ['hed fɜ:st] kopfüber III

headache ['hedeɪk] Kopfschmerzen; Kopfweh II

heading ['hedɪŋ] Überschrift; Titel <III>

headline ['hedlaɪn] Schlagzeile; Überschrift IV U4, 77

headphones *(pl)* ['hedfəʊnz] Kopfhörer IV U3, 59

health [helθ] Gesundheits-; gesundheitlich <IV U4, 88>

*to **hear** [hɪə] hören I

heard [hɜ:d] simple past von *to hear* I; past participle von *to hear* II

heartbeat ['hɑ:tbi:t] Herzschlag <IV U2, 35>

heat [hi:t] Hitze IV U5, 102

heavy ['hevi] schwer; stark II

height [haɪt] Höhe II

held [held] simple past, past participle von *to hold* III

helicopter ['helɪkɒptə] Helikopter; Hubschrauber I

Hello. [hə'ləʊ] Hallo. I

Hello there. [hə'ləʊ ˌðeə] Hallo.; Grüß dich. I

helmet ['helmət] Helm III

help [help] Hilfe II

to **help** [help] helfen I
  to help oneself [ˌhelp wʌnˈself] sich bedienen III
  I couldn't help but … [aɪ kʊdnt ˈhelp bʌt] Ich konnte nicht anders als … III
helper [ˈhelpə] Helfer; Helferin IV U4, 89
helpful [ˈhelpfl] hilfsbereit; hilfreich; nützlich IV U2, 38
her [hɜː] ihr, ihre; sie I
here [hɪə] hier I
  Here you are. [ˌhɪə juˈɑː] Bitte schön. I
hero (sg) [ˈhɪərəʊ], **heroes** (pl) [ˈhɪərəʊz] Held III
hers [hɜːz] ihre II
herself [hɜːˈself] sie selbst; sich selbst III
Hi. [haɪ] Hi.; Hallo. I
  to say hi to [ˌseɪ ˈhaɪ tə] grüßen; Grüße ausrichten I
hid [hɪd] simple past von to hide III
hidden [ˈhɪdn] past participle von to hide III
*to **hide** [haɪd] (sich) verstecken III
high [haɪ] hoch; groß I
  high school [ˈhaɪ ˌskuːl] Highschool (weiterführende Schule, Oberstufe) IV U1, 18
highlighted [ˈhaɪlaɪtɪd] markiert <III>
high-tech [ˌhaɪˈtek] Hightech- IV U4, 75
to **hike** [haɪk] wandern II
hiking [ˈhaɪkɪŋ] Wandern III
hill [hɪl] Berg; Hügel IV U4, 74
him [hɪm] ihm; ihn I
himself [hɪmˈself] sich (selbst); er selbst III
hip hop [ˈhɪphɒp] Hip-Hop (Musik) III
his [hɪz] sein I; seins; seiner II
History [ˈhɪstri] Geschichte I
history [ˈhɪstri] Geschichte III
*to **hit** [hɪt] treffen; schlagen II; (sich) stoßen; anstoßen; gegen etw. fahren III
hit [hɪt] simple past, past participle von to hit II
hobby [ˈhɒbi] Hobby III

*to **hold** [həʊld] halten; festhalten III
hole [həʊl] Loch I
holiday [ˈhɒlədeɪ] Ferien; Urlaub I
  national holiday [ˌnæʃnl ˈhɒlədeɪ] Nationalfeiertag <IV U1, 24>
home [həʊm] Zuhause; Heim; nach Hause I
  at home [ət ˈhəʊm] zu Hause I
  back home [bæk ˈhəʊm] zu Hause II
Homecoming (AE) [ˈhəʊmˌkʌmɪŋ] Ehemaligentreffen IV U2, 33
homepage [ˈhəʊmpeɪdʒ] Homepage <I>
homeroom [ˈhəʊmruːm] erste Stunde (in der Schule) IV U2, 45
homeschooling [ˈhəʊmˌskuːlɪŋ] Hausunterricht <IV U2, 34>
*to be **homesick** [biː ˈhəʊmsɪk] Heimweh haben III
homework [ˈhəʊmwɜːk] Hausaufgabe(n) I
  to do homework [ˌduː ˈhəʊmwɜːk] Hausaufgabe(n) machen I
honestly [ˈɒnɪstli] ehrlich IV U3, 63
honor (AE) [ˈɒnə] Ehre IV U1, 25
to **hoover** [ˈhuːvə] staubsaugen II
hope [həʊp] Hoffnung IV U1, 13
to **hope** [həʊp] hoffen I
hopeful [ˈhəʊpfl] hoffnungsvoll III
horrible [ˈhɒrəbl] schrecklich; furchtbar III
horse [hɔːs] Pferd I
  horse riding [ˈhɔːs ˌraɪdɪŋ] Reiten I
hospital [ˈhɒspɪtl] Hospital; Krankenhaus I
host [həʊst] Talkmaster; Gastgeber; Gastgeberin <IV U3, 69>
  host family [ˈhəʊst ˌfæmli] Gastfamilie IV U2, 34
hostel [ˈhɒstl] Herberge III
hot [hɒt] heiß I
  hot BBQ sauce [hɒt ˈbɑːbɪkjuː ˌsɔːs] scharfe Grillsoße <IV U5, 112>
  hot dog [ˈhɒt ˌdɒg] Hot Dog (Würstchen im Brötchen) IV U1, 14
hotel [həʊˈtel] Hotel II
hour [aʊə] Stunde I

rush hour [ˈrʌʃ ˌaʊə] Hauptverkehrszeit IV U1, 14
working hours (pl) [ˈwɜːkɪŋ ˌaʊəz] Arbeitszeit IV U2, 39
40 kilometres an hour [kɪˈlɒmɪtəz ənˈaʊə] 40 Kilometer pro Stunde I
house [haʊs] Haus I
  around the house [əˈraʊnd ðə haʊs] im Haus I
  State House (AE) [ˈsteɪt ˌhaʊs] Regierungsgebäude IV U5, 98
how [haʊ] wie I
  How about …? [haʊ əˈbaʊt] Wie wäre es mit …? II
  how are things going [ˌhaʊ ɑː ˌθɪŋz ˈgəʊɪŋ] wie läuft's; wie geht's IV U3, 55
  How are you? [ˌhaʊ ˈɑː jə] Wie geht es dir? I
  How are you doing? [ˌhaʊ ə jə ˈduːɪŋ] Wie geht es dir? IV U3, 54
  how do I get there [ˌhaʊ du aɪ ˈget ðeə] wie komme ich dahin III
  how many [ˌhaʊ ˈmeni] wie viele II
  How much (is/are) …? [ˌhaʊ ˈmʌtʃ ɪz/ɑː] Wie viel (kostet/kosten) …? I
  How old are you? [haʊ ˈəʊld ə juː] Wie alt bist du? I
  How to … [ˈhaʊ tə] Wie man … II
  How's it going? [ˌhaʊz ɪt ˈgəʊɪŋ] Wie geht's?; Wie läuft's? IV U3, 54
however [haʊˈevə] jedoch III
huge [hjuːdʒ] riesig; riesengroß IV ZI, 9
a/one **hundred** [ˈhʌndrəd] einhundert; hundert I
hung [hʌŋ] simple past, past participle von to hang II
hunger [ˈhʌŋgə] Hunger <IV U2, 136>
hungry [ˈhʌŋgri] hungrig I
to **hunt** [hʌnt] jagen <IV U2, 136>
hunter [ˈhʌntə] Jäger; Jägerin IV U4, 85
to **hurry** [ˈhʌri] sich beeilen II
*to **hurt** [hɜːt] weh tun; verletzen II
hurt [hɜːt] simple past, past participle von to hurt II; verletzt II
husband [ˈhʌzbənd] Ehemann IV U3, 54

husband

husky ['hʌski] Husky (*Schlittenhunderasse*) <IV U1, 30>

I

I [aɪ] ich I

I don't know! [aɪ ˌdəʊnt 'nəʊ] Ich weiß (es) nicht! I

I see. [aɪ 'siː] Ich verstehe. IV U5, 103

I wouldn't like (to) ... [aɪ 'wʊdnt laɪk (tə)] Ich möchte nicht ...; Ich würde nicht gerne ... I

I'd like (to) ... (= I would like to) [aɪd 'laɪk (tə)] Ich möchte ...; Ich würde gerne ... I

I'd rather [aɪd 'rɑːðə] ich würde lieber III

I'm from ... ['aɪm ˌfrɒm] Ich komme aus ... I

I'm sorry. [aɪm 'sɒrɪ] Es tut mir leid.; Entschuldigung. I

crushed ice ['krʌʃt ˌaɪs] zerstoßenes Eis <IV U5, 113>

ice cream [ˌaɪs 'kriːm] Eiscreme; Eis I

iceberg ['aɪsbɜːg] Eisberg III

ID [aɪ'diː] Ausweis; Personalausweis III

idea [aɪ'dɪə] Idee; Ahnung I

ideal [aɪ'dɪəl] ideal; optimal <IV U3, 72>

if [ɪf] wenn; falls II

ill [ɪl] krank; schlecht II

illegally [ɪ'liːgli] illegal; unrechtmäßig; rechtswidrig <IV U4, 88>

illness ['ɪlnəs] Krankheit <IV U2, 136>

to imagine [ɪ'mædʒɪn] sich vorstellen <IV U2, 39>

immigrant ['ɪmɪgrənt] Immigrant; Immigrantin; Einwanderer; Einwandererin IV U1, 13

to immigrate ['ɪmɪgreɪt] einwandern; immigrieren IV U1, 18

immigration [ˌɪmɪ'greɪʃn] Immigration; Zuwanderung IV U1, 22

impact ['ɪmpækt] Einfluss; Auswirkung IV U4, 80

speech impaired ['spiːtʃ ɪmˌpeərd] sprachbehindert IV U5, 102

important [ɪm'pɔːtnt] wichtig; einflussreich II

impossible [ɪm'pɒsəbl] unmöglich III

to impress [ɪm'pres] beeindrucken III

in [ɪn] in I; drinnen II

in August [ɪn 'ɔːgəst] im August I

in between [ˌɪn bɪ'twiːn] dazwischen <IV U4, 92>

in front of [ɪn 'frʌnt ˌəv] vor; davor II

in the afternoon [ɪn ði ˌɑːftə'nuːn] nachmittags I

in the background [ɪn ðə 'bækgraʊnd] im Hintergrund III

in the centre of [ˌɪn ðə 'sentər ˌəv] in der Mitte III

in the country [ɪn ðə 'kʌntri] auf dem Land I

in the distance [ɪn ðə 'dɪstns] in der Ferne IV U1, 15

in the end [ɪn ði 'end] schließlich; zum Schluss II

in the evenings [ɪn ði 'iːvnɪŋz] abends III

in the foreground [ɪn ðə 'fɔːgraʊnd] im Vordergrund III

in the middle [ɪn ðə 'mɪdl] in der Mitte III

in the south of [ˌɪn ðə 'saʊθ ˌəv] im Süden von III

in the world [ɪn ðə 'wɜːld] auf der Welt II

in time [ɪn 'taɪm] rechtzeitig I

inch [ɪnʃ] Zoll (Längenmaß: 2, 54 cm) <IV U5, 112>

to include [ɪn'kluːd] beinhalten; einschließen <IV U2, 48>

income ['ɪnkʌm] Einkommen <IV U4, 88>

independence [ˌɪndɪ'pendəns] Unabhängigkeit IV U1, 13

Indian ['ɪndɪən] indisch I; indisch II; Indianer; Indianerin <IV U3, 70>

individual [ˌɪndɪ'vɪdʒuəl] individuell; einzeln <IV U2, 48>

indoor [ˌɪn'dɔː] Hallen-; Innen- III

Industrial Revolution [ɪnˌdʌstrɪəl revl'uːʃn] industrielle Revolution III

industry ['ɪndəstri] Industrie III

influence ['ɪnfluəns] Einfluss IV U5, 98

information (*no pl*) [ˌɪnfə'meɪʃn] Information; Informationen I

information desk [ɪnfə'meɪʃn ˌdesk] Information II

informative [ɪn'fɔːmətɪv] informativ IV U4, 77

ingredient [ɪn'griːdɪənt] Zutat II

inhabitant [ɪn'hæbɪtnt] Einwohner; Einwohnerin; Bewohner; Bewohnerin III

injection [ɪn'dʒekʃn] Spritze III

injured ['ɪndʒəd] verletzt <IV U4, 88>

innocent ['ɪnəsnt] unschuldig IV U3, 63

insect ['ɪnsekt] Insekt III

inside [ɪn'saɪd] in ... hinein II; in; innen in; im Innern III; innen; drinnen IV U1, 25

instead [ɪn'sted] stattdessen; anstelle von IV U4, 80

instruction [ɪn'strʌkʃn] Unterricht; Anweisung <IV U2, 44>

instructor [ɪn'strʌktə] Lehrer; Lehrerin III

fitness instructor ['fɪtnəs ɪnˌstrʌktə] Fitnesstrainer; Fitnesstrainerin <IV U3, 72>

intelligent [ɪn'telɪdʒnt] intelligent; klug; vernünftig III

interest ['ɪntrəst] Interesse <IV U2, 137>

to interest ['ɪntrəst] interessieren <IV U4, 89>

*to be **interested** in [biː 'ɪntrəstɪd ˌɪn] sich interessieren für; interessiert sein an III

interesting ['ɪntrəstɪŋ] interessant I

internet ['ɪntənet] Internet II

to surf the internet [ˌsɜːf ði 'ɪntənet] im Internet surfen II

to interrupt [ˌɪntə'rʌpt] unterbrechen IV U4, 94

interview ['ɪntəvjuː] Interview; Befragung II; Vorstellungsgespräch IV U2, 38

to interview ['ɪntəvjuː] interviewen; befragen I

p pen • b bed • t ten • d dad • k cat • g grey • tʃ chair • dʒ joke • f fan • v very • θ three • ð the

interviewer [ˈɪntəvjuːə] Interviewer; Interviewerin; Befrager; Befragerin IV U1, 18

to **introduce** [ˌɪntrəˈdjuːs] einführen; einleiten <IV U2, 44>; zeigen <IV U2, 48>

introduction [ˌɪntrəˈdʌkʃn] Einleitung; Einführung III

to **invade** [ɪnˈveɪd] einmarschieren (in); eindringen (in) III

to **invent** [ɪnˈvent] erfinden III

invention [ɪnˈvenʃn] Erfindung III

inventor [ɪnˈventə] Erfinder; Erfinderin III

invincible [ɪnˈvɪnsəbl] unschlagbar; unbesiegbar <IV U2, 35>

invitation [ˌɪnvɪˈteɪʃn] Einladung I

to **invite** [ɪnˈvaɪt] einladen I

Irish [ˈaɪrɪʃ] irisch; Irisch III

is [ɪz] ist I

… is £1.25. [ɪz ˈwʌn paʊnd ˈtwentiˌfaɪv] … kostet ein Pfund fünfundzwanzig. I

Islam [ˈɪzlɑːm] Islam <IV U5, 206>

island [ˈaɪlənd] Insel II

isn't it? [ˈɪzntˌɪt] nicht wahr?; stimmt's? II

it [ɪt] es I

IT (Information Technology) [ˌaɪˈtiː, ɪnfəˌmeɪʃn tekˈnɒlədʒi] Informatik; Informationstechnik I

Italian [ɪˈtæliən] italienisch; Italienisch; Italiener; Italienerin II

its [ɪts] sein; ihr III

itself [ɪtˈself] (sich) selbst III

J

jacket [ˈdʒækɪt] Jacke II
jacket potato [ˌdʒækɪt pəˈteɪtəʊ] Ofenkartoffel II

jam [dʒæm] Marmelade; Konfitüre III
traffic jam [ˈtræfɪk ˌdʒæm] Stau IV U1, 14

Jamaican [dʒəˈmeɪkən] jamaikanisch II

January [ˈdʒænjuri] Januar I

Japanese [ˌdʒæpənˈiːz] japanisch; Japanisch; aus Japan; Japaner; Japanerin IV U5, 99

jar [dʒɑː] Glas III

jazz [dʒæz] Jazz *(Musikrichtung)* IV U5, 97

jealous [ˈdʒeləs] eifersüchtig; neidisch II

jeans *(pl)* [dʒiːnz] Jeans I

jersey [ˈdʒɜːzi] Trikot <IV U2, 50>

jewellery [ˈdʒuːəlri] Schmuck II

Jewish [ˈdʒuːɪʃ] jüdisch <IV U5, 206>

job [dʒɒb] Job I; Aufgabe; Tätigkeit; Arbeit; Beruf II
job title [ˈdʒɒb ˌtaɪtl] Stellenbezeichnung; Berufsbezeichnung IV U2, 38

to **join** [dʒɔɪn] sich anschließen III; verbinden <IV U2, 48>

joke [dʒəʊk] Witz I

journalism [ˈdʒɜːnlɪzm] Journalistik; Journalismus IV U2, 34

journalistic [ˈdʒɜːnlɪstɪk] journalistisch <IV U2, 49>

journey [ˈdʒɜːni] Fahrt; Reise III

to **joust** [dʒaʊst] einen Turnierzweikampf austragen; turnieren III

jousting [ˈdʒaʊstɪŋ] Turnierzweikampf III

joyful [ˈdʒɔɪfl] freudig <IV U5, 108>

judge [dʒʌdʒ] Juror; Jurorin II

juice [dʒuːs] Saft II

July [dʒʊˈlaɪ] Juli I

jumble sale [ˈdʒʌmbl ˌseɪl] Flohmarkt II

to **jump** [dʒʌmp] zusammenzucken; erschrecken III; springen IV U3, 63
jumping fitness [ˈdʒʌmpɪŋ ˌfɪtnəs] Jumping Fitness *(Trendsportart)* IV U4, 81

June [dʒuːn] Juni I

jungle [ˈdʒʌŋgl] Dschungel IV U4, 85

junior [ˈdʒuːniə] Nachwuchs- <IV U2, 137>

just [dʒʌst] gerade (eben); soeben; nur II

K

karate [kəˈrɑːti] Karate III

kebab [kɪˈbæb] Döner <IV U5, 206>

*to **keep** [kiːp] halten II
to keep cool [ˌkiːp ˈkuːl] Ruhe bewahren <III>
to keep going [kiːp ˈgəʊɪŋ] weitergehen; weitermachen IV U4, 85
to keep in touch [ˌkiːp ɪn ˈtʌtʃ] in Verbindung bleiben II
to keep out [kiːpˈaʊt] draußen halten III

kept [kept] simple past, past participle von *to keep* II

ketchup [ˈketʃʌp] Ketchup II

key word [ˈkiː ˌwɜːd] Stichwort; Schlüsselbegriff <IV U3, 68>

keyword [ˈkiːwɜːd] Schlüsselwort <IV U1, 31>

kid [kɪd] Kind II

kidney bean [ˈkɪdni ˌbiːn] Kidneybohne II

to **kill** [kɪl] töten III

kilogram (kg) [ˈkɪləgræm] Kilogramm (kg) I
7 kilograms a day [ˌkɪləgræmz ə ˈdeɪ] sieben Kilogramm täglich I

kilometre (km) [kɪˈlɒmɪtə] Kilometer (km) I
40 kilometres an hour [kɪˈlɒmɪtəzˌənˈaʊə] 40 Kilometer pro Stunde I

kilt [kɪlt] Schottenrock; Kilt III

kind [kaɪnd] freundlich; nett II

king [kɪŋ] König III

kiss [kɪs] Kuss II

kitchen [ˈkɪtʃɪn] Küche I

knee [niː] Knie III

knife *(sg)* [naɪf], **knives** *(pl)* [naɪvz] Messer II

knight [naɪt] Ritter III

*to **know** [nəʊ] wissen; kennen I; verstehen IV U5, 103
to get to know [ˌget tə ˈnəʊ] kennen lernen II
I don't know! [aɪ ˌdəʊnt ˈnəʊ] Ich weiß (es) nicht! I

knowledge *(no pl)* [ˈnɒlɪdʒ] Wissen; Kenntnisse <IV U1, 24>

*to be **known** as [bi: ˈnəʊn‿əz] bekannt sein als <IV U3, 70>

L

lab fee [ˈlæb ˌfi:] Laborgebühr <IV U2, 48>

label [ˈleɪbl] Etikett; Beschriftung <IV U1, 27>

to **label** [ˈleɪbl] beschriften <III>

ladder [ˈlædə] Leiter I

lady [ˈleɪdi] Dame; Frau II

laid [leɪd] simple past, past participle von *to lay* II

lake [leɪk] See III

lamb [læm] Lamm II

lamp [læmp] Lampe I

land [lænd] Land II

land of the free [ˌlænd‿əv ðə ˈfri:] Land der Freien IV U3, 53

to **land** [lænd] landen IV U3, 54

landlord [ˈlændlɔ:d] Eigentümer II

landowner [ˈlændˌəʊnə] Grundbesitzer; Grundbesitzerin IV U4, 84

landscape [ˈlændskeɪp] Landschaft IV ZI, 9

language [ˈlæŋgwɪdʒ] Sprache II

language detectives [ˈlæŋgwɪdʒ ˌdɪtektɪvz] Sprachdetektive <I>

language tip [ˌlæŋgwɪdʒ ˈtɪp] Grammatikhinweis <I>

sign language [ˈsaɪn ˌlæŋgwɪdʒ] Gebärdensprache; Zeichensprache III

laptop [ˈlæptɒp] Laptop I

large [lɑ:dʒ] groß II

lasagne [ləˈzænjə] Lasagne II

to **last** [lɑ:st] dauern; andauern; anhalten IV U4, 86

last [lɑ:st] letzte I

at last [ət ˈlɑ:st] endlich; zu guter Letzt II

late [leɪt] (zu) spät I

later [ˈleɪtə] später I

to **laugh** [lɑ:f] lachen II

to mow the **lawn** [ˌməʊ ðə ˈlɔ:n] den Rasen mähen <IV U2, 191>

*to **lay** [leɪ] legen; decken II

to lay the table [ˌleɪ ðə ˈteɪbl] den Tisch decken II

layout [ˈleɪaʊt] Layout; Anordnung IV U4, 77

lead [li:d] Leine I

leader [ˈli:də] Führer; Führerin; Anführer; Anführerin III

to **learn** [lɜ:n] lernen II

to learn about sth [ˌlɜ:n əˈbaʊt] etwas erfahren über III

least [li:st] geringste; am wenigsten <IV U3, 59>

leather [ˈleðə] Leder III

leave [li:v] lassen; verlassen; abfahren II

leaving [ˈli:vɪŋ] Abschieds- II

left [left] simple past, past participle von *to leave* II

left [left] links III

to turn left [ˌtɜ:n ˈleft] (nach) links abbiegen I

on the left [ɒn ðə ˈleft] auf der linken Seite; links I

leg [leg] Bein II

lemon [ˈlemən] Zitrone II

lemonade [ˌleməˈneɪd] Limonade II

*to **lend** [lend] leihen; verleihen II

length *(no pl)* [leŋθ] Dauer; Länge <IV U2, 44>

lent [lent] simple past von *to lend* II

less [les] weniger III

lesson [ˈlesn] Schulstunde; Unterricht I

let's [lets] lass uns I

Let's see … [ˌlets ˈsi:] Lass mal sehen …; Also … I

letter [ˈletə] Buchstabe; Brief III

lettuce [ˈletɪs] Kopfsalat II

water **level** [ˈwɔ:tə ˌlevl] Wasserpegel; Wasserstand <IV U5, 142>

library [ˈlaɪbri] Bibliothek; Bücherei III

driver's **license** *(AE)* [ˈdraɪvəz ˌlaɪsɪs] Führerschein IV U2, 38

lid [lɪd] Deckel <IV U3, 71>

life *(sg)* [laɪf], **lives** *(pl)* [laɪvz] Leben I

lifeboat [ˈlaɪfbəʊt] Rettungsboot III

lifestyle [ˈlaɪfstaɪl] Lebensart; Lifestyle IV U4, 74

lifetime [ˈlaɪftaɪm] Leben; Lebenszeit IV U4, 76

lift [lɪft] Aufzug; Lift <IV U1, 15>

light [laɪt] Licht IV U1, 13

light bulb [ˈlaɪt ˌbʌlb] Glühbirne III

tea light [ˈti: ˌlaɪt] Teelicht <IV U3, 71>

lights [laɪts] Ampel IV U1, 14

to **like** [laɪk] mögen I

to like … best [ˌlaɪk ˈbest] am meisten mögen; am liebsten mögen I

would like [wʊd ˈlaɪk] würde(n) gern; hätte(n) gern II

I wouldn't like (to) … [aɪ ˈwʊdnt laɪk (tə)] Ich möchte nicht …; Ich würde nicht gerne … I

I'd like (to) … (= I would like to) [aɪd ˈlaɪk (tə)] Ich möchte …; Ich würde gerne … I

Would you like (to) …? [ˌwʊd jə ˈlaɪk (tə)] Möchtest du? I

like [laɪk] wie I

like this [laɪk ˈðɪs] so; auf diese Weise I

line [laɪn] Zeile; Linie II

line dance [ˈlaɪn ˌdɑ:ns] Line Dance *(alle tanzen zusammen in einer Reihe)* <IV U5, 143>

lines *(pl)* [laɪnz] Text II

link [lɪŋk] Link; Verbindung IV U4, 80

linking word [ˌlɪŋkɪŋ ˈwɜ:d] Verbindungswort <IV U3, 73>

lion [ˈlaɪən] Löwe I

list [lɪst] Liste II

ranking list [ˈræŋkɪŋ lɪst] Rangliste; Rangfolge <IV U3, 59>

shopping list [ˈʃɒpɪŋ ˌlɪst] Einkaufszettel I

to **listen** (to) [ˈlɪsn] zuhören; anhören; hören I

listener [ˈlɪsənə] Zuhörer; Zuhörerin II

listening [ˈlɪsnɪŋ] Hörverstehen <I>

little [ˈlɪtl] klein II

a little [ə ˈlɪtl] ein bisschen II

to **live** [lɪv] wohnen; leben I

living room [ˈlɪvɪŋ ˌrʊm] Wohnzimmer I

loaf (sg) [ləʊf], **loaves** (pl) [ləʊvz] Brotlaib III

local [ˈləʊkl] hiesig; örtlich; lokal III

to **locate** [ləʊˈkeɪt] finden <IV U2, 48>

location [ləʊˈkeɪʃn] Drehort; Lage III; Aufenthaltsort; Standort <IV U5, 111>

to **lock** [lɒk] abschließen I

locker [ˈlɒkə] Schließfach; Spind IV U2, 34

lonely [ˈləʊnli] einsam III

long [lɒŋ] lang I

look [lʊk] Blick; Anblick; Sicht IV U1, 14
to have a look [ˌhæv ə ˈlʊk] anschauen II

to **look** [lʊk] schauen; nachschauen I; aussehen; sehen II
to look after [ˌlʊk ˈɑːftə] aufpassen; hüten II
to look at [ˈlʊk ət] anschauen I
to look for [ˈlʊk fə] suchen nach II
to look up [ˌlʊk ˈʌp] aufschauen; nachschauen II
Look … [lʊk] Schau mal …; Schau … nach. I

lookout point [ˈlʊkaʊt ˌpɔɪnt] Aussichtspunkt II

loose [luːs] locker; lose II

lorry driver [ˈlɒri ˌdraɪvə] LKW-Fahrer; LKW-Fahrerin II

*to **lose** [luːz] verlieren II

lost [lɒst] simple past von to lose II; past participle von to lose III
to get lost [get lɒst] sich verirren I

a **lot** [ə ˈlɒt] viel I; sehr II
a lot of [ə ˈlɒt əv] viel(e); eine Menge I

parking **lot** (AE) [ˈpɑːkɪŋ ˌlɒt] Parkplatz IV U1, 15

body **lotion** [ˈbɒdi ˌləʊʃn] Körperlotion III

lots [lɒts] viel; jede Menge III
lots of [ˈlɒts əv] viel; jede Menge I

loud [laʊd] laut III

love [lʌv] Liebe IV U4, 85

*to **fall** in **love** (with) [ˌfɔːl ɪn ˈlʌv] sich verlieben (in) III

to **love** [lʌv] lieben; gern mögen I

loved ones [ˈlʌvd ˌwʌnz] Angehörige; Nahestehende <IV U5, 108>

lovely [ˈlʌvli] schön; herrlich; hübsch II

low [ləʊ] niedrig II

lower [ˈləʊə] untere III

good **luck** [ˌɡʊd ˈlʌk] viel Glück II

luckily [ˈlʌkɪli] glücklicherweise II

*to be **lucky** [bi: ˈlʌki] Glück haben III

lucky day [ˌlʌki ˈdeɪ] Glückstag II

lucky number [ˌlʌki ˈnʌmbə] Glückszahl I

lunch [lʌnʃ] Mittagessen I
packed lunch [ˌpækt ˈlʌnʃ] Lunchpaket; Vesper II

lunchtime [ˈlʌnʃtaɪm] Mittagszeit; Mittagspause I

lyrics (pl) [ˈlɪrɪks] Liedtext <II>

M

machine [məˈʃiːn] Automat; Maschine II
payment machine [ˈpeɪmənt ˌməʃiːn] Bezahlautomat II

made [meɪd] simple past von to make I; past participle von to make II
to be made of [bi: ˈmeɪd əv] hergestellt sein aus III

magazine [ˌmæɡəˈziːn] Zeitschrift I

magic [ˈmædʒɪk] Magie; Zauberei II

magic [ˈmædʒɪk] magisch; Zauber- II

main course [ˌmeɪn ˈkɔːs] Hauptgericht II

major [ˈmeɪdʒə] Haupt-; wichtig; bedeutend IV ZI, 8

majority [məˈdʒɒrəti] Mehrheit IV U1, 23

*to **make** [meɪk] erstellen; machen; tun; bilden I
to make a cake [ˌmeɪk ə ˈkeɪk] einen Kuchen backen I

to **make** a reservation [ˌmeɪk ə ˈrezəveɪʃn] reservieren III

to **make** friends [ˌmeɪk ˈfrendz] Freundschaften schließen I

to **make** it [ˈmeɪk ɪt] es schaffen IV U3, 54

to **make** sb feel like sth [ˌmeɪk … ˈfiːl laɪk] jmdm. das Gefühl geben, etw. zu sein III

film **maker** [ˈfɪlm ˌmeɪkə] Filmemacher; Filmemacherin <III>

make-up [ˈmeɪkʌp] Make-up; Schminke IV U3, 58

mama [ˈmæmə] Mama II

man (sg) [mæn], **men** (pl) [men] Mann I

manager [ˈmænɪdʒə] Manager; Managerin; Geschäftsführer; Geschäftsführerin IV U2, 38

many [ˈmeni] viele II
how many [ˌhaʊ ˈmeni] wie viele II

map [mæp] Stadtplan; Landkarte III
mind map [ˈmaɪnd ˌmæp] Wörternetz <I>

March [mɑːtʃ] März I

to **march** [mɑːtʃ] marschieren <IV U5, 108>
marching band [ˈmɑːtʃɪŋ ˌbænd] Marschkapelle <IV U2, 190>

market [ˈmɑːkɪt] Markt II
farmers' market [ˌfɑːməz ˈmɑːkɪt] Bauernmarkt <IV U3, 72>
market stall [ˈmɑːkɪt ˌstɔːl] Marktstand; Marktbude <IV U2, 191>

marquee [mɑːˈkiː] Partyzelt; Festzelt <IV U1, 19>

*to get **married** [get ˈmærɪd] heiraten II

mashed potatoes [ˌmæʃt pəˈteɪtəʊz] Kartoffelbrei II

mast [mɑːst] Mast <IV U3, 71>

master [ˈmɑːstə] Herr; Meister <IV U3, 71>

match [mætʃ] Spiel I
final match [ˌfaɪnl ˈmætʃ] Endspiel <IV U2, 50>

to **match** [mætʃ] zuordnen I; zusammenpassen <IV U4, 95>

match

material [məˈtɪəriəl] Material; Stoff <III>

Math *(AE)* [mæθ] Mathematik; Mathe IV U2, 34

Maths [mæθs] Mathematik; Mathe I

It doesn't **matter.** [ɪt ˌdʌznt ˈmætə] Es ist egal. II

May [meɪ] Mai I

may [meɪ] vielleicht; können; dürfen II

maybe [ˈmeɪbi] vielleicht I

mayonnaise [ˌmeɪəˈneɪz] Mayonnaise II

me [mi:] mich; ich; mir I

meal [mi:l] Essen; Mahlzeit II

*to **mean** [mi:n] bedeuten; meinen III

mean [mi:n] gemein IV U3, 63

meaning [ˈmi:nɪŋ] Bedeutung; Sinn <III>

meant [ment] simple past, past participle von *to mean* III

meat [mi:t] Fleisch I

social **media** [ˌsəʊʃl ˈmi:diə] soziale Medien IV U4, 80

mediation [ˌmi:diˈeɪʃn] Sprachmittlung <I>

medicine [ˈmedsn] Medikamente; Medizin III

*to **meet** [mi:t] kennen lernen; treffen I

menu [ˈmenju:] Speisekarte II

mess [mes] Unordnung; Durcheinander I

message [ˈmesɪdʒ] Botschaft; Nachricht; SMS II

morning message [ˈmɔ:nɪŋ ˌmesɪdʒ] morgendliche Ansprache IV U2, 34

text message [ˈtekst ˌmesɪdʒ] SMS II

met [met] simple past von *to meet* I

metal [ˈmetl] Metall III

method [ˈmeθəd] Methode II

metre [ˈmi:tə] Meter I

microwave [ˈmaɪkrəweɪv] Mikrowelle IV U3, 59

middle [ˈmɪdl] Mitte III

in the middle [ɪn ðə ˈmɪdl] in der Mitte III

midnight [ˈmɪdnaɪt] Mitternacht III

migrant [ˈmaɪgrnt] Migrant; Migrantin <IV U4, 88>

mild [maɪld] mild I

mile [maɪl] Meile II

square mile (= sq. mi.) [ˌskweə ˈmaɪl] Quadratmeile IV ZI, 8

milk [mɪlk] Milch I

milkshake [ˈmɪlkˌʃeɪk] Milchmischgetränk; Milchshake III

million [ˈmɪljən] Million III

half a million [ˌhɑ:fˌə ˈmɪljən] eine halbe Million III

mind map [ˈmaɪnd ˌmæp] Wörternetz <I>

Never **mind.** [ˌnevə ˈmaɪnd] Macht nichts.; Schon gut.; Mach dir nichts draus. II

mine [maɪn] Bergwerk III

mine [maɪn] meins; meine II

of mine [əv ˈmaɪn] von mir II

miner [ˈmaɪnə] Bergarbeiter; Bergarbeiterin III

mineral water [ˈmɪnrl ˌwɔ:tə] Mineralwasser III

minimum [ˈmɪnɪməm] Minimum; minimal; Mindest- IV U2, 38

minority [maɪˈnɒrəti] Minderheit IV U1, 22

minute [ˈmɪnɪt] Minute II

mirror [ˈmɪrə] Spiegel III

miserable [ˈmɪzrəbl] elend; armselig; jämmerlich III

*to give sth a **miss** [ˌgɪv sʌmθɪŋˌə ˈmɪs] auf etw. verzichten; etw. bleiben lassen III

to **miss** [mɪs] verpassen; vermissen II

to **mix** [mɪks] mischen; vermischen; mixen IV U5, 98

mixed pickles [ˌmɪkst ˈpɪklz] gemischtes Essiggemüse <IV U5, 112>

mobile (phone) [ˈməʊbaɪl (ˌfəʊn)] Handy; Mobiltelefon I

modern [ˈmɒdn] modern I

moment [ˈməʊmənt] Moment; Augenblick II

Monday [ˈmʌndeɪ] Montag I

money [ˈmʌni] Geld I

monkey [ˈmʌŋki] Affe I

monster [ˈmɒnstə] Ungeheuer; Monster III

month [mʌnθ] Monat I

monthly [ˈmʌnθli] monatlich III

monument [ˈmɒnjəmənt] Denkmal II

moral [ˈmɒrl] moralisch <IV U1, 24>

more [mɔ:] mehr I

morning [ˈmɔ:nɪŋ] Morgen; Vormittag I

Good morning. [gʊd ˈmɔ:nɪŋ] Guten Morgen. II

morning message [ˈmɔ:nɪŋ ˌmesɪdʒ] morgendliche Ansprache IV U2, 34

mosque [mɒsk] Moschee II

most [məʊst] die meisten; die Mehrheit I; am meisten II

mostly [ˈməʊstli] hauptsächlich <IV U5, 108>

mother [ˈmʌðə] Mutter I

to **motivate** [ˈməʊtɪveɪt] motivieren <IV U2, 50>

motorbike [ˈməʊtəbaɪk] Motorrad I

mountain [ˈmaʊntɪn] Berg III

mouse *(sg)* [maʊs], **mice** *(pl)* [maɪs] Maus I

moussaka [muˈsɑ:kə] Moussaka II

mouth [maʊθ] Mund II

move [mu:v] Bewegung III

to **move** [mu:v] (sich) bewegen IV U1, 22

to move (house) [mu:v] umziehen II

movement [ˈmu:vmənt] Bewegung IV U5, 96

movie [ˈmu:vi] Film I

movie theater *(AE)* [ˈmu:vi ˌθi:ətə] Kino <IV U1, 134>

to **mow** the lawn [ˌməʊ ðə ˈlɔ:n] den Rasen mähen <IV U2, 191>

Mr [ˈmɪstə] Herr *(Anrede)* I

Mrs [ˈmɪsɪz] Frau *(Anrede)* I

Ms [mɪz] Frau *(Anrede)* I

much [mʌtʃ] viel I

so much [ˌsəʊ ˈmʌtʃ] so sehr III

too much [ˌtu: ˈmʌtʃ] zu sehr II

mud [mʌd] Schlamm; Matsch III

muddy [ˈmʌdi] schlammig I

multicultural [ˌmʌltiˈkʌltʃrl] multikulturell IV U5, 98

mum [mʌm] Mama I

mural [ˈmjʊərəl] Wandgemälde III

murderer [ˈmɜ:drə] Mörder; Mörderin III

museum [mjuˈzi:əm] Museum II

music [ˈmju:zɪk] Musik I
country and western music [ˌkʌntri ənd ˈwestən ˌmju:zɪk] Countrymusik <IV U5, 143>

musical [ˈmju:zɪkl] Musical <IV U1, 134>

musical [ˈmju:zɪkl] Musik-; musikalisch III

musician [mjuˈzɪʃn] Musiker; Musikerin <IV U4, 140>

Muslim [ˈmʊzlɪm] Muslim; Muslimin I; muslimisch <IV U5, 206>

must [mʌst] müssen I
must not/never [ˌmʌst ˈnɒt/ˈnevə] nicht/nie dürfen III
mustn't [ˈmʌsnt] nicht dürfen III

mustard [ˈmʌstəd] Senf II

my [maɪ] mein, meine I
My name is … [maɪ ˈneɪm ɪz] Ich heiße … I

myself [maɪˈself] selbst; selber III

mystery [ˈmɪstri] Rätsel; Geheimnis I

N

nacho [ˈnɑ:tʃəʊ] Nacho <IV U5, 112>

to nag [næg] nörgeln; meckern III

nail [neɪl] Nagel III
nail scissors [ˈneɪl ˌsɪzəz] Nagelschere III

name [neɪm] Name I

to name [neɪm] benennen IV ZI, 9
named after [ˈneɪmd ˌɑ:ftə] benannt nach <IV U3, 70>

napkin [ˈnæpkɪn] Serviette II

narrator [nəˈreɪtə] Erzähler; Erzählerin I

national [ˈnæʃnl] National-; national III

national holiday [ˌnæʃnl ˈhɒlədeɪ] Nationalfeiertag <IV U1, 24>

national park [ˌnæʃnl ˈpɑ:k] Nationalpark; Naturpark <IV U1, 30>

nationality [ˌnæʃnˈæləti] Nationalität; Staatsangehörigkeit <IV U5, 99>

Native American [ˌneɪtɪv əˈmerɪkən] Ureinwohner Amerikas; Ureinwohnerin Amerikas; Indianer; Indianerin; indianisch IV U2, 32

nature [ˈneɪtʃə] Natur III

naughty [ˈnɔ:ti] frech; böse III

near [nɪə] in der Nähe von I; nah III

to need [ni:d] brauchen I
needn't [ˈni:dnt] nicht brauchen; nicht müssen I

with special needs [wɪð ˌspeʃl ˈni:dz] mit Behinderung; mit besonderen Bedürfnissen III

neighbor (AE) [ˈneɪbə] Nachbar; Nachbarin IV U3, 54

neighbour [ˈneɪbə] Nachbar; Nachbarin III

nervous [ˈnɜ:vəs] nervös; aufgeregt II

net [net] Netz IV U4, 75
safety net [ˈseɪfti ˌnet] Sicherheitsnetz IV U4, 75

netball [ˈnetbɔ:l] Korbball I

never [ˈnevə] nie; niemals I
Never mind. [ˌnevə ˈmaɪnd] Macht nichts.; Schon gut.; Mach dir nichts draus. II

new [nju:] neu I
New Yorker [ˌnju: ˈjɔ:kə] New Yorker; New Yorkerin IV U1, 13

news [nju:z] Neuigkeit(en); Nachricht(en) II

newsagent's [ˈnju:zˌeɪdʒnts] Zeitschriftenladen III

newspaper [ˈnju:sˌpeɪpə] Zeitung II

next [nekst] nächste I; als Nächstes II
next to [ˈnekst tə] neben I

nice [naɪs] schön; nett I; lecker; gut III

nickname [ˈnɪkneɪm] Spitzname <IV U4, 141>

niece [ni:s] Nichte III

night [naɪt] Nacht I
night walk [ˌnaɪt ˈwɔ:k] Nachtwanderung I
that night [ðæt ˈnaɪt] an jenem Abend; in jener Nacht II

nightmare [ˈnaɪtmeə] Alptraum <IV U3, 68>

nine [naɪn] neun I

nineteen [ˌnaɪnˈti:n] neunzehn I

ninety [ˈnaɪnti] neunzig I

no [nəʊ] kein; keine; nein I
no one [ˈnəʊ wʌn] niemand I
No way! [ˌnəʊ ˈweɪ] Auf keinen Fall!; Was?!; Echt?! III

nobody [ˈnəʊbədi] niemand III

noise [nɔɪz] Geräusch I

noisy [ˈnɔɪzi] laut III

Norman [ˈnɔ:mən] Normanne; Normannin III

the Normans [ðə ˈnɔ:mənz] die Normannen III

north [nɔ:θ] Norden III
north of [ˈnɔ:θ əv] nördlich von IV ZI, 9

northwest [ˌnɔ:θˈwest] Nordwesten III
northwest of [ˌnɔ:θˈwest əv] nordwestlich III

nose [nəʊz] Nase I

not [nɒt] nicht I
not at all [ˌnɒt ət ˈɔ:l] überhaupt nicht; gar nicht II
not … any [ˌnɒt … eni] kein II
not … any more [ˌnɒt … eni ˈmɔ:] nicht mehr III
not … either [nɒt … ˈaɪðə] auch nicht III
not … yet [nɒt … ˈjet] noch nicht II

note [nəʊt] Geldschein II

notes [nəʊts] Notizen <IV U2, 37>

nothing [ˈnʌθɪŋ] nichts IV U3, 63

noun [naʊn] Nomen; Hauptwort <I>

November [nəˈvembə] November I

now [naʊ] jetzt; nun I; heutzutage II
right now [ˌraɪt ˈnaʊ] gerade; jetzt gleich; sofort III

nowhere [ˈnəʊweə] nirgendwo; nirgendwohin IV U2, 34

nowhere

s six • **z** zoo • **ʃ** she • **ʒ** revision • **h** her • **m** me • **n** no • **ŋ** sing • **ɪə** hear • **l** let • **r** red • **j** yes   235

nugget [ˈnʌgɪt] Klumpen; Nugget <IV U4, 92>

number [ˈnʌmbə] Nummer; Zahl I; Anzahl IV U4, 75

lucky number [ˌlʌki ˈnʌmbə] Glückszahl I

ordinal number [ˌɔːdɪnəl ˈnʌmbə] Ordinalzahl <I>

phone number [ˈfəʊn ˌnʌmbə] Telefonnummer III

nurse [nɜːs] Krankenschwester; Krankenpfleger II

nut [nʌt] Nuss I

O

o'clock [əˈklɒk] Uhr *(Zeitangabe bei vollen Stunden)* I

oak [əʊk] Eiche <IV U5, 142>

OAP [ˌəʊeɪˈpiː] Rentner; Rentnerin <IV U5, 207>

oat [əʊt] Hafer III

object [ˈɒbdʒɪkt] Objekt; Gegenstand <III>

observation [ˌɒbzəˈveɪʃn] Beobachtung <IV U2, 48>

ocean [ˈəʊʃn] Ozean; Meer IV ZI, 9

October [ɒkˈtəʊbə] Oktober I

the **odd** one out [ˌɒd wʌnˈaʊt] das Wort, das nicht in die Gruppe passt <III>

of [ɒv] von I

of course [əv ˈkɔːs] natürlich; selbstverständlich I

of mine [əv ˈmaɪn] von mir II

off [ɒf] abseits von <IV U1, 134>; von … weg IV U5, 107

special **offer** [ˌspeʃl ˈɒfə] Sonderangebot III

to **offer** [ˈɒfə] anbieten IV U2, 38

office [ˈɒfɪs] Büro II

post office [ˈpəʊst ˌɒfɪs] Postamt I

police **officer** [pəˈliːs ˌɒfɪsə] Polizeibeamter; Polizeibeamtin I

official [əˈfɪʃl] offiziell IV U4, 84

often [ˈɒfn] oft; häufig I

oh [əʊ] null *(bei Uhrzeiten und Telefonnummern)* I

oil [ɔɪl] Öl IV U5, 98

OK [ˌəʊˈkeɪ] okay I

old [əʊld] alt I

on [ɒn] auf; an I

to get on (the bus) [ˌget ˈɒn] einsteigen (in den Bus) IV U5, 106

to try on [ˌtraɪ ˈɒn] anprobieren II

on board [ˈɒn bɔːd] an Bord III

on foot [ɒn ˈfʊt] zu Fuß I

on purpose [ɒn ˈpɜːpəs] absichtlich II

on 7th July [ɒn ðə ˈsevnθ əv ˌdʒʊlaɪ] am 7. Juli I

on the bus [ɒn ðə ˈbʌs] im Bus II

on the left [ɒn ðə ˈleft] auf der linken Seite; links I

on the right [ɒn ðə ˈraɪt] auf der rechten Seite; rechts I

on the way [ˌɒn ðə ˈweɪ] auf dem Weg; unterwegs I

on time [ɒn ˈtaɪm] pünktlich III

on Tuesday [ɒn ˈtjuːzdeɪ] am Dienstag I

on TV [ɒn ˌtiːˈviː] im Fernsehen IV U1, 13

on Wednesdays [ɒn ˈwenzdeɪz] mittwochs I

on weekdays [ɒn ˈwiːkdeɪz] unter der Woche; an Werktagen III

once [wʌns] einst; einmal IV U1, 25

once more [ˈwʌns ˌmɔː] noch einmal II

one [wʌn] eins I

a/one hundred [ˈhʌndrəd] einhundert; hundert I

one day [wʌn ˈdeɪ] eines Tages III

one stop [ˌwʌn ˈstɒp] einmal Umsteigen <IV U3, 66>

one(s) [wʌn(z)] *Platzhalter für ein Nomen* III

loved ones [ˈlʌvd ˌwʌnz] Angehörige; Nahestehende <IV U5, 108>

one-way [ˈwʌnweɪ] einfach <IV U3, 66>

onion [ˈʌnjən] Zwiebel II

onion rings [ˈʌnjən ˌrɪŋz] Zwiebelringe <IV U5, 112>

online [ˌɒnˈlaɪn] online II

only [ˈəʊnli] nur I; einzige II

to **open** [ˈəʊpn] öffnen; aufmachen I

opening [ˈəʊpnɪŋ] Anfang; Eröffnung <IV U5, 111>

opening times [ˈəʊpnɪŋ ˌtaɪmz] Öffnungszeiten <IV U5, 207>

operation [ˌɒprˈeɪʃn] Operation III

operator [ˈɒpreɪtə] Vermittlung III

opinion [əˈpɪnjən] Meinung III

opposite [ˈɒpəzɪt] Gegenteil <II>

opposite [ˈɒpəzɪt] gegenüber I

optimistic [ˌɒptɪˈmɪstɪk] optimistisch III

or [ɔː] oder I

orange [ˈɒrɪndʒ] Orange I

orange [ˈɒrɪndʒ] orange I

orchestra [ˈɔːkɪstrə] Orchester III

order [ˈɔːdə] Reihenfolge <III>

to **order** [ˈɔːdə] bestellen II

ordinal number [ˌɔːdɪnəl ˈnʌmbə] Ordinalzahl <I>

organic [ɔːˈgænɪk] Bio-; organisch <IV U3, 72>

to **organize** [ˈɔːgənaɪz] organisieren II

original [əˈrɪdʒnl] original; ursprünglich <IV U1, 24>

other [ˈʌðə] andere; weitere I

each other [iːtʃ ˈʌðə] einander; sich; sich gegenseitig III

others [ˈʌðəz] andere II

the others [ðiˌˈʌðəz] die anderen I

ounce [aʊns] Unze (Maßeinheit: 28,35 Gramm) <IV U5, 112>

our [aʊə] unser, unsere I

ours [aʊəz] unsere III

ourselves [ˌaʊəˈselvz] selber; selbst III

out [aʊt] heraus II; aus; draußen; außerhalb <IV U3, 68>

to ask sb out [ˌɑːsk … ˈaʊt] sich mit jmdm. verabreden IV U2, 42

to fall out of [ˌfɔːl ˈaʊt əv] herausfallen aus IV U2, 42

to go out with [ˌgəʊ ˈaʊt wɪð] (aus) gehen mit IV U3, 58

to keep out [ˌkiːp ˈaʊt] draußen halten III

to point out [ˌpɔɪnt ˈaʊt] hinweisen auf <IV U1, 183>

out and about [ˌaʊt_ən_ə'baʊt] unterwegs I

out of [ˈaʊt_əv] aus ... heraus II; von <IV U2, 44>

out of fashion [ˌaʊt_əv 'fæʃn] altmodisch; nicht mehr aktuell <IV U3, 72>

outdated [ˌaʊt'deɪtɪd] veraltet IV U4, 81

outdoor [ˌaʊt'dɔ:] Freiluft-; Outdoor- III

outfit [ˈaʊtfɪt] Outfit; Kleidung III

outline [ˈaʊtlaɪn] Skizze; Kontur; Überblick <III>

outside [ˌaʊt'saɪd] draußen; im Freien II; außerhalb IV U2, 38

oven [ˈʌvn] Backofen II

over [ˈəʊvə] über IV U1, 12

over there [ˌəʊvə 'ðeə] da drüben; dort drüben II

to **own** [əʊn] besitzen II

own [əʊn] eigene II

P

p.m. [ˌpi:'em] nachmittags *(Uhrzeit)* II

to **pack** [pæk] packen; einpacken II

to pack up [ˈpæk_ʌp] packen; einpacken II

package [ˈpækɪdʒ] Paket IV U5, 102

packed lunch [ˈpækt 'lʌnʃ] Lunchpaket; Vesper II

packet [ˈpækɪt] Packung; Tüte I

pad [pæd] Polster; Schutz <IV U2, 50>

paddle [ˈpædl] Paddel <IV U3, 72>

paddle steamer [ˈpædl ˌsti:mə] Raddampfer <IV U5, 142>

standup **paddleboarding** [ˈstændʌp ˌpædlbɔ:dɪŋ] Stehpaddeln <IV U3, 72>

paddlewheel [ˈpædlˌwi:l] Schaufelrad <IV U5, 142>

page [peɪdʒ] Seite I

paid [peɪd] simple past, past participle von *to pay* II

to **paint** [peɪnt] streichen; anmalen; malen II

pair [peə] Paar <III>

a pair of [ə 'peər_əv] ein Paar II

pancake [ˈpænkeɪk] Pfannkuchen II

to **panic** [ˈpænɪk] panisch werden II

pantomime [ˈpæntəmaɪm] Weihnachtstheaterstück II

paper [ˈpeɪpə] Papier III

paperboy [ˈpeɪpəˌbɔɪ] Zeitungsausträger IV U2, 41

papergirl [ˈpeɪpəˌɡɜ:l] Zeitungsausträgerin IV U2, 41

papers *(pl)* [ˈpeɪpəz] Unterlagen; Papiere IV U1, 19

parade [pə'reɪd] Parade; Umzug III

paradise [ˈpærədaɪs] Paradies IV ZI, 9

paragraph [ˈpærəɡra:f] Paragraf; Absatz <IV U2, 43>

pardon [ˈpa:dn] Begnadigung; Entschuldigung; Verzeihung IV U3, 67

Pardon? [ˈpa:dn] Wie bitte? I

to **pardon** [ˈpa:dn] begnadigen; entschuldigen; verzeihen IV U3, 53

parent [ˈpeərnt] Elternteil <IV U1, 184>

parents *(pl)* [ˈpeərnts] Eltern II

park [pa:k] Park I

amusement park [ə'mju:zmənt ˌpa:k] Freizeitpark <IV U4, 201>

national park [ˌnæʃnl 'pa:k] Nationalpark; Naturpark <IV U1, 30>

theme park [ˈθi:m ˌpa:k] Freizeitpark I; Themenpark II

parking lot *(AE)* [ˈpa:kɪŋ ˌlɒt] Parkplatz IV U1, 15

parrot [ˈpærət] Papagei I

part [pa:t] Rolle; Teil II

to take part (in) [teɪk 'pa:t] teilnehmen (an) II

partner [ˈpa:tnə] Partnerin; Partner III

party [ˈpa:ti] Party; Feier I

to **pass** [pa:s] reichen II

passenger [ˈpæsndʒə] Passagier; Passagierin II

passive [ˈpæsɪv] Passiv; Passiv- <IV U5, 100>

past [pa:st] Vergangenheit III

past perfect [ˌpa:st 'pɜ:fɪkt] Plusquamperfekt <IV U1, 21>

past [pa:st] nach *(bei Uhrzeitangaben)* II; vorbei III

half past (two) [ˌha:f 'pa:st] halb (drei) I

pasta [ˈpæstə] Pasta; Nudeln II

pasta bake [ˌpæstə 'beɪk] Nudelauflauf II

to **paste** [peɪst] einfügen II

pasty [ˈpæsti] Pastete II

patient [ˈpeɪʃnt] Patient; Patientin II

patient [ˈpeɪʃnt] geduldig III

patterned [ˈpætənd] gemustert II

*to **pay** [peɪ] bezahlen II

to pay back [ˌpeɪ 'bæk] zurückzahlen II

to pay the bill [ˌpeɪ ðə 'bɪl] die Rechnung bezahlen III

pay phone [ˈpeɪ fəʊn] Münztelefon III

payment machine [ˈpeɪmənt ˌməʃi:n] Bezahlautomat II

PE (Physical Education) [ˌpi:'i:, ˌfɪzɪkl edʒʊ'keɪʃn] Sportunterricht I

peace [pi:s] Frieden III

peaceful [ˈpi:sfl] friedlich IV U5, 96

peach [pi:tʃ] Pfirsich I

peanut butter [ˌpi:nʌt 'bʌtə] Erdnussbutter III

pecan [ˈpi:kæn] Pekannuss IV U3, 67

pen [pen] Füller; Stift I

pence *(pl)* [pens], **penny** *(sg)* [ˈpeni] Pence *(brit. Währungseinheit)* I

... are 99p. [a: 'naɪntinaɪn ˌpens] ... kosten 99 Pence. I

pencil [ˈpensl] Bleistift; Buntstift I

pencil case [ˈpensl ˌkeɪs] Federmäppchen I

pencil sharpener [ˈpensl ˌʃa:pnə] Anspitzer I

penguin [ˈpeŋɡwɪn] Pinguin I

people *(pl)* [ˈpi:pl] Leute; Menschen I

pepper [ˈpepə] Pfeffer II

peppermint [ˈpepəmɪnt] Pfefferminz <IV U5, 113>

per [pɜ:] pro IV U2, 41

percent (%) [pə'sent] Prozent IV U1, 23

past perfect [ˌpa:st 'pɜ:fɪkt] Plusquamperfekt <IV U1, 21>

perfect

present **perfect** [ˌpreznt ˈpɜːfɪkt] das Perfekt <III>

perfect [ˈpɜːfɪkt] perfekt; vollkommen IV ZI, 9

performance [pəˈfɔːməns] Aufführung; Vorstellung <IV U2, 50>

perfume [ˈpɜːfjuːm] Parfüm III

period [ˈpɪəriəd] Stunde; Unterrichtsstunde IV U2, 34

study hall **period** [ˈstʌdi hɔːl ˌpɪəriəd] Freistunde IV U2, 34

permanent [ˈpɜːmnənt] permanent; dauerhaft <IV U1, 24>

person [ˈpɜːsn] Person; Mensch II

personal [ˈpɜːsnl] persönlich III

perspective [pəˈspektɪv] Perspektive; Blickwinkel <IV U3, 68>

pesticide [ˈpestɪsaɪd] Pestizid; Schädlingsbekämpfungsmittel <IV U4, 88>

pet [pet] Haustier I

phone [fəʊn] Telefon II

to answer the **phone** [ˌɑːnsə ðə ˈfəʊn] ans Telefon gehen III

mobile (**phone**) [ˈməʊbaɪl (ˌfəʊn)] Handy; Mobiltelefon I

pay **phone** [ˈpeɪ fəʊn] Münztelefon III

phone call [ˈfəʊn ˌkɔːl] Telefonanruf I

phone number [ˈfəʊn ˌnʌmbə] Telefonnummer III

to **phone** [fəʊn] anrufen; telefonieren II

photo [ˈfəʊtəʊ] Foto I

to take a **photo** [ˌteɪk ə ˈfəʊtəʊ] ein Foto machen I

to take **photos** [ˌteɪk ˈfəʊtəʊz] fotografieren; Fotos machen II

phrase [freɪz] Ausdruck; Redewendung; Satz <III>

PE (**Physical** Education) [ˌpiːˈiː, ˌfɪzɪkl edʒʊˈkeɪʃn] Sportunterricht I

to **pick** [pɪk] pflücken; herauslesen <IV U4, 88>; nehmen <IV U4, 93>

to **pick** up [ˌpɪk ˈʌp] aufheben II; abholen IV U2, 43

to **pick** up the pieces [ˌpɪk ʌp ðə ˈpiːsiːz] wieder in den Griff bekommen <IV U2, 137>

mixed **pickles** [ˌmɪkst ˈpɪklz] gemischtes Essiggemüse <IV U5, 112>

pick-up [ˈpɪkʌp] Abholung; Pick-up IV U5, 102

picnic [ˈpɪknɪk] Picknick I

picture [ˈpɪktʃə] Bild II; Film <IV U4, 140>

pie [paɪ] Kuchen; Pastete II

pie chart [ˈpaɪ ˌtʃɑːt] Kuchendiagramm; Tortendiagramm <IV U1, 26>

piece [piːs] Stück II

a **piece** of [ə ˈpiːs ˌəv] ein Stück <IV U1, 28>

piece of cake [ˈpiːs ˌəv keɪk] einfach <IV U3, 68>

pick up the pieces [ˌpɪk ʌp ðə ˈpiːsiːz] wieder in den Griff bekommen <IV U2, 137>

pierogi [pjɜːˈrɒgi] Pirogge II

guinea **pig** [ˈgɪni ˌpɪg] Meerschweinchen I

pile [paɪl] Stapel; Haufen <IV U4, 93>

pilgrim [ˈpɪlgrɪm] Pilger- <IV U3, 139>

pinch [pɪntʃ] Prise II

pineapple [ˈpaɪnæpl] Ananas III

pink [pɪŋk] pink; rosa I

pipe [paɪp] Rohr III

pirate [ˈpaɪrət] Seeräuber; Seeräuberin; Pirat; Piratin I

pizza [ˈpiːtsə] Pizza I

place [pleɪs] Platz; Stelle; Ort I

to take **place** [ˌteɪk ˈpleɪs] stattfinden <IV U5, 108>

plain [pleɪn] Ebene <IV U2, 136>

plain [pleɪn] schlicht; einfach II

plan [plæn] Plan II

to **plan** [plæn] planen III

plane [pleɪn] Flugzeug II

planet [ˈplænɪt] Planet <IV U2, 48>

plank [plæŋk] Brett; Planke II

plant [plɑːnt] Pflanze I

plantain [ˈplænteɪn] Kochbanane II

plantation [plænˈteɪʃn] Plantage IV U5, 97

plaster [ˈplɑːstə] Pflaster III

plastic [ˈplæstɪk] Plastik; Kunststoff III

plate [pleɪt] Teller II

play [pleɪ] Theaterstück II

role **play** [ˈrəʊl ˌpleɪ] Rollenspiel <II>

to **play** [pleɪ] spielen I

player [ˈpleɪə] Spieler; Spielerin II

playground [ˈpleɪgraʊnd] Schulhof; Pausenhof; Spielplatz I

playing card [ˈpleɪɪŋ ˌkɑːd] Spielkarte <IV U4, 92>

please [pliːz] bitte I

pledge [pledʒ] Versprechen IV U2, 45

pledge of allegiance [pledʒ əv əˈliːdʒns] Treueeid IV U2, 45

pocket [ˈpɒkɪt] Tasche; Hosentasche II

pocketful [ˈpɒkɪtfʊl] Tasche voll <IV U1, 19>

podcast [ˈpɒdkɑːst] Podcast IV U4, 94

poem [ˈpəʊɪm] Gedicht III

lookout **point** [ˈlʊkaʊt ˌpɔɪnt] Aussichtspunkt II

starting **point** [ˈstɑːtɪŋ ˌpɔɪnt] Ausgangspunkt <III>

to **point** (at) [ˌpɔɪnt ˈət] zeigen (auf) I

to **point** out [ˌpɔɪnt ˈaʊt] hinweisen auf <IV U1, 183>

police [pəˈliːs] Polizei III

police officer [pəˈliːs ˌɒfɪsə] Polizeibeamter; Polizeibeamtin I

Polish [ˈpəʊlɪʃ] polnisch; Polnisch; aus Polen IV U5, 99

polite [pəˈlaɪt] höflich II

polystyrene [ˌpɒliˈstaɪriːn] Styropor <IV U3, 71>

swimming **pool** [ˈswɪmɪŋ ˌpuːl] Schwimmbad I

poor [pɔː] arm IV U1, 18

pop [pɒp] Pop <IV U5, 143>

popcorn [ˈpɒpkɔːn] Popcorn I

popular [ˈpɒpjələ] beliebt III

population [ˌpɒpjəˈleɪʃn] Einwohner; Einwohnerzahl; Bevölkerung IV ZI, 8

pork [pɔːk] Schweinefleisch II

porridge [ˈpɒrɪdʒ] Haferbrei III

positive [ˈpɒzətɪv] positiv III

possessive pronoun [pə'sesɪv ˌprəʊnaʊn] Possessivpronomen <III>

post [pəʊst] Post *(online gestellte Nachricht)* IV U4, 80

  post office ['pəʊst ˌɒfɪs] Postamt I

to **post** [pəʊst] aufgeben *(einen Brief)*; abschicken *(einen Brief)* III; online stellen; posten IV U4, 80

postcard ['pəʊstkaːd] Postkarte I

poster ['pəʊstə] Poster I

pot [pɒt] Topf III; Becher <IV U3, 71>

potato *(sg)* [pə'teɪtəʊ], **potatoes** *(pl)* [pə'teɪtəʊz] Kartoffel II

  jacket potato [ˌdʒækɪt pə'teɪtəʊ] Ofenkartoffel II

  mashed potatoes [ˌmæʃt pə'teɪtəʊz] Kartoffelbrei II

pound [paʊnd] Pfund *(brit. Währungseinheit)* I

  … is £1.25. [ɪz 'wʌn paʊnd twentɪˌfaɪv] … kostet ein Pfund fünfundzwanzig. I

power ['paʊə] Energie; Kraft; Macht III

powerful ['paʊəfl] stark; mächtig; bedeutend; beeindruckend IV U1, 22

practical ['præktɪkl] praktisch IV U4, 89

practice ['præktɪs] Training; Übung I

to **practise** ['præktɪs] üben; trainieren III

prairie ['preəri] Prärie <IV U2, 136>

prayer [preə] Gebet IV U4, 85

to **prefer** [prɪ'fɜː] vorziehen II

preparation [ˌprepr'eɪʃn] Zubereitung <IV U5, 112>

to **prepare** [prɪ'peə] zubereiten; vorbereiten III

prerequisite [ˌpriː'rekwɪzɪt] Voraussetzung <IV U2, 48>

present ['preznt] Geschenk I; Gegenwart; Präsens <IV U4, 140>

  present perfect [ˌpreznt 'pɜːfɪkt] das Perfekt <III>

  present progressive [ˌpreznt prə'gresɪv] Verlaufsform der Gegenwart <III>

simple present [ˌsɪmpl 'preznt] Gegenwart; Präsens <III>

to **present** [prɪ'zent] vorstellen I; präsentieren <III>

presentation [ˌprezn'teɪʃn] Präsentation; Vortrag IV U2, 51

president ['prezɪdnt] Präsident; Präsidentin IV U3, 53

pretty ['prɪti] hübsch II

price [praɪs] Preis II

pride [praɪd] Stolz IV U5, 98

principal *(AE)* ['prɪnsɪpl] Schulleiter; Schulleiterin IV U2, 34

prison ['prɪzn] Gefängnis II

prize [praɪz] Preis II

probably ['prɒbəbli] wahrscheinlich III

problem ['prɒbləm] Problem I

process ['prəʊsəs] Prozess <IV U2, 48>

product ['prɒdʌkt] Produkt <III>

production [prə'dʌkʃn] Herstellung; Produktion <IV U4, 141>

profile ['prəʊfaɪl] Profil; Porträt; Steckbrief <III>

programme ['prəʊgræm] Programm; Sendung I

present progressive [ˌpreznt prə'gresɪv] Verlaufsform der Gegenwart <III>

project ['prɒdʒekt] Projekt III

to **promise** ['prɒmɪs] versprechen IV U3, 54

prompt card ['prɒmt ˌkaːd] Stichwortkarte <IV U2, 51>

possessive pronoun [pə'sesɪv ˌprəʊnaʊn] Possessivpronomen <III>

prop [prɒp] Requisit III

to **protect** [prə'tekt] schützen III

protective [prə'tektɪv] Schutz- <IV U2, 50>

protest ['prəʊtest] Protest; Demonstration IV U5, 96

to **protest** [prə'test] protestieren <IV U3, 138>

Protestant ['prɒtɪstnt] Protestant; Protestantin; protestantisch III

proud (of) [praʊd (əv)] stolz (auf) III

to **prove** [pruːv] beweisen IV U4, 84

pub [pʌb] Kneipe; Gasthaus III

public transport [ˌpʌblɪk 'trænspɔːt] öffentliche Verkehrsmittel III

published ['pʌblɪʃt] veröffentlicht <IV U3, 72>

pudding ['pʊdɪŋ] Nachspeise; Pudding II

to **pull** [pʊl] ziehen I

pumpkin ['pʌmpkɪn] Kürbis; Kürbis- <IV U3, 72>

purple ['pɜːpl] lila; violett I

on **purpose** [ɒn 'pɜːpəs] absichtlich II

to **push** [pʊʃ] schieben; drücken I; schubsen; drängeln III

*to **put** [pʊt] setzen; legen; stellen I

  to put a comment [ˌpʊt ə 'kɒment] einen Kommentar schreiben <I>

  to put in [ˌpʊt 'ɪn] einsetzen I

  to put in the right order [ˌpʊt ɪn ðə 'raɪt ɔːdə] in die richtige Reihenfolge bringen I

  to put on [ˌpʊt 'ɒn] anlegen; anziehen III

put [pʊt] simple past von *to put* I

puzzle ['pʌzl] Rätsel; Puzzle <I>

Q

qualification [ˌkwɒlɪfɪ'keɪʃn] Qualifikation; Abschluss; Schulabschluss <IV U4, 88>

better **quality** food [betə 'kwɒləti ˌfuːd] qualitativ besseres Essen <IV U3, 72>

quarter ['kwɔːtə] Viertel <IV U2, 50>

  quarter past ['kwɔːtə paːst] Viertel nach I

  quarter to ['kwɔːtə tə] Viertel vor I

queen [kwiːn] Königin III

question ['kwestʃən] Frage I

queue [kjuː] Warteschlange II

quick [kwɪk] schnell II

quiet ['kwaɪət] ruhig; leise; still III

quite [kwaɪt] ziemlich; ganz; völlig III

quiz [kwɪz] Quiz; Rätsel <I>

R

raccoon [rə'ku:n] Waschbär I
race [reɪs] Wettrennen; Rennen I
racism ['reɪsɪzm] Rassismus IV U5, 98
radiator ['reɪdieɪtə] Heizkörper
   IV U3, 59
radio ['reɪdiəʊ] Radio II
rafting ['ra:ftɪŋ] Rafting III
from rags to riches [frəm ˌrægz
   tə 'rɪtʃɪz] vom Tellerwäscher zum
   Millionär <IV U1, 28>
railway ['reɪlweɪ] Eisenbahn IV U4, 86
   railway track ['reɪlweɪ ˌtræk] Gleis
   IV U3, 64
rain [reɪn] Regen IV U4, 85
to rain [reɪn] regnen I
rainbow ['reɪnbəʊ] Regenbogen III
raincoat ['reɪnkəʊt] Regenmantel III
rainy ['reɪni] regnerisch I
ran [ræn] simple past von to run III
rang [ræŋ] simple past von to ring III
to rank [ræŋk] einstufen <IV U3, 59>
ranking list ['ræŋkɪŋ lɪst] Rangliste;
   Rangfolge <IV U3, 59>
rap [ræp] Rap <I>
to rap [ræp] rappen II
rapper ['ræpə] Rapper; Rapperin III
raspberry ['ra:zbri] Himbeere III
to rate [reɪt] bewerten; einstufen III
I'd rather [aɪd 'ra:ðə] ich würde lieber
   III
rating ['reɪtɪŋ] Bewertung <III>
razor ['reɪzə] Rasierer; Rasierapparat
   IV U3, 59
RE (Religious Education) [ˌa: ˈri:,
   rɪˌlɪdʒəs ˌedʒʊ'keɪʃn] Religionsunterricht I
*to read [ri:d] lesen I
reading ['ri:dɪŋ] Lesen <I>
ready ['redi] fertig; bereit I
   to get ready [ˌget 'redi] sich vorbereiten; sich fertig machen IV U3, 54
real [rɪəl] echt; richtig; wirklich II
reality [ri'æləti] Realität; Wirklichkeit
   <IV U1, 28>
really ['rɪəli] wirklich I; echt II
reason ['ri:zn] Grund III

to give reasons [ˌgɪv 'ri:znz]
   Gründe nennen; Gründe angeben
   III
*to rebuild [ˌri:'bɪld] wiederaufbauen
   <IV U2, 137>
receipt [ri'si:t] Quittung II
recipe ['resɪpi] Rezept II
to record [rɪ'kɔ:d] aufnehmen <III>
recording [rɪ'kɔ:dɪŋ] Aufnahme <III>
   recording studio [rɪ'kɔ:dɪŋ
   ˌstju:diəʊ] Tonstudio I
recyclable [ˌri:'saɪkləbl] wiederver-
   wertbar; recycelbar <IV U3, 71>
to recycle [ˌri:'saɪkl] recyceln; wieder-
   verwerten <IV U3, 71>
red [red] rot I
redwood (tree) ['redwʊd (tri:)] Mammutbaum IV U4, 74
to refuse [rɪ'fju:z] ablehnen; sich
   weigern IV U5, 99
region ['ri:dʒn] Region; Gegend
   <IV U4, 79>
registration [ˌredʒɪ'streɪʃn] Überprüfung der Anwesenheit I;
   Anmeldung II
regular ['regjələ] regelmäßig; normal;
   üblich; gleichmäßig IV U4, 89
to relax [rɪ'læks] sich entspannen
   <IV U2, 47>
relaxed [rɪ'lækst] entspannt; locker;
   gelassen IV U4, 74
reliable [rɪ'laɪəbl] verlässlich; zuverlässig; vertrauenswürdig IV U5, 109
RE (Religious Education) [ˌa: ˈri:,
   rɪˌlɪdʒəs ˌedʒʊ'keɪʃn] Religionsunterricht I
religious freedom [ˌrɪlɪdʒəs 'fri:dəm]
   Religionsfreiheit <IV U3, 70>
to remember [rɪ'membə] sich merken; sich erinnern (an) II
to remove [rɪ'mu:v] entfernen
   IV U5, 98
rent [rent] Miete II
to rent [rent] mieten III
to repair [rɪ'peə] reparieren III
to repeat [rɪ'pi:t] wiederholen III
to replace [rɪ'pleɪs] ersetzen IV U1, 12
report [rɪ'pɔ:t] Bericht IV U4, 84

to report [rɪ'pɔ:t] berichten; wieder-
   geben; melden; sich melden;
   anzeigen <IV U5, 104>
reporter [rɪ'pɔ:tə] Reporter; Reporterin III
republic [rɪ'pʌblɪk] Republik III
required [rɪ'kwaɪəd] erforderlich;
   notwendig <IV U2, 48>
   are required [rɪ'kwaɪəd] werden
   gebeten <IV U2, 48>
animal rescue shelter [ˌænɪml 'reskju:
   ˌʃeltə] Tierheim I
reservation [ˌrezə'veɪʃn] Reservierung
   IV U4, 76; Reservat IV U2, 32
   to make a reservation [ˌmeɪk ə
   'rezəveɪʃn] reservieren III
resident ['rezɪdnt] Bewohner; Bewohnerin; Anwohner; Anwohnerin; Einwohner; Einwohnerin <IV U1, 24>
to respect [rɪ'spekt] respektieren
   IV U4, 89
responsible [rɪs'pɒnsəbl] verantwortlich; verantwortungsvoll IV U2, 38
the rest [ðə 'rest] der Rest IV U1, 23
restaurant ['restrɒnt] Restaurant II
result [rɪ'zʌlt] Ergebnis II
*to retell [ˌri:'tel] nacherzählen; noch-
   mals erzählen <IV U2, 42>
return ticket [rɪ'tɜ:n ˌtɪkɪt] Hin- und
   Rückfahrkarte III
to return [rɪ'tɜ:n] zurückkehren
   IV U4, 85
review [rɪ'vju:] Kritik III
rice [raɪs] Reis II
rich [rɪtʃ] reich III
ridden ['rɪdn] past participle von to
   ride II
ride [raɪd] Fahrt; Ritt IV U1, 14
*to ride [raɪd] fahren; reiten II
horse riding ['hɔ:s ˌraɪdɪŋ] Reiten I
right [raɪt] Recht IV U5, 96
   civil rights (pl) [ˌsɪvl 'raɪts] Bürgerrechte IV U5, 96
right [raɪt] richtig; korrekt I; also II;
   rechts III; gerade; genau; in dem
   Moment als IV U2, 42
   right ahead [ˌraɪt ə'hed] geradeaus
   IV U1, 15

right away [ˌraɪt_əˈweɪ] sofort; gleich IV U4, 80

right now [ˌraɪt ˈnaʊ] gerade; jetzt gleich; sofort III

to be right [bi: ˈraɪt] recht haben II

to do the right thing [ˌdu: ðə ˈraɪt θɪŋ] das Richtige tun III

to turn right [ˌtɜ:n ˈraɪt] (nach) rechts abbiegen I

all right [ˌɔ:l ˈraɪt] in Ordnung; alles klar II

on the right [ɒn ðə ˈraɪt] auf der rechten Seite; rechts I

You're right. [jɔ: ˈraɪt] Du hast recht. I

*to **ring** [rɪŋ] läuten; klingeln III

river [ˈrɪvə] Fluss I

road [rəʊd] Straße I

roadwork (AE) [ˈrəʊdwɜ:k] Straßenbauarbeiten IV U1, 14

roast [rəʊst] gebraten <IV U3, 72>

roast beef [ˌrəʊst ˈbi:f] Roastbeef; Rinderbraten <IV U5, 112>

robotic [rəˈbɒtɪk] roboterhaft <IV U1, 134>

rock [rɒk] Fels; Stein III

rock climbing [ˈrɒk ˌklaɪmɪŋ] Klettern I

rock'n'roll [ˌrɒk ən ˈrəʊl] Rock 'n' Roll (Musikrichtung) IV U5, 97

rode [rəʊd] simple past von to ride II

role [rəʊl] Rolle IV U5, 107

role play [ˈrəʊl ˌpleɪ] Rollenspiel <II>

roller coaster [ˈrəʊlə ˌkəʊstə] Achterbahn II

the **Romans** [ðə ˈrəʊmənz] die Römer III

romance [ˈrəʊmæns] Liebesgeschichte III

Romanian [rʊˈmeɪniən] rumänisch; Rumänisch; aus Rumänien; Rumäne; Rumänin <IV U5, 206>

roof [ru:f] Dach II

room [ru:m] Zimmer; Raum I

rope [rəʊp] Seil I

rose [rəʊz] Rose IV ZI, 8

round trip [ˌraʊnd ˈtrɪp] Hin- und Rückflug; Hin- und Rückfahrt <IV U3, 66>

royal [ˈrɔɪəl] königlich II

rubber [ˈrʌbə] Gummi III

rubbish [ˈrʌbɪʃ] Müll; Abfall II

rude [ru:d] unhöflich; unverschämt IV U2, 39

rugby [ˈrʌgbi] Rugby III

to **ruin** [ˈru:ɪn] ruinieren; zerstören II

rule [ru:l] Regel III

ruler [ˈru:lə] Lineal I

*to **run** [rʌn] rennen; laufen I; betreiben; leiten; führen III

to run about [ˈrʌn əˌbaʊt] herumrennen II

to run away [ˈrʌn əˈweɪ] weglaufen III

to run out of [ˌrʌn ˈaʊt əv] ausgehen (Ware) III

run [rʌn] past participle von to run III

rung [rʌŋ] past participle von to ring III

gold **rush** [ˈgəʊld ˌrʌʃ] Goldrausch IV U4, 84

to **rush** [rʌʃ] eilen; sich beeilen; stürzen III

to rush down [rʌʃ ˈdaʊn] hinuntereilen II

rush hour [ˈrʌʃ ˌaʊə] Hauptverkehrszeit IV U1, 14

Russian [ˈrʌʃn] russisch; Russisch; aus Russland; Russe; Russin IV U5, 99

S

sad [sæd] traurig III

safe [seɪf] sicher; ungefährlich III

safety [ˈseɪfti] Sicherheit IV U4, 75

safety measure [ˈseɪfti ˌmeʒə] Sicherheitsmaßnahme; Schutzmaßnahme <IV U2, 48>

safety net [ˈseɪfti ˌnet] Sicherheitsnetz IV U4, 75

said [sed] simple past von to say I

sail [seɪl] Segel <IV U3, 71>

to **sail** [seɪl] segeln <IV U3, 70>

sailing ship [ˈseɪlɪŋ ʃɪp] Segelboot <IV U3, 70>

saint [seɪnt] Heilige; Heiliger <IV U5, 108>

salad [ˈsæləd] Salat II

sale [seɪl] Schlussverkauf; Ausverkauf II

jumble sale [ˈdʒʌmbl ˌseɪl] Flohmarkt II

sales associate (AE) [ˌseɪlz əˈsəʊʃiət] Verkäufer; Verkäuferin IV U2, 38

salsa [ˈsælsə] Salsasoße <IV U5, 112>

salt [sɔ:lt] Salz II

the **same** [ðə ˈseɪm] derselbe; gleich II

sample [ˈsa:mpl] Probe <IV U1, 24>

sandal [ˈsændl] Sandale <IV U4, 77>

sandwich [ˈsænwɪdʒ] Sandwich; belegtes Brot I

sang [sæŋ] simple past von to sing II

sank [sæŋk] simple past von to sink III

sat [sæt] simple past, past participle von to sit IV U3, 63

satnav [ˈsætnæv] Navi I

Saturday [ˈsætədeɪ] Samstag I

sauce [sɔ:s] Soße II

cocktail sauce [ˈkɒkteɪl ˌsɔ:s] Cocktailsoße <IV U5, 112>

sausage [ˈsɒsɪdʒ] Wurst; Bratwurst II

sausage roll [ˌsɒsɪdʒ ˈrəʊl] Blätterteig mit Wurstfüllung II

to **save** [seɪv] speichern II; retten; bergen III; aufheben IV U3, 54

saw [sɔ:] simple past von to see I

saxophone [ˈsæksəfəʊn] Saxofon I

*to **say** [seɪ] nachsprechen; nennen; sagen; sprechen I

to say hi to [ˌseɪ ˈhaɪ tə] grüßen; Grüße ausrichten I

to say sorry [ˌseɪ ˈsɒri] sich entschuldigen II

to **scan** [skæn] scannen; nach Details durchsuchen <III>

to **scare** [skeə] erschrecken II

scared [skeəd] verängstigt IV U3, 64

to be scared [bi: ˈskeəd] Angst haben; erschrocken sein II

scared

scarf *(sg)* [skɑːf], **scarves** *(pl)* [skɑːvz] Schal; Tuch I

scary [ˈskeəri] gruselig; beängstigend I

scene [siːn] Szene II
to set the scene [ˌset ðə ˈsiːn] beste Voraussetzungen schaffen <IV U3, 69>

schedule *(AE)* [ˈskedʒuːl] Stundenplan; Fahrplan IV U2, 33

school [skuːl] Schule I
at school [ət ˈskuːl] in der Schule I
boarding school [ˈbɔːdɪŋ ˌskuːl] Internat <IV U2, 137>
driving school [ˈdraɪvɪŋ ˌskuːl] Fahrschule <IV U2, 44>
high school [ˈhaɪ ˌskuːl] Highschool *(weiterführende Schule, Oberstufe)* IV U1, 18
school life [ˈskuːl ˌlaɪf] Schulalltag <I>
school trip [ˌskuːl ˈtrɪp] Klassenfahrt I

schoolyard [ˈskuːljɑːd] Schulhof <IV U1, 28>

Science [saɪəns] Wissenschaft; Naturwissenschaft I
science fiction [ˌsaɪəns ˈfɪkʃn] Science-Fiction I

scientist [ˈsaɪəntɪst] Wissenschaftler; Wissenschaftlerin <IV U2, 48>

scissors *(pl)* [ˈsɪzəz] Schere III
nail scissors [ˈneɪl ˌsɪzəz] Nagelschere III

scone [skɒn] Scone *(eine Art süßes Brötchen)* II

score [skɔː] Punktestand II; Punkten <IV U2, 50>

Scot [skɒt] Schotte; Schottin III

Scottish [ˈskɒtɪʃ] schottisch III

scrambled egg [ˌskræmbld ˈeg] Rührei II

to **scream** [skriːm] schreien; kreischen IV U3, 63

script [skrɪpt] Drehbuch; Skript <III>

sea [siː] Meer I

to **search** [sɜːtʃ] durchsuchen <III>

at the **seaside** [ət ðə ˈsiːsaɪd] am Meer I

season [ˈsiːzn] Saison; Jahreszeit <IV U2, 50>

seat [siːt] Sitz; Sitzplatz IV U5, 106
Please have a seat. [ˌpliːz hæv ə ˈsiːt] Bitte Platz nehmen. IV U3, 55

second [ˈseknd] Sekunde II

second [ˈseknd] zweite I

secret [ˈsiːkrət] Geheimnis II

secret [ˈsiːkrət] geheim II

section [ˈsekʃn] Abschnitt <III>

security [sɪˈkjʊərəti] Sicherheit <IV U1, 30>

*to **see** [siː] sehen I
to see friends [siː ˈfrendz] Freunde treffen I
I see. [aɪ ˈsiː] Ich verstehe. IV U5, 103
See you. [ˈsiː ˌjuː] Tschüss.; Bis bald. I
See you later. [ˌsiː jə ˈleɪtə] Tschüss.; Bis bald. I
See you soon! [ˈsiː ju ˌsuːn] Bis bald! I

seen [siːn] past participle von *to see* II

segregation [ˌsegrɪˈgeɪʃn] Rassentrennung; Trennung IV U5, 106

self [self] selbst; sich III

selfie [ˈselfi] Selfie *(Schnappschuss von sich selbst)* IV U4, 83

selfish [ˈselfɪʃ] selbstsüchtig IV U2, 39

*to **sell** [sel] verkaufen III

semester [sɪˈmestə] Halbjahr; Schulhalbjahr; Semester <IV U2, 48>

*to **send** [send] schicken; senden I

senior citizen [ˌsiːnjə ˈsɪtɪzn] Rentner; Rentnerin <IV U5, 207>

sensation [senˈseɪʃn] Sensation <IV U5, 143>

sent [sent] simple past von *to send* I; past participle von *to send* II

sentence [ˈsentəns] Satz <I>

September [sepˈtembə] September I

Serbian [ˈsɜːbiən] serbisch; Serbisch; aus Serbien; Serbe; Serbin <IV U5, 206>

serious [ˈsɪəriəs] ernst III

Are you serious? [ˌɑː ju ˈsɪəriəs] Im Ernst? III
to take sth seriously [ˌteɪk ˈsɪəriəsli] etw. ernst nehmen IV U1, 18

to **serve** [sɜːv] servieren IV U2, 33

service [ˈsɜːvɪs] Dienst III
emergency service [ɪˈmɜːdʒnsi ˌsɜːvɪs] Notdienst; Rettungsdienst III

set [set] Satz <IV U4, 92>; Kulisse <IV U4, 141>

*to **set** the scene [ˌset ðə ˈsiːn] beste Voraussetzungen schaffen <IV U3, 69>

settler [ˈsetlə] Siedler; Siedlerin IV U2, 32

seven [ˈsevn] sieben I

seventeen [ˌsevnˈtiːn] siebzehn I

seventy [ˈsevnti] siebzig I

several [ˈsevrl] einige; mehrere; verschiedene IV U4, 80

shampoo [ʃæmˈpuː] Shampoo III

shamrock [ˈʃæmrɒk] Kleeblatt III

shape [ʃeɪp] Form <III>

to **share** [ʃeə] teilen III

shark [ʃɑːk] Hai I

pencil **sharpener** [ˈpensl ˌʃɑːpnə] Anspitzer I

she [ʃiː] sie I

sheep *(sg)* [ʃiːp], **sheep** *(pl)* [ʃiːp] Schaf I

sheet of paper [ˈʃiːt əv ˌpeɪpə] Blatt Papier <IV U4, 92>

shelf *(sg)* [ʃelf], **shelves** *(pl)* [ʃelvz] Regal; Regalbrett I

walnut **shell** [ˈwɔːlnʌt ˌʃel] Walnussschale <IV U3, 71>

animal rescue **shelter** [ˌænɪml ˈreskju ˌʃeltə] Tierheim I

*to **shine** [ʃaɪn] scheinen; glänzen IV ZI, 8

ship [ʃɪp] Schiff I
sailing ship [ˈseɪlɪŋ ʃɪp] Segelboot <IV U3, 70>
ship builder [ˈʃɪp ˌbɪldə] Schiffsbauer; Schiffsbauerin III

shipyard [ˈʃɪpjɑːd] Werft III

shirt [ʃɜːt] Hemd; Shirt I

shoe [ʃuː] Schuh I

shone [ʃɒn] simple past, past participle von to shine IV ZI, 8

*****to shoot** (a film) [ˌʃuːt (ə 'fɪlm)] (einen Film) drehen <III>
to shoot (at) [ʃuːt (ət)] schießen (auf) IV U3, 63

shop [ʃɒp] Laden; Geschäft I
corner shop [ˈkɔːnə ˌʃɒp] Tante-Emma-Laden I
shop assistant [ˈʃɒp əˌsɪstnt] Verkäufer; Verkäuferin II
sports shop [ˈspɔːts ˌʃɒp] Sportgeschäft I

shopping [ˈʃɒpɪŋ] Einkaufen I
to do the shopping [ˌduː ðə ˈʃɒpɪŋ] Einkäufe machen; Besorgungen machen II
to go shopping [ˌgəʊ ˈʃɒpɪŋ] einkaufen gehen II
shopping centre [ˈʃɒpɪŋ ˌsentə] Einkaufszentrum I
shopping list [ˈʃɒpɪŋ ˌlɪst] Einkaufszettel I

short [ʃɔːt] kurz II

shortly [ˈʃɔːtli] kurz III

shorts (pl) [ʃɔːts] Shorts; kurze Hose I

shot [ʃɒt] simple past, past participle von to shoot IV U3, 63

should [ʃʊd] sollte III

shout [ʃaʊt] Schrei I
to **shout** [ʃaʊt] schreien; rufen II

show [ʃəʊ] Show; Wettbewerb I; Schau; Aufführung IV U5, 102
talent show [ˈtælənt ˌʃəʊ] Talentwettbewerb I
talk show [ˈtɔːk ˌʃəʊ] Talkshow <IV U3, 68>
TV show [ˌtiː ˈviː ˌʃəʊ] Fernsehsendung II

*****to show** [ʃəʊ] zeigen II
to show up [ˌʃəʊ ˈʌp] auftauchen; erscheinen IV U2, 42

shower [ˈʃaʊə] Dusche III
shower gel [ˈʃaʊə ˌdʒel] Duschgel III

shredded [ˈʃredɪd] gehackt; klein gemacht <IV U5, 112>

shrimp [ʃrɪmp] Krabbe; Garnele <IV U5, 112>

*****to shut** up [ˌʃʌt ˈʌp] die Klappe halten IV U3, 63

shy [ʃaɪ] schüchtern IV U2, 42

*****to be sick** [biː ˈsɪk] sich übergeben I; krank sein (AE) III

side [saɪd] Seite I

sidewalk (AE) [ˈsaɪdwɔːk] Gehweg; Bürgersteig IV U1, 15

sight [saɪt] Sehenswürdigkeit II

sightseeing [ˈsaɪtsiːɪŋ] Besichtigungstour <IV U4, 201>
to go sightseeing [ˌgəʊ ˈsaɪtsiːɪŋ] eine Besichtigungstour machen II

sign [saɪn] Schild; Zeichen III
sign language [ˈsaɪn ˌlæŋgwɪdʒ] Gebärdensprache; Zeichensprache III
to **sign** [saɪn] unterschreiben; unterzeichnen IV U3, 53
to sign autographs [ˌsaɪn ˈɔːtəgrɑːfs] Autogramme geben IV U3, 53

signal [ˈsɪgnl] Empfang; Signal; Zeichen III

signature [ˈsɪgnətʃə] Unterschrift <IV U2, 44>

silence [ˈsaɪləns] Stille; Schweigen; Ruhe III

silent [ˈsaɪlənt] stumm; schweigsam III

silk [sɪlk] Seide III

silly [ˈsɪli] albern II; dumm; doof III

simple [ˈsɪmpl] einfach III
simple present [ˌsɪmpl ˈpreznt] Gegenwart; Präsens <III>

since [sɪns] seit; seitdem IV U4, 80

*****to sing** [sɪŋ] singen I

singer [ˈsɪŋə] Sänger; Sängerin I

single ticket [ˈsɪŋgl ˌtɪkɪt] einfache Fahrkarte III

sink [sɪŋk] Becken; Spülbecken <IV U3, 71>

*****to sink** [sɪŋk] untergehen; sinken III

siren [ˈsaɪrən] Sirene; Martinshorn <IV U1, 19>

sister [ˈsɪstə] Schwester I

*****to sit** [sɪt] sitzen I

site [saɪt] Seite (im Internet) IV U4, 80
construction site [kənˈstrʌkʃn ˌsaɪt] Baustelle IV U1, 15

situation [ˌsɪtjuˈeɪʃn] Situation II

six [sɪks] sechs I

sixteen [ˌsɪkˈstiːn] sechzehn I

sixty [ˈsɪksti] sechzig I

size [saɪz] Größe II

skateboard [ˈskeɪtbɔːd] Skateboard III

to ski [skiː] Ski fahren II

skiing [ˈskiːɪŋ] Skifahren III

skill [skɪl] Fertigkeit <I>

to skim [skɪm] überfliegen <III>

skirt [skɜːt] Rock I

sky [skaɪ] Himmel <IV U2, 48>

skyline [ˈskaɪlaɪn] Skyline IV U1, 12

skyscraper [ˈskaɪskreɪpə] Wolkenkratzer IV U1, 14

slave [sleɪv] Sklave; Sklavin IV U4, 86

slavery [ˈsleɪvri] Sklaverei <IV U3, 138>

sled [sled] Schlitten <IV U1, 30>

sleep [sliːp] Schlaf III

*****to sleep** [sliːp] schlafen I

sleepover [ˈsliːpˌəʊvə] Übernachtung I

slept [slept] simple past, past participle von to sleep II

slice [slaɪs] Scheibe; Stück <IV U5, 113>

sliced bread [ˌslaɪst ˈbred] in Scheiben geschnittenes Brot III

slow [sləʊ] langsam III

small [smɔːl] klein I
small talk [ˈsmɔːl ˌtɔːk] Smalltalk <IV U3, 55>

smart [smɑːt] schlau; klug; intelligent III

smartphone [ˈsmɑːtˌfəʊn] Smartphone IV U4, 80

*****to smell** [smel] riechen III

smelt [smelt] simple past, past participle von to smell III

to smile [smaɪl] lächeln <IV U1, 184>

smoke [sməʊk] Rauch III

smoked tofu [ˈsməʊkt ˌtəʊfuː] geräucherter Tofu <IV U5, 112>

smoothie [ˈsmuːði] Smoothie <IV U3, 72>

smuggler ['smʌglə] Schmuggler; Schmugglerin II

smurf [smɜːf] Schlumpf I

snack [snæk] Snack; Imbiss I

snake [sneɪk] Schlange I

snow [snəʊ] Schnee IV U1, 14

so [səʊ] deshalb; also I; so II
   so much [ˌsəʊ 'mʌtʃ] so sehr III

soap [səʊp] Seife III

social ['səʊʃl] sozial; gesellschaftlich <IV U1, 134>
   social media [ˌsəʊʃl 'miːdiə] soziale Medien IV U4, 80
   Social Studies ['səʊʃl ˌstʌdiz] Gesellschaftslehre; Sozialkunde I

society [sə'saɪəti] Gesellschaft <IV U2, 48>

sock [sɒk] Socke I

sofa ['səʊfə] Sofa II

software ['sɒftweə] Software II

solar ['səʊlə] Sonnen-; Solar-; solar III
   solar system ['səʊlə] Sonnensystem <IV U2, 48>

sold [səʊld] simple past, past participle von to sell III

soldier ['səʊldʒə] Soldat; Soldatin III

solid ['sɒlɪd] fest III

solution [sə'luːʃn] Lösung IV U5, 98

to solve [sɒlv] lösen I

some [sʌm] einige; ein paar I; etwas II

somebody ['sʌmbədi] jemand IV U2, 38
   somebody else [ˌsʌmbədi 'els] jemand anderes II

something ['sʌmθɪŋ] etwas I

sometimes ['sʌmtaɪmz] manchmal I

son [sʌn] Sohn III

song [sɒŋ] Lied I

soon [suːn] bald II
   as soon as [əz 'suːn ˌəz] sobald IV U4, 89
   See you soon! ['siː ju ˌsuːn] Bis bald! I

sore [sɔː] schmerzhaft; wund II
   sore throat [ˌsɔː 'θrəʊt] Halsschmerzen II

Sorry. ['sɒri] Tut mir leid.; Entschuldigung. I
   to be sorry [bi 'sɒri] leidtun III
   to feel sorry for [ˌfiːl 'sɒri] Mitleid haben mit; bedauern III
   I'm sorry. [aɪm 'sɒri] Es tut mir leid.; Entschuldigung. I
   Sorry about … ['sɒri ˌəbaʊt] Es tut mir leid wegen … I

sort [sɔːt] Sorte; Art II

to sort [sɔːt] sortieren <III>

sound [saʊnd] Ton; Laut; Geräusch III

to sound [saʊnd] klingen II

soup [suːp] Suppe II

sweet and sour [ˌswiːt ən 'saʊə] süßsauer <IV U5, 206>

south [saʊθ] Süden III
   south of ['saʊθ ˌəv] südlich von IV ZI, 9
   in the south of [ɪn ðə 'saʊθ ˌəv] im Süden von III

southern ['sʌðən] südlich IV U5, 96

Southerner ['sʌðnə] Südstaatler; Südstaatlerin IV U5, 97

souvenir [ˌsuːvn'ɪə] Souvenir; Andenken III
   souvenir shop ['suːvnɪə ˌʃɒp] Souvenirladen III

soy bean ['sɔɪ ˌbiːn] Sojabohne IV ZI, 9

spaghetti [spə'geti] Spaghetti II

Spanish ['spænɪʃ] spanisch; Spanisch; aus Spanien IV U5, 98

to speak [spiːk] sprechen II

speaking ['spiːkɪŋ] Sprechen <I>

special ['speʃl] besonders; speziell I
   special offer [ˌspeʃl 'ɒfə] Sonderangebot III
   with special needs [wɪð ˌspeʃl 'niːdz] mit Behinderung; mit besonderen Bedürfnissen III

spectacular [spek'tækjələ] spektakulär IV U4, 77

speech [spiːtʃ] Sprache; Rede III
   direct speech [dɪˌrekt 'spiːtʃ] direkte Rede <IV U5, 110>
   farewell speech [feə'wel spiːtʃ] Abschiedsrede II

speech bubble ['spiːtʃ ˌbʌbl] Sprechblase <III>

speech impaired ['spiːtʃ ɪmˌpeəd] sprachbehindert IV U5, 102

to spell [spel] buchstabieren I

spelling ['spelɪŋ] Rechtschreibung I

to spend [spend] ausgeben (Geld); verbringen (Zeit) II

spent [spent] simple past, past participle von to spend II

spice [spaɪs] Gewürz II

spicy ['spaɪsi] würzig; pikant II

spider ['spaɪdə] Spinne III

splash [splæʃ] Platsch I

spoke [spəʊk] simple past von to speak II

spoken ['spəʊkn] past participle von to speak II

spoon [spuːn] Löffel II

sport [spɔːt] Sport I; Sportart III
   sports shop ['spɔːts ˌʃɒp] Sportgeschäft I

sporting event ['spɔːtɪŋ ɪˌvent] Sportereignis; Sportveranstaltung <IV U2, 50>

to spread [spred] streichen <IV U5, 112>

spring roll [ˌsprɪŋ 'rəʊl] Frühlingsrolle II

square [skweə] Platz II
   square mile (= sq. mi.) [ˌskweə 'maɪl] Quadratmeile IV ZI, 8

stadium ['steɪdiəm] Stadion II

stage [steɪdʒ] Bühne II
   at this stage [æt ðɪs 'steɪdʒ] zu diesem Zeitpunkt <IV U5, 108>

stairs (pl) [steəz] Treppe II

food stall ['fuːd ˌstɔːl] Essensstand II

market stall ['maːkɪt ˌstɔːl] Marktstand; Marktbude <IV U2, 191>

stallholder ['stɔːlˌhəʊldə] Standinhaber; Standinhaberin II

stamp [stæmp] Briefmarke III

to stand [stænd] stehen II
   to stand up [stænd ˌʌp] aufstehen; stehen IV U3, 63

standup paddleboarding [ˈstændʌp
ˌpædlbɔːdɪŋ] Stehpaddeln
<IV U3, 72>

star [stɑː] Star I; Stern III

start [stɑːt] Start; Anfang III

to **start** [stɑːt] anfangen; beginnen;
starten II; gründen III

to start a band [ˌstɑːt ə ˈbænd] eine
Band gründen II

starting point [ˈstɑːtɪŋ ˌpɔɪnt] Ausgangspunkt <III>

to get **started** [ˌget ˈstɑːtɪd] anfangen <III>

starter [ˈstɑːtə] Vorspeise II

state [steɪt] Staat; Bundesstaat; Land
IV ZI, 8

state government [ˈsteɪt
ˌgʌnmənt] Landesregierung
IV U5, 98

State House (AE) [ˈsteɪt ˌhaʊs]
Regierungsgebäude IV U5, 98

statement [ˈsteɪtmənt] Aussage;
Behauptung <IV U3, 196>; Erklärung <IV U4, 87>

station [ˈsteɪʃn] Haltestelle; Station;
Bahnhof III

status [ˈsteɪtəs] Status IV U4, 81

to **stay** [steɪ] übernachten; bleiben II

*to **steal** [stiːl] stehlen IV U2, 38

steam engine [ˈstiːm ˌendʒɪn] Dampfmaschine III

paddle **steamer** [ˈpædl ˌstiːmə] Raddampfer <IV U5, 142>

steel [stiːl] Stahl III

step [step] Schritt III; Stufe II

stereotype [ˈsteriəʊtaɪp] Stereotyp;
Klischee IV U2, 42

stick [stɪk] Stock II

sticker [ˈstɪkə] Aufkleber II

still [stɪl] noch; immer noch I; dennoch III

to **stir** [stɜː] rühren; umrühren II

stocks [stɒks] Pranger III

stole [stəʊl] simple past von to steal
IV U2, 38

stolen [ˈstəʊlən] past participle von
to steal IV U2, 38

stomach [ˈstʌmək] Magen; Bauch II

stomach ache [ˈstʌmək ˌeɪk] Bauchweh; Bauchschmerzen II

stone [stəʊn] Stein III

stood [stʊd] simple past, past participle von to stand II

stop [stɒp] Haltestelle; Halt II

bus stop [ˈbʌs ˌstɒp] Bushaltestelle
II

one stop [ˌwʌn ˈstɒp] einmal
Umsteigen <IV U3, 66>

to **stop** [stɒp] aufhören I

store (AE) [stɔː] Laden; Geschäft
IV U2, 33

department store [dɪˈpɑːtmənt
ˌstɔː] Kaufhaus II

storm [stɔːm] Sturm IV U2, 32

story [ˈstɔːri] Geschichte I

feature story [ˈfiːtʃə ˌstɔːri] Leitartikel; Sonderbericht <IV U5, 110>

straight [streɪt] gerade <IV U2, 47>

straight on [streɪt ˈɒn] geradeaus I

hair **straightener** [ˈheə ˌstreɪtnə]
Haarglätter I

strange [streɪndʒ] merkwürdig;
seltsam II

straw [strɔː] Trinkhalm II

drinking straw [ˈdrɪŋkɪŋ ˌstrɔː]
Trinkhalm <IV U3, 71>

strawberry [ˈstrɔːbri] Erdbeere II

stream [striːm] Bach <IV U2, 136>

to **stream** [striːm] streamen (im
Internet) IV U4, 80

street [striːt] Straße III

street art [ˈstriːt ˌɑːt] Straßenkunst
IV U1, 13

street gang [ˈstriːt ˌgæŋ] Straßengang <IV U1, 134>

strict [strɪkt] streng; strikt IV U2, 34

striking [ˈstraɪkɪŋ] bemerkenswert;
auffallend III

comic **strip** [ˈkɒmɪk strɪp] Comicstrip
<IV U2, 42>

strong [strɒŋ] stark III

structure [ˈstrʌktʃə] Aufbau; Struktur
III

to **structure** [ˈstrʌktʃə] strukturieren;
gliedern <IV U2, 46>

*to be **stuck** [biː ˈstʌk] feststecken;
nicht weg können I

*to get **stuck** [ˌget ˈstʌk] stecken
bleiben IV U3, 54

student [ˈstjuːdnt] Schüler; Schülerin;
Student; Studentin I

studio [ˈstjuːdiəʊ] Studio IV U4, 75

recording studio [rɪˈkɔːdɪŋ
ˌstjuːdiəʊ] Tonstudio I

TV studio [ˌtiːˈviː ˌstjuːdiəʊ] Fernsehstudio II

study hall period [ˈstʌdi hɔːl ˌpɪəriəd]
Freistunde IV U2, 34

study skills [ˌstʌdi ˈskɪlz] Fertigkeit
Lern- und Arbeitstechniken <I>

stunt [stʌnt] Stunt <IV U2, 50>

stuntman [ˈstʌntmæn] Stuntman
IV U3, 53

style [staɪl] Stil III

subject [ˈsʌbdʒɪkt] Schulfach I

core subject [ˌkɔː ˈsʌbdʒɪkt] Pflichtfach IV U2, 35

submarine [ˌsʌbmrˈiːn] U-Boot I

to **subscribe** [səbˈskraɪb] abonnieren
IV U4, 81

subtotal [ˈsʌbˌtəʊtl] Zwischensumme
<IV U3, 66>

suburb [ˈsʌbɜːb] Vorort IV U1, 15

subway (AE) [ˈsʌbweɪ] U-Bahn
IV U1, 14

success [səkˈses] Erfolg IV U5, 107

successful [səkˈsesfl] erfolgreich III

suddenly [ˈsʌdnli] plötzlich; auf
einmal II

sugar [ˈʃʊgə] Zucker I

to **suit** [suːt] stehen; passen II

suitable [ˈsuːtəbl] geeignet; passend
<IV U2, 51>

suitcase [ˈsuːtkeɪs] Koffer II

to **sum** up [ˌsʌm ˈʌp] zusammenfassen IV U3, 73

to **summarize** [ˈsʌmraɪz] zusammenfassen <IV U3, 73>

summary [ˈsʌmri] Zusammenfassung
<III>

summer [ˈsʌmə] Sommer II

sun [sʌn] Sonne III

to **sunbathe** [ˈsʌnbeɪð] sonnenbaden II

Sunday [ˈsʌndeɪ] Sonntag I

sunglasses *(pl)* [ˈsʌnˌglɑːsɪz] Sonnenbrille II

sunk [sʌŋk] past participle von *to sink* III

sunny [ˈsʌni] sonnig I

super [ˈsuːpə] super II

superhero [ˈsuːpəˌhɪərəʊ] *(sg)*, **superheroes** [ˈsuːpəˌhɪərəʊz] *(pl)* Superheld <IV U1, 135>

supermarket [ˈsuːpəˌmɑːkɪt] Supermarkt II

support [səˈpɔːt] Unterstützung; Hilfe IV U1, 19

supporter [səˈpɔːtə] Anhänger; Anhängerin; Fan <IV U2, 50>

sure [ʃʊə] sicher I
  sure of oneself [ˈʃʊərˌəv ˌwʌnself] selbstsicher III

to **surf** [sɜːf] surfen; wellenreiten II
  to surf the internet [ˌsɜːf ði ˈɪntənet] im Internet surfen II

surfboard [ˈsɜːfbɔːd] Surfbrett IV U4, 76

surfer [ˈsɜːfə] Wellenreiter; Wellenreiterin; Surfer; Surferin IV ZI, 9

surfing [ˈsɜːfɪŋ] Wellenreiten; Surfen IV U4, 74

surprise [səˈpraɪz] Überraschung I

surprised [səˈpraɪzd] überrascht II

survey [ˈsɜːveɪ] Umfrage II

to **survive** [səˈvaɪv] überleben III

sushi [ˈsuːʃi] Sushi <IV U5, 206>

swam [swæm] simple past von *to swim* II

swamp [swɒmp] Sumpf IV ZI, 9

to **swap** [swɒp] tauschen <IV U4, 92>

sweatshirt [ˈswetʃɜːt] Sweatshirt I

*to **sweep** [swiːp] fegen II

sweet [swiːt] Süßigkeit; Bonbon I

sweet [swiːt] süß III
  sweet and sour [ˌswiːt ən ˈsaʊə] süßsauer <IV U5, 206>

swept [swept] simple past, past participle von *to sweep* II

*to **swim** [swɪm] schwimmen II

*to go **swimming** [ˌgəʊ ˈswɪmɪŋ] schwimmen gehen I

swimming pool [ˈswɪmɪŋ ˌpuːl] Schwimmbad I

Swiss [swɪs] schweizerisch; aus der Schweiz; Schweizer; Schweizerin IV U4, 84

sword [sɔːd] Schwert III

swum [swʌm] past participle von *to swim* II

symbol [ˈsɪmbl] Symbol IV U1, 13

Syrian [ˈsɪriən] syrisch; aus Syrien; Syrer; Syrerin <IV U5, 206>

T

table [ˈteɪbl] Tisch I; Tabelle <III>
  table tennis [ˈteɪbl ˌtenɪs] Tischtennis II

tablespoon [ˈteɪblspuːn] Esslöffel <IV U5, 113>

tablet [ˈtæblət] Tablette II

tactic [ˈtæktɪk] Taktik; Vorgehensweise III

take [teɪk] Aufnahme <III>

*to **take** [teɪk] nehmen; mitnehmen I; hinbringen II; dauern III; bringen IV U2, 43
  to take a break [ˌteɪk ə ˈbreɪk] Pause machen II
  to take a photo [ˌteɪk ə ˈfəʊtəʊ] ein Foto machen I
  to take a test [ˌteɪk ə ˈtest] eine Prüfung machen <IV U2, 44>
  to take a trip [ˌteɪk ə ˈtrɪp] eine Fahrt machen III
  to take notes [ˌteɪk ˈnəʊts] sich Notizen machen I
  to take off [ˌteɪk ˈɒf] ausziehen III
  to take out [ˌteɪk ˈaʊt] herausnehmen I
  to take part (in) [ˌteɪk ˈpɑːt] teilnehmen (an) II
  to take photos [ˌteɪk ˈfəʊtəʊz] fotografieren; Fotos machen II
  to take place [ˌteɪk ˈpleɪs] stattfinden <IV U5, 108>

to take sth seriously [ˌteɪk ˈsɪəriəsli] etw. ernst nehmen IV U1, 18

to take the dog for a walk [ˌteɪk ðə ˌdɒg fər ə ˈwɔːk] den Hund spazieren führen II

to take turns [ˌteɪk ˈtɜːnz] sich abwechseln <II>

Take care. [ˈteɪk ˌkeə] Macht's gut. I

takeaway [ˈteɪkəweɪ] Essen zum Mitnehmen II

takeaway [ˈteɪkəweɪ] zum Mitnehmen II

taken [ˈteɪkn] past participle von *to take* II

talent [ˈtælənt] Talent I
  talent show [ˈtælənt ˌʃəʊ] Talentwettbewerb I

talk [tɔːk] Gerede II; Vortrag; Rede <III>
  to give a talk [ˌgɪv ə ˈtɔːk] einen Vortrag halten <III>
  small talk [ˈsmɔːl ˌtɔːk] Smalltalk <IV U3, 55>
  talk show [ˈtɔːk ˌʃəʊ] Talkshow <IV U3, 68>

to **talk** (to) [ˈtɔːk tə] sprechen (mit); reden (mit) I
  to talk about [ˈtɔːk əˌbaʊt] sprechen über II

tall [tɔːl] groß; hoch II

tape [teɪp] Klebeband <IV U3, 71>

task [tɑːsk] Aufgabe; Auftrag <I>

taste [teɪst] Geschmack <IV U5, 112>

tasty [ˈteɪsti] lecker; schmackhaft III

tax [tæks] Steuer <IV U3, 66>

taxi [ˈtæksi] Taxi II

tea [tiː] Tee; (frühes) Abendessen I
  tea bag [ˈtiː ˌbæg] Teebeutel <IV U5, 113>
  tea light [ˈtiː ˌlaɪt] Teelicht <IV U3, 71>

teacher [ˈtiːtʃə] Lehrer; Lehrerin I

team [tiːm] Team; Mannschaft I

teamwork [ˈtiːmwɜːk] Teamwork II

to **tease** [tiːz] hänseln; sticheln; reizen IV U2, 38

teaspoon *(tsp)* [ˈtiːspuːn] Teelöffel *(TL)* II

technology [tekˈnɒlədʒi] Technologie <IV U4, 90>

Design Technology (DT) [dɪˌzaɪn tekˈnɒlədʒi, ˌdiːˈtiː] Technik I

Welding Technology [ˈweldɪŋ ˌteknɒlədʒi] Schweißtechnik <IV U2, 48>

teen [tiːn] Jugend-; Teenager; Jugendliche; Jugendlicher II

teenager [ˈtiːnˌeɪdʒə] Teenager; Jugendliche; Jugendlicher III

telephone [ˈtelɪfəʊn] Telefon III

telephone box [ˈtelɪfəʊn ˌbɒks] Telefonzelle II

***to tell** [tel] erzählen; sagen I

ten [ten] zehn I

tennis [ˈtenɪs] Tennis I

tent [tent] Zelt III

tepee [ˈtiːpiː] Tipi <IV U2, 136>

terrible [ˈterəbl] schrecklich; schlimm; furchtbar I

territory [ˈterɪtri] Gebiet; Revier; Territorium <IV U5, 142>

test [test] Test; Klassenarbeit I

to take a test [ˌteɪk ə ˈtest] eine Prüfung machen <IV U2, 44>

to test [test] testen; prüfen II

text [tekst] Text II

text message [ˈtekst ˌmesɪdʒ] SMS II

to text [tekst] eine SMS schreiben II

texter [ˈtekstə] SMS-Schreiber; SMS-Schreiberin II

than [ðæn] als II

thank God [ˌθæŋkˈɡɒd] Gott sei Dank <IV U3, 70>

Thank you. [ˈθæŋk ju] Danke. I

thanks [θæŋks] danke I

Thanks so much. [ˌθæŋk_səʊ ˈmʌtʃ] Vielen Dank.; Herzlichen Dank. IV U4, 94

Thanksgiving [ˌθæŋksˈɡɪvɪŋ] Erntedankfest IV U3, 53

that [ðæt] das I; dass III

after that [ˈɑːftə ðət] danach I

that night [ˌðæt ˈnaɪt] an jenem Abend; in jener Nacht II

That's £2.24. [ðæts ˈtuː paʊndz ˌtwenti ˈfɔː] Das macht zwei Pfund und 24 Pence. I

the [ðə] der; die (auch Pl.); das I

the same [ðə ˈseɪm] derselbe; gleich II

theater (AE) [ˈθɪətə] Theater IV U1, 13

movie theater (AE) [ˈmuːvi ˌθiːətə] Kino <IV U1, 134>

theatre [ˈθɪətə] Theater II

their [ðeə] ihr, ihre (Pl.) I

theirs [ðeəz] ihre III

them [ðem; ðəm] sie (Pl.); ihnen I

theme park [ˈθiːm ˌpɑːk] Freizeitpark I; Themenpark II

themselves [ðəmˈselvz] selber; sie selbst; sich selbst; selbst III

then [ðen] dann; danach I; damals III

there [ðeə] da; dort I

down there [ˌdaʊn ˈðeə] dahin; da unten <IV U1, 183>

over there [ˌəʊvə ˈðeə] da drüben; dort drüben II

there are [ðeərˈɑː] da sind; es gibt I

there is [ðeə ˈɪz] da ist; dort ist; es gibt I

these [ðiːz] diese (hier) II

they [ðeɪ] sie (Pl.) I

thing [θɪŋ] Sache; Ding I

***to think** [θɪŋk] denken; glauben I

to think of [ˈθɪŋk_əv] sich ausdenken; sich etwas einfallen lassen <III>

third [θɜːd] dritte I

thirsty [ˈθɜːsti] durstig II

thirteen [θɜːˈtiːn] dreizehn I

thirty [ˈθɜːti] dreißig I

this [ðɪs] das; dies I

like this [ˌlaɪk ˈðɪs] so; auf diese Weise III

this way [ˌðɪs ˈweɪ] in diese Richtung II

those [ðəʊz] jene II

thought [θɔːt] simple past, past participle von to think II

a/one thousand [əˈwʌn ˈθaʊznd] eintausend; tausend II

three [θriː] drei I

threw [θruː] simple past von to throw IV U2, 38

throat [θrəʊt] Hals II

sore throat [ˌsɔː ˈθrəʊt] Halsschmerzen II

through [θruː] durch II

***to throw** [θrəʊ] werfen IV U2, 38

thrown [θrəʊn] past participle von to throw IV U2, 38

Thursday [ˈθɜːzdeɪ] Donnerstag I

ticket [ˈtɪkɪt] Karte II; Fahrschein; Eintrittskarte III

return ticket [rɪˈtɜːn ˌtɪkɪt] Hin- und Rückfahrkarte III

single ticket [ˈsɪŋɡl ˌtɪkɪt] einfache Fahrkarte III

to tidy (up) [ˌtaɪdi ˈʌp] aufräumen; in Ordnung bringen II

tiger [ˈtaɪɡə] Tiger I

tight [taɪt] eng; fest II

time [taɪm] Zeit; Uhrzeit I; Mal III

brewing time [ˈbruːɪŋ ˌtaɪm] Brühzeit <IV U5, 113>

free time [ˌfriː ˈtaɪm] Freizeit I

in time [ɪn ˈtaɪm] rechtzeitig I

on time [ɒn ˈtaɪm] pünktlich III

opening times [ˈəʊpnɪŋ ˌtaɪmz] Öffnungszeiten <IV U5, 207>

time travel [ˈtaɪm ˌtrævl] Zeitreise III

time zone [ˈtaɪm ˌzəʊn] Zeitzone IV ZI, 8

timeline [ˈtaɪmlaɪn] Zeitstrahl <IV U4, 87>

timetable [ˈtaɪmˌteɪbl] Stundenplan I; Fahrplan III

tin [tɪn] Dose; Büchse; Mülleimer IV U3, 63

tiny [ˈtaɪni] klein; winzig III

tip [tɪp] Tipp; Ratschlag II

tired [taɪəd] müde I

to get tired of sth [ˌget ˈtaɪəd_əv] etw. sattbekommen; etw. satthaben IV U1, 14

tissue [ˈtɪʃuː] Taschentuch III

title [ˈtaɪtl] Titel; Überschrift <II>

title

job title ['dʒɒb ˌtaɪtl] Stellenbezeichnung; Berufsbezeichnung
IV U2, 38

to [tuː; tʊ; tə] in; nach; zu; vor *(bei
Uhrzeitangaben)* I; bis II

toast [təʊst] Toast II

today [təˈdeɪ] heute I

together [təˈgeðə] zusammen;
gemeinsam I

toilet ['tɔɪlət] Toilette I

told [təʊld] simple past von *to tell* I

to tolerate ['tɒlreɪt] tolerieren;
dulden IV U5, 98

tomato *(sg)* [təˈmaːtəʊ], tomatoes
(pl) [təˈmaːtəʊz] Tomate II

tomorrow [təˈmɒrəʊ] morgen II

tongue twister ['tʌŋ ˌtwɪstə]
Zungenbrecher <III>

tonight [təˈnaɪt] heute Abend; heute
Nacht II

tonne [tʌn] Tonne II

too [tuː] auch I; zu II

too much [ˌtuː ˈmʌtʃ] zu sehr II

took [tʊk] simple past von *to take* II

tool [tuːl] Werkzeug; Gerät II

tooth *(sg)* [tuːθ], teeth *(pl)* [tiːθ] Zahn
III

toothbrush ['tuːθbrʌʃ] Zahnbürste III

toothpaste ['tuːθpeɪst] Zahnpasta III

toothpick ['tuːθpɪk] Zahnstocher II

top [tɒp] Top; Oberteil II; Spitze
IV U1, 13

topic ['tɒpɪk] Thema IV U2, 51

torch [tɔːtʃ] Taschenlampe I

torn [tɔːn] zerrissen; aufgerissen
IV U4, 83

tornado [tɔːˈneɪdəʊ] Tornado;
Wirbelsturm IV U2, 33

total ['təʊtl] Summe <IV U3, 66>

total ['təʊtl] Gesamt-; gesamt IV ZI, 8

*to keep in touch [ˌkiːp ɪn ˈtʌtʃ] in
Verbindung bleiben II

touchdown ['tʌtʃdaʊn] Touchdown
<IV U2, 50>

tough [tʌf] hart III

tour [tʊə] Tour; Fahrt; Reise IV U4, 76

guided tour ['gaɪdɪd ˌtɔː] Führung
<IV U1, 13>

tourist ['tʊərɪst] Tourist; Touristin I

Tourist Information Centre ['tʊərɪst
ɪnfəˈmeɪʃn ˌsentə] Touristeninformation I

towel ['taʊəl] Handtuch III

tower ['taʊə] Turm II

clock tower ['klɒk ˌtaʊə] Uhrenturm
II

town [taʊn] Stadt I

town centre [ˌtaʊn ˈsentə]
Stadtzentrum; Stadtmitte
<IV U1, 15>

town hall [ˌtaʊn ˈhɔːl] Rathaus II

toy [tɔɪ] Spielzeug III

cuddly toy ['kʌdli ˌtɔɪ] Kuscheltier
III

track [træk] Strecke IV U5, 102

railway track ['reɪlweɪ ˌtræk] Gleis
IV U3, 64

tractor ['træktə] Traktor I

trader ['treɪdə] Händler; Händlerin
<IV U2, 136>

tradition [trəˈdɪʃn] Tradition III

traditional [trəˈdɪʃnl] traditionell
<IV U2, 136>

traffic ['træfɪk] Verkehr III

traffic jam ['træfɪk ˌdʒæm] Stau
IV U1, 14

tragic ['trædʒɪk] tragisch <IV U2, 136>

trail [treɪl] Wanderweg; Spur
IV U5, 102

train [treɪn] Zug I

trainer ['treɪnə] Turnschuh I; Trainer;
Trainerin IV U5, 103

training ['treɪnɪŋ] Training III

tram [træm] Straßenbahn III

transcontinental [ˌtræns͵kɒntɪˈnentl]
transkontinental *(über den
Kontinent hinweg)* IV U4, 86

transfer [trænsˈfɜː] Transport;
Transfer IV U5, 102

to translate [trænzˈleɪt] übersetzen
IV U5, 102

transparency [trænˈspærnsi] Folie
<IV U2, 51>

transport ['trænspɔːt] Transport
<IV U1, 30>

public transport [ˌpʌblɪk ˈtrænspɔːt]
öffentliche Verkehrsmittel III

travel ['trævl] (das) Reisen <IV U1, 30>

time travel ['taɪm ˌtrævl] Zeitreise III

to travel ['trævl] reisen II; fahren III

tray [treɪ] Tablett II

treasure ['treʒə] Schatz II

tree [triː] Baum I

trend [trend] Trend; Entwicklung;
Richtung IV U4, 80

tribe [traɪb] Stamm; Volksstamm
<IV U1, 24>

trick [trɪk] Trick; Streich I; Kunststück
III

Trick or treat! [ˌtrɪk ə ˈtriːt] Süßes,
sonst gibt's Saures! I

trip [trɪp] Ausflug I; Trip; Fahrt; Reise
III

boat trip ['bəʊt ˌtrɪp] Bootsfahrt;
Schiffsfahrt II

outgoing trip [aʊtgəʊɪŋ ˈtrɪp]
Hinfahrt <IV U3, 66>

return trip [ˌrɪtɜːn ˈtrɪp] Rückfahrt
<IV U3, 66>

round trip [ˌraʊnd ˈtrɪp] Hin- und
Rückflug; Hin- und Rückfahrt
<IV U3, 66>

school trip [ˌskuːl ˈtrɪp]
Klassenfahrt I

to take a trip [teɪk ə ˈtrɪp] eine
Fahrt machen III

trouble ['trʌbl] Schwierigkeiten;
Problem; Ärger III

trousers *(pl)* ['traʊzəz] Hose I

truck [trʌk] Wagen; Karre III

true [truː] wahr II

to trust [trʌst] vertrauen IV U5, 109

to try [traɪ] probieren; versuchen II;
ausprobieren III

to try on [traɪ ˈɒn] anprobieren II

to try out [traɪ ˈaʊt] ausprobieren
III

T-shirt ['tiːʃɜːt] T-Shirt I

tube [tjuːb] Schlauch; Rohr III

Tuesday ['tjuːzdeɪ] Dienstag I

on Tuesday [ˌɒn ˈtjuːzdeɪ] am
Dienstag I

tuna ['tjuːnə] Thunfisch II

tunnel [ˈtʌnl] Tunnel III
(wind) turbine [(wɪnd) ˈtɜːbaɪn]
  Windrad III
turkey [ˈtɜːki] Truthahn; Pute IV U3, 53
Turkish [ˈtɜːkɪʃ] türkisch; Türkisch; aus
  der Türkei IV U5, 99
*****to take turns** [ˌteɪk ˈtɜːnz] sich
  abwechseln <II>
to turn [tɜːn] abbiegen III
  to turn into [ˌtɜːn ˈɪntə] umwandeln
  in; verwandeln in <IV U1, 28>
  to turn left [ˌtɜːn ˈleft] (nach) links
  abbiegen I
  to turn right [ˌtɜːn ˈraɪt] (nach)
  rechts abbiegen I
tutor [ˈtjuːtə] Klassenlehrer;
  Klassenlehrerin I
  tutor group [ˈtjuːtə ˌgruːp] Klasse
  (in einer englischen Schule) I
tutorial [tjuːˈtɔːriəl] Anleitung;
  Tutorial IV U4, 80
TV [tiːˈviː] Fernseher; Fernsehen I
  TV show [ˌtiːˈviː ˌʃəʊ]
  Fernsehsendung II
  TV studio [ˌtiːˈviː ˌstjuːdiəʊ]
  Fernsehstudio II
  to watch TV [ˌwɒtʃ tiːˈviː]
  fernsehen I
  on TV [ɒn ˌtiːˈviː] im Fernsehen
  IV U1, 13
tweet [twiːt] Pieps III
twelve [twelv] zwölf I
twenty [ˈtwenti] zwanzig I
  twenty-one [ˌtwentiˈwʌn]
  einundzwanzig I
to twist [twɪst] verdrehen; verzerren
  II
two [tuː] zwei I
type [taɪp] Sorte; Typ; Art III
to type [taɪp] tippen <III>
typical [ˈtɪpɪkl] typisch <IV U2, 35>
tyre [taɪə] Reifen III

U

umbrella [ʌmˈbrelə] Regenschirm II
umpire [ˈʌmpaɪə] Schiedsrichter;
  Schiedsrichterin <III>

unappealing [ˌʌnəˈpiːlɪŋ]
  uninteressant IV U4, 77
uncle [ˈʌŋkl] Onkel I
uncomfortable [ʌnˈkʌmftəbl]
  unbequem; unangenehm II
under [ˈʌndə] unter I
underground [ˈʌndəɡraʊnd] U-Bahn
  II
underlined [ˌʌndəˈlaɪnd]
  unterstrichen <III>
*****to understand** [ˌʌndəˈstænd]
  verstehen II
understood [ˌʌndəˈstʊd] simple past
  von *to understand* II
unemployed [ˌʌnɪmˈplɔɪd] arbeitslos
  IV U1, 18
unfair [ʌnˈfeə] unfair III
unfashionable [ʌnˈfæʃnəbl]
  unmodisch II
to unfriend [ʌnˈfrend] entfreunden
  *(jmdn. von seiner Freundesliste
  streichen)* IV U4, 81
unfriendly [ʌnˈfrendli] unfreundlich
  III
unhappy [ʌnˈhæpi] unglücklich II
uniform [ˈjuːnɪfɔːm] Uniform I
unit [ˈjuːnɪt] Lektion; Kapitel <I>
unmotivated [ʌnˈməʊtɪveɪtɪd]
  unmotiviert IV U2, 39
until [ʌnˈtɪl] bis I
unusual [ʌnˈjuːʒl] ungewöhnlich <II>;
  außergewöhnlich IV U4, 77
up [ʌp] hinauf; oben II
  to pick up [ˌpɪkˈʌp] abholen
  IV U2, 43
  to show up [ˌʃəʊˈʌp] auftauchen;
  erscheinen IV U2, 42
  to shut up [ˌʃʌtˈʌp] die Klappe
  halten IV U3, 63
  to stand up [ˌstændˈʌp] aufstehen;
  stehen IV U3, 63
  to wash up [ˌwɒʃˈʌp] abwaschen;
  abspülen <IV U2, 191>
to update [ˈʌpdeɪt] updaten; auf den
  neuesten Stand bringen IV U4, 81
updated [ʌpˈdeɪtɪd] aktualisiert
  <IV U1, 30>

to upload [ˈʌpləʊd] hochladen; ins
  Internet stellen II
upper [ˈʌpə] obere III
upset [ʌpˈset] aufgebracht; bestürzt I
upside-down [ˌʌpsaɪd ˈdaʊn]
  umgedreht; auf den Kopf gestellt
  <IV U4, 92>
us [ʌs] wir; uns I
US [juːˈes] US-amerikanisch IV U1, 18
to use [juːz] benutzen; verwenden II
  to get used to (sth) [ɡet ˈjuːzd tə]
  sich an (etw.) gewöhnen IV U1, 18
  used to (live) [ˈjuːst tə] (wohnte)
  früher III
useful [ˈjuːsfl] nützlich; hilfreich III
usually [ˈjuːʒli] normalerweise;
  gewöhnlich II

V

vacation (AE) [vəˈkeɪʃn] Ferien;
  Urlaub <IV U1, 15>
vacuum cleaner [ˈvækjuːm ˌkliːnə]
  Staubsauger IV U3, 59
valid [ˈvælɪd] gültig III
van [væn] Lieferwagen; Transporter
  III
variety [vəˈraɪəti] Auswahl <IV U5, 112>
veganism *(no pl)* [ˈviːɡənɪzm]
  Veganismus IV U4, 83
vegetable (veg) [ˈvedʒtəbl] Gemüse II
vegetarian [ˌvedʒɪˈteəriən] Vegetarier;
  Vegetarierin I
veggie bean cake [ˌvedʒi ˈbiːn keɪk]
  vegetarisches Bohnengericht II
version [ˈvɜːʃn] Version <IV U1, 135>
very [ˈveri] sehr I
vet [vet] Tierarzt; Tierärztin II
victim [ˈvɪktɪm] Opfer <IV U5, 108>
Victorian era [vɪkˌtɔːriən ˈɪərə]
  viktorianisches Zeitalter III
video [ˈvɪdiəʊ] Video IV U4, 80
  video chat [ˈvɪdiəʊ ˌtʃæt] Video-
  Chat III
Vietnamese [ˌvjetnəˈmiːz] vietnamesisch; Vietnamesisch; aus Vietnam; Vietnamese; Vietnamesin
  IV U5, 98

view [vjuː] Aussicht; Sicht; Ausblick; Blick IV U1, 14

viewing [ˈvjuːɪŋ] Hör-/Sehverstehen <I>

the **Vikings** [ðə ˈvaɪkɪŋz] die Wikinger III

village [ˈvɪlɪdʒ] Dorf III

to **visit** [ˈvɪzɪt] besuchen II

visitor [ˈvɪzɪtə] Besucher; Besucherin II

vocabulary [vəˈkæbjələri] Vokabular; Wortschatz II

voice [vɔɪs] Stimme III

volleyball [ˈvɒlibɔːl] Volleyball IV U4, 74

volunteer [ˌvɒlənˈtɪə] Freiwilliger; Freiwillige; ehrenamtlicher Helfer; ehrenamtliche Helferin III

to **vote** [vəʊt] abstimmen; wählen IV U2, 49

to vote for [ˈvəʊt fə] abstimmen über; wählen IV U2, 33

voyage [ˈvɔɪɪdʒ] Reise; Fahrt III

W

wage [weɪdʒ] Lohn IV U2, 38

to **wait** [weɪt] warten II

to wait for [ˈweɪt fɔː] warten auf II

waiter [ˈweɪtə] Kellner II

waitress [ˈweɪtrəs] Kellnerin; Bedienung IV U4, 89

*to **wake** up [ˌweɪkˈʌp] aufwachen II

walk [wɔːk] Spaziergang III

night walk [ˌnaɪt ˈwɔːk] Nachtwanderung I

to take the dog for a walk [ˌteɪk ðə ˌdɒg fər ə ˈwɔːk] den Hund spazieren führen II

a five minute walk [ə ˈfaɪv mɪnɪt ˌwɔːk] fünf Minuten zu Fuß III

to **walk** [wɔːk] gehen I; laufen II

dog **walker** [ˈdɒg ˌwɔːkə] Hundeausführer; Hundeausführerin IV U2, 41

walking [ˈwɔːkɪŋ] Wandern III

wall [wɔːl] Mauer; Wand II

walnut shell [ˈwɔːlnʌt ˌʃel] Walnussschale <IV U3, 71>

to **want (to)** [wɒnt (tə)] wollen I

war [wɔː] Krieg <IV U1, 184>

Civil War [ˌsɪvl ˈwɔː] Bürgerkrieg <IV U3, 138>

wardrobe [ˈwɔːdrəʊb] Kleiderschrank I

warm [wɔːm] warm I

warning [ˈwɔːnɪŋ] Warnung IV U2, 33

was [wɒz] simple past von *to be* I

to **wash** [wɒʃ] (sich) waschen; spülen III

to wash up [wɒʃˈʌp] abwaschen; abspülen <IV U2, 191>

*to do the **washing** up [ˌduː ðə ˈwɒʃɪŋ ʌp] abspülen II

to **watch** [wɒtʃ] anschauen; ansehen I; aufpassen auf; zuschauen; beobachten II

to watch TV [ˌwɒtʃ tiːˈviː] fernsehen I

bird **watching** [ˈbɜːd ˌwɒtʃɪŋ] Vogelbeobachtung III

water [ˈwɔːtə] Wasser I

bucket of water [ˈbʌkɪt əv ˌwɔːtə] Eimer Wasser I

mineral water [ˈmɪnrl ˌwɔːtə] Mineralwasser III

water level [ˈwɔːtə ˌlevl] Wasserpegel; Wasserstand <IV U5, 142>

waterproof [ˈwɔːtəpruːf] wasserfest <IV U3, 71>

wave [weɪv] Welle IV ZI, 9

to **wave** [weɪv] winken II

way [weɪ] Art und Weise III; Weg IV U2, 34

way in [ˌweɪ ˈɪn] Einstieg <I>

way to go [ˈweɪ tə ˌgəʊ] super II

asking the way [ˈɑːskɪŋ ðə ˌweɪ] nach dem Weg fragen I

No way! [ˌnəʊ ˈweɪ] Auf keinen Fall!; Was?!; Echt?! III

on the way [ɒn ðə ˌweɪ] auf dem Weg; unterwegs I

this way [ðɪs ˈweɪ] in diese Richtung II

we [wiː; wi] wir I

weak [wiːk] schwach III

wealth [welθ] Reichtum III

*to **wear** [weə] tragen *(Kleidung)* I

weather [ˈweðə] Wetter I

web [web] Spinnennetz; Netz III

website [ˈwebsaɪt] Website II

wedding [ˈwedɪŋ] Hochzeit II

Wednesday [ˈwenzdeɪ] Mittwoch I

on Wednesdays [ɒn ˈwenzdeɪz] mittwochs I

week [wiːk] Woche I

on **weekdays** [ɒn ˈwiːkdeɪz] unter der Woche; an Werktagen III

weekend [ˈwiːkend] Wochenende I

at the weekend [ət ðə ˈwiːkend] am Wochenende I

weekly [ˈwiːkli] wöchentlich III

to **weigh** [weɪ] wiegen II

to **welcome** [ˈwelkəm] willkommen heißen IV U4, 80

You're **welcome.** [jɔː ˈwelkəm] Gern geschehen. I

welcome (to) [ˈwelkəm (tʊ)] willkommen (bei/in) I

Welding Technology [ˈweldɪŋ ˌteknɒlədʒi] Schweißtechnik <IV U2, 48>

well [wel] na ja I; gut II

Well done! [ˌwel ˈdʌn] Gut gemacht! I

welly [ˈweli] Gummistiefel I

Welsh [welʃ] walisisch; Walisisch; Waliser; Waliserin III

went [went] simple past von *to go* I

were [wɜː] simple past von *to be* I

west [west] Westen III

west of [ˈwest əv] westlich von IV ZI, 9

country and **western** music [ˌkʌntri ənd ˈwestən ˌmjuːzɪk] Countrymusik <IV U5, 143>

wet [wet] nass I

what [wɒt] was I; welche II; wie III

What a … [ˈwɒt ə] Was für ein/eine … I

What about …? [ˈwɒt əˌbaʊt] Was ist mit …? I

What about you? [ˌwɒt əbaʊt ˈjuː] Und du? II

what else [ˌwɒt ˈels] was sonst; was noch <I>

What else can you …? [ˌwɒt ˈels kæn juː] Was kannst du noch …? <I>

What time is it? [ˌwɒt ˈtaɪm ˌɪz ˌɪt] Wie spät ist es?; Wie viel Uhr ist es? I

What to … [ˈwɒt tə] Was man … II

What's up? [ˌwɒts ˈʌp] Wie geht's? IV U3, 54

What's wrong? [ˌwɒts ˈrɒŋ] Was ist los?; Was stimmt nicht? II

What's your name? [ˌwɒts jə ˈneɪm] Wie heißt du? I

wheel [wiːl] Rad II

big wheel [ˌbɪg ˈwiːl] Riesenrad II

wheelchair [ˈwiːltʃeə] Rollstuhl III

when [wen] wann I; wenn; als II

where [weə] wo; wohin; woher I

Where are you from? [ˌweər ˌə ju ˈfrɒm] Woher kommst du? I

wherever [weəˈrevə] wo(hin) auch immer; egal wo(hin); überall wo(hin) III

which [wɪtʃ] welche II; die; der; dem; den; das III

while [waɪl] während II

to whisper [ˈwɪspə] flüstern <IV U5, 104>

white [waɪt] weiß I

who [huː] wer I; die; welche II; der; dem; den III

whole [həʊl] ganz IV U3, 63

whom [huːm] wem; wen IV U3, 58

whose [huːz] dessen; deren III

why [waɪ] warum I

wife Ehefrau IV U4, 85

the wild [ðə ˈwaɪld] Wildnis; freie Wildbahn IV U5, 102

wild [waɪld] wild IV U3, 63

wilderness [ˈwɪldənəs] Wildnis IV U4, 85

wildlife [ˈwaɪldlaɪf] Tierwelt (in freier Wildbahn) IV U5, 102

will [wɪl] werden II

*to win [wɪn] gewinnen; siegen I

wind [wɪnd] Wind I

wind farm [ˈwɪnd fɑːm] Windpark III

window [ˈwɪndəʊ] Fenster I

windy [ˈwɪndi] windig I

wine [waɪn] Wein IV U3, 62

winner [ˈwɪnə] Sieger; Siegerin; Gewinner; Gewinnerin I

winter [ˈwɪntə] Winter I

wish [wɪʃ] Wunsch <III>

Best wishes, [ˌbest ˈwɪʃɪz] Viele Grüße, I

to wish [wɪʃ] wünschen III

witch [wɪtʃ] Hexe I

with [wɪð] mit I

with special needs [wɪð ˌspeʃl ˈniːdz] mit Behinderung; mit besonderen Bedürfnissen III

within [wɪˈðɪn] innerhalb <IV U2, 136>

without [wɪˈðaʊt] ohne III

witness [ˈwɪtnəs] Zeuge; Zeugin IV U5, 107

woke up [ˌwəʊk ˈʌp] simple past von to wake up II

woman (sg) [ˈwʊmən], women (pl) [ˈwɪmɪn] Frau I

won [wʌn] simple past von to win I; past participle von to win II

won't (= will not) [wəʊnt] nicht werden II

wonderful [ˈwʌndəfl] wunderbar III

wood [wʊd] Holz I; Wald III

wood [wʊd] Holz III

wool [wʊl] Wolle I

word [wɜːd] Wort <I>

key word [ˈkiː ˌwɜːd] Stichwort; Schlüsselbegriff <IV U3, 68>

linking word [ˌlɪŋkɪŋ ˈwɜːd] Verbindungswort <IV U3, 73>

work [wɜːk] Arbeit I

to work [wɜːk] arbeiten I; funktionieren II

workbook [ˈwɜːkbʊk] Arbeitsheft I

worker [ˈwɜːkə] Arbeiter; Arbeiterin II

working hours (pl) [ˈwɜːkɪŋ ˌaʊəz] Arbeitszeit IV U2, 39

workshop [ˈwɜːkʃɒp] Workshop II

acting workshop [ˈæktɪŋ ˌwɜːkʃɒp] Schauspielworkshop II

world [wɜːld] Welt II

in the world [ɪn ðə ˈwɜːld] auf der Welt II

world-class [ˈwɜːldˌklɑːs] weltklasse <IV U1, 134>

worn [wɔːn] past participle von to wear II

worried [ˈwʌrid] beunruhigt; besorgt II

to worry [ˈwʌri] sich Sorgen machen I

worst [wɜːst] schlimmste; schlechteste III

would [wʊd] würde(n) II

would like [wʊd ˈlaɪk] würde(n) gern; hätte(n) gern II

I wouldn't like (to) … [aɪ ˈwʊdnt laɪk (tə)] Ich möchte nicht …; Ich würde nicht gerne … I

Would you like (to) …? [wʊd jə ˈlaɪk (tə)] Möchtest du? I

wrap [ræp] Wrap II

bubble wrap [ˈbʌbl ˌræp] Luftpolsterfolie <IV U3, 71>

wrist [rɪst] Handgelenk IV U3, 63

*to write [raɪt] schreiben I

writer [ˈraɪtə] Schriftsteller; Schriftstellerin II; Verfasser; Verfasserin; Autor; Autorin III

writing [ˈraɪtɪŋ] Schreiben <I>

written [ˈrɪtn] past participle von to write <IV U3, 72>; schriftlich <IV U2, 44>

wrong [rɒŋ] falsch I

wrote [rəʊt] simple past von to write I

Y

year [jɪə] Jahr; Jahrgangsstufe; Klasse I

yearbook [ˈjɪəbʊk] Jahrbuch <IV U2, 49>

yellow [ˈjeləʊ] gelb I

yes [jes] ja I

yesterday [ˈjestədeɪ] gestern I

yet [jet] schon II

not … yet [nɒt … ˈjet] noch nicht II

yogurt [ˈjɒgət] Joghurt II

you [juː] du; Sie; ihr; euch; dich; dir; Ihnen I

You're right. [jɔ ˈˌraɪt] Du hast recht. I

You're welcome. [jɔ ˈwelkəm] Gern geschehen. I

young [jʌŋ] jung II

your [jɔː] dein, deine; euer, eure; Ihr, Ihre I

yours [jɔːz] deine; eure; Ihre I

Yours, [jɔːz] Eure *(als Briefabschluss)* I

yourself [jɔːˈself] dich selbst II

by yourself [baɪ ˈjɔːself] allein II

yourselves [jɔːˈselvz] selber; ihr/euch/ Sie/sich (selbst) III

youth *(no pl)* [juːθ] Jugend-; Jugend III

Z

zebra [ˈzebrə] Zebra I

zero [ˈzɪərəʊ] null I

zip line [ˈzɪp ˌlaɪn] Seilrutsche III

ZIP Code [ˈzɪp kəʊd] Postleitzahl <IV U2, 44>

time zone [ˈtaɪm ˌzəʊn] Zeitzone IV ZI, 8

zoo [zuː] Zoo; Tierpark I

zookeeper [ˌzuːˈkiːpə] Tierpfleger; Tierpflegerin I

to zoom in [ˈzuːm ˌɪn] heranzoomen <I>

Boys' names

Alaqua [ˈælækwə] <IV U2, 137>
Chris [krɪs] IV U3, 62
CJ [ˈsiːˌdʒeɪ] IV U2, 45
Daniel [ˈdænjəl] IV U4, 76
David [ˈdeɪvɪd] IV U1, 14
Derek [ˈderɪk] IV U4, 80
Edward [ˈedwəd] IV U4, 85
Ethan [ˈiːθn] IV U5, 102
Finn [fɪn] <IV U3, 72>
Gordie [ˈɡɔːdi] IV U3, 62
Jacob [ˈdʒeɪkəb] IV U3, 54
José [həʊˈzeɪ] IV U1, 18
Matt [mæt] IV U5, 102
Matteo [məˈtɪəʊ] <IV U4, 88>
Michael [ˈmaɪkl] IV U2, 38
Pablo [ˈpæbləʊ] IV U1, 20
Ramon [rəˈmɒn] <IV U4, 88>
Robert [ˈrɒbət] IV U3, 54
Ronan [ˈrəʊnən] IV U1, 25
Roy [rɔɪ] IV U2, 45
Teddy [ˈtedi] IV U3, 63
Vern [vɜːn] IV U3, 63
Warren [ˈwɒrn] IV U2, 33
Wesley [ˈwezli] IV U1, 25

Girls' names

Amy [ˈeɪmi] <IV U2, 44>
Angela [ˈændʒlə] IV U1, 19
Anna [ˈænə] IV U5, 98
Becky [ˈbeki] IV U4, 79
Brenda [ˈbrendə] IV U3, 54
Caitlin [ˈkeɪtlɪn] <IV U2, 44>
Claudette [klɔːˈdet] IV U5, 106
Emma [ˈemə] <IV U3, 72>
Jennifer [ˈdʒenɪfə] IV U3, 58
Jessica [ˈdʒesɪkə] IV U1, 25
Julia [ˈdʒuːliə] IV U3, 54
Lily [ˈlɪli] IV U3, 54
Linda [ˈlɪndə] IV U2, 40
Marie [məˈriː] IV U2, 39
Pam [pæm] <IV U3, 72>
Pat [pæt] <IV U2, 137>
Ruby [ˈruːbi] IV U2, 45
Ruth [ruːθ] IV U3, 58
Sandy [ˈsændi] IV U4, 79
Stacey [ˈsteɪsi] IV U2, 39

Surnames

Beeman [ˈbiːmən] IV U3, 64
Blanco [ˈblæŋkəʊ] IV U1, 18
Colvin [ˈkɒlvɪn] IV U5, 106
Lachance [ˈlæʃɑːns] IV U3, 63
Lee [liː] IV U4, 80
Miller [ˈmɪlə] IV U3, 54
Singh [sɪŋ] IV U1, 14
Sutter [ˈsʌtə] IV U4, 84
Warner [ˈwɔːnə] <IV U3, 72>
Williams [ˈwɪljəmz] IV U5, 98

Place names

Africa [ˈæfrɪkə] Afrika II
Alabama (AL) [æləˈbæmə] *Bundesstaat in den USA* IV ZI, 9
Alaska (AK) [əˈlæskə] Alaska IV ZI, 8
America [əˈmerɪkə] Amerika II
Arkansas (AR) [ˈɑːkənsɔː] *Fluss und Bundesstaat in den USA* <IV U2, 136>
Asia [ˈeɪʒə] Asien IV U4, 74
Australia [ɒsˈtreɪliə] Australien I
Bishop [ˈbɪʃəp] *Ortsname* IV U4, 76
Bodie [ˈbəʊdi] *Ortsname* IV U4, 86
Boston [ˈbɒstən] *Stadt in den USA* III
The British Isles [ðə ˌbrɪtɪʃ ˈaɪlz] die Britischen Inseln III
the Bronx [ðə ˈbrɒŋks] *Stadtteil von NYC* IV U1, 12
Brooklyn [ˈbrʊklɪn] *Stadtteil von NYC* IV U1, 12
California (CA) [ˌkælɪˈfɔːniə] Kalifornien IV ZI, 9
Canada [ˈkænədə] Kanada III
Cape Cod [ˌkeɪp ˈkɒd] *Ortsname* <IV U3, 70>
Cardiff [ˈkɑːdɪf] *Hauptstadt von Wales* III
Charleston [ˈtʃɑːlstən] *Stadt in den USA* IV U5, 98
Chicago [ʃɪˈkɑːɡəʊ] *Stadt in den USA* <IV U2, 44>
China [ˈtʃaɪnə] China IV U1, 23
Clearwater [ˈklɪəwɔːtə] *Stadt in den USA* IV U5, 104
Coloma [kəˈləʊmə] *Ortsname* IV U4, 84

Colorado (CO) [ˌkɒləˈrɑːdəʊ] *Bundesstaat in den USA* IV ZI, 10
Cuba [ˈkjuːbə] Kuba IV U1, 18
The Czech Republic [ðə ˌtʃek rɪˈpʌblɪk] Tschechien II
Daytona [deɪˈtəʊnə] *Stadt in den USA* IV U5, 102
Del Mar [ˌdel ˈmɑː] *Ortsname* <IV U4, 77>
Denmark [ˈdenmɑːk] Dänemark III
Doheny [dəˈhiːni] *Strand in Kalifornien* <IV U4, 77>
Dominican Republic [ðə dəˌmɪnɪkn rɪˈpʌblɪk] Dominikanische Republik IV U1, 23
Eastern Europe [ˈiːstn ˌjʊərəp] Osteuropa IV U1, 23
England [ˈɪŋɡlənd] England I
Europe [ˈjʊərəp] Europa II
Florida (FL) [ˈflɒrɪdə] *Bundesstaat in den USA* IV U5, 96
Florida Keys [ˈflɒrɪdə ˌkiːz] *Inselkette in den USA* IV U5, 143
France [frɑːns] Frankreich II
Germany [ˈdʒɜːməni] Deutschland I
Great Britain [ˌɡreɪt ˈbrɪtn] Großbritannien III
Greece [ɡriːs] Griechenland IV U1, 23
Harlow [ˈhɑːləʊ] *Stadt in den USA* IV U3, 64
Hawaii [həˈwaɪiː] *Inselkette im Pazifischen Ozean* IV ZI, 9
Huntsville [ˈhʌntsvɪl] *Ort in den USA* IV ZI, 10
Illinois (IL) [ˌɪlɪˈnɔɪ] *Bundesstaat in den USA* <IV U2, 44>
India [ˈɪndiə] Indien I
Indiana (IN) [ˌɪndiˈænə] *Bundesstaat in den USA* IV ZI, 10
Ireland [ˈaɪələnd] Irland IV U1, 23
Italy [ˈɪtəli] Italien II
Jamaica [dʒəˈmeɪkə] Jamaika II
Japan [dʒəˈpæn] Japan <IV U4, 90>
Kentucky (KY) [kenˈtʌki] *Bundesstaat in den USA* IV ZI, 10
Las Vegas [ˌlæs ˈveɪɡəs] *Großstadt in den USA* IV ZI, 10

Las Vegas

Latin America

Latin America [ˌlætɪn əˈmerɪkə] Lateinamerika IV U1, 18

Little Italy [ˌlɪtl ˈɪtli] *Stadtteil von NYC* IV U1, 25

London [ˈlʌndən] London I

Los Angeles [lɒsˌˈændʒɪliːz] *Stadt in den USA* IV U3, 52

Louisiana (LA) [luˌiːziˈænə] *Bundesstaat in den USA* IV ZI, 9

Maine (ME) [meɪn] *Bundesstaat in den USA* IV U3, 53

Manhattan [mænˈhætn] *Stadtteil von NYC* IV U1, 12

Massachusetts [ˌmæsəˈtʃuːsɪts] *Bundesstaat in den USA* <IV U3, 66>

Mexico [ˈmeksɪkəʊ] Mexiko IV U1, 23

Miami [maɪˈæmi] *Stadt in den USA* IV U3, 57

The Midwest [ðə ˈmɪdwest] der Mittlere Westen IV ZI, 8

Mississippi (MS) [ˌmɪsɪˈsɪpi] *Bundesstaat in den USA* IV ZI, 9

Montgomery [mɑːntˈgʌmri] *Stadt in den USA* IV U5, 106

Narrabeen [ˈnærəbiːn] *Strand in Australien* <IV U4, 77>

Nashville [ˈnæʃvɪl] *Ort in den USA* IV U5, 97

The Netherlands [ðə ˈneðələndz] die Niederlande II

Nevada (NV) [nəˈvɑːdə] *Bundesstaat in den USA* IV ZI, 10

New England [ˌnjuːˌˈɪŋglənd] Neuengland IV ZI, 8

New Mexico (NM) [njuː ˈmeksɪkəʊ] *Bundesstaat in den USA* IV ZI, 10

New Orleans [ˌnjuːˌɔːˈliənz] *Stadt in den USA* IV U5, 97

New York City (NYC) [njuː jɔːk ˈsɪti] *Großstadt in den USA* IV U1, 12

North America [ˌnɔːθˌəˈmerɪkə] Nordamerika IV ZI, 8

North Dakota (ND) [ˌnɔːθ dəˈkəʊtə] *Bundesstaat in den USA* IV ZI, 10

Northern Ireland [ˌnɔːðn ˈaɪələnd] Nordirland III

Norway [ˈnɔːweɪ] Norwegen III

Oklahoma (OK) [ˌəʊkləˈhəʊmə] *Bundesstaat in den USA* <IV U2, 137>

Panama [ˌpænəˈmaː] *Ortsname* IV U4, 85

Park Ridge [ˈpɑːk ˌrɪdʒ] *Ortsname* <IV U2, 44>

Pennsylvania (PA) [ˌpensɪlˈveɪniə] *Bundesstaat in den USA* IV ZI, 10

Philadelphia [ˌfɪləˈdelfiə] *Stadt in den USA* <IV U3, 66>

The Philippines [ðə ˈfɪlɪpiːnz] die Philippinen IV U1, 19

Plymouth [ˈplɪməθ] *Ortsname* <IV U3, 70>

Poland [ˈpəʊlənd] Polen II

Queens [kwiːnz] *Stadtteil von NYC* IV U1, 12

The Republic of Ireland [ðə rɪˌpʌblɪkˌ əvˌˈaɪələnd] Irland III

Russia [ˈrʌʃə] Russland IV U1, 23

Sacramento [ˌsækrəˈmentəʊ] *Ortsname* IV U4, 84

San Francisco [ˌsæn frənˈsɪskəʊ] *Stadt in den USA* IV U4, 74

Santa Cruz [ˌsæntə ˈkruːz] *Stadt in den USA* <IV U4, 77>

Scandinavia [ˌskændɪˈneɪviə] Skandinavien IV U1, 23

Scotland [ˈskɒtlənd] Schottland III

Seattle [siˈætl] *Großstadt in den USA* IV ZI, 10

Siberia [saɪˈbɪəriə] Sibirien <IV U2, 136>

South Carolina (SC) [ˌsaʊθ kærˈlaɪnə] *Bundesstaat in den USA* IV U5, 98

South Dakota (SD) [ˌsaʊθ dəˈkəʊtə] *Bundesstaat in den USA* IV U2, 34

Spain [speɪn] Spanien II

Staten Island [ˌstætn ˈaɪlənd] *Stadtteil von NYC* IV U1, 12

Trestles [ˈtreslz] *Strand in Kalifornien* <IV U4, 77>

Turkey [ˈtɜːki] Türkei II

The United Kingdom (UK) [ðə juːˌnaɪtɪd ˈkɪŋdəm] Vereinigtes Königreich von Großbritannien und Nordirland III

USA (United States of America) [juːesˈeɪ (juːˌnaɪtɪd ˌsteɪtsˌəv əˈmerɪkə)] USA (Vereinigte Staaten von Amerika) III

Venice Beach [ˌvenɪs ˈbiːtʃ] *Stadtteil von Los Angeles* <IV U1, 26>

Vietnam [ˌvjetˈnæm] Vietnam IV U1, 23

Wales [weɪlz] Wales III

Washington (WA) [ˈwɒʃɪŋtən] *Bundesstaat in den USA* IV ZI, 10

Washington, D.C. [ˌwɒʃɪŋtən ˌdiːˈsiː] *Hauptstadt der USA* IV ZI, 8

West Coast [ˌwest ˈkəʊst] Westküste <IV U1, 24>

p pen • **b** bed • **t** ten • **d** dad • **k** cat • **g** grey • **tʃ** chair • **dʒ** joke • **f** fan • **v** very • **θ** three • **ð** the

Other names

Academy Award [əˌkædəmiˌəˈwɔːd] *Filmpreis* <IV U4, 140>

The **Appalachian Mountains** [ðə ˌæpəleɪʃən ˈmaʊntɪnz] Die Appalachen IV ZI, 8

Batman [ˈbætmæn] *Filmtitel* <IV U1, 135>

Baxendale Road [ˈbæksndeɪl ˌrəʊd] *Straßenname* <IV U2, 44>

bento [ˈbentəʊ] *Kästchen für Speisen* <IV U4, 90>

Bird Highway [ˌbɜːd ˈhaɪweɪ] *Straßenname* <IV U2, 44>

Bollywood [ˈbɒliwʊd] *indische Filmindustrie: Bombay + Hollywood* II

Broadway [ˈbrɔːdweɪ] *Straße in NYC* IV U1, 14

Brooklyn Bridge [ˌbrʊklɪn ˈbrɪdʒ] *Brücke in NYC* IV U1, 14

California Star [ˌkælɪfɔːniəˈstɑː] *Name einer Zeitung* IV U4, 84

Census Bureau [ˈsensəsˌbjʊərəʊ] Statistisches Bundesamt <IV U1, 26>

Central Park [ˌsentrl ˈpɑːk] *Park in NYC* IV U1, 14

Chief Ten Bears [ˌtʃiːf ˈten beəz] Häuptling Zehn Bären <IV U2, 136>

Chinatown [ˈtʃaɪnətaʊn] *chinesisches Stadtviertel* IV U4, 74

Colorado River [ˌkɒlərɑːdəʊ ˈrɪvə] *Fluss in den USA* IV ZI, 8

Christopher **Columbus** [ˌkrɪstəfə kəˈlʌmbəs] *Personenname* <IV U2, 136>

Columbus Day [kəˌlʌmbəs ˈdeɪ] *Feiertag in den USA* <IV U3, 139>

The **Confederate Flag** [ðə kənˈfedrət ˌflæg] Konföderiertenflagge IV U5, 98

Declaration of Independence [ˌdekləreɪʃn̩ˌəv ˌɪndɪˈpendəns] Unabhängigkeitserklärung IV ZI, 10

Denali [dəˈnɑːli] *höchster Berg in Nordamerika (neuer Name)* IV ZI, 8

Department of Homeland Security [dɪˌpɑːtmənt ˌəv ˌhəʊmlænd

sɪˈkjʊərəti] Heimatschutzbehörde IV U1, 23

Ellis Island [ˌelɪsˌ ˈaɪlənd] *Insel vor NYC* IV U1, 20

Empire State Building [ˌempaɪə steɪt ˈbɪldɪŋ] *Gebäude in NYC* IV U1, 14

Empire State of Mind (Part II) Broken Down [ˌempaɪə ˌsteɪtˌəv ˈmaɪnd (pɑːt ˈtuː) ˌbrəʊkn ˈdaʊn] *Liedname* <IV U1, 19>

European Union [ˌjʊərəpiːən ˈjuːnjən] Europäische Union III

The **Everglades** [ði ˈevəgleɪdz] *Nationalpark in den USA* IV U5, 102

Fort Knox [ˌfɔːt ˈnɒks] *Lager für die Goldreserven des Schatzamtes der USA* IV ZI, 10

Fruit4U [ˌfruːtfəˈjuː] *Firmenname* IV U2, 39

Mahatma **Gandhi** [məˌhɑːtmə ˈgændi] *Personenname* IV U5, 108

Gold Rush [ˈgəʊld ˌrʌʃ] **Goldrausch in Kalifornien** IV U4, 75

The **Golden Gate Bridge** [ðə ˌgəʊldn ˌgeɪt ˈbrɪdʒ] *berühmte Brücke in San Francisco* IV U4, 74

Gotham City [ˌgɒθəm ˈsɪti] *fiktiver Ort im Film Batman* <IV U1, 135>

Grand Canyon [ˌgrænd ˈkænjən] *Sehenswürdigkeit in den USA* IV U4, 76

Grand Central Station [ˌgrænd sentrl ˈsteɪʃn] *Hauptbahnhof in NYC* IV U1, 14

Grand Central Terminal [ˈgrænd ˌsentrl ˌtɜːmɪnl] *alter Name des Hauptbahnhofs in NYC* IV U1, 16

Gulf Coast [ˈgʌlf ˌkəʊst] Golfküste IV U5, 96

Hollywood [ˈhɒliwʊd] *Zentrum der amerikanischen Filmindustrie (in Los Angeles)* II

Huarache [ˌhuːəˈrɑːtʃə] *Name einer Schuhfirma* <IV U4, 77>

Hurricane Katrina [ˌhʌrɪkən kəˈtriːnə] *Name eines Wirbelsturms* <IV U5, 108>

Independence Day [ˌɪndɪˈpendəns ˌdeɪ] amerikanischer Unabhängigkeitstag <IV U3, 138>

Indy 500 [ˌɪndi faɪvˈhʌndred] *Name eines Autorennens* IV ZI, 10

Iron Man [ˈaɪən ˌmæn] *Filmtitel* <IV U1, 135>

Martin Luther **King** [ˌmɑːtɪn ˌluːθə ˈkɪŋ] *Personenname* <IV U3, 138>

Stephen **King** [ˌstiːvn ˈkɪŋ] *US-amerik. Schriftsteller* IV U3, 62

King Kong [ˈkɪŋ ˌkɒŋ] King Kong <IV U4, 141>

Ku Klux Klan [ˌkuː klʌks ˈklæn] *ein rassistischer Geheimbund in den Südstaaten der USA* IV U5, 107

Lexington Avenue [ˈleksɪŋtn ˌævənjuː] *Straße in NYC* IV U1, 14

Abraham **Lincoln** [ˌeɪbrəhæm ˈlɪŋkən] *16. Präsident der USA (1861–1865)* <IV U3, 138>

Long Island [ˌlɒŋˈaɪlənd] *Teilort von NYC* <IV U1, 135>

Malcolm X [ˌmælkəm ˈeks] *Personenname* <IV U5, 108>

Mardi Gras [ˌmɑːdi ˈgrɑː] Faschingsdienstag IV U5, 98

Martin Luther King Day [ˌmɑːtɪn ˌluːθə ˌkɪŋ ˈdeɪ] *Feiertag in den USA zu Ehren Martin Luther Kings* <IV U3, 138>

Mayflower [ˈmeɪflaʊə] *Schiffsname* <IV U3, 70>

Mesa Verde [ˌmeɪsə ˈvɜːdi] *US-Nationalpark* IV ZI, 10

Mississippi River [ˌmɪsɪsɪpi ˈrɪvə] *Fluss in den USA* IV ZI, 8

Missouri River [mɪˌzʊəri ˈrɪvə] *Fluss in den USA* IV ZI, 8

Mt. McKinley [ˌmaʊnt məˈkɪnli] *höchster Berg in Nordamerika (alter Name)* IV ZI, 8

NASCAR (National Association for Stock Car Racing) [ˈnæzkɑː] *amerikanischer Motorsportverband* IV U5, 102

NASCAR

New World [ˌnjuː ˈwɜːld] *alter Name für Amerika* <IV U3, 70>

Niagara Falls [naɪˌægrə ˈfɔːlz] *Niagarafälle* IV U3, 52

One World Trade Center [ˌwʌn ˈwɜːld ˌtreɪd ˌsentə] *Gebäude in NYC* IV U1, 12

Oscar [ˈɒskə] *Filmpreis* <IV U4, 140>

Pacific Ocean [pəˌsɪfɪk ˈəʊʃn] *Pazifischer Ozean* IV ZI, 9

Rosa **Parks** [ˌrəʊzə ˈpɑːks] *amerikanische Bürgerrechtlerin* IV U5, 107

Presidents' Day [ˌprezɪdnts ˈdeɪ] *Feiertag in den USA* <IV U3, 138>

Rio Grande [ˌriːəʊˈgrænd] *Fluss in den USA* <IV U2, 136>

River Thames [ˌrɪvə ˈtemz] *Fluss in London* II

the **Rockies** (= the Rocky Mountains) [ðə ˈrɒkiz] *Gebirge in Nordamerika* <IV U4, 89>

Rocky Mountains [ˌrɒki ˈmaʊntɪnz] *Gebirge in Nordamerika* IV ZI, 9

Silicon Valley [ˌsɪlɪkən ˈvæli] *Ort, wo viele Computerfirmen ihren Sitz haben* IV U4, 75

Sitting Bull [ˌsɪtɪŋ ˈbʊl] *Name des Häuptlings eines Indianerstammes* IV ZI, 10

Space Needle [ˈspeɪs ˌniːdl] *Sehenswürdigkeit in Seattle* IV ZI, 10

Statue of Liberty [ˌstætʃuː əv ˈlɪbəti] *Freiheitsstatue in NYC* IV U1, 13

Joseph **Strauss** [ˌdʒəʊzɪf ˈstraʊs] *Architekt* IV U4, 75

Super Bowl [ˈsuːpə bəʊl] *Meisterschaftsendspiel des NFL* <IV U2, 50>

Surfin' USA [ˈsɜːfɪn ˌjuːesˈeɪ] *Liedtitel* <IV U4, 77>

Taylor **Swift** [ˌteɪlə ˈswɪft] *Personenname* IV U5, 97

Universal Studios [ˌjuːnɪˈvɜːsl ˌstjuːdiəʊz] *bekanntes Filmstudio in den USA* <IV U4, 141>

US Space & Rocket Center [ˌjuːes ˌspeɪs ən ˈrɒkɪt ˌsentə] *Raumfahrtmuseum in den USA* IV ZI, 10

Ventura County Line [venˌtʊərə ˌkaʊnti ˈlaɪn] *Name einer Bahnlinie* <IV U4, 77>

Very Large Array [ˌveri lɑːdʒ əˈreɪ] *Radioteleskop in den USA* IV ZI, 10

Walk of Fame [ˌwɔːk əv ˈfeɪm] *Straße in Hollywood mit Sternen für bekannte Leute* IV U4, 75

Wall Street [ˈwɔːl ˌstriːt] *Straße in NYC* IV U1, 14

George **Washington** [ˌdʒɔːdʒ ˈwɒʃɪŋtən] *1. Präsident der USA (1789–1797)* <IV U3, 138>

The **White House** [ðə ˈwaɪt ˌhaʊs] *das Weiße Hause* IV U3, 53

World Trade Center [ˌwɜːld ˈtreɪd ˌsentə] *Gebäude in NYC bis 2001* IV U1, 12

World Wide Web [ˌwɜːld waɪd ˈweb] *ein über das Internet abrufbares System* IV U4, 80

Malala **Yousafzai** [ˌməlælæ ˈjuːsæfzaɪ] *Personenname* IV U5, 108

A

abbiegen to turn III
abdecken to cover IV U3, 58
Abend evening I
    an jenem Abend that night II
    heute Abend tonight II
Abendessen dinner II
(frühes) **Abendessen** tea I
abends in the evenings III
Abenteuer adventure I
aber but I
abfahren leave II
Abfall rubbish II
abholen to pick up IV U2, 43
Abholung pick-up IV U5, 102
ablehnen to refuse IV U5, 99
abonnieren to subscribe IV U4, 81
abräumen to clear IV U2, 33
    den Tisch abräumen to clear the
    table II
abschicken (einen Brief) to post III
Abschieds- leaving II
Abschiedsrede farewell speech II
abschließen to lock I
sich **abseilen** to abseil II
absichtlich on purpose II
absolut absolutely IV U3, 59
abspülen to do the washing up II
abstimmen über to vote for IV U2, 33
Abteilung department II
acht eight I
Achterbahn roller coaster II
achtzehn eighteen I
achtzig eighty I
Ackerboden farmland IV U2, 32
Ackerland farmland IV U2, 32
Adapter adaptor III
Adjektiv adjective III
Adresse address II
Affe monkey I
Afroamerikaner African American
    IV U5, 96
afroamerikanisch African-American
    IV U5, 106
Ahnung idea I
Aktenkoffer briefcase III
Aktentasche briefcase III

Aktivität activity I
akzeptieren to accept IV U5, 99
albern silly II
Alkohol alcohol (no pl) IV U3, 58
alle all I; everyone II; every III; every-
    body IV U2, 43
Allee avenue IV U1, 14
allein alone I; by yourself II
    ganz allein all alone I
Allergie allergy II
allergisch gegen allergic to II
alles everything II
    alles klar all right II
Alligator alligator IV ZI, 9
Alphabet alphabet I
als than; as II; when II
also so I; right II
alt old I
Alter age I
Altglascontainer bottle bank II
am Dienstag on Tuesday I
am Schluss by the end II
am Wochenende at the weekend I
Amerikaner American IV ZI, 9
Amerikanerin American IV ZI, 9
Amerikanisch American IV ZI, 9
amerikanisch American IV ZI, 9
amisch Amish IV U3, 58
die **Amischen** the Amish IV U3, 53
Ampel lights IV U1, 14
amüsiert amused IV U3, 63
an on; at I; by IV U3, 63
    an Bord on board III
    an der Spitze (von) at the front
    of II
Ananas pineapple III
anbauen to grow IV U3, 58
anbieten to offer IV U2, 38
Anblick look IV U1, 14
andauern to last IV U4, 86
Andenken souvenir III
andere other I; others II
    ein anderer another II
    die anderen the others I
    anderer Meinung sein to disagree
    II
(sich) **ändern** to change III

    seine Meinung ändern to change
    one's mind III
anders different I
Anfang start; beginning III
anfangen to start II
Anführer leader III
Anführerin leader III
angenehm comfortable II
angezogen (wie) dressed III
angreifen to attack IV U2, 42
Angriff attack IV U1, 12
Angst haben to be scared; to be
    afraid I
ängstlich afraid II
anhalten to last IV U4, 86
anhören to listen (to) I
ankommen to arrive II
Ankündigung announcement II
anlegen to put on III
Anleitung tutorial IV U4, 80
anmalen to paint II
Anmeldeformular entry form II
Anmeldung registration II
annehmen to accept IV U5, 99
Annonce ad(vert) (= advertisement)
    IV U4, 76
Anordnung layout IV U4, 77
anprobieren to try on II
Anruf call III
anrufen to call I; to phone II
Anrufer caller II
Anruferin caller II
anschauen to watch; to look at I; to
    have a look II
sich **anschließen** to join III
ansehen to watch I
Anspitzer pencil sharpener I
morgendliche **Ansprache** morning
    message IV U2, 34
ansprechend appealing IV U4, 77
anstelle von instead IV U4, 80
anstoßen to hit III
(sich) **stoßen** to hit III
Antenne antenna III
Antwort answer II
antworten to answer I
Anzahl number IV U4, 75
Anzeige advertisement II

anziehen to put on III
   sich **anziehen** to get dressed II
April April I
Arbeit work I; job II
arbeiten to work I
Arbeiter worker II
Arbeiterin worker II
Arbeitsheft workbook I
Arbeitskollege co-worker IV U2, 38
Arbeitskollegin co-worker IV U2, 38
arbeitslos unemployed IV U1, 18
arbeitsreich busy I
Arbeitszeit working hours (pl)
   IV U2, 39
Architekt architect IV U4, 75
Architektin architect IV U4, 75
Archiv archive II
Areal area IV ZI, 9
Ärger trouble III
Arm arm I
arm poor IV U1, 18
Armee army III
armselig miserable III
Art sort II; type III
   Art und Weise way III
Arzt doctor II
Ärztin doctor II
Astronomie astronomy IV U2, 34
atmen to breathe III
Attacke attack IV U1, 12
auch too; also I
   auch nicht not either III
auf on; at I
   auf dem Land in the country I
   auf dem Weg on the way I
   auf der linken Seite on the left I
   auf der rechten Seite on the right I
   auf der Welt in the world II
   auf diese Weise like this III
   auf einmal suddenly II
   Auf keinen Fall! No way! III
   Auf Wiedersehen! Goodbye. I
Aufbau structure III
auffallend striking III
Aufführung show IV U5, 102
Aufgabe job II
aufgeben to give up IV U1, 18
aufgeben (einen Brief) to post III

aufgebracht upset I
aufgeregt excited; nervous II
aufgerissen torn IV U4, 83
aufheben to pick up II; to save
   IV U3, 54
jmdn. **aufheitern** to cheer sb up III
aufhören to stop I; to finish II
Aufkleber sticker II
aufmachen to open I
jmdn. **aufmuntern** to cheer sb up III
aufpassen to look after II
   aufpassen auf to watch II
aufräumen to tidy (up) II
aufregend exciting I
aufschauen to look up II
aufstehen to get up I; to stand up
   IV U3, 63
auftauchen to show up IV U2, 42
aufwachen to wake up II
aufwachsen to grow up III
Aufzug elevator (AE) IV U1, 13
Auge eye II
Augenblick moment II
August August I
   im August in August I
aus from I
   aus … heraus out of II
Ausbildung education IV U2, 38
Ausblick view IV U1, 14
auschecken to check out III
Auseinandersetzung argument II;
   conflict IV U5, 99
ausfallen to fail IV U1, 19
Ausflug trip I
ausgeben (Geld) to spend II
ein **ausgefüllter** Tag a busy day I
ausgehen (Ware) to run out of III
   (aus)gehen mit to go out with
   IV U3, 58
ausländisch foreign IV U1, 18
ausleihen to borrow II
ausprobieren to try; to try out III
ausräumen to clear IV U2, 33
Ausrüstung equipment III
aussehen to look II
außer except III
außergewöhnlich unusual IV U4, 77
außerhalb outside IV U2, 38

außerhalb des Lehrplans
   extracurricular IV U2, 34
Außerirdische alien I
Außerirdischer alien I
außerunterrichtlich (Zusatzunter-
   richt) extracurricular IV U2, 34
Aussicht view IV U1, 14
Aussichtspunkt lookout point II
aussteigen to get off II
Austausch exchange IV U2, 34
Ausverkauf sale II
auswählen to choose II
auswandern to emigrate IV U1, 19
Ausweis ID III
Auswirkung impact IV U4, 80
Auto car I
Autofahrt drive III
Autogramm autograph IV U3, 53
   Autogramme geben to sign auto-
   graphs IV U3, 53
Automat machine II
Autor writer III
Autorin writer III

B

Baby baby II
Babysitter babysitter IV U2, 41
Babysitterin babysitter IV U2, 41
einen Kuchen **backen** to make a
   cake I
Bäcker baker III
Bäckerei baker's III
Bäckerin baker III
Backofen oven II
Bad bathroom I
Badezimmer bathroom I
Bahnhof station I
bald soon II
Ball ball II
Banane banana I
Band band II
Bank bench III
Bär bear I
Bargeld cash II
Baseball baseball IV U1, 13
Basketball basketball II
Bauarbeiter builder II

Bauarbeiterin builder II
Bauch stomach II
Bauchschmerzen stomach ache II
Bauchweh stomach ache II
bauen to build II
Bauer farmer I
Bäuerin farmer I
Bauernhof farm I
Baum tree I
Baumwolle cotton III
Baustelle construction site IV U1, 15
beängstigend scary I
beantworten to answer I
bedauern to feel sorry for III
bedecken to cover IV U3, 58
bedeuten to mean III
bedeutend major IV ZI, 8; powerful
    IV U1, 22
sich **bedienen** to help oneself III
Bedienung waitress IV U4, 89
Bedingung condition IV U1, 22
mit besonderen **Bedürfnissen** with
    special needs III
sich **beeilen** to hurry II; to rush III
beeindrucken to impress III
beeindruckend powerful IV U1, 22
beenden to finish II
befolgen to follow III
befördern to carry II
befragen to interview I
Befrager interviewer IV U1, 18
Befragerin interviewer IV U1, 18
Befragung interview II
befreunden (*jmdn. zu seiner Freundes-
    liste hinzufügen*) to friend IV U4, 81
begeistert excited II
Beginn beginning III
beginnen to start II; to begin IV U1, 18
begnadigen to pardon IV U3, 53
Begnadigung pardon IV U3, 67
mit **Behinderung** with special needs
    III
bei at I
    bei Bewusstsein awake III
Bein leg II
beinahe almost III
Beispiel example IV U5, 98
    zum Beispiel for example IV U2, 34

sich **beklagen** to complain IV U1, 18
Bekleidungsvorschriften dress code
    IV U2, 36
bekommen to get I
bekräftigen to confirm IV U4, 84
beliebt popular III
bemerkenswert striking III
benennen to name IV ZI, 9
benutzen to use II
beobachten to watch II
bequem comfortable II
bereit ready I
bereits already II
Berg mountain III; hill IV U4, 74
Bergarbeiter miner III
Bergarbeiterin miner III
bergen to save III
Bergwerk mine III
Bericht report IV U4, 84
Beruf job II; career IV U1, 18
Berufsbezeichnung job title IV U2, 38
berühmt famous I
Besatzung crew III
beschäftigt busy I
sich **beschweren** to complain
    IV U1, 18
eine **Besichtigungstour** machen to
    go sightseeing II
besitzen to own; to have got II
mit **besonderen** Bedürfnissen with
    special needs III
besonders special I; especially II
besorgt worried II
Besorgungen machen to do the
    shopping II
besser better I
bestätigen to confirm IV U4, 84
bestbezahlt best-paid IV U5, 97
beste best II
    die besten the best II
besteigen to climb III
bestellen to order II
bestürzt upset I
besuchen to visit II
Besucher visitor II
Besucherin visitor II
Beton concrete III
betreiben to run III

betreten to enter IV U3, 54
betrunken drunk IV U3, 62
Bett bed I
    ins Bett gehen to go to bed I
Bettdecke blanket IV U3, 62
beunruhigt worried II
Bevölkerung population IV ZI, 8
bevor before II
(sich) **bewegen** to move IV U1, 22
Bewegung move III; movement
    IV U5, 96
beweisen to prove IV U4, 84
sich **bewerben** (für/um) to apply
    (for) IV U2, 38
bewerten to rate III
Bewohner inhabitant III
Bewohnerin inhabitant III
bei **Bewusstsein** awake III
Bezahlautomat payment machine II
bezahlen to pay II
Bezirk borough IV U1, 12
Bibliothek library III
Bild picture II
bilden to make I
Bildung education IV U2, 38
billig cheap II
Biologie Biology I
bis to II; until I
    bis zu before II
    Bis bald! See you soon! I
    Bis bald. See you later.; See you. I
    bis (spätestens) by III
ein **bisschen** a little; a bit II
bitte please I
    Bitte schön. Here you are. I
bitten um to ask for II
blau blue I
bleiben to stay II
    etw. bleiben lassen to give sth a
    miss III
    in Verbindung bleiben to keep in
    touch II
    stecken bleiben to get stuck
    IV U3, 54
Bleistift pencil I
Blick look; view IV U1, 14
Blog blog II
Blume flower III

Blume

Bluse blouse I
bluten to bleed III
Boden ground III
Bonbon sweet I
Boot boat II
Bootsfahrt boat trip II
an **Bord** on board III
böse angry II; naughty III
Boss boss II
Botschaft message II
Boulevard avenue IV U1, 14
Bowlen bowling IV U3, 58
Box box I
braten to fry IV U5, 98
Bratwurst sausage II
brauchen to need I
   nicht brauchen needn't I
braun brown I
brechen to break II
brennen to be on fire II; to burn III
Brett plank II
Brief letter III
Briefmarke stamp III
bringen to bring II; to take IV U2, 43
britisch British II
Broschüre brochure III; booklet
   IV U5, 102
Brot bread II
   belegtes Brot sandwich I
Brotlaib loaf III
Brücke bridge II
Bruder brother I
Buch book I
buchen to book IV U4, 76
Bücherei library III
Büchse tin IV U3, 63
Buchstabe letter III
buchstabieren to spell I
Bucht bay IV U4, 75
Büfett buffet III
Bühne stage II
Bundesstaat state IV ZI, 8
bunt colourful II
Buntstift pencil I
Burg castle II
Bürgerrechte civil rights *(pl)* IV U5, 96
Bürgersteig sidewalk *(AE)* IV U1, 15
Büro office II

Bus bus I
   im Bus on the bus II
Bushaltestelle bus stop II
Butter butter I

C

Café café I
Cafeteria cafeteria I
Camp camp II
campen gehen to go camping II
Camping camping III
Campingplatz campsite III
Cartoon cartoon IV U4, 81
Center centre III; center *(AE)* IV U1, 13
Chance chance II
chatten to chat II
Cheerleader *(Mädchen, das in einer*
   Gruppe eine Sportmannschaft
   anfeuert) cheerleader IV U2, 34
Chef boss II
Chefin boss II
Chefkoch head chef II
Chefköchin head chef II
Chili chilli II
chillen to chill out IV U4, 76
Chinese Chinese IV U5, 99
Chinesin Chinese IV U5, 99
Chinesisch Chinese IV U5, 99
chinesisch Chinese IV U5, 99
christlich Christian IV U3, 53
circa about II
Cola coke I
College college IV U1, 19
Comic(heft) comic II
Computer computer I
Courage courage IV U5, 107
Cousin cousin II
Cousine cousin II
Crew crew III
Curry curry II
Cyber-Mobbing cyberbullying
   IV U4, 80

D

da there I
   da drüben over there II

   da ist there is I
   da sind there are I
da because I
Dach roof II
Dachboden attic I
damals then III
Dame lady II
Dampfmaschine steam engine III
danach then; after that I; after III
Herzlichen **Dank.** Thanks so much.
   IV U4, 94
Vielen **Dank.** Thanks so much.
   IV U4, 94
danke thanks I
Danke. Thank you. I
dann then I
das the; this; that I; which III
dass that III
Date date IV U2, 42
Datei file II
Datum date I
dauern to take III; to last IV U4, 86
davor in front of II
Decke blanket IV U3, 62
decken to lay II
dein your I
deine yours I; your I
dem who; which III
Demonstration protest IV U5, 96
den who; which III
denken to think I
Denkmal monument II
dennoch still III
deprimiert down III
der the I; who; which III
deren whose III
derselbe the same II
Desaster disaster III
deshalb so I
dessen whose III
Detail detail IV U5, 102
deutlich clear IV U4, 77
Deutsch German I
deutsch German III
Dezember December I
dich you I
   dich selbst yourself II
die *(auch Pl.)* the I; who II; which III

Diele hall II
Dienst service III
Dienstag Tuesday I
  am Dienstag on Tuesday I
dies this I
diese (hier) these II
Ding thing I
dir you I
Distanz distance IV ZI, 9
Dollar *(amer. Währungseinheit)* dollar
  IV ZI, 8
Donnerstag Thursday I
doof silly III
Dorf village III
dort there I
  dort drüben over there II
  dort ist there is I
Dose can I; tin IV U3, 63
Dr. *(Anrede)* Dr III
Drama drama III
drängeln to push III
Draufgänger daredevil IV U3, 53
Draufgängerin daredevil IV U3, 53
draußen outside II
  draußen halten to keep out III
dreckig dirty I
Drehort location III
drei three I
dreißig thirty I
dreizehn thirteen I
drinnen in II; inside IV U1, 25
dritte third I
drücken to push I
Dschungel jungle IV U4, 85
du you I
Dudelsack bagpipes *(pl)* III
dulden to tolerate IV U5, 98
dumm silly III
dunkel dark I
Dunkelheit the dark III
durch through II
  quer durch across IV U3, 54
Durcheinander mess I
Durchsage announcement II
durchschnittlich average IV U3, 58
dürfen may II; to be allowed to
  IV U2, 34
  nicht dürfen mustn't III

nicht/nie dürfen must not/never
III
  Darf es sonst noch etwas sein?
  Anything else? I
durstig thirsty II
Dusche shower III
Duschgel shower gel III

E

echt real II; really II
  Echt?! No way! III
Ecke corner III
  Es ist egal. It doesn't matter. II
egal wo(hin) wherever III
Ehefrau wife IV U4, 85
Ehemaligentreffen Homecoming
  (AE) IV U2, 33
Ehemann husband IV U3, 54
Ehre honor *(AE)* IV U1, 25
ehrenamtliche Helferin volunteer III
ehrenamtlicher Helfer volunteer III
ehrlich honestly IV U3, 63
Ei egg I
eifersüchtig jealous II
eigene own II
Eigenschaftswort adjective III
eigentlich actually III; anyway
  IV U1, 14
Eigentümer landlord II
eilen to rush III
Eimer Wasser bucket of water I
ein a; an I
  ein bisschen a bit II
  ein paar a few III
  ein wenig a bit II
einander each other III
Einbrecher burglar I
Einbrecherin burglar I
einchecken to check in III
eindeutig clear IV U4, 77
eindringen (in) to invade III
einfach easy I; plain II; simple III
einfache Fahrkarte single ticket III
Einfluss impact IV U4, 80; influence
  IV U5, 98
einflussreich important II
einfügen to paste II

eingängig catchy IV U4, 77
Eingangstor gateway IV U1, 12
einhundert a/one hundred I
einige some I; a few III; several
  IV U4, 80
Einkäufe machen to do the shopping
  II
Einkaufen shopping I
einkaufen gehen to go shopping II
Einkaufszentrum shopping centre I
Einkaufszettel shopping list I
einladen to invite I
Einladung invitation I
einmal once IV U1, 25
  noch einmal once more II
einmarschieren (in) to invade III
einpacken to pack; to pack up II
einprägsam catchy IV U4, 77
eins one I
einsam lonely III
einschlafen to fall asleep III
einsetzen to put in I
einst once IV U1, 25
einsteigen (in den Bus) to get on
  (the bus) IV U5, 106
Einstellung attitude IV U4, 89
einstufen to rate III
Eintrag entry IV U4, 86
eintreten to enter IV U3, 54
Eintrittskarte ticket III
nicht **einverstanden** sein to disagree
  II
Einwanderer immigrant IV U1, 13
Einwandererin immigrant IV U1, 13
einwandern to immigrate IV U1, 18
Einwohner inhabitant III; population
  IV ZI, 8
Einwohnerin inhabitant III
Einwohnerzahl population IV ZI, 8
Einzelheit detail IV U5, 102
einzige only II
Eis ice cream I
Eisberg iceberg III
Eiscreme ice cream I
Eisenbahn railway IV U4, 86
Elefant elephant I
elegant chic I
elektrisch electric IV U3, 59

elektrisch

261

Elektrizität electricity III
elend miserable III
elf eleven I
Eltern parents (pl) II
E-Mail e-mail I
emigrieren to emigrate IV U1, 19
Empfang signal III
Ende end II; ending III
enden to finish II; to end IV U5, 107
endlich at last II
Energie power III
eng tight II
die **Engländer** the English III
Englisch English I
englisch English I
Entdeckung discovery IV U4, 84
entfernen to remove IV U5, 98
entfernt away II
Entfernung distance IV ZI, 9
entfreunden (jmdn. von seiner Freundesliste streichen) to unfriend IV U4, 81
entlang along I; down III
(sich) **entscheiden** to decide III
Entscheidung decision IV U1, 18
entschuldigen to pardon IV U3, 53
   sich entschuldigen to say sorry II
Entschuldigung pardon IV U3, 67
Entschuldigung! Excuse me! I
Entschuldigung. Sorry.; I'm sorry. I
sich **entspannen** to chill out IV U4, 76
entspannt relaxed IV U4, 74
Entwicklung trend IV U4, 80
Enzyklopädie encyclopedia IV U4, 86
er he I
   er selbst himself III
Erdbeere strawberry II
Erdboden ground III
Erdkunde Geography I
Erdnussbutter peanut butter III
Ereignis event IV U4, 86
etwas **erfahren** über to learn about sth III
erfinden to invent III
Erfinder inventor III
Erfinderin inventor III
Erfindung invention III
Erfolg success IV U5, 107

erfolgreich successful III
erforschen to explore II
Ergebnis result II
ergreifen to grab III
sich **erinnern** (an) to remember II
erklären to explain III
erkunden to explore II
sich **erkundigen** nach to ask about II
erlauben to allow IV U4, 84
ernst serious III
   etw. ernst nehmen to take sth seriously IV U1, 18
   Im Ernst? Are you serious? III
Erntedankfest Thanksgiving IV U3, 53
erraten to guess II
erscheinen to show up IV U2, 42
erschöpft exhausted III
erschrecken to scare II; to jump III
erschrocken sein to be scared II
ersetzen to replace IV U1, 12
erstaunlich amazing II
erste first I
   erste Stunde (in der Schule) homeroom IV U2, 45
erstellen to make I
als **Erstes** first I
Erwachsene adult III
Erwachsener adult III
erwarten to expect III
erzählen to tell I
Erzähler narrator I
Erzählerin narrator I
Erziehung education IV U2, 38
es it I
   es gibt there are; there is I
   Es tut mir leid wegen … Sorry about … I
   Es tut mir leid. I'm sorry. I
Essen food I; meal II; dinner IV U3, 53
   Essen zum Mitnehmen takeaway II
essen to eat I; to have II
Essensstand food stall II
Esszimmer dining room I
etwa about II
etwas something I; some II
euch you I
euer your I

eure yours I; your I
Eure (als Briefabschluss) Yours, I
Euro (Währung) euro III
Europäer European IV U2, 32
Europäerin European IV U2, 32
europäisch European IV U2, 32
Europäisch European IV U2, 32
ewig forever II
exakt exact III
existieren to be around IV U4, 80
explodieren to explode III
Explosion explosion III

F

Fabel fable III
Fabrik factory III
Fahne flag II
fahren to go I; to ride II; to travel III; to drive IV U3, 52
   gegen etw. fahren to hit III
   Ski fahren to ski II
Fahrer driver III
Fahrerin driver III
einfache **Fahrkarte** single ticket III
Fahrplan timetable III; schedule (AE) IV U2, 33
Fahrpreis fare III
Fahrrad bike I
Fahrschein ticket III
Fahrt ride IV U1, 14; drive; trip; voyage; journey III; tour IV U4, 76
   eine Fahrt machen to take a trip III
Fakt fact II
Fall case IV U5, 107
fallen to fall I; to fall (over) III
falls if II
falsch wrong I
Faltblatt flyer II
Familie family I
Fan fan I
fangen to catch II
Fantasie fantasy II
fantastisch fantastic II
Fantasy fantasy II
Farbe colour I; color (AE) IV ZI, 8
Fasching carnival IV U5, 98

Fass barrel IV U3, 53
fast almost III
Fastfood fast food I
faszinierend fascinating IV U4, 77
Februar February I
Federmäppchen pencil case I
Feedback feedback IV U2, 39
fegen to sweep II
fehlschlagen to fail IV U1, 19
Feier party I; celebration IV U3, 52
feiern to celebrate I
Feind enemy III
Feindin enemy III
Feld field IV ZI, 9
Fels rock III
Fenster window I
Ferien holiday I
in der **Ferne** in the distance IV U1, 15
Fernsehen TV I
    im Fernsehen on TV IV U1, 13
fernsehen to watch TV I
Fernseher TV I
Fernsehsendung TV show II
Fernsehstudio TV studio II
fertig ready I
    sich fertig machen to get ready
    IV U3, 54
fertigstellen to finish II
fest tight II; solid III
festhalten to hold III
festnehmen to arrest IV U5, 107
feststecken to be stuck I
Feuer fire I
Feuerwehrauto fire engine II
Fieber fever IV U4, 86
Film film; movie I
Filzstift felt-tip I
Finanz- financial IV U1, 14
finanziell financial IV U1, 14
finden to find I
Finger finger III
Fingerabdruck fingerprint II
Firma company II
Fisch fish I
fit fit III
Fitnessraum gymnasium III
Fläche area IV ZI, 9
Flagge flag II

Flamingo flamingo I
Flasche bottle I
Fledermaus bat I
Fleisch meat I
fleißig hard-working IV U2, 39
fliegen to fly II
fließend fluent III
Flohmarkt jumble sale II
Flug flight II
Flughafen airport II
Flugzeug plane II
Flur hall; corridor II
Fluss river I
flüssig fluent III
Flyer flyer II
folgen to follow III
Fön hairdryer III
in **Form** fit III
Foto photo I
    ein Foto machen to take a photo I
    Fotos machen to take photos II
fotografieren to take photos II
Frage question I
fragen to ask I
    fragen nach to ask about II
    nach dem Weg fragen asking the
    way I
die **Franzose**n the French (pl)
    IV U5, 98
Französisch French I
Frau woman I; lady II
Frau (Anrede) Mrs; Ms I
frech cheeky; naughty III
freie Wildbahn the wild IV U5, 102
Land der **Freien** land of the free
    IV U3, 53
Freiheit freedom (no pl) IV U1, 23
Freiland- free range II
Freiluft- outdoor III
Freistunde study hall period IV U2, 34
Freitag Friday I
Freiwillige volunteer III
Freiwilliger volunteer III
Freizeit free time I
Freizeitpark theme park I
fremd foreign IV U1, 18
Freude fun I
Freund friend I

    Freunde treffen to see friends I
Freund (in einer Paarbeziehung)
    boyfriend IV U2, 42
Freundin friend I
Freundin (in einer Paarbeziehung)
    girlfriend IV U2, 38
freundlich kind II; friendly III
Freundschaften schließen to make
    friends I
Frieden peace III
friedlich peaceful IV U5, 96
frieren to freeze; to get cold III
Frisbee frisbee I
Frisbeescheibe frisbee I
frisch fresh II
Friseur hairdresser II
Friseurin hairdresser II
frittieren to fry IV U5, 98
froh glad IV U3, 54
Frucht fruit I
früh early I
    früher earlier I
    (wohnte) früher used to (live) III
Frühlingsrolle spring roll II
Frühstück breakfast I
frühstücken to have breakfast I
Frühstückspension bed and break-
    fast (B & B) III
(sich) **fühlen** to feel II
führen to run III
Führer guide II; leader III
Führerin guide II; leader III
Führerschein driver's license
    (AE) IV U2, 38
Füller pen I
fünf five I
fünfzehn fifteen I
fünfzig fifty I
funktionieren to work II
für for I
    für immer forever II
furchtbar awful; terrible I; horrible;
    dreadful III
sich **fürchten** to be afraid II
Fuß foot I
    zu Fuß on foot I
Fußball football I
Fußboden floor I

Fußboden

Fußgelenk ankle II
Fußknöchel ankle II
füttern to feed I

G

Gabel fork II
Gang corridor II
ganz all II; quite III; whole IV U3, 63
   ganz allein all alone I
   den ganzen Tag all day III
gar nicht not at all II
Garten garden I
Gas gas III
Gast guest III
Gastfamilie host family IV U2, 34
Gasthaus pub III
Gebärdensprache sign language III
Gebäude building II
geben to give I; to be around
   IV U4, 80
   Autogramme geben to sign autographs IV U3, 53
   jmdm. das Gefühl geben, etw. zu
   sein to make sb feel like sth III
   es gibt there are; there is I
Gebet prayer IV U4, 85
Gebiet area IV ZI, 9
geboren werden to be born III
(in der Pfanne) gebraten fried II
Geburtstag birthday I
   Alles Gute zum Geburtstag! Happy
   birthday! I
Gedicht poem III
geduldig patient III
gefährlich dangerous III
Gefängnis prison II
gefrieren to freeze III
jmdm. das **Gefühl** geben, etw. zu
   sein to make sb feel like sth III
gegen against II; around III
   gegen etw. fahren to hit III
Gegend area IV ZI, 9
sich **gegenseitig** each other III
gegenüber opposite I
geheim secret II
Geheimnis mystery I; secret II
gehen to go; to walk I

gehen um to be about III
   ins Bett gehen to go to bed I
gehörlos deaf III
Gehweg sidewalk *(AE)* IV U1, 15
Geist ghost II
Gel gel III
gelassen relaxed IV U4, 74
gelb yellow I
Geld money I
Geldschein note II
Gelegenheit chance II
gemein mean IV U3, 63
Gemeinde community IV U1, 18
gemeinsam together I
Gemeinschaft community IV U1, 18
Gemüse vegetable (veg) II
Obst- und **Gemüseladen**
   greengrocer's III
gemustert patterned II
gemütlich cosy III
genannt werden to be called II
genau exact III; right IV U2, 42
   Genau. Exactly. IV U3, 59
genießen to enjoy II
genug enough III
genügend enough III
Geocaching geocaching I
Geografie Geography I
gerade right now III; right IV U2, 42
   gerade (eben) just II
geradeaus straight on I; right ahead
   IV U1, 15
Gerät tool II; device IV U3, 58
Geräusch noise I; sound III
Gerede talk II; gossip IV U3, 58
Gericht dish II; court IV U5, 107
Gerichtsverhandlung court case
   IV U5, 107
Gern geschehen. You're welcome. I
gern mögen to love I
   hätte(n) gern would like II
   Ich würde nicht gerne … I
   wouldn't like (to) … I
   würde(n) gern would like II
gesamt total IV ZI, 8
Gesamt- total IV ZI, 8
Geschäft shop I; store *(AE)* IV U2, 33
Geschäftsführer manager IV U2, 38

Geschäftsführerin manager IV U2, 38
Geschäftsmann businessman
   IV U4, 84
geschehen to happen II
Geschenk present I
Geschichte History; story I; history III
Geschoss bullet IV U3, 63
Gesellschaft company II
Gesellschaftslehre Social Studies I
gestatten to allow IV U4, 84
gestern yesterday I
Getränk drink II
Getreide corn IV ZI, 9
gewinnen to win I
Gewinner winner I
Gewinnerin winner I
sich an (etw.) **gewöhnen** to get used
   to (sth) IV U1, 18
gewöhnlich usually II
Gewürz spice II
Gips cast III
Giraffe giraffe I
Gitarre guitar III
glänzen to shine IV ZI, 8
Glas glass II; jar III
glauben to think I; to believe II
gleich the same II; right away
   IV U4, 80
   jetzt gleich right now III
gleichmäßig regular IV U4, 89
Gleis railway track IV U3, 64
Glocke bell II
Glück haben to be lucky III
viel **Glück** good luck II
glücklich happy I
glücklicherweise luckily II
Glückstag lucky day II
Glückszahl lucky number I
Glückwunsch! Congratulations! II
Glühbirne light bulb III
Gold gold III
Gold- gold III; golden IV U5, 98
golden gold III; golden IV U5, 98
Goldrausch gold rush IV U4, 84
Grab grave III
Gras grass I
grau grey I
greifen to grab III

Grenze border IV U3, 52
Griechisch Greek IV U5, 99
griechisch Greek IV U5, 99
Grill barbecue I
Grillparty barbecue I
groß big; high I; tall; large II
großartig great I; fantastic II
Größe size II
Großeltern grandparents *(pl)* II
Großmutter grandmother III
Großstadt city II
Großvater grandfather II
großzügig generous IV U2, 39
grün green I
Grund reason III
    Gründe angeben to give reasons III
    Gründe nennen to give reasons III
Grundbesitzer landowner IV U4, 84
Grundbesitzerin landowner IV U4, 84
gründen to start III; to found IV U5, 98
Gruppe group I
gruselig scary I; creepy IV U3, 53
Grüß dich. Hello there. I
Grüße ausrichten to say hi to I
Viele Grüße, Best wishes, I
grüßen to say hi to I
gültig valid III
Gummi rubber III
Gummistiefel welly I
gut good I; fine II; well; nice III
    gut sein in/bei to be good at I
    Guten Morgen. Good morning. II
    Gut gemacht! Well done! I

H

Haar hair III
Haare hair III
    sich die Haare schneiden lassen to have a haircut II
Haargel hair gel III
Haarglätter hair straightener I
Haarschnitt haircut II
haben to have I; to have got II
    Glück haben to be lucky III
    hätte(n) gern would like II

    Mitleid haben mit to feel sorry for III
    Du hast recht. You're right. I
Hafen harbour II; harbor *(AE)* IV U1, 22
Hafer oat III
Haferbrei porridge III
Hai shark I
halb half III
    halb (drei) half past (two) I
    eine halbe Million half a million III
(die) Hälfte half IV U4, 80
Hallen- indoor III
Hallo. Hello.; Hi.; Hello there. I
Hals throat II
Halsband collar I
Halsschmerzen sore throat II
Halt stop II
halten to keep II; to hold III
    die Klappe halten to shut up IV U3, 63
    draußen halten to keep out III
Haltestelle stop II
Haltung attitude IV U4, 89
Hamburger burger II
Hand hand I
handeln von to be about III
Handgelenk wrist IV U3, 63
Handtuch towel III
Handy mobile (phone) I
hängen to hang II
hänseln to tease IV U2, 38
hart hard II; tough III
hassen to hate I
häufig often I
Haupt- major IV ZI, 8
Hauptgericht main course II
Hauptstadt capital (city) III
Hauptverkehrszeit rush hour IV U1, 14
Haus house I
    im Haus around the house I
    nach Hause home I
    zu Hause at home I
Hausaufgabe(n) homework I
    Hausaufgabe(n) machen to do homework I
Häuschen cottage III

Hausmeister caretaker I
Hausmeisterin caretaker I
Haustier pet I
Heer army III
Heft book I; booklet IV U5, 102
Heim home I
Heimweh haben to be homesick III
heiraten to get married II
heiß hot I
heißen to be called II
    willkommen heißen to welcome IV U4, 80
Heizkörper radiator IV U3, 59
Held hero III
helfen to help I
Helfer helper IV U4, 89
Helferin helper IV U4, 89
Helikopter helicopter I
hell bright IV ZI, 8
Helm helmet III
Hemd shirt I
heraus out II
    aus … heraus out of II
herausfallen aus to fall out of IV U2, 42
herausfinden to find; to find out I
herauskommen to get out III
herausnehmen to take out I
Herberge hostel III
Herbst fall *(AE)* IV ZI, 8
hereinkommen to get in I; to enter IV U3, 54
hergestellt sein aus to be made of III
Herr *(Anrede)* Mr I
herrlich lovely II
herüber across IV U3, 54
herum around I
herumkommen to get around III
herumrennen to run about II
herunter down III
herunterladen to download II
Herzlichen Dank. Thanks so much. IV U4, 94
heute today I
    heute Abend tonight II
    heute Nacht tonight II
heutzutage now II
Hexe witch I

Hi. Hi. I
hier here I
hiesig local III
Highschool *(weiterführende Schule, Oberstufe)* high school IV U1, 18
Hightech- high-tech IV U4, 75
Hilfe help II; support IV U1, 19
hilfreich useful III; helpful IV U2, 38
hilfsbereit helpful IV U2, 38
Himbeere raspberry III
Hin- und Rückfahrkarte return ticket III
hinauf up II
hinbringen to take II
in … hinein inside II
hineingehen to go on II; to enter IV U3, 54
hineingelangen to get into IV U1, 14
hineinkommen to get into IV U1, 14
hinfallen to fall (over) III
hinnehmen to accept IV U5, 99
hinter behind II
Hinter- back IV U3, 62
Hintergrund background III
im Hintergrund in the background III
Hinterteil back IV U5, 106
hinüber across IV U3, 54
hinunter down III
hinuntereilen to rush down II
Hinweis clue I
hinzufügen to add II
zu … hinzufügen to bookmark II
Hip-Hop *(Musik)* hip hop III
Hitparade charts *(pl only)* IV U5, 97
Hitze heat IV U5, 102
Hobby hobby III
hoch high I; tall II
hochladen to upload II
Hochzeit wedding II
hoffen to hope I
Hoffnung hope IV U1, 13
hoffnungsvoll hopeful III
höflich polite II
Höhe height II
Höhle cave II
holen to get II
Holz wood III

hören to listen (to); to hear I
Hose trousers *(pl)* I
kurze Hose shorts *(pl)* I
Hosentasche pocket II
Hospital hospital I
Hot Dog *(Würstchen im Brötchen)* hot dog IV U1, 14
Hotel hotel II
Hotelfachschule catering college II
hübsch beautiful I; pretty; lovely II
Hubschrauber helicopter I
Hügel hill IV U4, 74
Huhn chicken I
Hühnchen chicken II
Hund dog I
Hundeausführer dog walker IV U2, 41
Hundeausführerin dog walker IV U2, 41
Hundekeks dog biscuit II
hundert a/one hundred I
hungrig hungry I
husten to cough III
Hut hat II
hüten to look after II

I

ich I; me I
Ich heiße … My name is … I
Ich komme aus … I'm from … I
Ich weiß (es) nicht! I don't know! I
ich würde lieber I'd rather III
Idee idea I
ihm him I
ihn him I
Ihnen you I
ihnen them I
ihr you I; her I; its III
Ihr your I
ihr *(Pl.)* their I
Ihre yours I; your I
ihre their I; her I; hers II; theirs III
im August in August I
im Bus on the bus II
Im Ernst? Are you serious? III
im Freien outside II
im Haus around the house I

im Stadtzentrum downtown *(AE)* IV U1, 14
im Süden von in the south of III
im vorderen Bereich at the front of II
Imbiss snack I
immer always I
für immer forever II
immer noch still I
Immigrant immigrant IV U1, 13
Immigrantin immigrant IV U1, 13
Immigration immigration IV U1, 22
immigrieren to immigrate IV U1, 18
in in; to; at I; inside III
in der Ferne in the distance IV U1, 15
in der Mitte in the centre of III
in der Pause at break I
in der Schule at school I
in Form fit III
in Ordnung fine; all right II
in … hinein inside II
Indianer Native American IV U2, 32
Indianerin Native American IV U2, 32
indianisch Native American IV U2, 32
indisch Indian II
indisch Indian I
Industrie industry III
industrielle Revolution Industrial Revolution III
Informatik IT (Information Technology) I
Information information *(no pl)* I; information desk II
Informationen information *(no pl)* I
informativ informative IV U4, 77
Ingenieur engineer II
Ingenieurin engineer II
Inhalt content III
innen in inside III
innen inside IV U1, 25
Innen- indoor III
im Innern inside III
Insekt insect III
Insel island II
Institut college IV U1, 19
intelligent clever I; smart; intelligent III
interessant interesting I

sich **interessieren** für to be interested in III

interessiert sein an to be interested in III

Internet internet II
   im Internet surfen to surf the internet II
   ins Internet stellen to upload II

Internettagebuch blog II

Interview interview II

interviewen to interview I

Interviewer interviewer IV U1, 18

Interviewerin interviewer IV U1, 18

irgendein any II

irgendetwas anything II

irgendwelche any II

Irisch Irish III

irisch Irish III

Italiener Italian II

Italienerin Italian II

Italienisch Italian II

italienisch Italian II

J

ja yes I
   na ja well I

Jacke coat I; jacket II

Jäger chaser IV U2, 33; hunter IV U4, 85

Jägerin chaser IV U2, 33; hunter IV U4, 85

Jahr year I

Jahrgangsstufe year I

Jahrhundert century III

jamaikanisch Jamaican II

jämmerlich miserable III

Januar January I

Japaner Japanese IV U5, 99

Japanerin Japanese IV U5, 99

Japanisch Japanese IV U5, 99

japanisch Japanese IV U5, 99

Jeans jeans *(pl)* I

jeder every; everyone I; everybody IV U2, 43

jedoch however III

jemals ever II

jemand somebody IV U2, 38
   jemand anderes somebody else II

jene those II

jetzt now I
   jetzt gleich right now III

Job job I

Joghurt yogurt II

Journalismus journalism IV U2, 34

Journalistik journalism IV U2, 34

Jugend youth *(no pl)* III

Jugend- teen II; youth *(no pl)* III

Jugendliche teen II; teenager III

Jugendlicher teen II; teenager III

Jugendzentrum activity centre III

Juli July I

jung young II

Junge boy I

Juni June I

Juror judge II

Jurorin judge II

K

Käfig cage I

kalt cold I

Kamel camel I

Kamm comb III

Kampf fight; battle III

kämpfen to fight III

Kanarienvogel canary III

Kanone cannon II

Kanonenkugel cannon ball II

Kanufahren canoeing I

Kapitän captain I

Kapitänin captain I

Kappe cap I

Karate karate III

Karneval carnival IV U5, 98

Karotte carrot II

Karre truck III

Karriere career IV U1, 18

Karte card I; ticket II

Kartoffel potato II

Kartoffelbrei mashed potatoes II

Kartoffelchip crisp I

Karton cardboard III

Käse cheese I

Käsekuchen cheesecake II

Katastrophe disaster III

Katholik Catholic III

Katholikin Catholic III

katholisch Catholic III

Katze cat I

kaufen to buy I

Kaufhaus department store II

Kaugummi chewing gum I

kein no I; not … any II

Keks biscuit II

Kellner waiter II

Kellnerin waitress IV U4, 89

kennen to know I
   kennen lernen to meet I; to get to know II

Kerl guy IV U2, 42

Kerze candle I

Ketchup ketchup II

Kidneybohne kidney bean II

Kilogramm (kg) kilogram (kg) I
   sieben Kilogramm täglich 7 kilograms a day I

Kilometer (km) kilometre (km) I
   40 Kilometer pro Stunde 40 kilometres an hour I

Kilt kilt III

Kind child; kid II

Kinder children *(pl)* II

Kinderzimmer bedroom I

Kino cinema I

Kirche church II

Kiste box I

die **Klappe** halten to shut up IV U3, 63

klar clear IV U4, 77
   alles klar all right II

Klasse year I; class III; grade *(AE)* IV U2, 33

Klasse *(in einer englischen Schule)* tutor group I

Klassenarbeit test I

Klassenfahrt school trip I

Klassenlehrer tutor I

Klassenlehrerin tutor I

Klassenzimmer classroom I

Klatsch gossip IV U3, 58

Klebstoff glue I

Kleeblatt shamrock III

Kleid dress I

Kleider *(Pl.)* clothes *(pl)* I

Kleiderordnung dress code IV U2, 36

Kleiderschrank wardrobe I
Kleidung clothes *(pl)*; outfit III
klein small I; little II; tiny III
Klettern rock climbing I
klettern to climb III
klicken to click I
klingeln to ring III
klingen to sound II
Klischee stereotype IV U2, 42
Kloß dumpling II
Klub club II
Klubhaus clubhouse IV U3, 62
klug clever I; smart; intelligent III
Kneipe pub III
Knie knee III
Knoblauch garlic II
knuddelig cuddly III
Koch chef II
Kochbanane plantain II
Kochen cooking II
kochen to cook II
Köchin chef II
Koffer suitcase II
Kohl cabbage II
Kohle coal III
Kokosnuss coconut II
Kombination combination II
kommen to come I
Kommentar comment IV U4, 80
Komödie comedy III
Kompromiss compromise IV U5, 99
Konfitüre jam III
Konflikt conflict IV U5, 99
König king III
königlich royal II
Konkurrenz competition IV U2, 34
können can I; may II
  nicht können can't I; cannot III
  nicht weg können to be stuck I
konnte could III
  Ich konnte nicht anders als … I
  couldn't help but … III
könnte could III
Konto account IV U4, 80
Kontrolle check IV U1, 22
kontrollieren to check III
(sich) **konzentrieren** to concentrate
  IV U3, 58

Konzert concert II
Kopf head II
Kopfhörer headphones *(pl)* IV U3, 59
Kopfsalat lettuce II
Kopfschmerzen headache II
kopfüber head first III
Kopfweh headache II
Kopie copy II
kopieren to copy II
Korbball netball I
Korn corn IV ZI, 9
Körper body III
Körperlotion body lotion III
korrekt right I
Korridor hall II
kosten to cost III
  … kosten 99 Pence. … are 99p. I
  … kostet ein Pfund fünfundzwan-
  zig. … is £1.25. I
kostenlos free III
köstlich delicious II
Kostüm costume; fancy dress I
Kraft power III
krank sein *(AE)* to be sick III
krank ill II
Krankenhaus hospital I
Krankenpfleger nurse II
Krankenschwester nurse II
Krankenwagen ambulance III
Krankheit disease IV U1, 22
Kraut cabbage II
Kreis circle III
kreischen to scream IV U3, 63
Kricket cricket II
Kritik review III
Krokodil crocodile I
Kubaner Cuban IV U1, 18
Kubanerin Cuban IV U1, 18
kubanisch Cuban IV U1, 18
Küche kitchen I
Kuchen cake I; pie II
  einen Kuchen backen to make a
  cake I
Kugel bullet IV U3, 63
Kuh cow III
kühl cool I
kühlen to cool III
Kühlschrank fridge III

Kultur culture IV U1, 13
sich **kümmern** (um) to care (for) III
Kumpel buddy *(infml)* IV U2, 45
Kunde customer III
Kundin customer III
Kunst Art I
Kunststoff plastic III
Kunststück trick III
Kuppel dome II
Kurs course III; class IV U2, 34
kurz short II; shortly III
  kurze Hose shorts *(pl)* I
Kuscheltier cuddly toy III
Kuss kiss II
Küste coast III
  an der Küste on the coast III

L

lachen to laugh II
Ladegerät charger III
Laden shop I; store *(AE)* IV U2, 33
  Tante-Emma-Laden corner shop I
Lage location III
Lager camp II
Lamm lamb II
Lampe lamp I
Land country I; land II; countryside
  III; state IV ZI, 8
  auf dem Land in the country I
  Land der Freien land of the free
  IV U3, 53
landen to land IV U3, 54
Landesregierung state government
  IV U5, 98
Landkarte map III
ländliche Gegend country I
Landschaft countryside III; land-
  scape IV ZI, 9
Landwirt farmer I
Landwirtin farmer I
Landwirtschaftsflächen farmland
  IV U2, 32
lang long I
langsam slow III
langweilig boring I
Laptop laptop I
Lasagne lasagne II

lassen leave II
  etw. bleiben lassen to give sth a miss III
  lass uns let's I
Laufbahn career IV U1, 18
laufen to run I; to walk II
  Wie läuft's? How's it going? IV U3, 54
Laut sound III
laut noisy; loud III
läuten to ring III
Layout layout IV U4, 77
Leben life I; lifetime IV U4, 76
leben to live I
Lebensart lifestyle IV U4, 74
Lebensmittel food I; groceries (pl) IV U4, 89
Lebenszeit lifetime IV U4, 76
lecker nice; tasty III
Leder leather III
leer empty IV U4, 86
legen to put I; to lay II
Lehrer teacher I; instructor III
Lehrerin teacher I; instructor III
Leiche body IV U3, 62
leicht easy I
Es tut mir **leid**. I'm sorry. I
Es tut mir **leid** wegen … Sorry about … I
Tut mir **leid**. Sorry. I
leidtun to be sorry III
leihen to lend II
Leine lead I
leise quiet III
leiten to run III
Leiter ladder I
lernen to learn II
  kennen lernen to get to know II
lesen to read I
zu guter **Letzt** at last II
letzte last I
leuchtend bright IV ZI, 8
Leute people (pl) I; guys II
Lexikon encyclopedia IV U4, 86
Licht light IV U1, 13
Liebe/Lieber …, (Anrede in Briefen)
  Dear …, I
Liebe love IV U4, 85

lieben to love I
ich würde **lieber** I'd rather III
Liebesgeschichte romance III
Lieblings- favourite I; favorite (AE) IV U3, 53
Lied song I
Lieferwagen van III
Lifestyle lifestyle IV U4, 74
Lift elevator (AE) IV U1, 13
lila purple I
Limonade lemonade II
Lineal ruler I
Linie line II
Link link IV U4, 80
links on the left I; left III
Liste list II
LKW-Fahrer lorry driver II
LKW-Fahrerin lorry driver II
Loch hole I
locker relaxed IV U4, 74; loose II
Löffel spoon II
Lohn wage IV U2, 38
lokal local III
lose loose II
lösen to solve I
Lösung solution IV U5, 98
Löwe lion I
Luft air IV U1, 22
Luftballon balloon I
Lunchpaket packed lunch II
lustig funny I

M

machen to do; to make I
  ein Foto machen to take a photo I
  Hausaufgabe(n) machen to do homework I
  sich Notizen machen to take notes I
  Gut gemacht! Well done! I
  Mach dir nichts draus. Never mind. II
  Macht nichts. Never mind. II
  Macht's gut. Take care. I
Macht power III
mächtig powerful IV U1, 22
Mädchen girl I

Magen stomach II
Magie magic II
magisch magic II
Mahlzeit meal II
Mai May I
Mais corn IV ZI, 9
Make-up make-up IV U3, 58
Mal time III
malen to paint II
Mama mum I; mama II
Mammutbaum redwood (tree) IV U4, 74
Manager manager IV U2, 38
Managerin manager IV U2, 38
manchmal sometimes I
Mann man I
Mannschaft team I; crew III
Märchen fable III
Marke brand III
Markt market II
Marmelade jam III
März March I
Maschine machine II
Mathe Maths I; Math (AE) IV U2, 34
Mathematik Maths I; Math (AE) IV U2, 34
Matsch mud III
Mauer wall II
Maus mouse I
Mayonnaise mayonnaise II
meckern to nag III
soziale **Medien** social media IV U4, 80
Medikamente medicine III
Medizin medicine III
Meer sea I; ocean IV ZI, 9
  am Meer at the seaside I
Meerschweinchen guinea pig I
Mehl flour II
  in Mehl wenden to cover in flour IV U5, 98
mehr more I
  nicht mehr not … any more III
mehrere several IV U4, 80
Mehrheit majority IV U1, 23
  die Mehrheit most I
Meile mile II
mein my I
meine my I; mine II

meine

269

meinen to mean III
Meinung opinion III
   einer Meinung sein (mit) to agree (with) III
   seine Meinung ändern to change one's mind III
   anderer Meinung sein to disagree II
am **meisten** most II
die **meisten** most I
eine **Menge** a lot of I
jede **Menge** lots of I; lots III
Mensa cafeteria I
Mensch person II
Menschen people (pl) I
Menschenmenge crowd II
sich **merken** to remember II
merkwürdig strange; funny II
Messer knife II
Metall metal III
Meter metre I
Methode method II
Metzgerei butcher's III
mich me I
Miete rent II
Mikrowelle microwave IV U3, 59
Milch milk I
Milchmischgetränk milkshake III
Milchshake milkshake III
mild mild I
Milliarde billion IV U1, 13
Million million III
   eine halbe Million half a million III
Minderheit minority IV U1, 22
Mindest- minimum IV U2, 38
Mineralwasser mineral water III
minimal minimum IV U2, 38
Minimum minimum IV U2, 38
Minute minute II
mir me I
   von mir of mine II
mischen to mix IV U5, 98
mit with I
   mit (dem Zug) by (train) I
   mit Behinderung with special needs III

mit besonderen Bedürfnissen with special needs III
mitbringen to bring II
Mitleid haben mit to feel sorry for III
zum **Mitnehmen** takeaway II
mitnehmen to take I
Mittagessen lunch I
Mittagspause lunchtime I
Mittagszeit lunchtime I
Mitte centre; middle III; center (AE) IV U1, 13
   in der Mitte in the centre of; in the middle III
Mitternacht midnight III
Mittwoch Wednesday I
mittwochs on Wednesdays I
mixen to mix IV U5, 98
Mobiltelefon mobile (phone) I
Mode fashion (no pl) IV U3, 58
modern modern I
modisch fashionable II
mögen to like I; to enjoy III
   am liebsten mögen to like … best I
   am meisten mögen to like … best I
   gern mögen to love I
   nicht mögen to hate I; to dislike IV U4, 81
   Ich möchte … I'd like (to) … (= I would like to) I
   Ich möchte nicht … I wouldn't like (to) … I
   Möchtest du? Would you like (to) …? I
Möglichkeit chance IV U1, 18
Moment moment II
   in dem Moment als right IV U2, 42
Monat month I
monatlich monthly III
Monster monster III
Montag Monday I
Mörder murderer III
Mörderin murderer III
Morgen morning I
   Guten Morgen. Good morning. II
morgen tomorrow II

morgendliche Ansprache morning message IV U2, 34
Moschee mosque II
Motorrad motorbike I
Moussaka moussaka II
müde tired I
Müll rubbish II
Mülleimer tin IV U3, 63
multikulturell multicultural IV U5, 98
Mund mouth II
Münze coin III
Münzgeld change II
Münztelefon pay phone III
Museum museum II
Musik music I
Musik- musical III
musikalisch musical III
Musikgruppe band II
Müsli cereal III
Muslim Muslim I
Muslimin Muslim I
müssen must I; to have to II
   nicht müssen needn't I
Mut courage IV U5, 107
mutig brave III
Mutter mother I
Mütze cap I

N

nach to; after I
   nach Hause home I
   nach dem Weg fragen asking the way I
   nach (bei Uhrzeitangaben) past II
Nachbar neighbour III; neighbor (AE) IV U3, 54
Nachbarin neighbour III; neighbor (AE) IV U3, 54
Nachmittag afternoon I
nachmittags in the afternoon I
nachmittags (Uhrzeit) p.m. II
Nachricht message II
Nachricht(en) news II
nachschauen to look I; to look up II
Nachsitzen detention IV U2, 45
Nachspeise dessert; pudding II
nachsprechen to say I

nächste next I
als **Nächstes** next II
Nacht night I
  heute Nacht tonight II
  in jener Nacht that night II
Nachtwanderung night walk I
Nagel nail III
Nagelschere nail scissors III
nah near III
in der **Nähe** close IV U3, 53
in der **Nähe** von near I
nahe close IV U3, 53
Nahrung food I
Name name I
Nase nose I
  die Nase voll haben (von) to be
  fed up (with) III
nass wet I
national national III
National- national III
Natur nature III
natürlich of course I
Naturwissenschaft Science I
Navi satnav I
neben next to I
neblig foggy I
nehmen to take I
  etw. ernst nehmen to take sth
  seriously IV U1, 18
  Bitte Platz nehmen. Please have a
  seat. IV U3, 55
neidisch jealous II
nein no I
nennen to say I
nervös nervous II
nett nice I; kind II; friendly III
Netz web III; net IV U4, 75
neu new I
  auf den neuesten Stand bringen
  to update IV U4, 81
Neuigkeit(en) news II
neun nine I
neunzehn nineteen I
neunzig ninety I
nicht not I
  auch nicht not either III
  nicht brauchen needn't I

nicht dürfen mustn't III
nicht einverstanden sein to
  disagree II
nicht können can't I; cannot III
nicht mehr not … any more III
nicht mögen to hate I; to dislike
  IV U4, 81
nicht müssen needn't I
nicht wahr? isn't it? II
nicht werden won't (= will not) II
Nichte niece III
nichts nothing IV U3, 63
nie never I
niederbrennen to burn down II
niedlich cute I
niedrig low II
niemals never I
niemand no one I; nobody III
nirgendwo nowhere IV U2, 34
nirgendwohin nowhere IV U2, 34
noch still I; even II
  noch ein another II
  noch einmal again; once more II
  noch nicht not … yet II
Norden north III
nördlich von north of IV ZI, 9
Nordwesten northwest III
nordwestlich northwest of III
nörgeln to nag III
normal regular IV U4, 89
normalerweise usually II
die **Normannen** the Normans III
Normanne Norman III
Normannin Norman III
Notdienst emergency service III
Note grade (AE) IV U2, 33
Notfall emergency III
sich **Notizen** machen to take notes I
Notruf emergency call III
November November I
Nudelauflauf pasta bake II
Nudeln pasta II
null zero I
null (bei Uhrzeiten und
  Telefonnummern) oh I
Nummer number I
nun now I
nur only I; just II

Nuss nut I
nützlich useful III; helpful IV U2, 38

O

oben up II
obere upper III
Oberteil top II
Obst fruit I
  Obst- und Gemüseladen
  greengrocer's III
oder or I
Ofenkartoffel jacket potato II
öffentliche Verkehrsmittel public
  transport III
offiziell official IV U4, 84
öffnen to open I
oft often I
ohne without III
Ohr ear II
okay OK I
Oktober October I
Öl oil IV U5, 98
Oma grandma II
Onkel uncle I
online online II
  online stellen to post IV U4, 80
Opa grandad III
Operation operation III
optimistisch optimistic III
Orange orange I
orange orange I
Orchester orchestra III
in **Ordnung** fine; all right II
  in Ordnung bringen to tidy (up) II
organisieren to organize II
Ort place I
örtlich local III
Osten east III
östlich von east of IV ZI, 9
Outdoor- outdoor III
Outfit outfit III
Ozean ocean IV ZI, 9

P

ein **Paar** a pair of II
ein **paar** some I; a few III

packen to pack; to pack up II
Packung packet I
Paket package IV U5, 102
panisch werden to panic II
Papa dad I
Papagei parrot I
Papier paper III
Papiere papers *(pl)* IV U1, 19
Pappe cardboard III
Parade parade III
Paradies paradise IV ZI, 9
Parfüm perfume III
Park park I
Parkplatz parking lot *(AE)* IV U1, 15
Partner partner III
Partnerin partner III
Party party I
Passagier passenger II
Passagierin passenger II
passen to suit; to fit II
passieren to happen II
Pasta pasta II
Pastete pasty; pie II
Patient patient II
Patientin patient II
Pause break I
   in der Pause at break I
   Pause machen to take a break II
Pausenhof playground I
peinlich embarrassing IV U2, 42
Pekannuss pecan IV U3, 67
Pence *(brit. Währungseinheit)* pence I
   Das macht zwei Pfund und 24
   Pence. That's £2.24. I
   … kosten 99 Pence. … are 99p. I
perfekt perfect IV ZI, 9
Person person II
Personalausweis ID III
persönlich personal III
Pfannkuchen pancake II
Pfeffer pepper II
Pferd horse I
Pfirsich peach I
Pflanze plant I
Pflaster plaster III
Pflichtfach core subject IV U2, 35
Pfund *(brit. Währungseinheit)*
   pound I

   Das macht 2 Pfund und 24 Pence.
   That's £2.24. I
   … kostet ein Pfund fünfund-
   zwanzig. … is £1.25. I
Picknick picnic I
Pick-up pick-up IV U5, 102
Pieps tweet III
pikant spicy II
Pinguin penguin I
pink pink I
Pirat pirate I
Piratin pirate I
Pirogge pierogi II
Pizza pizza I
Plan plan II
planen to plan III
Planke plank II
Plantage plantation IV U5, 97
Plastik plastic III
Platsch splash I
Platz place I; square II
   Bitte Platz nehmen. Please have a
   seat. IV U3, 55
plaudern to chat II
plötzlich suddenly II
Podcast podcast IV U4, 94
Polizei police III
Polizeibeamter police officer I
Polizeibeamtin police officer I
polnisch Polish IV U5, 99
Polnisch Polish IV U5, 99
Pommes frites chips *(pl)* I
Popcorn popcorn I
positiv positive III
Post *(online gestellte Nachricht)* post
   IV U4, 80
Postamt post office I
posten to post IV U4, 80
Poster poster I
Postkarte postcard I
praktisch practical IV U4, 89
Praline chocolate IV U3, 54
Pranger stocks III
Präsentation presentation IV U2, 51
Präsident president IV U3, 53
Präsidentin president IV U3, 53
Preis prize; price II
Prise pinch II

pro per IV U2, 41
   pro Stück each II
probieren to try II
Problem problem I; trouble III
Programm programme I
Projekt project III
Propellerboot airboat IV U5, 102
Prospekt brochure III
Protest protest IV U5, 96
Protestant Protestant III
Protestantin Protestant III
protestantisch Protestant III
Prozent percent (%) IV U1, 23
prüfen to test II
Pudding pudding II
Punktestand score II
pünktlich on time III
Pute turkey IV U3, 53
putzen to clean I

Q

Quadratmeile square mile (= sq. mi.)
   IV ZI, 8
quer durch across IV U3, 54
Quittung receipt II

R

Rad wheel II
Radfahren cycling III
Radiergummi eraser I
Radio radio II
Rafting rafting III
rappen to rap II
Rapper rapper III
Rapperin rapper III
Rasierapparat razor IV U3, 59
Rasierer razor IV U3, 59
Rassentrennung segregation
   IV U5, 106
Rassismus racism IV U5, 98
Rat advice III
raten to guess II
Rathaus town hall II
Ratschlag advice III; tip II
Rätsel mystery I
Rauch smoke III

Raum room I
Rechner calculator I
Rechnung bill III
Recht right IV U5, 96
   recht haben to be right II
   Du hast recht. You're right. I
rechts on the right I; right III
Rechtschreibung spelling I
Rechtsfall court case IV U5, 107
rechtzeitig in time I
Rede speech III
reden (mit) to talk (to) I
Regal shelf I
Regalbrett shelf I
Regel rule III
regelmäßig regular IV U4, 89
Regen rain IV U4, 85
Regenbogen rainbow III
Regenmantel raincoat III
Regenschirm umbrella II
Regierungsgebäude State House
   (AE) IV U5, 98
Regisseur director II
Regisseurin director II
regnen to rain I
regnerisch rainy I
reich rich III
reichen to pass II
Reichtum wealth III
Reifen tyre III
in die richtige **Reihenfolge** bringen
   to put in the right order I
Reis rice II
Reise trip; voyage; journey III; tour
   IV U4, 76
reisen to travel II
Reiten horse riding I
reiten to ride II
reizen to tease IV U2, 38
Religionsunterricht RE (Religious
   Education) I
rennen to run I
reparieren to repair III
Reporter reporter III
Reporterin reporter III
Republik republic III
Requisit prop III
Reservat reservation IV U2, 32

reservieren to make a reservation III;
   to book IV U4, 76
Reservierung reservation IV U4, 76
respektieren to respect IV U4, 89
der **Rest** the rest IV U1, 23
Restaurant restaurant II
retten to save III
Rettungsboot lifeboat III
Rettungsdienst emergency service
   III
Rezept recipe II
richtig right I; real II
das **Richtige** tun to do the right
   thing III
Richtung trend IV U4, 80
   in diese Richtung this way II
riechen to smell III
Riese giant III
Riesen- giant IV U4, 74
riesengroß huge IV ZI, 9
Riesenrad big wheel II
riesig huge IV ZI, 9; giant IV U4, 74
Rindfleisch beef II
Ring circle III
Ritt ride IV U1, 14
Ritter knight III
Rock skirt I
Rohr tube; pipe III
Rolle part II; role IV U5, 107
Rollstuhl wheelchair III
Rolltreppe escalator II
die **Römer** the Romans III
rosa pink I
Rose rose IV ZI, 8
rot red I
Hin- und **Rückfahrkarte** return ticket
   III
Rückmeldung feedback IV U2, 39
Rucksack backpack IV U3, 62
Ruf call III
rufen to call I; to shout II
Rugby rugby III
Ruhe silence III
ruhig quiet III
Rührei scrambled egg II
rühren to stir II
ruinieren to ruin II
Russe Russian IV U5, 99

Russin Russian IV U5, 99
Russisch Russian IV U5, 99
russisch Russian IV U5, 99
Rüstung armour III

S

Sache thing I
Sack bag I
Saft juice II
sagen to say; to tell I
Salat salad II
Salz salt II
sammeln to collect I
   (sich) sammeln to gather IV U3, 64
Samstag Saturday I
Sandwich sandwich I
Sänger singer I
Sängerin singer I
etw. **sattbekommen** to get tired of
   sth IV U1, 14
etw. **satthaben** to get tired of sth
   IV U1, 14
sauber clean I
   sauber machen to clean I
sauer sein to be fed up (with) III
Saxofon saxophone I
Schachtel box I
Schaf sheep I
Schal scarf I
Schälchen bowl II
Schale bowl II
Schatz treasure II
schätzen to guess IV U3, 59
Schau show IV U5, 102
schauen to look I
Schauspielen acting III
Schauspieler actor II
Schauspielerei acting III
Schauspielerin actor II
Schauspielworkshop acting work-
   shop II
scheinen to shine IV ZI, 8
Schere scissors *(pl)* III
schick chic I
schicken to send I
schieben to push I
schießen (auf) to shoot (at) IV U3, 63

Schiff ship I
Schiffsbauer ship builder III
Schiffsbauerin ship builder III
Schiffsfahrt boat trip II
Schild sign III
Schimmelkäse blue cheese II
Schinken ham II
Schlacht battle III
Schlaf sleep III
schlafen to sleep I; to be asleep III
Schlafzimmer bedroom I
schlagen to hit II; to beat III
Schlagzeile headline IV U4, 77
Schlamm mud III
schlammig muddy I
Schlange snake I
schlau clever I; smart III
Schlauch tube III
schlecht bad I; ill II
schlechteste worst III
schleifen to drag IV U5, 107
schleppen to drag IV U5, 107
schlicht plain II
schließen to close I
Schließfach locker IV U2, 34
schließlich in the end; finally II
schlimm terrible I
schlimmste worst III
Schloss castle II
Schlumpf smurf I
Schluss end II; ending III
   am Schluss by the end II
   zum Schluss in the end; finally II
Schlussfolgerung conclusion III
Schlussverkauf sale II
schmackhaft tasty III
schmerzhaft sore II
Schminke make-up IV U3, 58
Schmuck jewellery II
Schmuggler smuggler II
Schmugglerin smuggler II
schmutzig dirty I
Schnäppchen bargain II
schnappen to grab III
Schnee snow IV U1, 14
(sich) schneiden to cut II
   sich die Haare schneiden lassen to
   have a haircut II

schnell fast; quick II
   der/die/das schnellste the
   fastest I
Schokolade chocolate I
   Tafel Schokolade bar of
   chocolate I
schon already; yet II
   Schon gut. Never mind. II
schön nice; beautiful I; fine; lovely II
Schotte Scot III
Schottenrock kilt III
Schottin Scot III
schottisch Scottish III
Schrank cupboard III
schrecklich awful; terrible I; horrible
   III
Schrei shout I
schreiben to write I
   eine SMS schreiben to text II
Schreibtisch desk IV U3, 62
schreien to shout II; to scream
   IV U3, 63
Schriftsteller writer II
Schriftstellerin writer II
Schritt step III
schubsen to push III
schüchtern shy IV U2, 42
Schuh shoe I
Schule school I
   in der Schule at school I
Schüler student I
Schülerin student I
Schulfach subject I
Schulhof playground I
Schulleiter principal (AE) IV U2, 34
Schulleiterin principal (AE) IV U2, 34
Schulstunde lesson I
Schüssel bowl II
Schusswaffe gun IV U3, 62
schützen to protect III
schwach weak III
schwarz black I
Schweigen silence III
schweigsam silent III
Schweinefleisch pork II
Schweizer Swiss IV U4, 84
Schweizerin Swiss IV U4, 84
schweizerisch Swiss IV U4, 84

schwer heavy; hard II
schwerhörig deaf III
Schwert sword III
Schwester sister I
schwierig difficult III; hard II
Schwierigkeiten trouble III
Schwimmbad swimming pool I
schwimmen to swim II
   schwimmen gehen to go
   swimming I
Science-Fiction science fiction I
Scone (eine Art süßes Brötchen)
   scone II
sechs six I
sechzehn sixteen I
sechzig sixty I
See lake III
Seeräuber pirate I
Seeräuberin pirate I
sehen to see I; to look II
Sehenswürdigkeit sight II
sehr very I; a lot II
   so sehr so much III
   zu sehr too much II
Seide silk III
Seife soap III
Seil rope I
Seilbahn cable car IV U4, 74
Seilrutsche zip line III
sein to be I
   sauer sein to be fed up (with) III
sein his I; its III
seit for IV U4, 80; since IV U4, 80
seitdem since IV U4, 80
Seite page; side I
Seite (im Internet) site IV U4, 80
Sekunde second II
selber myself; ourselves; themselves;
   yourselves III
selbst myself; self III
   dich selbst yourself II
   ihr/euch/Sie/sich (selbst) yourselves III
   sie selbst themselves; herself III
selbstbewusst confident III
selbstsicher confident; sure of
   oneself III
selbstsüchtig selfish IV U2, 39

selbstverständlich of course I
Selfie *(Schnappschuss von sich selbst)* selfie IV U4, 83
seltsam strange; funny II
senden to send I
Sendung programme I
Senf mustard II
September September I
servieren to serve IV U2, 33
Serviette napkin II
setzen to put I
Shampoo shampoo III
Shirt shirt I
Shorts shorts *(pl)* I
Show show I
sich each other; self III
   sich **beeilen** to rush III
   sich **beklagen** to complain IV U1, 18
   sich **beschweren** to complain IV U1, 18
   sich **gegenseitig** each other III
sicher sure I; safe III
Sicherheit safety IV U4, 75
Sicherheitsnetz safety net IV U4, 75
Sicht look; view IV U1, 14
Sie you I
sie her; she I
sie *(Pl.)* they; them I
   sie selbst herself III
sieben seven I
siebzehn seventeen I
siebzig seventy I
Siedler settler IV U2, 32
Siedlerin settler IV U2, 32
siegen to win I
Sieger winner I
Siegerin winner I
Signal signal III
singen to sing I
sinken to sink III
Situation situation II
Sitz seat IV U5, 106
Sitzbank bench III
sitzen to sit I
Sitzplatz seat IV U5, 106
Skateboard skateboard III
Ski fahren to ski II
Skifahren skiing III

Sklave slave IV U4, 86
Sklavin slave IV U4, 86
Skyline skyline IV U1, 12
Smartphone smartphone IV U4, 80
SMS message; text message II
   eine SMS schreiben to text II
SMS-Schreiber texter II
SMS-Schreiberin texter II
Snack snack I
so like this I; so II
   so … wie as … as II
   so sehr so much III
sobald as soon as IV U4, 89
Socke sock I
soeben just II
Sofa sofa II
sofort right now III; right away IV U4, 80
Software software II
sogar even II
Sohn son III
Sojabohne soy bean IV ZI, 9
solar solar III
Solar- solar III
Soldat soldier III
Soldatin soldier III
sollte should III
Sommer summer II
Sonderangebot special offer III
Sonne sun III
Sonnen- solar III
sonnenbaden to sunbathe II
Sonnenbrille sunglasses *(pl)* II
sonnig sunny I
Sonntag Sunday I
sich **Sorgen machen** to worry I
sorgfältig careful II
Sorte sort II; type III
Soße sauce II
Souvenir souvenir III
Souvenirladen souvenir shop III
soweit as far as IV U3, 59
soziale Medien social media IV U4, 80
Sozialkunde Social Studies I
Spaghetti spaghetti II
spanisch Spanish IV U5, 98
Spanisch Spanish IV U5, 98
spannend exciting I

Spaß fun I
   zum Spaß for fun III
(zu) spät late I
später later I; after III
den Hund **spazieren** führen to take the dog for a walk II
Spaziergang walk III
speichern to save II
Speise dish II
Speisekarte menu II
spektakulär spectacular IV U4, 77
speziell special I
Spiegel mirror III
Spiel match; game I
spielen to play I; to act II
Spieler player II; gamer II
Spielerin player II; gamer II
Spielfeld court III
Spielkarte card I
Spielplatz playground I
Spielzeug toy III
Spind locker IV U2, 34
Spinne spider III
Spinnennetz web III
Spitze top IV U1, 13
   an der Spitze (von) at the front of II
spitze awesome IV U2, 34
Sport sport I
Sportart sport III
Sportgeschäft sports shop I
Sportunterricht PE (Physical Education) I
sprachbehindert speech impaired IV U5, 102
Sprache language II; speech III
sprechen to say I; to speak II
   sprechen (mit) to talk (to) I
   sprechen über to talk about II
springen to jump IV U3, 63
Spritze injection III
spülen to wash III
Spülmaschine dishwasher IV U3, 59
Spur clue I; trail IV U5, 102
Staat state IV ZI, 8
Staatsangehörige citizen IV U1, 18
Staatsangehöriger citizen IV U1, 18
Staatsbürger citizen IV U1, 18

Staatsbürger

Staatsbürgerin citizen IV U1, 18
Stadion stadium II
Stadt town I; city II
Stadtmitte city centre III
Stadtplan map III
Stadtteil borough IV U1, 12
Stadtzentrum city centre III
   im Stadtzentrum downtown *(AE)*
   IV U1, 14
Stahl steel III
auf den neuesten **Stand** bringen to
   update IV U4, 81
Standinhaber stallholder II
Standinhaberin stallholder II
Star star I
stark heavy II; powerful IV U1, 22
Start start III
starten to start II
stattdessen instead IV U4, 80
Status status IV U4, 81
Stau traffic jam IV U1, 14
staubsaugen to hoover II
Staubsauger vacuum cleaner
   IV U3, 59
stecken bleiben to get stuck IV U3, 54
stehen to suit; to stand II; to stand
   up IV U3, 63
stehlen to steal IV U2, 38
steigen to climb III
Stein brick II; rock; stone III
Stelle place I
stellen to put I
   online stellen to post IV U4, 80
Stellenbezeichnung job title IV U2, 38
sterben to die III
Stereotyp stereotype IV U2, 42
Stern star III
sticheln to tease IV U2, 38
Stiefel boot II
Stift pen I
Stil style III
still quiet III
Stille silence III
Stimme voice III
stimmt's? isn't it? II
Stock stick II
Stockwerk floor II
Stolz pride IV U5, 98

stolz (auf) proud (of) III
strahlend bright IV ZI, 8
Strand beach I
   den Strand nach Strandgut
   absuchen to go beach combing II
Straße road I; street III
Straßenbahn tram III
Straßenbauarbeiten roadwork *(AE)*
   IV U1, 14
Straßenkunst street art IV U1, 13
streamen *(im Internet)* to stream
   IV U4, 80
Strecke track IV U5, 102
Streich trick I
streichen to paint II
Streit argument II; fight III
(sich) streiten to fight III
streng strict IV U2, 34
strikt strict IV U2, 34
Strom electricity III
Struktur structure III
Stück piece II
   pro Stück each II
Student student I
Studentin student I
Studio studio IV U4, 75
Stufe step II
Stuhl chair I
stumm silent III
Stunde hour I; period IV U2, 34
   erste Stunde *(in der Schule)*
   homeroom IV U2, 45
   40 Kilometer pro Stunde 40 kilo-
   metres an hour I
Stundenplan timetable I; schedule
   (AE) IV U2, 33
Stuntman stuntman IV U3, 53
Sturm storm IV U2, 32
stürzen to rush III
suchen nach to look for II
Süden south III
   im Süden von in the south of III
südlich southern IV U5, 96
   südlich von south of IV ZI, 9
Südstaatler Southerner IV U5, 97
Südstaatlerin Southerner IV U5, 97
Sumpf swamp IV ZI, 9

super cool I; super; way to go II;
   awesome IV U2, 34
Supermarkt supermarket II
Suppe soup II
Surfbrett surfboard IV U4, 76
Surfen surfing IV U4, 74
surfen to surf II
   im Internet surfen to surf the
   internet II
Surfer surfer IV ZI, 9
Surferin surfer IV ZI, 9
süß sweet III; cute I
Süßes, sonst gibt's Saures! Trick or
   treat! I
Süßigkeit sweet I
Sweatshirt sweatshirt I
Symbol symbol IV U1, 13
Szene scene II

T

Tablett tray II
Tablette tablet II
Tafel board I
   Tafel Schokolade bar of choco-
   late I
Tag day I
   eines Tages one day III
   den ganzen Tag all day III
   ein ausgefüllter Tag a busy day I
Tagebuch diary I
täglich daily III
   vier Stunden täglich four hours a
   day I
Taktik tactic III
Talent talent I
Talentwettbewerb talent show I
Tante aunt II
Tanz dance III
Tanz- dancing IV U2, 43
Tanzen dancing IV U2, 43
tanzen to dance I
Tänzer dancer I
Tänzerin dancer I
tapfer brave III
Tapferkeit courage IV U5, 107
Tasche bag I; pocket II
Taschenlampe torch I

Taschenrechner calculator I

Taschentuch tissue III

Tasse cup II

Tätigkeit job II

tatkräftig energetic IV U4, 89

Tatsache fact II

tatsächlich actually III

taub deaf III

tausend a/one thousand II

Taxi taxi II

Team team I

Teamwork teamwork II

Technik Design Technology (DT) I

Techniker engineer II

Technikerin engineer II

Tee tea I

Teelöffel (TL) teaspoon (tsp) II

Teenager teen II; teenager III

Teil part II

teilen to share III

teilnehmen (an) to take part (in) II

Telefon phone II; telephone III

ans Telefon gehen to answer the phone III

Telefonanruf phone call I

telefonieren to phone II

Telefonnummer phone number III

Telefonzelle telephone box II

Teller plate II

Tennis tennis I

Teppich carpet I

Test test I

testen to test II

teuer expensive II

Text lines (pl); text II

Theater theatre; drama II; theater (AE) IV U1, 13

Theaterstück play II

Thema topic IV U2, 51

Themenpark theme park II

Thunfisch tuna II

Tier animal I

Tierarzt vet II

Tierärztin vet II

Tierheim animal rescue shelter I

Tierpark zoo I

Tierpfleger zookeeper I

Tierpflegerin zookeeper I

Tierwelt (in freier Wildbahn) wildlife IV U5, 102

Tiger tiger I

Tipp tip II

Tisch table I

den Tisch decken to lay the table II

Tischler carpenter II

Tischlerin carpenter II

Tischtennis table tennis II

Toast toast II

Tochter daughter I

tod- deadly III

tödlich deadly III

Toilette toilet I

tolerieren to tolerate IV U5, 98

toll great; brilliant I; amazing II

Tomate tomato II

Ton sound III

Tonne tonne II; barrel IV U3, 53

Tonstudio recording studio I

Top top II

Topf pot III

Tor gateway IV U1, 12

Tornado tornado IV U2, 33

tot dead III

töten to kill III

Tour tour IV U4, 76

Tourist tourist I

Touristin tourist I

Touristeninformation Tourist Information Centre I

Tradition tradition III

tragen to carry II

tragen (Kleidung) to wear I

Trainer trainer IV U5, 103

Trainerin trainer IV U5, 103

trainieren to practise III

Training practice I; training III

Traktor tractor I

Transfer transfer IV U5, 102

transkontinental (über den Kontinent hinweg) transcontinental IV U4, 86

Transport transfer IV U5, 102

Transporter van III

Tratsch gossip IV U3, 58

Traum dream I

träumen to dream III

traurig sad III

treffen to meet I; to hit II

Freunde treffen to see friends I

treiben to drive IV U3, 52

Trend trend IV U4, 80

Trennung segregation IV U5, 106

Treppe stairs (pl) II

Treue allegiance IV U2, 45

Treueeid pledge of allegiance IV U2, 45

Trick trick I

trinken to drink II

Trinkhalm straw II

Trip trip III

trocken dry III

trocknen to dry IV U5, 98

Trommel- drumming III

Truthahn turkey IV U3, 53

Tschüss. See you later.; Bye.; See you. I

T-Shirt T-shirt I

Tuch scarf I

tun to do; to make I

Tut mir leid. Sorry. I

Tunnel tunnel III

Tür door I

Türkisch Turkish IV U5, 99

türkisch Turkish IV U5, 99

Türklingel doorbell IV U3, 54

Turm tower II

Turnhalle gym(nasium) IV U2, 42

turnieren to joust III

Turnierzweikampf jousting III

Turnschuh trainer I

Tüte bag; packet I

Tutorial tutorial IV U4, 80

Typ type III; guy IV U2, 42

U

U-Bahn underground II; subway (AE) IV U1, 14

U-Boot submarine I

üben to practise III

über about I; over IV U1, 12; across IV U3, 54

überall all over IV U4, 85

überall wo(hin) wherever III

überfüllt crowded IV U1, 22

sich **übergeben** (BE) to be sick III

    sich **übergeben** to be sick I

überhaupt nicht not at all II

überleben to survive III

überlegen to guess II

übernachten to stay II

Übernachtung sleepover I

überprüfen to check III

Überprüfung der Anwesenheit

    registration I

überqueren to cross III

überrascht surprised II

Überraschung surprise I

Überschrift headline IV U4, 77

übersetzen to translate IV U5, 102

überzeugt convinced IV U3, 59

üblich regular IV U4, 89

Übung exercise; practice I

Übungsheft exercise book I

Uhr clock II

Uhr *(Zeitangabe bei vollen Stunden)*

    o'clock I

Uhrenturm clock tower II

Uhrzeit time I

um at I

    um … herum around IV U1, 14

    ungefähr **um** around III

umfallen to fall (over) III

Umfrage survey II

umher around I

umrühren to stir II

umsteigen to change III

umziehen to move (house) II

Umzug parade III

Unabhängigkeit independence

    IV U1, 13; freedom *(no pl)* IV U1, 23

unangenehm uncomfortable II

unbequem uncomfortable II

und and I

unfair unfair III

Unfall accident III

unfreundlich unfriendly III

ungefähr about II

    ungefähr um around III

ungefährlich safe III

Ungeheuer monster III

ungewöhnlich unusual IV U4, 77

unglaublich amazing II

Unglück disaster III

unglücklich unhappy II

unhöflich rude IV U2, 39

Uniform uniform I

uninteressant unappealing IV U4, 77

unmodisch unfashionable II

unmöglich impossible III

unmotiviert unmotivated IV U2, 39

Unordnung mess I

uns us I

unschuldig innocent IV U3, 63

unser our I

unsere ours III; our I

unter under I

    unter der Woche on weekdays III

unterbrechen to interrupt IV U4, 94

untere lower III

untergehen to sink III

Unterlagen papers *(pl)* IV U1, 19

Unterricht class; lesson I

Unterrichtsstunde class; period

    IV U2, 34

unterschiedlich different I

unterschreiben to sign IV U3, 53

Unterstützung support IV U1, 19

unterwegs on the way; out and

    about I

unterzeichnen to sign IV U3, 53

unverschämt rude IV U2, 39

updaten to update IV U4, 81

Ureinwohner Amerikas Native

    American IV U2, 32

Ureinwohnerin Amerikas Native

    American IV U2, 32

Urgroßeltern great-grandparents

    IV U1, 25

Urlaub holiday I

Ururopa great-great-grandad I

US-amerikanisch US IV U1, 18

V

Vanillesauce custard II

Vater father I

Veganismus veganism *(no pl)*

    IV U4, 83

Vegetarier vegetarian I

Vegetarierin vegetarian I

Ventilator fan IV U3, 59

sich mit jmdm. **verabreden** to ask sb

    out IV U2, 42

Verabredung date IV U2, 42

veraltet outdated IV U4, 81

verändern to change III

verängstigt scared IV U3, 64

Veranstaltung event IV U4, 86

verantwortlich responsible IV U2, 38

verantwortungsvoll responsible

    IV U2, 38

verärgert angry II; annoyed III

Verband bandage III

verbessern to correct I

verbinden to attach; to connect III

Verbindung link IV U4, 80

    in **Verbindung** bleiben to keep in

    touch II

verboten forbidden IV U3, 58

verbrennen to burn down II; to burn

    III

verbringen *(Zeit)* to spend II

verdienen to earn IV U2, 38

verdrehen to twist II

Verein club II

Vereinsheim clubhouse IV U3, 62

Verfasser writer III

Verfasserin writer III

Verfolger chaser IV U2, 33

Verfolgerin chaser IV U2, 33

Vergangenheit past III

vergessen to forget I

vergleichen to compare I

vergnügt amused IV U3, 63

verhaften to arrest IV U5, 107

sich **verirren** to get lost I

verkaufen to sell III

Verkäufer shop assistant II; assistant

    III; sales associate *(AE)* IV U2, 38

Verkäuferin shop assistant II;

    assistant III; sales associate *(AE)*

    IV U2, 38

Verkehr traffic III

öffentliche **Verkehrsmittel** public

    transport III

verkleidet (als) dressed III

Verkleidung fancy dress I

verlassen leave II
verlässlich reliable IV U5, 109
verlegen embarrassed II
verletzen to hurt II
verletzt hurt II
sich **verlieben** (in) to fall in love (with) III
verlieren to lose II
vermischen to mix IV U5, 98
vermissen to miss II
Vermittlung operator III
vermuten to guess IV U3, 59
vernünftig intelligent III
verpassen to miss II
verrückt crazy I
jmdn. **verrückt** machen to drive sb crazy III
versagen (in/bei) to fail (at) IV U1, 19
verschiedene several IV U4, 80
verschwinden to disappear IV U3, 62
Versprechen pledge IV U2, 45
versprechen to promise IV U3, 54
(sich) **verstecken** to hide III
verstehen to understand II; to get III; to know IV U5, 103
etw. **verstehen** to get sth IV U5, 102
Versuch experiment II
versuchen to try II
vertrauen to trust IV U5, 109
vertrauenswürdig reliable IV U5, 109
vervollständigen to complete I; to finish II
verwenden to use II
verwirrt confused III
verzeihen to pardon IV U3, 53
Verzeihung pardon IV U3, 67
verzerren to twist II
auf etw. **verzichten** to give sth a miss III
Vesper packed lunch II
Video video IV U4, 80
Video-Chat video chat III
viel a lot; much; lots of I; a lot of I; lots III
viel Glück good luck II
viele many II
wie viele how many II
Viele Grüße, Best wishes, I

Vielen Dank. Thanks so much. IV U4, 94
vielleicht maybe I; may II
vier four I
vierte fourth I
Viertel nach quarter past I
Viertel vor quarter to I
vierzehn fourteen I
vierzig forty I
Vietnamese Vietnamese IV U5, 98
Vietnamesin Vietnamese IV U5, 98
Vietnamesisch Vietnamese IV U5, 98
vietnamesisch Vietnamese IV U5, 98
viktorianisches Zeitalter Victorian era III
violett purple I
Vogel bird I
Vogelbeobachtung bird watching III
Vokabular vocabulary II
voll full IV U5, 106
Volleyball volleyball IV U4, 74
völlig quite III; absolutely IV U3, 59
vollkommen perfect IV ZI, 9
von from; of I; by II
von hinten from behind I
von … weg off IV U5, 107
vor ago; in front of II; before IV U3, 61
vor *(bei Uhrzeitangaben)* to I
vor allem especially II
vorbei past III
vorbereiten to prepare III
sich vorbereiten to get ready IV U3, 54
Vordergrund foreground III
im Vordergrund in the foreground III
Vorgehensweise tactic III
vorhaben to be up to III
vorher before II
vorhersagen to foretell III
Vormittag morning I
vormittags *(Uhrzeit)* a.m. II
Vorort suburb IV U1, 15
Vorrichtung device IV U3, 58
vorsichtig careful II
Sei vorsichtig! Be careful! I
Vorsingen audition II
Vorspeise starter II

Vorspielen audition II
Vorsprechen audition II
vorstellen to present I
Vorstellungsgespräch interview IV U2, 38
Vortanzen audition II
Vortrag presentation IV U2, 51
vorziehen to prefer II

W

wach awake III
wachsen to grow IV U3, 58
Wagen truck III
wählen to choose II; to vote for IV U2, 33
Wahlfach elective IV U2, 34
wahr true II
während while II; during III
wahrscheinlich probably III
Währung currency IV ZI, 8
Wald wood III; forest IV U3, 53
Waliser Welsh III
Waliserin Welsh III
walisisch Welsh III
Walisisch Welsh III
Wand wall II
Wandern hiking; walking III
wandern to hike II
Wanderweg trail IV U5, 102
Wandgemälde mural III
wann when I
warm warm I
Warnung warning IV U2, 33
warten to wait II
warten auf to wait for II
Warteschlange queue II
warum why I
was what I
Was?! No way! III
Was für ein/eine … What a … I
Was ist los? What's wrong? II
Was ist mit …? What about …? I
Was man … What to … II
Was stimmt nicht? What's wrong? II
Waschbär raccoon I
(sich) **waschen** to wash III

waschen

Wasser water I
   Eimer **Wasser** bucket of water I
Website website II
Wechselgeld change II
wechseln to change II
Wecker alarm clock I
Weg way IV U2, 34
   auf dem **Weg** on the way I
weg away II
   nicht **weg** können to be stuck I
wegen because of III
weglaufen to run away III
weh tun to hurt II
Weide field IV ZI, 9
sich **weigern** to refuse IV U5, 99
Weihnachten Christmas I
Weihnachtstheaterstück pantomime
   II
weil because I
Wein wine IV U3, 62
Art und **Weise** way III
auf diese **Weise** like this I; like this
   III
weiß white I
Weißkopfseeadler bald eagle IV ZI, 8
weit far III
weitere other I
weitergehen to keep going IV U4, 85
weitermachen to keep going
   IV U4, 85
welche which; what; who II
Welle wave IV ZI, 9
Wellenreiten surfing IV U4, 74
wellenreiten to surf II
Wellenreiter surfer IV ZI, 9
Wellenreiterin surfer IV ZI, 9
Welt world II
   auf der **Welt** in the world II
wem whom IV U3, 58
wen whom IV U3, 58
in Mehl **wenden** to cover in flour
   IV U5, 98
ein **wenig** a bit II
wenige a few III
weniger less III
wenn when; if II
wer who I

Werbespot advertisement II; ad(vert)
   IV U4, 76
werden to get I; will; to become II
   genannt **werden** to be called II
   nicht **werden** won't (= will not) II
werfen to throw IV U2, 38
Werft shipyard III
Werk factory III
an **Werktagen** on weekdays III
Werkzeug tool II
Westen west III
westlich von west of IV ZI, 9
Wettbewerb show I; competition II
Wetter weather I
wichtig important II; major IV ZI, 8
wie like I; how I; as II; what III
   Wie alt bist du? How old are you? I
   Wie bitte? Pardon? I
   Wie geht es dir? How are you? I;
   How are you doing? IV U3, 54
   wie geht's how are things going
   IV U3, 55
   Wie geht's? What's up?; How's it
   going? IV U3, 54
   Wie heißt du? What's your name? I
   wie läuft's how are things going
   IV U3, 55
   Wie läuft's? How's it going?
   IV U3, 54
   Wie man … How to … II
   Wie spät ist es? What time is it? I
   Wie viel (kostet/kosten) …? How
   much (is/are) …? I
   Wie viel Uhr ist es? What time is
   it? I
   wie viele how many II
   Wie wäre es mit …? How about
   …? II
   so … wie as … as II
wieder again II
wiederholen to repeat III
Auf **Wiedersehen.** Goodbye. I
wiegen to weigh II
Wiese field IV ZI, 9
die **Wikinger** the Vikings III
wild wild IV U3, 63
freie **Wildbahn** the wild IV U5, 102

Wildnis wilderness IV U4, 85; the wild
   IV U5, 102
willkommen (bei/in) welcome (to) I
   willkommen heißen to welcome
   IV U4, 80
Wind wind I
windig windy I
Windpark wind farm III
Windrad (wind) turbine III
winken to wave II
Winter winter I
winzig tiny III
wir we; us I
Wirbelsturm tornado IV U2, 33
wirklich really I; real II; actually III
wirr confused III
wissen to know I
   Ich weiß (es) nicht! I don't know! I
Wissenschaft Science I
Witz joke I
witzig funny I
wo where I
   wo(hin) auch immer wherever III
Woche week I
   unter der Woche on weekdays III
Wochenende weekend I
   am Wochenende at the weekend I
wöchentlich weekly III
woher where I
   Woher kommst du? Where are you
   from? I
wohin where I
wohnen to live I
Wohnung flat I
Wohnwagen caravan III
Wohnzimmer living room I
Wolke cloud IV U2, 33
Wolkenkratzer skyscraper IV U1, 14
wolkig cloudy I
Wolldecke blanket IV U3, 62
Wolle wool I
wollen to want (to) I
Workshop workshop II
Wortschatz vocabulary II
Wrap wrap II
wund sore II
wünschen to wish III
würde(n) would II

würde(n) gern would like II
Ich würde gerne … I'd like (to) …
(= I would like to) I
Ich würde nicht gerne … I
wouldn't like (to) … I
Wurst sausage II
würzig spicy II
wütend angry II; furious III

Z

Zahl number I
Zahn tooth III
Zahnbürste toothbrush III
Zahnpasta toothpaste III
Zahnstocher toothpick II
Zauber- magic II
Zauberei magic II
Zebra zebra I
zehn ten I
Zeichen sign; signal III
Zeichensprache sign language III
Zeichentrickfilm cartoon IV U4, 81
zeichnen to draw II
zeigen to show II
Zeile line II
Zeit time I
viktorianisches **Zeitalter** Victorian
era III
Zeitreise time travel III
Zeitschrift magazine I
Zeitschriftenladen newsagent's III
Zeitung newspaper II
Zeitungsausträger paperboy IV U2, 41
Zeitungsausträgerin papergirl
IV U2, 41
Zeitzone time zone IV Zl, 8
Zelt tent II
Zelten camping III
zelten to go camping II
Zeltplatz campsite III
Zentimeter (cm) centimetre (cm) I
Zentrum centre III; center (AE)
IV U1, 13
zerbrechen to break II
zerrissen torn IV U4, 83
zerstören to ruin II
Zeuge witness IV U5, 107

Zeugin witness IV U5, 107
Ziege goat III
Ziegelstein brick II
ziehen to pull I; to grow IV U3, 58; to
drag IV U5, 107
Ziel ambition II
ziemlich quite III
Zimmer room I
Zimmerdecke ceiling I
Zimmerin carpenter II
Zimmermann carpenter II
Zitrone lemon II
Zoo zoo I
zornig angry II
zu to I; too II
zu Fuß on foot I
zu Hause at home I; back home II
zu sehr too much II
zubereiten to prepare III
züchten to grow IV U3, 58
Zucker sugar I
zuerst first I
Zug train I
Zuhause home I
zuhören to listen (to) I
Zuhörer listener II
Zuhörerin listener II
Zukunft future IV U1, 18
zum Schluss finally II
zum Spaß for fun III
zumachen to close I
zuordnen to match I
zurück back I
zurückkehren to return IV U4, 85
zurückzahlen to pay back II
zusammen together I; everyone II
zusammenfassen to sum up IV U3, 73
zusammenzucken to jump III
Zusatz- extra II
zusätzlich extra II
zuschauen to watch II
Zustand condition IV U1, 22
zustimmen to agree II; to agree
(with) III
Zutat ingredient II
zuverlässig reliable IV U5, 109
zuvor before II
Zuwanderung immigration IV U1, 22

zwanzig twenty I
zwei two I
zweite second I
Zwiebel onion II
zwischen between II
zwölf twelve I

Lösungen

Lösungen Mediation

1. It said that the United States is free (from Great Britain).
2. President …
3. November
4. political, religious, economic reasons
5. Africans; people from Africa
6. New Hampshire, Massachusetts, Rhode Island, Connecticut, New York, New Jersey, Pennsylvania, Delaware, Maryland, Virginia, North Carolina, South Carolina, Georgia
7. Cherokee, Navajo, Sioux, Chippewa, Choctaw, Pueblo, Apache, Iroquois, Creek, Blackfeet, Seminole, Cheyenne, Arawak, Shawnee, Mohegan, Huron, Oneida, Lakota, Crow, Teton, Hopi, Inuit
8. Pacific (Ocean)
9. because there are 50 states
10. New Year's Day, Martin Luther King, Jr. Day, Presidents' Day, Memorial Day, Independence Day, Labor Day, Columbus Day, Veterans Day, Thanksgiving, Christmas

Lösungen Grammatik – TEST YOURSELF

G1
1. had
2. liked
3. did not / didn't take
4. did … do
5. Were
6. was not / wasn't

G2
1. had left
2. had not / hadn't done
3. had … started
4. had watched
5. had lived
6. had not / hadn't seen

G3
1. could not / couldn't / was not allowed to / wasn't allowed to
2. had to
3. could / was allowed to
4. did not / didn't have to
5. could / were allowed to
6. could not / couldn't

G4
1. will / 'll help
2. will / 'll be
3. does not / doesn't come
4. will not / won't find
5. meet
6. read

G5
1. Do
2. does
3. will
4. Did
5. –
6. did

G6
1. would be
2. would not / wouldn't meet
3. was / were
4. did not / didn't come
5. would not / wouldn't worry
6. would be

G7
1. goes
2. is not / isn't surfing
3. Are … listening
4. do not / don't like
5. do … do
6. meet

G8
1. has … met
2. have not / haven't seen
3. hasn't … called
4. Have … forgotten
5. have not / haven't been
6. Have … watched

G9
1. is cooked
2. is made
3. are not / aren't cooked
4. are organized
5. is not / isn't accepted
6. are not / aren't grown

G10
1. Anna says (that) they prefer the Everglades.
2. She says (that) she wants to go on a boat tour.
3. She says (that) she doesn't like all those crowds.
4. She says (that) she doesn't want to feed the alligators.
5. She says (that) she knows Florida.
6. She says (that) they can't visit the zoo at night.

Bildquellennachweis

Cover.1 Getty Images (The Image Bank), München; **Cover.2** Getty Images (Photographer's Choice), München; **2.1** Getty Images (Photolibrary/Maremagnum), München; **3.1** Alamy Stock Photo (World History Archive), Abingdon, Oxon; **3.2** plainpicture GmbH & Co. KG (Michael Runkel), Hamburg; **4.1** Getty Images (Lonely Planet/jean pierre lescourret), München; **5.1** Getty Images (Stockbyte), München; **5.2** Getty Images (Daniel Zuchnik), München; **8.6** Getty Images (Corbis), München; **8.7** Getty Images RF (The Image Bank), München; **8.3** Getty Images (Perspectives), München; **8.4** Getty Images (First Light), München; **8.8** plainpicture GmbH & Co. KG (Ableimages/David Harrigan), Hamburg; **8.5** Getty Images (National Geographic Magazines), München; **8.9** plainpicture GmbH & Co. KG (Aurora Photos/Josh Miller), Hamburg; **8.1** Getty Images (Iconica), München; **8.2** Getty Images (E+/Ron Thomas), München; **10.10** By Orlando Scott Goff, Bismarck, Dakota Territory - Heritage Auctions, Public Domain, https://commons.wikimedia.org/w/index.php?curid=27530348; **10.5** By John Dunlap, text by Thomas Jefferson et al. - http://lcweb2.loc.gov/cgi-bin/ampage?collId=rbc3&fileName=rbc0001_2004pe76546page.db, Public Domain, https://commons.wikimedia.org/w/index.php?curid=33408334; **10.6** Getty Images (The Image Bank), München; **10.12** Getty Images (Lonely Planet), München; **10.3** Getty Images (Bettmann), München; **10.11** Getty Images (Lonely Planet), München; **10.13** Getty Images (Universal Images Group), München; **10.1** Getty Images (DigitalGlobe), München; **10.2** Getty Images (The Image Bank), München; **10.9** Getty Images (Tim Fitzharris), München; **10.7** plainpicture GmbH & Co. KG (Image Source/Gu), Hamburg; **10.14** Getty Images (Science Source), München; **10.15** Getty Images (Photodisc), München; **10.16** Getty Images (Alan Copson), München; **10.17** Getty Images (David Sucsy), München; **10.4** plainpicture GmbH & Co. KG (Fancy Images/Whisson/Jordan), Hamburg; **10.8** Getty Images (Corbis Documentary), München; **10.18** Getty Images (Cameron Davidson), München; **12.1** Getty Images (Photolibrary/Maremagnum), München; **12.2** plainpicture GmbH & Co. KG (Gine Seitz), Hamburg; **13.1** Avenue Images GmbH (ponton), Hamburg; **13.2** Getty Images (Lonely Planet/Michael Marquand), München; **13.3** Getty Images (Moment/© 2014 Noppon Umnajwannaphan), München; **14.2** Alamy Stock Photo (Etcheverry Images), Abingdon, Oxon; **14.1** Thinkstock (LUNAMARINA), München; **18.1** Corbis (Duane Osborn/Somos Images), Berlin; **19** Song: Empire State of Mind, Text: CARTER, SHAWN/HUNTE, ANGELA/KEYES, BERT/Keys, Alicia/Robinson, Sylvia/SEWELL, JANET ANDREA/SHUCKBURGH, ALEXANDER WILLIAM, Verlag: Carter Boys Music / EMI April Music / Foray Music / Gambi Music Inc / Global Talent Publishing / J Sewell Publishing / Lellow Productions Inc / Masani El Shabazz EMI Music Publishing Germany GmbH, Berlin / Rolf Budde Musikverlag GmbH, Berlin / Neue Welt Musikverlag GmbH, Hamburg; **19.1** Corbis (PT Images/Tetra Images), Berlin; **19.2** plainpicture GmbH & Co. KG (Kniel Synnatzschke), Hamburg; **21.1** Corbis (Duane Osborn/Somos Images), Berlin; **22.1** Alamy Stock Photo (The Print Collector), Abingdon, Oxon; **25.2** Alamy Stock Photo (Michael Dwyer), Abingdon, Oxon; **25.1** shutterstock (Vacclav), New York, NY; **25.3** Thinkstock (stu99), München; **25.4** Thinkstock (iStockphoto), München; **26.1** Getty Images (Lonely Planet/jean pierre lescourret), München; **27.1** Ulrike Beutel, Mitarbeiterin, Stuttgart; **28.1** Getty Images (Hulton Archive), München; **29.2** Fotolia.com (Robert Wilson), New York; **29.4** Fotolia.com (tharun15), New York; **29.3** Fotolia.com (gguy), New York; **29.1** Alamy Stock Photo (Randy Duchaine), Abingdon, Oxon; **30.2** Getty Images (Gallo Images), München; **30.1** Getty Images (First Light), München; **30.3** Thinkstock (mlharing), München; **32.2** Alamy Stock Photo (World History Archive), Abingdon, Oxon; **32.1** Thinkstock (welcomia), München; **33.1** Thinkstock (IPGGutenbergUKLtd), München; **33.2** Alamy Stock Photo (Martin Shields), Abingdon, Oxon; **33.3** Getty Images (J. Meric), München; **34.1** plainpicture GmbH & Co. KG (Fancy Images/Hero), Hamburg; **35.3** Getty Images (E+/Pamela Moore), München; **35.5** Alamy Stock Photo (Marjorie Kamys Cotera/Bob Daemmrich Photography /), Abingdon, Oxon; **35.2** Getty Images (Universal Images Group), München; **35.1** Thinkstock (alexfedo), München; **35** Song: Cool Kids, Text: Dzwonek, Jesiah/Sierota, Graham/Sierota, Jamie/Sierota, Jefery/Sierota, Noah/Sierota Sydney, Verlag: Echosmith Songs/WB Music Corp./Jeffery David Songs/Upcast Music D/A/CH Neue Welt Musikverlag GmbH, Hamburg/Roba Music Verlag GmbH, Hamburg, Reach Music Publishing, Burbank CA; **35.6** shutterstock (Jim Lopes), New York, NY; **36.6** Thinkstock (Ramsey), München; **36.5** Thinkstock (StandbyPictures), München; **36.4** Thinkstock (Jupiterimages), München; **36.2** Thinkstock (xantuanx), München; **36.1** Thinkstock (Wylius), München; **36.3** Thinkstock (Antonius_), München; **45.1** JDM Productions Inc, New York; **47.1** Getty Images (E+/Steve Debenport), München; **48.2** Thinkstock (michal-rojek), München; **48.1** Thinkstock (Digital Vision.), München; **49.1** Getty Images (Roger Lecuyer), München; **50.1** Thinkstock (Mike Watson Images), München; **50.2** Thinkstock (Enterline Design Services LLC), München; **50.3** plainpicture GmbH & Co. KG (Image Source), Hamburg; **52.1** plainpicture GmbH & Co. KG (Michael Runkel), Hamburg; **52.2** Getty Images (Corbis), München; **53.1** plainpicture GmbH & Co. KG (NaturePL/Edwin Giesbers), Hamburg; **53.2** Getty Images (Aurora), München; **53.3** f1 online digitale Bildagentur, Frankfurt; **56.1** Getty Images (Thomas M. Barwick INC), München; **58.2** Thinkstock (Flying Colours Ltd), München; **58.1** Alamy Stock Photo (brt PHOTO), Abingdon, Oxon; **59.1** iStockphoto (RF/Sascha Burkard), Calgary, Alberta; **59.3** Thinkstock (Oleksiy Mark), München; **59.5** MEV Verlag GmbH, Augsburg; **59.2** Avenue Images GmbH (stock disc), Hamburg; **59.4** shutterstock (Maxx-Studio), New York, NY; **61.1** Getty Images (Taxi/Troy Aossey), München; **62** From: The body, Stephen King, retold by Robin Waterfield; **62.1** Ullstein Bild GmbH (United Archives / KPA), Berlin; **63.1** Ullstein Bild GmbH (United Archives), Berlin; **67.3** JDM Productions Inc, New York; **67.1** JDM Productions Inc, New York; **67.2** JDM Productions Inc, New York; **67.4** JDM Productions Inc, New York; **68.1** Alamy Stock Photo (Hero Images Inc.), Abingdon, Oxon; **70.1** Alamy Stock Photo (North Wind Picture Archives), Abingdon, Oxon; **74.1** shutterstock (mariakraynova), New York, NY; **74.2** plainpicture GmbH & Co. KG (CI2/Joel Bear Studios), Hamburg; **75.3** Getty Images (Lonely Planet/jean pierre lescourret), München; **75.1** Getty Images (E+/Johnny Greig), München; **75.2** Getty Images (Kiyoshi Ota/Bloomberg), München; **76.4** Getty

Images (Blend Images), München; **76.1** shutterstock (bikeriderlondon), New York, NY; **76.2** Thinkstock (1001Love), München; **76.3** Thinkstock (somchaij), München; **77** Song: Surfin' U.S.A., Text: Brian Wilson, Verlag: ARC Music Corp. Good Tunes Music AG; **77.1** Ullstein Bild GmbH (Rolf Schulten), Berlin; **79.3** Beutel, Ulrike, Stuttgart; **79.4** Beutel, Ulrike, Stuttgart; **79.2** Beutel, Ulrike, Stuttgart; **79.1** Reis, Axel, Oberderdingen; **80.1** Getty Images (Hero Images), München; **81.1** Getty Images (South_agency), München; **83.1** Thinkstock (McIninch), München; **85.1** Alamy Stock Photo (Granger Historical Picture Archive), Abingdon, Oxon; **86.1** Alamy Stock Photo (Russ Bishop), Abingdon, Oxon; **87.1** Getty Images (E+/Steve Debenport), München; **88.1** Alamy Stock Photo (nik wheeler), Abingdon, Oxon; **89.1** JDM Productions Inc, New York; **91.1** Thinkstock (littlewormy), München; **93.1** Reis, Axel, Oberderdingen; **94.2** Reis, Axel, Oberderdingen; **94.1** Reis, Axel, Oberderdingen; **96.2** Alamy Stock Photo (World History Archive), Abingdon, Oxon; **96.1** Getty Images (Stockbyte), München; **97.3** Getty Images (2013 Kevin Mazur), München; **97.1** Getty Images (Hulton Archive/The Print Collector), München; **97.2** Getty Images (Blend Images), München; **98.2** Thinkstock (emarto), München; **98.1** shutterstock (Michael Rosebrock), New York, NY; **99.4** Geoatlas, Hendaye; **99.2** Klett-Archiv-RF-HF, Stuttgart; **99.3** Klett-Archiv-RF-HF, Stuttgart; **99.5** Geoatlas, Hendaye; **99.1** Klett-Archiv-RF-HF, Stuttgart; **102.1** Getty Images (Jon Feingersh Photography 2011), München; **102.2** Getty Images (Stocktrek Images), München; **104.1** Getty Images (The Image Bank), München; **105.1** Getty Images (kristian sekulic), München; **106.1** laif (Richard Harbus/Polaris), Köln; **106.2** Picture-Alliance (Everett Collection), Frankfurt; **108.1** Getty Images (Sean Gardner), München; **109.3** February Films, London; **109.4** JDM Productions Inc, New York; **109.2** JDM Productions Inc, New York; **109.1** JDM Productions Inc, New York; **112.1** Fotolia.com (lubashi), New York; **113.^6;** "shutterstock (Suslik1983), New York, NY; **113.5** shutterstock (jultud), New York, NY; **113.1** iStockphoto (RF/Dmitry Bezkorovayny), Calgary, Alberta; **113.3** Corbis (Matthias Kulka), Berlin; **113.4** shutterstock (George W. Bailey), New York, NY; **113.2** iStockphoto (sspopov), Calgary, Alberta; **113.7** Thinkstock (pilipphoto), München; **116.1** plainpicture GmbH & Co. KG (Kniel Synnatzschke), Hamburg; **118.1** plainpicture GmbH & Co. KG (Fancy Images/Hero), Hamburg; **119.1** Getty Images (Fuse), München; **119.3** Alamy Stock Photo (Marjorie Kamys Cotera/Bob Daemmrich Photography), Abingdon, Oxon; **119.5** Getty Images (E+/Pamela Moore), München; **119.2** Alamy Stock Photo (Image Source Plus), Abingdon, Oxon; **119.4** Getty Images (View Pictures/UIG), München; **125.1** iStockphoto (RF/Sascha Burkard), Calgary, Alberta; **125.2** Avenue Images GmbH (stock disc), Hamburg; **125.5** MEV Verlag GmbH, Augsburg; **125.4** shutterstock (Maxx-Studio), New York, NY; **125.3** Thinkstock (Oleksiy Mark), München; **127.4** Getty Images (Blend Images), München; **127.1** shutterstock (bikeriderlondon), New York, NY; **127.3** Thinkstock (somchaij), München; **127.2** Thinkstock (1001Love), München; **129.1** Getty Images (Hero Images), München; **131.5** Geoatlas, Hendaye; **131.4** Geoatlas, Hendaye; **131.2** Klett-Archiv-RF-HF, Stuttgart; **131.3** Klett-Archiv-RF-HF, Stuttgart; **131.1** Klett-Archiv-RF-HF, Stuttgart; **133.1** Getty Images (Moment Mobile), München; **134.1** Getty Images RF (The Image Bank), München; **134.6** Getty Images (WireImage), München; **134.5** Alamy Stock Photo (PYMCA), Abingdon, Oxon; **134.4** Getty Images (Hulton Archive), München; **134.3** Getty Images (Michael Ochs Archives), München; **134.2** Corbis (Owaki - Kulla), Berlin; **135.1** Corbis (Bo Zaunders), Berlin; **135.2** Getty Images (Daniel Zuchnik), München; **136.1** Getty Images RF (The Image Bank), München; **136.3** Getty Images (Dorling Kindersley RF), München; **136.2** Kansas Historical Society, Topeka; **137.1** Getty Images (The Image Bank), München; **138.1** Getty Images RF (The Image Bank), München; **138.2** Getty Images (Popperfoto), München; **138.3** Getty Images (National Geographic Magazines), München; **138.4** Getty Images (M_a_y_a), München; **139.2** iStockphoto (circlePS), Calgary, Alberta; **139.1** Getty Images (De Agostini Picture Library), München; **140.1** Getty Images RF (The Image Bank), München; **140.2** Getty Images (Corbis Documentary), München; **140.3** Getty Images (Jemal Countess), München; **140.4** Getty Images (Albert L. Ortega), München; **141.2** Getty Images (DreamPictures), München; **141.1** Alamy Stock Photo (FORRAY Didier/SAGAPHOTO.COM), Abingdon, Oxon; **142.1** Getty Images RF (The Image Bank), München; **142.2** Getty Images (Lonely Planet), München; **142.3** Getty Images (Corbis Documentary), München; **143.1** Getty Images (Photographer's Choice), München; **143.2** Getty Images (Corbis Documentary), München; **144.1** Getty Images (Spencer Sutton), München; **144.3** Getty Images (Lonely Planet), München; **144.2** Getty Images (Photolibrary), München; **144.4** Getty Images (Jiji Press / AFP), München; **145.1** Getty Images (Gary S. Chapman), München; **147.1** Getty Images (Blend Images), München; **148.1** The Absolutely True Diary of a Part-Time Indian, Author: Sherman Alexie, Illustrator: Ellen Forney, Andersen Press.; **148** The Absolutely True Diary of a Part-Time Indian, Sherman Alexie, Andersen Press; **149.1** The Absolutely True Diary of a Part-Time Indian, Author: Sherman Alexie, Illustrator: Ellen Forney, Andersen Press.; **150.1** The Absolutely True Diary of a Part-Time Indian, Author: Sherman Alexie, Illustrator: Ellen Forney, Andersen Press.; **150.2** The Absolutely True Diary of a Part-Time Indian, Author: Sherman Alexie, Illustrator: Ellen Forney, Andersen Press.; **182.9** Fotolia.com (naughtynut), New York; **182.8** Fotolia.com (blondsteve), New York; **182.7** iStockphoto (Dominic Burke RF), Calgary, Alberta; **182.6** Fotolia.com (thorabeti), New York; **182.5** Fotolia.com (Pavel Losevsky), New York; **182.4** iStockphoto (Marcel Pfost), Calgary, Alberta; **182.3** Fotolia.com (axeldrosta), New York; **182.2** iStockphoto (Michael Utech), Calgary, Alberta; **182.1** iStockphoto (stockcam), Calgary, Alberta; **183.3** Bananastock, Watlington / Oxon; **183.2** Das Fotoarchiv RF (RF), Essen; **183.1** Thinkstock (Owat Tasai), München; **188.11** iStockphoto (Alejandro Rivera), Calgary, Alberta; **188.10** Klett-Archiv (Weccard), Stuttgart; **188.9** Avenue Images GmbH (StockDisc), Hamburg; **188.8** shutterstock (igor.stevanovic), New York, NY; **188.7** Thinkstock (Stockbyte), München; **188.6** Avenue Images GmbH (Digital Vision), Hamburg; **188.5** Fotolia.com (Michael Shake), New York; **188.4** iStockphoto (Steve Debenport), Calgary, Alberta; **188.1** Fotosearch Stock Photography (Digital Vision), Waukesha, WI; **188.3** iStockphoto (herreid), Calgary, Alberta; **188.2** shutterstock (bikeriderlondon), New York, NY;

Textquellennachweis

S. 19: Song: Empire State of Mind, Text: CARTER, SHAWN/HUNTE, ANGELA/KEYES, BERT/Keys, Alicia/Robinson, Sylvia/SEWELL, JANET ANDREA/SHUCKBURGH, ALEXANDER WILLIAM, Verlag: Carter Boys Music / EMI April Music / Foray Music / Gambi Music Inc / Global Talent Publishing / J Sewell Publishing / Lellow Productions Inc / Masani El Shabazz EMI Music Publishing Germany GmbH, Berlin / Rolf Budde Musikverlag GmbH, Berlin / Neue Welt Musikverlag GmbH, Hamburg

S. 35: Song: Cool Kids, Text: Dzwonek, Jesiah/Sierota, Graham/Sierota, Jamie/Sierota, Jefery/Sierota, Noah/Sierota Sydney, Verlag: Echosmith Songs/WB Music Corp./Jeffery David Songs/Upcast Music D/A/CH Neue Welt Musikverlag GmbH, Hamburg/ Roba Music Verlag GmbH, Hamburg, Reach Music Publishing, Burbank CA

S. 62: From: The body, Stephen King, retold by Robin Waterfield

S. 77: Song: Surfin' U.S.A., Text: Brian Wilson, Verlag: ARC Music Corp. Good Tunes Music AG

S. 148–151: The Absolutely True Diary of a Part-Time Indian, Sherman Alexie, Andersen Press

ALASKA
Denali▲
CANADA

CANADA

Seattle
Portland   WASHINGTON
OREGON
Rocky

MONTANA
NORTH DAKOTA

IDAHO
WYOMING
SOUTH DAKOTA

NEVADA
Mountains
NEBRASKA

UTAH
Denver
COLORADO
KA

San Francisco
CALIFORNIA

Las Vegas

HOLLYWOOD

ARIZONA
OKLAHO
Los Angeles
Phoenix
San Diego
NEW MEXICO

Pacific Ocean

TEXAS

HAWAII
MEXICO

THE UNITED STATES OF AMERICA

MINNESOTA
polis

WISCONSIN

MICHIGAN

Great

Lakes

Milwaukee

Chicago

IOWA

ILLINOIS

INDIANA

OHIO

MISSOURI

KENTUCKY

Nashville

TENNESSEE

ARKANSAS

Mississippi

MISSIS-
SIPPI

ALABAMA

LOUISIANA

New Orleans

as

n

Detroit

NEW YORK

PENNSYLVANIA

Philadelphia

WEST
VIRGINIA

VIRGINIA

Washington, D.C.

NORTH CAROLINA

SOUTH
CAROLINA

Atlanta

GEORGIA

MAINE

1 2

3 Boston

4 5

6

7   8

New
York
City

1 VERMONT
2 NEW HAMPSHIRE
3 MASSACHUSETTS
4 CONNECTICUT
5 RHODE ISLAND
6 NEW JERSEY
7 MARYLAND
8 DELAWARE

Atlantic Ocean

FLORIDA

Miami

Everglades

Gulf of Mexico

NORTH

WEST   EAST

SOUTH

0   500   1000 km

0   500 miles